INTEREST GROUPS AND LOBBYING

INTEREST GROUPS AND LOBBYING

Pursuing Political Interests in America

THOMAS T. HOLYOKE

California State University, Fresno

WESTVIEW
PRESS

A MEMBER OF THE PERSEUS BOOKS GROUP

Westview Press was founded in 1975 in Boulder, Colorado, by notable publisher and intellectual Fred Praeger. Westview Press continues to publish scholarly
titles and high-quality undergraduate- and graduate-level textbooks in core
social science disciplines. With books developed, written, and edited with the
needs of serious nonfiction readers, professors, and students in mind, Westview Press honors its long history of publishing books that matter.

Copyright © 2014 by Westview Press
Published by Westview Press,
A Member of the Perseus Books Group

Find us on the World Wide Web at www.westviewpress.com.

Every effort has been made to secure required permissions for all text, images,
maps, and other art reprinted in this volume.

Westview Press books are available at special discounts for bulk purchases in
the United States by corporations, institutions, and other organizations. For
more information, please contact the Special Markets Department at the Perseus Books Group, 2300 Chestnut Street, Suite 200, Philadelphia, PA 19103, or
call (800) 810–4145, ext. 5000, or e-mail special.markets@perseusbooks.com.

A CIP catalog record for the print version of this book is available from the
Library of Congress.

ISBN (paperback): 978-0-8133-4581-9
ISBN (ebook): 978-0-8133-4582-6
10 9 8 7 6 5 4 3 2 1

FOR

Mom, Dad, and Melanie

CONTENTS

PREFACE

A recent article in the *Washington Post* quoted several professional lobbyists saying that lobbying was a profession that could not really be taught (Goldman 2012). It had to be experienced—meaning those who practiced the profession could only learn it by doing it. As Mike House, who works for the private for-hire lobbying firm Hogan Lovells, said to the *Post*, "It's all about good instincts. And instincts can never be taught." Having worked for interest groups on and off for about eight years, as well as having been an occasional lobbying target when I worked on the staff of the New York State Senate, I am inclined to agree with Mr. House's assessment. That makes writing a college textbook about lobbying intimidating. Actually none of the lobbyists I know, and I have known many, ever intended to become lobbyists when they were in college. When life suddenly deposited them into the profession, they *had* to learn it by instinct, though most of them also benefited from mentoring by older, more experienced lobbyists. Still, I doubt that I can teach anybody how to lobby, and this book is in no way a lobbying manual.

I can, however, teach college students a fair amount about what interest groups are and why they exist, as well as what lobbyists are and how lobbying works in the most generalized sense. That is what this book is about, and I think it is worthwhile to know. The number of interest groups and lobbyists in national politics—and, I strongly suspect, at the state and local levels—is rapidly growing. Even organizations that traditionally stayed out of blatant advocacy politics are now jumping into the advocacy game. An obvious recent example is the Heritage Foundation, the formerly academic-like think tank that is reorienting itself as a bold advocate for conservative ideas and policies (Milbank 2012). American citizens are abandoning their traditional political parties, and too often they do not vote, but they are supporting ever more interest groups, either through their direct participation or with their money. The US political system is a system of interest group politics—that is, policy being made by competing interest groups—and every student should realize this fact and try to understand it, even if they are not political science majors or do not want to be lobbyists. After all, nearly every student will go on to join one or more interest groups in their lives, if they are not already members! In this book I lay out and explore the basic ideas of interest group politics and provide details on how it works. For students who do go on to be lobbyists, I hope this means the gap that instinct must fill between knowing and professionally doing will now be smaller.

If I have made mistakes in my facts or in how I understand prevailing theories, I accept all of the blame. None goes to Toby Wahl at Westview Press, who asked me to write this book. Thank you very much for the wonderful opportunity to distill nearly everything I know about interest groups and lobbying, academic learning and personal experience, into a book for undergraduate and graduate students. I was so excited about the prospect that I laid out this book's basic structure within five minutes of being asked to write it! Special thanks also to Ada Fung at Westview Press, who took over the project and drove it forward with an enthusiasm and efficiency that helped me sustain my own enthusiasm. Good editors terrify me because they show me how inadequate my own writing can be, and my initial development editor, Brooke Maddeford, was exceptionally harsh while also being very nice. The same can be said of my project editor, Rachel King, and my copyeditor, Beth Wright of Trio Bookworks. Thanks for all of your help.

I want to thank my colleagues Jeff Cummins, Mike Heaney, Melanie Ram, and Heath Brown, who were all kind enough to read through parts of this manuscript and give me their insightful comments. Then there were the fourteen people who reviewed my manuscript. Fourteen! I'd like to thank for their invaluable feedback Mark Brewer (University of Maine), William Byrne (St. John's University), David Damore (University of Nevada, Las Vegas), Rodd Freitag (University of Wisconsin, Eau Claire), Bryan McQuide (University of Idaho), Chapman Rackaway (Fort Hays State University), Laura Woliver (University of South Carolina), and the seven reviewers who chose to remain anonymous.

I have a few last points to make about writing this book. First, I must acknowledge the interest group textbooks already on the market that are very good and written by people I deeply respect. I believe my book is different in many ways from theirs and values their contributions while also adding to them. Second, because a lot of interest group politics and lobbying must be experienced to be understood, not only have I tried to include lots of direct quotations in this book, but I also felt it important to do a little field research for it, even though the book is not a work of primary research. So thanks go to the many lobbyists, interest group staff, legislative staff, and administrative agency staff who gave me their time when I was in Washington, DC. Thanks to the Office of the Provost and the Henry Madden Library at California State University, Fresno, for funding the trip and the sabbatical. And thanks to the American Political Science Association for giving me office space in the Centennial Center during my time in Washington. Third, I have never written for students before. Although I had ideas of how I might do it, I decided to actually have my students read an early draft of the manuscript and provide feedback on whether it made any sense at all to them. I teach a course on interest groups and lobbying, so it was easy to assign my manuscript. Not only did this give me an opportunity to see how it worked in an actual class, but I also encouraged my students (yes, by offering extra credit) to provide me with comments on the manuscript and how they thought it might be improved. That turned out to be surprisingly valuable (and a little painful), so thanks to Brooke Smith, Caitlin Ryan, Xavier Vasquez, Jessica Boujikian, Rebecca Levers, Juan Santiago, Patrick Simon, Brittani Smith, and Roxanne Castillo.

Finally, while a lot of people argue that much of our nation's problems with governing come from interest groups and lobbyists, I do not share that belief. Yes, there is too much money in American politics today, but I think a ban on lobbying would do a lot more harm than good. Interest groups and lobbyists provide an important type of political representation. The United States is so diverse that no political party, not even lawmakers elected to serve constituents in geographic regions, can effectively articulate the needs of all the groups of citizens sharing common interests whom they are supposed to represent. Interest groups can, and most of them do it well. The lobbyists I know may be a little stuck in narrow visions of what policy should be and whom it should serve, and they may believe their own rhetoric a little too much, but in that sense they are no different from the rest of us. In any case, that is what they are hired to do. Faithfully representing the people who employ you is the hallmark of a good, professional, and *ethical* lobbyist. We should not punish lobbyists for doing a good job representing the groups of people who hire them. We should find ways to best use their representational skills for the greater good of our representative republic.

Very special thanks to Melanie Ram for putting up with all of this. I don't think you were expecting me to write another book quite so soon. Thanks for your patience, encouragement, and all-around support!

FIGURES AND TABLES

First Shoot All the Lobbyists?

In 2006 a man named Jack Abramoff was sentenced to six years in federal prison for fraud and conspiracy involving the corruption of government officials (he actually served three and a half), but in the minds of most people tuning in to the congressional investigation, Abramoff was prosecuted for being a lobbyist. And they probably approved of that. *Washington Post* writer Jan Witold Baran, who covered the Abramoff investigation, wrote of the public's view of lobbying, "If Shakespeare lived today, perhaps he would write, 'First shoot all the lobbyists'" (Baran 2006). Baran, though, went on to actually defend the lobbying profession, emphasizing that most of the tens of thousands of people practicing it are ethical and honorable. That opinion was not shared by a letter to the editor in my hometown newspaper, which said of 2012 Republican Party presidential hopefuls that "the nominee will be a mere puppet for the man who is possibly the most dangerous man in America: [lobbyist] Grover Norquist. . . . He is much more than [the man who heads Americans for Tax Reform], however. He holds huge influence over the tea party and other ultra-conservative zealots."[1] A dim view of lobbying also comes from the good-government organization Citizens for Responsibility and Ethics in Washington, which issued a study in 2012 reporting that several once-powerful lawmakers were now lobbying for special interest groups they had helped fund with public money while still in Congress. Said the center's executive director Melanie Sloan, "This is part of the reason why the public is so disgusted by the revolving door" (Farnam 2012b). Of course, Sloan's detractors probably say that she is just another lobbyist herself.

Who and what are these lobbyists that the public is so disgusted with? In the 2012 Republican primary, former House Speaker Newt Gingrich was accused of being one for Freddie Mac, the government-backed housing finance company many conservatives blamed for the housing market crash of 2008. The accusation must have been serious because Gingrich vehemently denied ever having been one, and by the letter of the law he was right. Why be afraid of being labeled a lobbyist, though, when by all accounts hiring one is good for business? A team of tax experts calculated that in 2004 lobbyists for corporations working on the American Jobs Creation Act produced a return of over $220 for their clients for every $1 spent (Alexander, Scholz, and Mazza 2010). Whatever lobbyists are doing, and whether for good or for ill, apparently they do it well.

What about the special interest groups these lobbyists work for? Some are obscure, such as the Organic Consumers Association or the International Association of Fish and Wildlife Agencies, while others are virtually household names and feared by lawmakers. Washington journalist Jeffrey Birnbaum used to survey prominent Washingtonians about which groups were the most powerful, with famous organizations such as the American Association of Retired Persons (AARP) and the National Rifle Association (NRA) usually vying for the top spot.[2] Another journalist, Jonathan Rauch (1994), argues that there are so many of them, demanding so many special benefits and favorable policies from Congress, that they threaten the very existence of the US government. Lawmakers, he says, are so beholden to these interests that they cannot react to a crisis without offending them. There is actually a whole cottage industry of books by journalists, former lawmakers, and scholars condemning the proliferation of interest groups in American politics (e.g., Gardner 1972; Birnbaum 1992; Drew 1999; Kaiser 2009). They find evidence of interest group influence in places one might not even expect, such as an effort by the McDonald's Corporation to lobby the Oxford English Dictionary. In 2007 McDonald's joined forces with the British Chambers of Commerce and Conservative Party to pressure the venerable dictionary to modify or drop its unflattering definition of the word "McJob" (Thompson 2007). The dictionary's editors successfully resisted.

Interest groups and lobbying are perhaps the hardest subjects to define, study, and teach in political science. Most people, including students, come to the subject predisposed to disliking them. It is easy to identify and define members of Congress, legislative bodies, administrative agencies, judges, the courts, and even political parties, but what exactly is an interest group? And would you know one if you saw one? Americans for Tax Reform perhaps, and maybe even Citizens for Responsibility and Ethics in Washington. But what about the Rotary Club? Or the American Automobile Association? Or the

Camp Fire Girls? All three have taken positions on public policy at one time or another. Does that make them interest groups? Are you in an interest group and do not even know it? Lots of people are. Many corporations, perhaps a majority, also lobby. In fact they employ more lobbyists in Washington, DC, than anybody else. Are they interest groups?

It is because interest groups are so hard to define and identify that scholars are not even sure how many of them there are. A conservative estimate is at least seven thousand working in Washington, DC, but I suspect that drastically undercounts even just the number active in national politics. Tens of thousands more work at the state and local levels. Scholars cannot even agree on what the exact term is for them. Interest group? Organized interest? Pressure group? Special interest? Are there any *un*-special interests?

The same problem exists with lobbyists. Who are they? One reason they might be hard to spot is because they themselves often avoid the title, printing "government affairs associate" or something equally vague on their business cards. Many like the term "advocate," but that could include a lot of other people you might not associate with lobbying. If Jack Abramoff is like Grover Norquist, then is he also like Ralph Nader, the founder of Public Citizen who wrestled with General Motors in the 1960s? Or like John Muir and David Brower, respectively the founder and political reorganizer of the Sierra Club? Muir and Brower at times both led the famous hiking club on political crusades against the government. They would probably describe themselves as advocates, but does that mean they are also lobbyists?

Whatever lobbyists are, we should probably not shoot them, outlaw their profession, or suppress the interest groups they work for. James Madison did not think so, arguing in Federalist No. 10 that suppression of any faction of citizens with a common interest is a remedy "worse than the disease." Suppressing them would also be illegal under the First Amendment of the US Constitution, which guarantees the right to freely assemble and petition the government for a redress of grievances. Even if outlawing lobbyists and interest groups were possible, it would be unwise. They provide representation for parts of the public that care intensely about political issues or have strongly held beliefs they feel must be pursued through the policy-making apparatus of the state. Since American society is so heterogeneous with many groups organized, or at least with the potential to be organized, around a wide range of issues and beliefs, there is no way they can be represented by any political party. To win majorities, parties must assemble and represent many interests, but trying to represent everybody means they represent nobody well. US presidents and senators have the same problem. Even House members represent too many competing interests in their districts to be effective advocates for them all. Private organizations speaking for distinct groups of people have no need to represent any majority.

The upside of interest groups is that they can and do provide focused representation for small groups of people organized around narrow, well-defined interests that could probably not ever be priorities for political parties. The downside is that there are so many private organizations representing group interests in national politics today that the relatively small number of public officials whose attention they compete for cannot possibly respond to them all. Nor do interest groups represent all factions of the public equally. Some simply have more resources than others with which they can make their constituent members' voices heard more loudly by policy-makers. And some potential constituent members simply cannot get organized, or even realize that they had better be organized, if they want to avoid being hurt by the policies advanced by competing interest groups. What groups *do* share with parties and constituent-based representation in government is a disregard for the public interest.

One book on groups and lobbying cannot do justice to all of the motivations and concerns connected to interest group representation—not even close. Instead I try to provide a broad overview of the subject. This book starts, in Chapter 1, by defining interest groups and explaining why they are so prominent in the United States. Then I explore in Chapters 2 and 3 how and why interest groups form, why they fail to form, and why they sometimes emerge out of social movements. In Chapter 4, I describe how lobbyists interface with the members of interest groups, the people they are supposed to represent, and problems with representation quality as groups grow older and larger. I try to assemble all of these pieces together in a coherent manner in Chapter 5 to provide a foundation for the second half of the book. In Part II, I explore how interest group lobbyists gain influence in the institutions of the national government, such as Congress in Chapter 6, the executive branch (president and bureaucracy) in Chapter 7, and the judicial branch in Chapter 8. In these three chapters I show how employing various methods of influence can enhance or detract from the basic representative function of interest groups. In Chapter 9 I discuss how group lobbyists interact with each other through bargaining, conflict, and strategically choosing where to lobby. Chapter 10 focuses on campaign finance, a subject that could (and does) fill whole books. While my overview of interest groups in electoral politics could be considered a little thin, since the subject of electoral politics is so vast, interest groups are also becoming smaller players in this arena, especially when compared to the new super PACs that have sprung up.

In Chapter 11 I return to the book's overarching theme of political representation. I do not believe that interest groups provide the fairest form of representation, though they may provide the *fairest possible* form of representation. Their lobbyists are supposed to be vigorous advocates for their members, and only their members, though sometimes political pressures prevent them from fulfilling even that role particularly well. Yet, like them or not, interest groups may have to be accepted as vehicles for representation because they already exist in large numbers, and these numbers are increasing. They actually appear to be the only form of political participation that is increasing, if indeed joining an interest group is participation (though it is no harder than voting). The real key in the representation problem, though, is the lobbyist. They are supposed to be the spokespersons for a faction of citizens sharing an interest, and how well they provide representation before government is an important question.

Notes

1. Letter to the editor, *Fresno Bee* (Fresno, CA), February 20, 2012.
2. I have Birnbaum's lists for 1997, 1998, 1999, and 2001 and will share them on request. I have not heard that he has made any since.

PART ONE

Origins and Structure

CHAPTER ONE

Interests and Interest Groups

What is an interest group? Would you recognize an interest group if one called you and asked for money? Or if you saw its logo on a fundraising letter? Perhaps you have seen the logo of the American Bankers Association on one of your local bank's walls, and even suspected that it refers to some kind of organization representing banks and the people whose profession is banking. Checking ABA's Web site would probably remove any doubt, for it says, "The American Bankers Association is the voice of America's $13 trillion banking industry, representing banks of all sizes and charters, from the smallest community bank to the largest bank holding companies."[1] The Web site also lays out a variety of problems the multitrillion-dollar banking industry apparently has with current government policy, and describes what ABA leaders are doing to convince lawmakers in Congress, the White House, and regulatory agencies to solve them. That sounds like lobbying, and you, like most people, probably associate lobbying with interest groups. If so, then the Center for Education Reform must also be an interest group: its home page says its purpose is to urge lawmakers to enact policies promoting consumer choice in K-12 education because that is what its supporters want.[2] Both the center and ABA represent a group of Americans who have needs and desires, what we call "interests," that can only be fulfilled by changing public policy. It feels right to call them interest groups.

But what about the Alliance to Protect Nantucket Sound, which describes itself as a "nonprofit environmental organization dedicated to the long term preservation of Nantucket Sound"?[3] Made up of residents of Hyannis, Massachusetts, along with their elected officials and civic associations, the alliance's goal is to convince the Federal Aviation Administration to deny approval of a giant solar wind farm on the shores of Nantucket Sound. Does that make this environmental organization an interest group? What about the Trans Canada Company or the nonprofit organization Consumer Energy Alliance? From 2012 to 2013 both tried to convince President Barack Obama to permit the construction of the Keystone Pipeline to move oil from Canada to Texas. Or what about Bold Nebraska, which represents people who do *not* want Obama to approve the pipeline because it might pollute water in the underground Ogallala Aquifer?[4] Are they all interest groups?

What about American Crossroads, organized under the federal tax code as a 527 nonprofit by President George W. Bush's former advisor Karl Rove to raise money for conservative candidates in elections? Is it an interest group even though it does not appear to have any actual members? How about former House majority leader Dick Armey's Tea Party–tied FreedomWorks, which organized resistance to President Obama's 2009 health care plan? What about the Tea Party itself? Or any political party? Are they *not* interest groups because they try to influence policy by changing the ideological composition of elected legislatures rather than changing the minds of people already elected to those legislatures? Is Haliburton, a corporation subsisting on government contracts, an interest group because it aggressively pushes lawmakers to give them these contracts? Is BP Oil an interest group? Citibank? The United Way? What about Southern California's Metropolitan Water District, a giant public agency that provides municipal water but also spends money to shape policy in the state legislature and battles other political groups such as the Mono Lake Committee for control of water resources? Universities solicit lawmakers for grants to fund large research projects. Are they interest groups too?

Defining Interests and Interest Groups

It is easy to identify members of Congress because the process of becoming one is clearly laid out in the Constitution. Regulatory agencies are also pretty easy to distinguish from other organizations because they are created by acts of Congress. Even political parties can be identified without too much trouble. Interest groups, though, are harder. In fact, scholars cannot even agree on what to call them. Is an "interest group" the same as an "organized interest," "social movement organization," "special interest group," "private interest," "pressure group," "lobby," "nongovernmental organization," or "political organization"? Perhaps it would be easier to start by thinking about why some entities are not interest groups. Presidents and executive branch officials often pressure Congress to pass (or to not pass) legislation, and members of Congress try to pressure them in return, and they all try to influence the decisions of Supreme Court justices. These policy makers lobby in that they try to persuade each other to enact policies they desire, but they are not working for interest groups. They serve in institutions created by public law to formally make policies benefitting all citizens within their jurisdictions. They wield powers that flow directly or indirectly from the nation's most fundamental law, the Constitution. So while government officials and lawmakers lobby each other, no government institution is an interest group. Apologies to the Metropolitan Water District.

Political parties are not interest groups either. Apologies to Democrats, Republicans, and all of America's small third parties. Parties gain political power by trying to get enough of their members elected to office to command a majority and thus directly control lawmaking institutions. To do that, they need the support of a majority of voting citizens, which means trying to represent many different groups of people at once, often bitterly realizing that trying to represent everyone usually results in failing to represent anyone well. When we talk about an **interest group**, we refer to a singular **interest**. Each group represents one need or desire, or at most a few very closely related needs or desires, held by only a small number of people. Consequently, most interest groups cannot gain formal political power by electing their members to public office. They represent too few people. Whatever influence interest groups have in government, it is *informal* rather than formal.

Corporations are not interest groups either. They exist first and foremost to make a profit in the marketplace and return that profit to their shareholders, not lobby for government largesse and favorable policy. Nor do they represent any definable group of people with a common interest. Their shareholders might be considered constituents, but most of them are involved with the company to make money, not influence policy. Corporations often do wade into the political arena, usually because a change in policy (or lack of policy change) will have a direct impact on their financial bottom lines. Moreover, some corporate executives have tried to claim they actually represent the interests of their employees and customers, sometimes even persuading them to contact lawmakers on the company's behalf, as Allstate Insurance did with its forty-five thousand employees in the 2011 fight over whether to raise the nation's debt ceiling (Dash and Schwartz 2011) and as Caterpillar did when the fight happened again in 2013 (Yang and Hamburger 2013). CEOs, however, are not accountable to their employees and customers and thus cannot be said to represent them in the political process. The same is true of universities, hospitals, and similar nonprofit organizations. They are not interest groups. Apologies to Citibank and the United Way. Corporations and nonprofits do collectively employ more lobbyists in Washington, DC, than true interest groups (Salisbury 1984), but they tend to only lobby sporadically (Brasher and Lowery 2006). Real interest groups represent some portion of the public, not just their own leaders and CEOs.

Interest groups, then, are private organizations, not formal parts of the government. This is why they are sometimes called nongovernmental organizations. They primarily exist to provide informal political representation to citizens, usually by persuading lawmakers that it would be valuable to enact policies that help these citizens pursue strongly felt interests. A person's interest is fundamental to their character and is often grounded in economic need, aspects of personal identity (e.g., profession, ethnicity, sexual orientation), perceptions of fairness and justice, desires to acquire or achieve, and even metaphysical beliefs and values including religion. More broadly, interests define a person's perception of who they are and what they believe so strongly, so intensely, that its absence would change that person's identity. They would be a different person without that interest. Interest groups are thus formal aggregations of people sharing the same interest.

American society is extremely diverse, and so the number of different interests that are felt intensely enough to motivate people to form an interest group is probably unknowable. Not every individual interest leads to a mobilized interest group, often only because there are not enough other people who share the same interest to form a group, or because people with similar interests are too geographically dispersed (though today this is not the barrier it used to be). Those who do find enough soul mates who share their interest, who believe the interest should be embedded in the nation's laws (and thus also apply to everyone else), and who are willing to dedicate enough time and money might then form an interest group. This is the beginning of a workable definition of "interest group," but further development requires exploring the concept of self-interest.

A Culture of Self-Interest

Interest groups only exist to represent their members' self-interests. People join or otherwise support an interest group because they want it to advocate for policies that make it easier for them to pursue their personal interests, even though public policy is supposed to treat everyone equally. While some interest groups do claim to advocate for the *public* interest or *common* good rather than just the good of their members, that is still simply their point of view. Ask coal miners and users of energy from coal-fired plants in West Virginia whether the common interest is served when environmental laws force their mines to shut down, putting them out of work. Ask Louisiana's shrimping industry if it is well served by offshore oil drilling that is supposed to make the United States energy independent even though oil spills kill marine life. Coal miners and shrimpers benefit from cleaner air and cheaper oil but are hurt by lack of income. Policy that serves one person's idea of what ought to be true for everyone benefits only that person's self-interest, often at the expense of somebody else's self-interest.

Simply put, we create interest groups to help us further our personal interests through the nation's lawmaking process. This should not be surprising. Our political and economic systems are based on the fundamental belief that everyone has a right to pursue his or her own self-interest, and that no one's interest is more or less legitimate than anybody else's. We expect our government to protect this right to pursue our self-interest, and we often look to public officials to help us out by enacting policy prioritizing our self-interest, even when it is harmful to a majority of other citizens. We may talk about the virtues of compromise and the public interest, but then we denounce our leaders as incompetent or corrupt when new policy in any way threatens our self-interest. Compromises are only "obvious" and "sensible" when they give us what we want. In other words, we recognize no public interest in our political system, only many individual interests that sometimes aggregate into interest groups. Could it be any other way?

Democracy and Interests in the Classical World

In her book *Beyond Adversary Democracy* (1980), political theorist Jane Mansbridge argues that it once *was* different, and how our political beliefs subsequently changed to make individual self-interest almost sacred tells us a lot about why interest groups are both numerous and legitimate in the United States today.

Smaller, simpler societies have common interests because their needs are general, even universal. Everyone must eat, drink, and have shelter. But as societies more easily satisfy these basic needs and become larger, more complex, and more affluent, other common interests become harder to discern.

Common interests may even cease to exist as citizens become more concerned with their own idiosyncratic needs and desires, or find that they want the riches and pleasures others have. They become driven by the contentious pursuit of individual self-interest.

For instance, Mansbridge argues, members of prehistoric hunter-gatherer groups had no real concept of individual interests. Resources for survival were acquired together and shared together so that decisions for the group were made by consensus for the common good of the group (10). Of course, these tribes were very small and very homogenous. From birth to death people lived with the same tribe and spent nearly all of their time working with fellow tribal members to acquire the food and water they all needed to survive. Each person's individual interest was the group's interest because everyone had a common interest in survival (12).

Collective decision making in the common interest survived the birth of civilization and was central to democracy in classical Athens of the fifth century BCE. All Athenian citizens (men descended from citizens and who had completed military service) were expected to participate in the Assembly, where decisions were debated until the collective good was determined and policy was made by unanimous consent. What benefitted one citizen was assumed to benefit everyone, so unanimous consent was desirable and possible to achieve (Mansbridge 1980, 9). Politics, said Aristotle, was not about satisfying personal needs but the process of discovering the common interest (Graziano 2001, 108). Participation and deliberation should be every citizen's way of life, not something to be opted out of. Those who did not participate were scornfully called "idiots" and, if we believe Aristophanes's play *The Acharnians*, fined for not attending the Assembly.

Yet sometimes the Assembly had to fall back on majority rule because achieving consensus was impossible (Mansbridge 1980, 13). This was an important change from more primitive societies. Majority rule means there must be one or more minorities whose interests are so different that they cannot be persuaded to accept the majority's view of the common good. In such cases there arguably is no common good, just conflict between the interests of the majority and those of the minority, with the latter getting hurt. These differences tend to emerge in larger, more affluent societies, Mansbridge argues (13), because enduring differences in wealth and privilege create different experiences and expectations—what is often called "social hierarchy" or a class system. Enduring differences between the wealthy, the military, and poorer citizens led to clashes of interests in the Assembly that ultimately weakened Athens. Pericles rose to power in 461 by promising the lower classes more political influence at the expense of wealthier citizens and more spending on public works (such as the Acropolis), but the internal divisions he created weakened Athens as it entered the disastrous Peloponnesian War with Sparta (Fornara and Samons 1991).

Pericles's supporters and rivals acted more like political parties than interest groups because they sought power through elections, but it was the size, complexity, and affluence of Athens that made it harder to discern the common good and pushed it into factional conflict. This is perhaps why Aristotle warned in his *Politics* that city-states should not be too large, fearing that factions would tear them apart. Yet it happened again in republican Rome. Differences in wealth and ancestry created a strong social hierarchy in Rome, but Romans still believed that all citizens should participate in lawmaking and elections. This guaranteed that conflicting class interests would emerge in the political arena. From the fifth to the last century BCE, the Romans tried to cope with competing social factions by building an increasingly complicated system of checks and balances to give each interest a voice in policy making (Abbott 1901).

Originally the two elected executive offices of consul, and the senators they appointed to recommend laws, were held by the wealthy patrician class descended from ancient Roman nobility. Yet because majority rule was used to elect consuls, some from the lower plebeian class won consular offices and went on to become senators. They won office by promising to create new political offices and institutions serving the interests of just their class. Examples of this were the Plebian Council, which made laws advancing their interests, and the offices of the public tribunes, who could veto any laws threatening plebeian interests. Ultimately this led to the emergence of wealthy plebeians disconnected from the interests of the poor, increasing the emphasis on self-interest rather than the good of the republic. Empowering these contentious interests resulted in a political system of separated powers so full of faction-controlled vetoes that the republic could no longer function (Abbott 1901). Military leaders like Julius Caesar and Pompey took advantage of the dysfunction by using their personal wealth and popularity to gain permanent control of high offices (Holland 2005). The result was a civil war creating so much instability that these competing factions finally supported a wholesale transfer of political power into the hands of Augustus Caesar, the first Roman emperor (Everitt 2007).

That the complicated webs of factional interests brought down democratic Athens and republican Rome was not lost on the men who wrote the US Constitution. In Federalist No. 51 James Madison defended the system of checks and balances they created as the best solution to the "mischief of factions" he warned about in Federalist No. 10. Time will tell whether he and his peers were wise to create a system of balancing powers as Rome had tried to do, but for all his concern about factions driven by self-interest, Madison could not endorse any government that suppressed them. He and his colleagues were too deeply embedded in political and economic beliefs that glorified individual self-interest. Factions of people driven by self-interest might be dangerous, but the Founders believed it was natural human behavior (Mansbridge 1990). Factions supporting populists like Pericles and Caesar may have hurt Athens and Rome, but they had to be endured and controlled, not destroyed. In the Founders' view, self-interest was tied to liberty, and liberty was sacred.

Self-Interest and the Social Contract

The political and economic philosophy that assigned such a fundamental role to individual self-interest emerged after Europe had achieved enough political stability that factions grounded in economic differences could emerge (Mansbridge 1980, 15). In the Dark Ages following the collapse of the Western Roman Empire in the fifth century CE, the strongest remaining institution was the Roman Catholic Church, but its message, articulated by Saint Augustine, was stoic submission rather than political participation. A person's only interest was in achieving salvation after death, not trying to understand disputes between the church and young monarchies, or wondering why there was sometimes more than one pope.

When more earthly interests did reappear, they were an economic response to the new political stability of the High Middle Ages in the twelfth and thirteenth centuries. Explorers and merchants established trade routes to the Middle and Far East, which, in turn, allowed many Europeans to enjoy a standard of living higher than subsistence, demanding goods imported from Asia or items created at home by skilled artisans (Bishop 1968). Once established, these artisans aggressively protected their economic interests by forming guilds to control entry into their professions and guard production secrets to ensure minimum prices and job security. Merchant houses formed to provide systems of insurance and credit that were essential for making world trade possible and also helped form a wealthy new business class. Though not interest groups per se, trade guilds and merchant houses bore more than passing resemblance to modern labor unions and trade associations (Bonnett 1935).

The Enlightenment that swept Europe in the seventeenth and eighteenth centuries allowed philosophers to ask what the purpose of government really was and why any government had the right to rule beyond claims to a divine right. Yet most of the political and economic theory that Enlightenment thinkers produced ended up, intentionally or not, justifying the commercial foundations of European empires. Adam Smith's economic theory in *The Wealth of Nations* (1776) asserted that individual choice in the pursuit of one's self-interest by acquiring wealth and property led to a healthy and productive society. Similarly, the political theory that emerged even before Smith's book, and that so informed the authors of the US Constitution, argued that the legitimate role of government was to protect individual self-interest (Mansbridge 1990).

This theory is found in the works of Great Britain's political theorists Thomas Hobbes, John Locke, and David Hume (Mansbridge 1980, 15). Hobbes argued in *Leviathan* (1651) that everyone is driven by self-interest, which, in the absence of government and society, leads them into deadly conflict with each other over scarce resources. People consent to be ruled because, in exchange, the ruler is obligated to protect them from each other so they can pursue their interests in relative safety. In other words, people are naturally self-interested, and in Hobbes's state of nature, where there is no government, people are free to make choices purely aimed at fulfilling their needs, wants, and desires. Often they take what they want from each other by force. By submitting to government in exchange for some security, they sacrifice some of this freedom to pursue their self-interest.

In his *Second Treatise on Government* (1689), John Locke expanded on this notion of a social contract between ruler and ruled and the obligations of each, especially as it related to the protection of property. In the state of nature one is only responsible for one's self, and pursuing self-interest through labor creates property rights. Everyone is equal because there is no society and government to impose hierarchy, so all self-interests are equally valid, and everyone is free to acquire property. Because the property acquired is always threatened by others in the state of nature, civil society is created through the social contract as an arena for pursuing self-interest under a set of rules determined by the state, often by majority rule. In return for sacrificing part of their absolute liberty for security, the remaining liberty of citizens to pursue their self-interests had to be guaranteed. That indeed was the purpose of government. These ideas would probably have been alien to the Athenians, but they made sense to the Founding Fathers of the United States and were the intellectual foundations of the Declaration of Independence and the Constitution.

The Founders also understood the risks embedded in social contract theory from the work of Scottish philosopher David Hume. In *On the First Principles of Government* (1777), Hume argued that there were enough similar individual interests in society that people might well end up pursuing them together in factions. Because the House of Commons, eighteenth-century Britain's dominant political institution, now elected its members and made laws though majority rule, it was possible that a large enough faction might take control of the House and use the lawmaking process for its own advantage. But because factionalism was a byproduct of people's natural proclivity to pursue self-interest, factional strife was inevitable in free societies with representative political systems and could not be repressed. Hume's solution, reminiscent of republican Rome, was to create a web of checks and balances to minimize the influence of factions without suppressing them.

This fear of factions surfaced in the writings of James Madison, especially Federalist No. 10, and the importance of checks and balances was stressed in Federalist No. 51 as well as in John Adams's *Thoughts on Government*. Reflecting British political theory, Madison argued that political factions are a natural consequence of self-interested human behavior. As he wrote in Federalist No. 10, "By faction, I understand a number of citizens, whether amounting to a majority or a minority of the whole, who are united and actuated by some common impulse of passion, or of interest, adverse to the rights of other citizens, or to the permanent and aggregate interests of the community." But because individual self-interests, and therefore factional interests, are natural, they must be respected. Of eliminating factions he wrote in the same paper, "It could never be more truly said than of [this] remedy, that it was worse than the disease."

This historical overview provides a foundation for understanding what interest groups are and why they are a part of the American political system. They are collections of people, each of whose individual self-interest is similar to those of others, all of whom see the political arena as the best place to pursue their mutual self-interest and so form an organization to pursue those interests. But organizations are not built around just any kind of interest. As I show in Figure 1.1, some interests, like interests in eating food, drinking water, and having shelter, are so universal (lower on the vertical axis) that they cannot be held by just one group in the population. Interests that are so esoteric they are unique to an individual (higher on the vertical axis) also do not lead

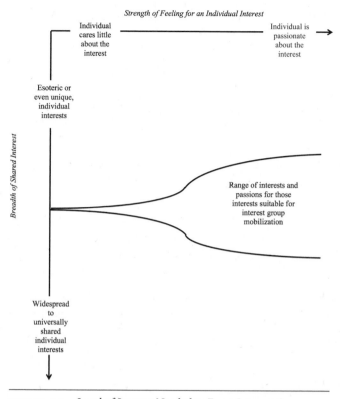

FIGURE 1.1   Level of Interest Needed to Form Interest Groups

to group formation. Groups form around "mid-range" interests, those that are shared by many but rarely by a majority. Also, the more intensely people feel about a particular interest, the more likely they are to take the time to promote or defend it in the political arena. So, as I show with the horizontal axis in Figure 1.1, more universal or esoteric interests might still be the foundation for forming a group if people feel strongly enough about them to commit some resources. That is why the area showing the range of interests capable of leading to group formation expands on the right side of Figure 1.1.

Larger, more diverse societies like the United States produce a greater variety of interests that are intensely felt by a minority of its citizens. These interests are strong enough that the people who hold them are willing to commit time and money to form organizations that use politics to promote them. Social contract theory, so familiar to the Founders, makes pursuit of self-interest a legitimate basis for political action. Every person has a natural right to pursue their wants and desires through the political process. Since the state has a fundamental responsibility to acknowledge and protect these interests, it is acceptable for citizens, including citizens organized into groups, to make demands on government. The founders guaranteed it in the **First Amendment** to the Constitution.

Lobbying: The Right of Interests to Petition

The First Amendment's last clause reads: "Congress shall make no law . . . abridging . . . the right of the people to freely assemble and petition government for a redress of grievances." It captures the two key parts of interest group politics: collective action (the right to freely assemble) and lobbying government to answer the demands of citizens (petition for redress of grievances). The idea of citizens with similar interests proactively or reactively demanding that their government protect their self-interest is the cornerstone of democratic government, and using intermediaries to press these demands is the very definition of representation. Where did these constitutional rights to assemble and petition come from? Unsurprisingly, they evolved right along with social contract theory.

Evolution of the Right to Petition in Great Britain

The origin of the right to assemble and petition can be traced back to the signing of the Magna Carta in 1215. The Great Charter hardly granted new rights to English citizens, but it did stipulate that the barons of England had a right to petition the crown for a redress of their grievances and even expect the monarch to respond (Lawson and Seidman 1999). It was from this duty of the king to consult the nobility and respond to petitions that the institution of Parliament (which simply means "discussion group") evolved (Holt 1992). When Parliament grew to include appointed county and city representatives after 1265, the idea that a legislative body had an obligation to hear and respond to the concerns of citizens, rather than just the nobility, was established.

The famous legal scholar Sir William Blackstone argued in his *Commentaries on the Laws of England* (1766) that expanding the power of the House of Commons in the seventeenth century, as well as giving more citizens the right to vote for their representatives in the Commons, led to a greater emphasis on citizen petitioning. Often it was the only way legislators knew what the interests of the public were (Lawson and Seidman 1999). Petitioning was an individual right, though, not a collective right. In 1640, after several attempts to present petitions to Parliament were rejected, riots resulted. Afterward, no more than twenty people could sign a petition, no more than ten were allowed to present it, and all petitions had to be approved first by a variety of public officers. At least these conditions were superior to those in Imperial Russia, Blackstone argues, where the czar executed petitioners whose petitions failed. After the Glorious Revolution of 1688 brought constitutional government to Great Britain, the importance of allowing individual petitioning to protect self-interest as a civil right was made very clear with the enactment of the English Bill of Rights (Holt 1992).

The Right to Petition in America

English civil liberties and political theory found their way across the Atlantic Ocean as colonization of North America took place, with the right of individual petitioning enshrined by the Puritans in the Massachusetts Body of Liberties in 1642 (Lawson and Seidman 1999). The right in Massachusetts was astonishingly broad, granted to all people subject to the colony's laws, including women, bondsmen, and Native Americans. It appears many actually did exercise this right to seek redress of grievances from the colonial government.[5] A century later, it was the failure of King George III and Prime Minister Lord North to address, or even acknowledge, petitioned grievances that justified revolt by the American colonists. In the Declaration of Independence, Thomas Jefferson wrote, "In every stage of these Oppressions, We have Petitioned for Redress in the most humble terms: Our repeated petitions have been answered only by repeated injury. A Prince, whose character is thus marked by every act which may define a Tyrant, is unfit to be the ruler of a free People." Such violations of rights under the English Bill of Rights, Jefferson argued in the Declaration, broke the covenant of the social contract between colonists and king and justified breaking away from the British Empire.

To ensure that respect for the right to petition would endure in the United States, and at the urging of four states as a condition for constitutional ratification, James Madison incorporated it into the First Amendment of the Bill of Rights (Lawson and Seidman 1999). Petitioning was already a regular part of government in Madison's home state of Virginia, and he would make sure it was embedded in the Bill of Rights (Thomas 1993, 149). In fact, his original draft of the First Amendment *only* articulated rights to assemble and petition; the more famous rights of freedom of worship, speech, and press were added later.[6]

The right to petition may be in the same clause of the First Amendment as the freedom to assemble, but no assembly is required to petition. Grounded in the belief that people naturally pursue individual self-interest, petitioning is an individual right, but it may be done collectively. The amendment also places no limit on what form the petitioning might take, or what individuals might petition for, though "redress of grievances" suggests seeking relief from actions the government has already taken, rather than demanding that it take an action. Early efforts to demand redress, however, backfired. In 1830 the right to petition was used by abolitionists in an effort to end slavery in the District of Columbia, with a massive petition to the House of Representatives.[7] Rather than grant any actual redress, the House, under pressure from Southern interests, responded by banning petitioning until 1844 (Thomas 1993, 182–183).

Most petitioning is done today by employing professional agents, or lobbyists. While initially condemning lobbying for special legislative favors in 1875's *Trist v. Child* (Susman 2008), the Supreme Court upheld the First Amendment protection for lobbyists under the right to petition in *United States v. Rumely* (1953) and *United States v. Harriss* (1954). Hiring these lobbyists, though, is expensive, so for most Americans the freedom to petition can only be pursued in conjunction with the freedom to assemble. Thus, while it is not legally necessary, petitioning is often done collectively by a multitude with a common grievance. People combine resources to employ lobbyists to seek redress of whatever grievance is preventing them from pursuing their common interest. That too has been validated by the Court in *NAACP v. Alabama* (1959). But the First Amendment does not guarantee that the government will actually provide any redress, so the collective had better employ a good agent to lobby on their behalf.

A Very Brief History of Interest Groups in the United States

In 2005 the *Congressional Quarterly Researcher* published a report on the rapid growth of the Washington, DC, lobbying profession (Katel 2005): "Lobbying is a growth industry. . . . The number of registered lobbyists in Washington has more than doubled during the past decade, to 26,013 (up from about 10,000 in 1996), and last year clients paid lobbyists an unprecedented $2 billion to help influence Congress." Another count places the number of lobbyists at 35,000 in 2008 (Allard 2008). There are also well over seven thousand organizations that might be comfortably labeled interest groups, and they too rapidly increased in number in the twentieth century. Indeed, special-interest lobbying in the nation's capital always appears to be booming, just as it has always been associated with political corruption, the buying and selling of influence, and flagrant disregard for the public interest.

Lobbying in the Early Republic

What drives people to form interest groups is explored in the next chapter, but one reason is to take advantage of the government's growing interest in solving particular economic or social problems (Leech et al. 2005). This is why interest groups do not appear in significant numbers in Washington until the late nineteenth century. Why form a group to petition in Washington if the national government shows no interest in solving, or even recognizing, any problems? French philosopher Alexis de Tocqueville found in the 1830s as he toured the country to write *Democracy in America* (1835) that instead of looking to their government to redress grievances, Americans preferred to form groups to solve problems *in place of* government action. Local problem solving was easier for nonpolitical groups to do in small-town, agrarian antebellum America, where all problems and politics were truly local. The national government was a distant and comfortably theoretical abstraction.

Lobbying, however, did accompany the very first Congress of the United States. Even in the beginning the federal government had responsibilities for national finance, foreign policy, and defense. Agents representing banking interests fought hard to shape the fiscal policies of first Treasury secretary Alexander Hamilton, especially his proposal for the government to assume the debts of the states after the Revolutionary War (Herring 1929, 31–32). Thomas Jefferson complained to President George Washington about New England legislators pressuring Hamilton (whom Jefferson reviled) at the bidding of financial interests, even though Jefferson believed it came at the expense of their own constituents' interests (Truman 1951, 6). Also of great concern to many was Hamilton's proposal to create a Bank of the United States, which was desired by Northern financiers and merchants who wanted a stable currency, but was opposed by speculators profiting off the existing system of multiple currencies with no fixed value, as well as Southern farmers who saw a national bank as an attack on states' rights (McDonald 1979).

The agents these people employed to influence Hamilton may have even been called "lobbyists," for one version of the word's history claims that it was already being used in Great Britain to refer to petitioners waiting in the lobbies of the houses of Parliament in London (Hansen 2006). The other popular account is that the word was coined in the 1870s by President Ulysses S. Grant in reference to influence seekers lying in wait for him in the lobby of Washington's Willard Hotel (McKean 2004, 3). Regardless of the term's true origin, lobbyists have been spending a lot of time waiting around for lawmakers ever since.

There were reputedly plenty of them focusing their efforts on the small national government of the antebellum era. Most lobbied on behalf of individuals and corporations, rather than anything like today's interest groups. The interests of steamship companies seeking rights—often monopoly rights—to control trade on rivers and canals, the interests of early railroad companies trying to secure government financing, and even early weapons manufacturers seeking military contracts were represented before Congress by men like Thurlow Weed, Collis Huntington, Samuel Colt, and even famous sitting senators like Daniel Webster. In the 1850s, the bribes these lobbyists allegedly paid to members of Congress in return for votes on trade tariff levels led to the first real investigation of undue corporate influence (Susman 2006; Jacob 2010, 16–17).

The Gilded Age

The political, economic, and social fabric of the nation transformed dramatically after the Civil War, and so did lobbying. The Gilded Age (roughly the 1870s and 1880s) is now remembered, with a fair amount of dramatic license, as a time of corruption and excess. In other words, it was the golden age of lobbying. A collection of semisovereign states were being fused into a single nation as the United States underwent industrialization. The new economic and social problems this change brought could only be efficiently resolved with uniform national policy, not a patchwork of state laws (when there was any law at all). New territory was being added to the nation, and it was up to the federal government to figure out how best to use it. Harnessing the West's potential as a vast supply of natural resources and new markets required large-scale infrastructure development: the building of canals and nation-spanning railroads. The private sector was unable or unwilling to pay these development costs, especially since the federal government could be persuaded to do it for them (Thompson 1985). And persuasion meant lobbying.

Designing policy to meet these new demands for infrastructure and financing was well beyond the capabilities of the poorly educated, amateurish, and understaffed Congress of the time (Thompson 1985). Coming to help this suddenly important but rather unready body were the agents of industrialists: colorful men who used their legal and social talents to secure public contracts, favorable policy, and general largesse for their well-heeled employers. Around Washington moved larger-than-life lobbyists like William Chandler and self-styled King of the Lobby Sam Ward. If the yellow journalism of the late nineteenth century is to be believed, Ward and Chandler left a legacy of a Congress corrupted by wine, food, and women as they sought votes and government subsidies benefitting "fat cat" industrialists such as Astor, Carnegie, Vanderbilt, and Rockefeller. Ward's influence was allegedly so great that he did business out of the conference room of the Senate Appropriations Committee in the Capitol (Jacob 2010).

Much of this corruption may well have been exaggerated by the likes of David Graham Phillips, whose "The Treason of the Senate" series in *Cosmopolitan Magazine* (not the one known today!) in 1906 described senators being bribed with money and lucrative corporate directorships in return for enormous land grants and contracts by the vague but decidedly sinister "Interests." Looking back at the Gilded Age from a time not too far removed, political scientist Pendleton Herring wrote of the "old lobby" that actual bribery was not nearly as pervasive as people like Phillips would have it, though the influence of men like Ward and Chandler was profound. Sam Ward in fact boasted that he never gave a bribe because he never needed to. His influence came from his skill at building personal relationships. Legislators had plenty of time on their hands. They were living far from home and family; looking for food, drink, and entertainment; and were perhaps a little awed by the opulent lifestyles of the great industrial families and their lobbyists (Jacob 2010). Who would not want to spend an evening at the lavish high-society dinners thrown by that famous gourmet chef Sam Ward? Or enjoy a little game of cards where a congressman might win big when playing against a lobbyist? Or perhaps spend time with a "lobbyess," even if it meant missing crucial hearings and votes on Capitol Hill (Herring 1929, 36)?

While fun nights out might have helped them build impressive portfolios of relationships, Gilded Age historian Margaret Susan Thompson (1985) argues that lobbyists were also valued by legislators because they helped with the important district-relations work that kept elected officials in office, especially patronage decisions. There were scandals and bribery—such as the noxious Credit Mobilier mess of 1872, where shares of stock in a company building the First Transcontinental Railroad were handed out by lobbyists and even by members of Congress to other congressmen in return for votes—but clear vote buying was hard to find. An investigation pushed by President Woodrow Wilson in 1913 failed to uncover any clear corruptive connection between senators and lobbyists, at least none anybody would admit to (Katel 2005, 624).

The Gilded Age, however, was still not a period of interest group formation; these lobbyists were agents for personal or corporate interests, or for individuals seeking patronage jobs from their members of Congress (Herring 1929, 36–37). Studying the historical record, political scientists Daniel Tichenor and Richard Harris (2002) found quite a few individual business leaders testifying before Congress between 1833 and 1880, but virtually nobody representing anything that could be called an interest group. In the 1880s, however, organized groups began to appear. In the last decade of the nineteenth century, Tichenor and Harris identified roughly 400 group representatives appearing at hearings, and about 1,600 from 1900 to 1920. Partially this was because scandals like Credit Mobilier and the inflammatory journalism of Phillips convinced many businessmen it would be safer to work through trade associations rather than be seen lobbying directly (Herring 1929, 41). But new demands for more far-ranging national policy-making were just as responsible for the creation and boom of organized groups—perhaps even more so.

The Age of Organization

In Figure 1.2 I use data from the Web site Lobbyists.info to chart the birth rates of American interest groups.[8] The solid line shows the number of organizations engaged in national and state politics established each year, whereas the broken line shows the number of births of groups only lobbying the federal government. Consistent with what Tichenor and Harris discovered, the lines only really start to rise at the end of the nineteenth century.

Most of these newcomers were trade associations for industries, such as manufacturing companies and railroads, as well as a variety of professions, such as tailors, builders, shop owners, lawyers, and doctors. Business leaders sponsored many of these trade groups because it was not cost effective to lobby individually when the new workplace safety and monopoly-busting laws coming out of Washington concerned whole industries (Aldrich et al. 1994, 224). Highly skilled professions organized associations, such as the American Bar Association (founded in 1878) to represent the collective interests of lawyers. Formerly nonpolitical associations chose to become politically active, as the American Medical Association (founded in 1847) decided to do in 1899.[9]

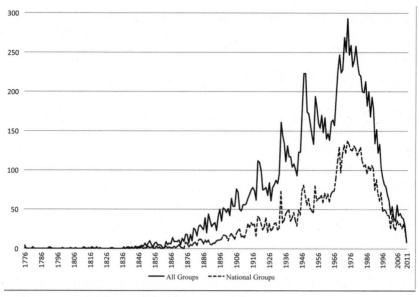

FIGURE 1.2   Interest Group Birth Rates, 1776–2011
Source: Lobbyists.info and *Washington Representatives*

As the twentieth century dawned, bakers, bankers, candlestick makers, miners, cobblers, textile manufacturers, brewers, lumberjacks, bond dealers, pet sellers, printers, and pickle canners (among others) all sought political representation through associations. Many were actually encouraged to form associations by the government as part of its efforts to organize American industry for World War I. Most of these associations initially operated on shoestring budgets, working out of office space and with staff supplied by their member businesses. Still, by the 1920s, Herring claimed that it was just about impossible to think of any business or profession not represented in Washington by some interest group (1929, 2, 78).

Farmers across the South, Midwest, and even the far West were also organizing. Price instabilities, unstable economic conditions, railroad transportation costs, and overall fears that industrialization and modernization were going to leave rural America behind sparked the creation of the National Grange and the National Farmers Alliance (Browne 2001, 63–64). Founded in 1870, the Grange mobilized so many farmers that even strict free-market devotees in Congress agreed to provide price supports or price floors and ceilings for most crops rather than risk being booted from office. For a time the Grange, which flirted for a while with the idea of becoming a political party, was even able to influence Senate confirmation of federal judges (Ainsworth and Maltese 1996).

But not all of the turn-of-the-century organizing shown in Figure 1.2 occurred around economic interests. Out of the abolitionist movement of the mid-nineteenth century came advocacy groups more tied to social causes than businesses and professions. While John Gardner, founder of the archetypal social activist group Common Cause, says, "Future historians may remember the 1970s as the decade when citizen action emerged as a revitalizing force in American society" (Gardner 1972, 72), what citizen activist group was more successful than the early twentieth century's Women's Christian Temperance Union or the Anti-Saloon League? After a brutal advocacy war (see Odegard 1928), these groups achieved the greatest political victory of all: amending the Constitution to ban alcohol. Other women's rights activist groups went on to further amend it to give women the right to vote in 1920.

Growing public concern about the physical and social health of America during the Industrial Revolution also spurred the formation of cause-oriented interest groups. They pressed lawmakers for child labor restrictions, antimonopoly laws, safer working conditions, immigration reform, and some small amount of social insurance support for the elderly and unemployed (Clemens 1997; Gamm and Putnam 1999). Tichenor and Harris found about 150 such organizations testifying before Congress from 1900 to 1909, and then over 400 during the next decade (2002, 598).

Mindful of the alleged excesses of Gilded Age lobbying, many viewed all of these new political organizations with suspicion. President Theodore Roosevelt and congressional lawmakers tried to use the power and resources of the federal government to improve society by banning business contributions in elections with the Tillman Act of 1907 (Katel 2005, 624). Then their good-government Progressive Era, as we now call it, began to run out of steam. In 1913, investigations of corrupt lobbying practiced by these new interest groups, especially by the National Association of Manufacturers, failed to uncover anything substantial, and interest in regulating groups and lobbyists began to dwindle (Herring 1929, 42–45). Reform even remained elusive after the 1923 Teapot Dome scandal, in which oil companies bribed President Warren Harding's Interior secretary, Albert Fall, to gain lucrative oil production contracts for the navy without going through a competitive bidding process.

The New Deal Burst

The great economic stimulation from government employment and building programs, along with the new pro-regulatory environment in the 1930s, all enacted to combat the Great Depression, created another burst of group formation seen in Figure 1.2 (Aldrich et al. 1994, 232). New business associations formed to resist the wave of legislation and regulation coming out of President Franklin Roosevelt's administration, while other associations formed at the administration's insistence in order to make the distribution of resources and operation of employment programs easier. Cause-oriented groups also emerged to support Roosevelt's National Recovery Act, Social Security Act, National Labor Relations Act, and Glass-Steagall Act (this last one separated the banking and investing industries from each other). Trade and industrial labor unions, which had largely avoided politics in favor of strikes, now saw enormous opportunity in Roosevelt and congressional Democrats and mobilized their members to support the president's New Deal policies (Greenstone 1977, Ch. 1; Hannan and Freeman 1977).

Ironically, some of Roosevelt's top aides, men who had reveled in being the enemies of business, went on to enjoy highly successful lobbying careers working for those very same business interests once the heady days of the New Deal faded after World War II. Progressive idealism did not stand in the way of Tom "Tommy the Cork" Corcoran and Abe Fortas building lucrative careers from the many connections they had built up in Washington during their years with Roosevelt (McKean 2004). They survived investigations into their lobbying practices because Congress decided that making phone calls on behalf of wealthy clients to friends in government who owed them favors was not corruption, just as Congress exonerated Sam Ward of similar charges in the prior century (McKean 2004, 165; Jacob 2010, 3). Efforts to regulate lobbying in 1946 also largely failed because Congress could not figure out how to define the profession (a recurring problem), and much of what it did enact was struck down by the US Supreme Court in *United States v. Harriss* in 1954 because it infringed on the First Amendment right to petition (Milbrath 1963, 7, 13).

The Postwar Explosion

In 1983, political scientist Jack Walker published a famous (to political scientists anyway) article charting the birth rates of interest groups. He found a burst of unusually high group formation in the late 1960s and early 70s (see Figure 1.2). More importantly, Walker found that this **advocacy explosion** (as scholars like to call it; see Knoke 1986) largely produced cause-oriented groups—those lobbying for social change rather than the protection of economic and professional interests. Whereas most people during the Depression were concerned with economic matters, or solving social problems stemming from the economic collapse, Americans in the 1950s focused on new social problems because of economic growth. As political scientist Jeff Berry explains it, in a time when most Americans did not have to worry about layoffs and keeping food on the table and roofs over the heads of their families, many began to think more critically about the impact of postwar economic growth on consumers and the environment (1999, Ch. 3). They wanted to ensure that America's growing prosperity was shared by everyone and that the world's wealthiest society set an example by making sure that all of its less fortunate citizens were cared for. Government was seen as a positive force in this mission, and political entrepreneurs like Ralph Nader, who founded Public Citizen, and John Gardner, of Common Cause, were among those who established new citizen groups and public interest groups to help President Lyndon Johnson enact his Great Society program.

I explain the differences between trade associations and citizen and public interest groups in the next chapter, but the emergence of so many cause-oriented groups in the 1970s rounds out the broad contours of today's Washington interest group community. Today there are thousands of interest groups lobbying on hundreds of issues in the nation's capital city. Figure 1.3 shows the breakdown of issues lobbied by interest groups in 2010, created from information in the Lobbyists.info database. Clearly some issues attract far more interest group attention than others. Only 24 groups claim to be lobbying on dairy issues, and only 34 are interested in trucking, while 827 lobby on banking and finance and a whopping 2,052 on health care. But here is the larger point: not only is just about every profession organized in an association, and not only is almost every conceivable social cause being pursued by an interest group, but almost *every* issue one can think of is being vigorously lobbied today in the halls of Congress, in the West Wing of the White House, in the hundreds of executive branch agencies, and even in the federal courts. New interest groups are pushing even more new issues, and old issues are attracting even more new interest groups. Yet we actually do not know just how many groups there are, for there is no comprehensive register of them all. Lobbyists.info and similar databases are almost certainly undercounting the total number of groups pursuing the interests of some collection of Americans in national (to say nothing of state, local, and international) politics. We are a nation of citizens pursuing our individual self-interest through interest groups.

There are so many interest groups and lobbyists that they even have their own professional associations, such as the American Society of Association

Number of interest groups and client industries lobbying each issue

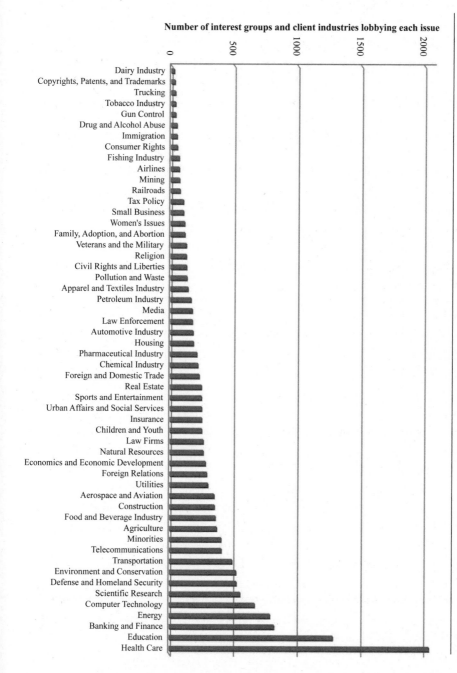

FIGURE 1.3 Lobbying Groups and Client Organization by Issue in 2010

Source: Washington Representatives

Executives and the American League of Lobbyists. Interest groups and lobbying are significant and, if you accept social contract theory like Madison, quite natural. They are a legitimate part of our contemporary political landscape. Participating in interest groups, in fact, is the only form of political participation that seems to be growing. Americans are abandoning their political parties, and frequently fewer than half vote in elections, but they seem to love the idea of representation through interest groups (even though they tell pollsters they do not)! Madison seems to have expected this when he wrote in Federalist No. 10 that "Liberty is to faction what air is to fire" and "the latent causes of faction are sown in the nature of man." While he had deep reservations about so many small factions being active in American politics, he believed that forming factions was natural for people driven by self-interest, so inhibiting their formation was "the cure worse than the disease." Instead he protected free association and lobbying in the First Amendment. Were he alive today, he might not be thrilled to see thousands of interest groups lobbying Washington, but he also might not be surprised.

In Summary

So what is most important to remember in this chapter? Here is a quick summary:

- Interest groups are collections of people with essentially the same self-interest, about which they feel so strongly that they collectively form an organization to promote and defend it through the political process.
- The development of the political philosophy of the social contract underlying our civilization prioritizes individual self-interest and protects the pursuit of that self-interest through politics.
- Large-scale interest group formation began in the late nineteenth century and continued dramatically through the twentieth century.
- Scholars have a hard time defining interest groups; therefore we do not even know for certain how many there are.
- Some interest groups represent businesses, trades, and professions, while others represent social causes.

Finally, keep this in mind as you read the rest of the book: interest groups are considered legitimate because we believe the pursuit of self-interest is close to sacred. It probably could not be any other way in an economic system that assumes the best result for society comes when people compete with each other to satisfy their self-interest. As Jane Mansbridge observes, democratic politics in a free-market economy are usually adversarial, and this leaves no room for thinking about the common good. Indeed, there may be no common good or public interest in such a system. If we wished to eliminate interest groups and lobbying, as Madison understood, we would have to fundamentally rethink who we are and what rights and liberties we expect to enjoy in our political system. Barring such an unlikely change, it may be best to think more about how we can use interest groups and their adversarial impulse—which itself is just a reflection of our own adversarial nature—to achieve the greatest good for the greatest number of people. I will return to this idea at the end of the book.

Notes

1. See "About the American Bankers Association," American Bankers Association, 2013, http://www.aba.com/About/Pages/default.aspx.

2. See the home page of the Center for Education Reform, http://www.edreform.org.

3. See "About Us," Save Our Sound: Alliance to Protect Nantucket Sound, 2013, http://www.saveoursound.org/about_us/.

4. See "TransCanada Pipeline," Bold Nebraska, 2013, http://boldnebraska.org/transcanada-pipeline.

5. I am indebted to the First Amendment Center for providing me with much of this information. See Adam Newton, "Petition Overview," First Amendment Center, October 10, 2002, http://www.firstamendmentcenter.org/petition-overview.

6. See Newton, "Petition Overview."

7. Ibid.

8. The data from Lobbyists.info is on groups and associations and is probably the best database of political organizations in existence. It was supplemented by additional interest groups listed in *Washington Representatives* (2010 edition), a companion publication that includes many citizen groups and public interest groups not in the Lobbyists.info database. These sources are superior to lobbying registration data because the latter only capture organizations directly lobbying Congress, not those that only lobby the bureaucracy or judiciary. Nor does lobbying registration data normally include organizations that indirectly lobby through grassroots advocacy. Also, some of the organizations in the Lobbyist.info database only lobby sporadically as issues important to them come up, and this means they may not be included in the registration database if they did not register to lobby that year. One drawback of all of these datasets is that they only include groups still alive today, not those that have closed down.

9. See "Our History," American Medical Association, 2013, http://www.ama-assn.org/ama/pub/about-ama/our-history.page?.

CHAPTER TWO

Collective Action and Interest Group Organization

In his 1972 manifesto, *In Common Cause*, founder of the organization Common Cause John Gardner dramatically condemned the state of the American political system.

> Under present conditions, our political and governmental machinery cannot serve *anybody*—neither poor people nor the middle class, neither black nor white, neither young nor old. . . . But a good many citizens have worked with great energy and little success on the substantive problems of education, health, poverty, housing, employment, equal rights, the environment, and war and peace. And it is gradually beginning to dawn on them that many of those problems are made harder to solve—or rendered wholly unsolvable—by breakdowns in the structure and process of government. (17–18)

Gardner made no secret of who the villains behind this breakdown were. He wrote: "Today good citizens leave the voting booth, pat themselves on the back for doing their civic duty, and then go home and forget the whole thing. But the political machines don't forget. The oil lobby doesn't forget it. Nor the agribusiness lobby. Representatives of those and all the other special interests are in their offices the morning after election day figuring out the next step. . . . And the taxpayers will pay and pay and pay—and wonder why the more they pay, the less they get" (19–21). But attacking these special interests head-on was not Gardner's solution, for he felt that would not bring about the dramatic reform of government institutions and the people in them that was required to fix the underlying problem. Instead, Gardner recommended citizen action through organizations led by professional advocates, such as his own new group. As he said, "In matters of social action, citizens have some lessons to learn. Citizens can repair that [government] breakdown—but only through organization. Common Cause has proven that it can be done. The basic ailments that are making invalids of our political and governmental institutions will only be cured by tough, sustained pressure. And that pressure must come from citizens" (18–20).

What makes Common Cause different from the entrenched lobbies Gardner marked as enemies? Clearly he believes that the differences between his "citizen lobby" and industry and trade associations were profound. Is he right? Are groups like Common Cause better at mobilizing the public for political participation than business interests? Do they lobby for something nobler, like the elusive public interest? Do many people even *want* to join and participate in these kinds of interest groups? Or are these individuals just writing the occasional check to yet another self-interested advocacy organization masquerading as an advocate of the public interest? In this chapter I explore the odd logic of interest group membership. People join interest groups for different reasons, and these reasons can shape the structure of a group and the kinds of political goals it fights for.

Collective Action in an Individualistic Nation

When Alexis de Tocqueville, author of *Democracy in America* (1835), travelled the United States, two observations left impressions on him. First, Americans, more than Europeans, embodied the capitalistic spirit of entrepreneurship and individualism. Second, while Americans frequently formed groups, they were usually small, ad hoc, and structured to solve problems *without* turning to government for help. Americans were only group-oriented in situations in which individuals had certain goals to achieve, like asking for better or more roads and schools, and knew that they could only achieve these goals if they pooled time and resources with each other. In other words, people formed groups when they had to, not because they wanted to. Americans, Tocqueville concluded, were fundamentally individualists. Twentieth-century scholars, though, were unwilling to accept this conclusion. Social-psychologist Arthur Bentley (1908) argued that a person's interest—his or her wants, needs, and outlook on life—could not be understood outside of his or her "group-context." People are defined by those around them, he argued, and often those around them are individuals who have similar backgrounds, needs, beliefs, and ideas—their "group," so to speak. Society is little more than an aggregation of these groups. And because the collective interests of one group might be harmful to the interests of other groups, politics is necessary to determine how these interests are met (or not) and to divide resources accordingly.

Political scientist David Truman built a whole theory of politics and government around this assumption that society is a plurality of groups and that each of these groups are composed of people who share interests. Grounded in the ideas of Bentley, as well as those of David Hume and James Madison discussed in the last chapter, this theory of **pluralism** argues that politics is conflict between cohesive groups—or *pluralities*—rather than simple majorities of people. Latent groups of citizens sharing common interests mobilize to fight back when they perceive political conflict as threatening to their interests. Mobilization begets countermobilization, and thus the range of interest groups active in American politics inexorably expands like ripples from a drop of water in a pool (Truman 1951, 106–107). In this view, existing policy reflects the balance of power between groups, though it typically favors the stronger group.

However, there are a couple of serious criticisms of this theory on why interest groups form. One is that unmobilized people are often unable to perceive dangers to their interests because opposing interest groups and their allies in government keep those threats hidden (Mills 1956; Bachrach and Baratz 1962). A tougher criticism came from the economist Mancur Olson (1965). He argued that truly self-interested people will not pay to join and support an organization even when they do see threats to their interests. Why should they? If other people are willing to pay the costs of organizing the interest group, then the rational nonjoiner gets the benefit of having his or her interests defended with the added benefit of not paying the requisite fee to belong to the group. Of course Olson's prediction that self-interested people will free ride on the efforts of others has a perverse consequence. If everyone is rationally self-interested, then nobody will pay the cost of forming and running the interest group. They all believe somebody else will do it. The result is that the interest group never forms and the rational individual's interest is never defended!

Olson's argument must be taken seriously. Like Tocqueville, he believed that Americans are avid individualists inclined to compete even with others who hold similar interests. Interest groups advocate for changes in policy that affects everyone whether they are members of the group or not because public policy is a **public good**. An individual whose interests are aligned with a mobilized group reaps the benefits of its lobbying even if he or she is not a member and does not contribute to its effort. Most groups charge membership dues, so in a cost-benefit analysis it is logical for a competitive individual not to pay when he or she will still enjoy the public benefits. Nonmembers get a free ride on the backs of those (suckers?) who pay to join.

Olson's great insight is not identifying this **free-rider problem** but his explanation of why interest groups exist *in spite* of those who ride on the tails of their dues-paying peers. Obviously interest groups exist and millions of people support them, so there must be some compensation for membership that tips the scale in Olson's cost-benefit analysis. The group must provide *something* that members value but cannot get, or at least not get easily, if they do not join the group.

Think about the American Automobile Association (AAA), which boasts a membership of over fifty million.[1] AAA is a political organization that maintains a large office in Washington, DC, where its staff lobbies for greater highway funding and other pro-car policies. Yet it would not be too great of a stretch to say that few AAA members know much about its lobbying activities and probably would not care if they did. Drivers join AAA to get their keys out when they accidentally lock them inside their cars, to get gas delivered to their stalled vehicle when they accidentally run out of it, and to get their cars hauled out of ditches. They only get these benefits if they pay advocacy-supporting membership dues. Towing and other roadside assistance is a **material incentive**, a private tangible benefit that members get for belonging to an organization that also happens to lobby for public benefits such as highways without potholes. This changes the cost-benefit analysis and makes it rational for self-interested people to join. Thus, Olson argued, interest groups are formed and maintained.

Other Incentives and the Free-Rider Problem's Problems

Olson's insight is profound yet incomplete: profound because even though his utilitarian logic is hardly the reason for all political activism, every other explanation for interest group formation must still confront it; incomplete because scholars (and presumably group executives) know that while people have to get something for membership, lots of groups do not seem to offer anything as valuable as AAA's road services. Yet people still join those interest groups. A typology of incentives proposed in 1961 by political scientists Peter Clark and James Q. Wilson shows the weakness in Olson's assumption that activism can be explained by cost-benefit analyses. Political activism, Clark and Wilson understood, is driven by passion to change policy and society as much as it is by cold reason, and probably more so. As they were surrounded by the political unrest of the 1960s, it is hard to imagine how they could have come to any other conclusion.

Some individuals and businesses pay the fee to join political associations because they value services the group offers, but other members are driven more by political passion. In exchange for membership dues, many organizations offer the opportunity for political involvement to people who want and need a sense of political purpose. Unlike members who join because they want to get the restricted, material benefits of membership, these members are attracted by the intangible reward of feeling like their contributions to, and participation in, the group makes a positive difference in society, like aiding the poor or improving the business climate (Berry 1999; Drutman 2012). Clark and Wilson call this a **purposive incentive**, and groups that primarily attract members by offering this kind of reward are fundamentally different in how they operate and what they advocate for from organizations that attract members primarily by offering material incentives (see Chapter 4).

Groups relying primarily on purposive incentives to attract members may also have a harder time recruiting them than organizations relying on material incentives. While the steady provision of material benefits keep memberships relatively stable, groups relying on more purposive-driven members often have a harder time recruiting when issues important to potential members are not on the government's agenda. But when the issues do come up, their ranks can swell. When it became obvious that Congress was going to take up legislation in 2013 increasing the number of immigrants coming into the United States, the leader of a group opposing the bill, NumbersUSA, reported that his historically three-hundred-thousand-person membership abruptly swelled to two million (Bolton 2013)!

Clark and Wilson also identified a third incentive: people sometimes join groups to fulfill a need to socialize with others who hold interests similar to their own. This may seem to describe social clubs and civic associations more than political advocacy organizations, but consider that some otherwise purposive-driven groups have long histories of recruiting members by promising opportunities to socialize. The Sierra Club does this by offering members hiking trips with others who enjoy nature. The National Rifle Association provides its members opportunities to meet and socialize as they shoot targets. Separating this **solidary incentive** from the purposive incentive is difficult, though, because individuals with an interest in bringing about political change would probably also want to meet others who feel strongly about the same thing. They are all kindred spirits in the group.

In fact, joining social clubs may still lead to interest group membership and activism. Tocqueville noted that Americans frequently joined local civic associations; the social skills they learned there disposed them toward political participation. Research by political scientists Henry Brady, Sidney Verba, and Kay Lehman Schlozman (1995; 1999) found evidence supporting his observation. Participation in nonpolitical civic associations teaches activism and crucial group-building skills such as organizing protests, public speaking, and fundraising. Moreover, they found that it is within social circles of individuals sharing common interests that recruitment for political groups often takes place. While, all things being equal, people of higher socioeconomic status (SES) are more likely to participate in politics, civic group membership compensates because the skills and networks people of lower SES develop make them more likely to participate as well (Holyoke 2013b). A great example of this was seen in the churches, social clubs, and small colleges of the South where African Americans learned to organize for civil rights (McAdam 1982).

Who Joins Interest Groups?

So some people join interest groups because they feel passionately about the interests the group represents. Others want to socialize with people who share similar interests. Still others just want the perks and goodies of membership, and some join for all these reasons. This is useful to know, but it still tells us nothing about *who* actually joins interest groups. What do we know about them? Only a little, but a 2008 survey by Zogby does provide some insight.[2] They found that 38 percent of people in interest groups are between the ages of thirty-five and fifty-four, while 21 percent are between fifty-five and sixty-nine, and 12 percent are over the age of seventy. So the plurality of group members are in their prime working years, and membership tapers off in the older and younger strata. They are a fairly educated bunch: 66 percent of group members have a bachelor's degree, while only 30 percent of nonmembers had not finished (or even started) their undergraduate education.

While 78 percent of interest group members are Caucasian, 12 percent are African American (13 percent of Americans are African American according to the Census Bureau), and 5 percent are Hispanic (17 percent of Americans are Hispanic). Joiners are also somewhat wealthier than average, though this may only mean that they have more dispensable income to spend on supporting political groups. Twenty-five percent of group members earn an annual income of between $50,000 and $75,000, and while only 14 percent earn $75,000 to $100,000, 26 percent earn over $100,000 annually. Interest group members are only a little more ideologically liberal than nonmembers. Of all group members, 30 percent describe themselves as ideological moderates, which is also true of 28 percent of nonmembers. Only 36 percent of members describe themselves as "conservative" or "very conservative," while 43 percent of nonmembers describe themselves in this way. As for liberals and self-described "progressives," 29 percent of members place themselves in this category, while that is true of only 22 percent of nonmembers. Conservatives apparently are less inclined to join interest groups than liberals.

For several characteristics there are no real differences between members and nonmembers. Having children (age seventeen or younger) makes no differences, nor does being single, married, or divorced. Men and women are equally likely to join, as are rural folk and suburbanites, while city dwellers are less likely (perhaps because they have more social alternatives). Retirees are no more or less likely to join, AARP notwithstanding. In sum, the typical interest group joiner is white, middle-aged, well educated, and upper-income.

Starting Up Interest Groups

Incentives explain why members join interest groups that already exist, but who starts them up and funds them before there are members to pay any dues? Even the most politically passionate, purposive-driven, would-be members who are eager to organize a group to pursue their political interests still need somebody to do the mundane logistical work of incorporation, fundraising, member recruitment, and strategy development. Most groups can trace their origins back to a skillful political entrepreneur who took it upon themselves to organize members (Salisbury 1969). Public Citizen founder Ralph Nader is perhaps the most famous example, but others are John Muir for the Sierra Club, John Gardner for Common Cause, David Brower for Friends of the Earth (after being fired from Sierra Club), and lesser known figures such as George Maxwell for the National Irrigation Association, James Howenstein for the American Bankers Association, and John Taylor for the National Community Reinvestment Coalition.

Where do these visionaries find the money to get their organizations going? The popular image may be bands of concerned citizens pooling meager resources to start a group on a shoestring budget in a David versus Goliath struggle against well-heeled, faceless corporate interests. Or of noble, civic-minded businesspeople giving their time and money to promote their industry's or community's fortunes against an overregulating, job-killing government (another David versus Goliath). These images are more myth than reality. In one of the first thorough surveys of interest group origins and finances, political scientist Jack Walker found that to start and fund an interest group, it's not sufficient that charismatic entrepreneurs bring together small but highly motivated groups of politically passionate people with some spare change. A fledgling group needs a major infusion of start-up capital from some type of patron to create and sustain it through those critical first years of collective action (Walker 1983; 1991, 49).

Walker and others point to the socially turbulent 1960s as a time that was especially conducive to group formation because ideologically motivated foundations wanted to promote their visions of the public good by funding new advocacy organizations (Walker 1991, 48–49). Philanthropies like the Ford Foundation wanted to solve the nation's social and environmental ills by using public policy to harness and channel the wealth of American business into social programs. To that end they provided the seed capital that got many of the left-leaning activist groups of that era off the ground (Vogel 1989, Ch. 5; Berry 1999). The government itself has been many groups' financial patron, giving funds through contracts that provide services on the state's behalf, which in turn encourages these organizations to lobby policy makers for ongoing financial support and policy change (Salamon 1995). Even today many interest groups remain dependent on these various patrons. Walker found that 89 percent of cause-oriented groups not only depended on philanthropies, government, or private individuals for start-up support, but years later were still more reliant on them than on member dues for funding (King and Walker 1991, 78–81).

Types of Organized Interests

It is now clear that interest groups come in many forms and have different kinds of members and goals. Some are concerned with business issues, others with social issues, and sometimes they fight over whether the issue is social or business-related. Some groups are large, with members in state and local chapters all over the nation, advocating for a host of issues in many areas of policy making. Others are very small and only interested in a few issues. Some can turn out tens of thousands of passionate, purposive-driven members to protest on the steps of the Capitol, while others can barely get their members to send them an occasional check without promising glitzy conventions in Las Vegas and lots of exclusive, material goodies. Some groups represent people, while others represent corporations or nonprofits. Some do not even have actual dues-paying members at all but still claim to advocate on behalf of a discernible group of people with a common interest. This is why some scholars prefer omitting the word "group" and instead use the term **organized interest** (e.g., Baumgartner and Leech 1998).

Figure 2.1 shows a variety of types of organizations, only some of which are true interest groups, that lobby the national government. This 2010 data comes from the same *Washington Representatives* and Lobbyists.info data used in Chapter 1. Associations, defined and explained below, are the plurality, though some only lobby on rare occasions. Corporations also lobby in large numbers, though large firms do so more frequently than small businesses because they tend to attract more government attention (Lux, Crook, and Woehr 2011). Despite the disdain corporate CEOs reputedly have toward government, thousands of them have decided that public policy has enough impact on their bottom line to hire lobbying firms, or even to open their own corporate lobbying offices in Washington, to pursue the interests of their shareholders. Sometimes their goals fly in the face of public demand, such as the efforts of music recording companies to prosecute Web sites and software makers that facilitate the popular practice of peer-to-peer music file sharing, and to push legislation that bans the practice (Lardner 2009). I talk more about corporate lobbying in Chapter 3.

Another significant organization category in Figure 2.1 is hospitals and universities, which lobby to shape health care policy, education funding, and intellectual property laws, and to gain government grants. Add them together with corporations, along with state and local governments, foreign governments, and Indian nations, and it becomes clear that the majority of organizations lobbying in Washington are not groups trying to represent some portion of the public at all (Salisbury 1984). Interest groups are a minority in the community of organized interests!

Genuine interest groups fall into a few basic categories, which I explain using two membership characteristics laid out in Figure 2.2. The first dimension relates to how inclusive the interests of the organization are. Some groups

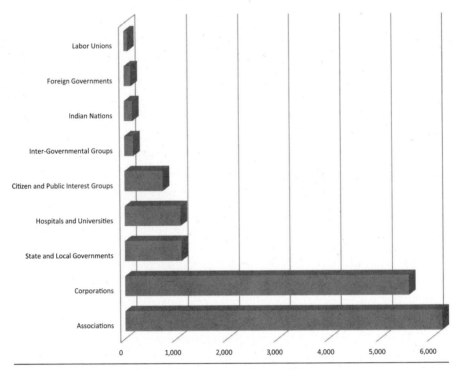

FIGURE 2.1   Number and Type of Lobbying Entities in 2010

seek to serve small, tightly defined social or economic interests and have no desire to contribute to the general well-being of anybody else. Associations representing professions are the obvious example. If you do not design buildings for a living, you cannot join the American Institute of Architects. On the other hand, some interests will represent anybody and everybody. Anybody can join the Audubon Society; an interest in birds is not required. Often the policies interest groups seek will affect everyone, and thus the group may claim to be representing all Americans and therefore the public interest. Whether all citizens want the organization to represent them is another matter.

The other dimension is the intensity of passion members have for the interest binding them together. It seems to be a fact of political life in America that many people just do not feel all that strongly about their political interests, at least not strong enough to promote or defend them by participating in interest groups, even if they are members. Of course even social clubs are having a hard time getting people to participate these days (Putnam 2001). As Mancur Olson argued, many would simply prefer to sit back and let others do the advocacy work for them.

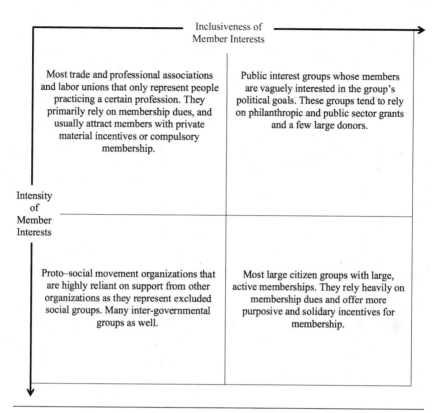

Inclusiveness of
Member Interests

Most trade and professional associations
and labor unions that only represent people
practicing a certain profession. They
primarily rely on membership dues, and
usually attract members with private
material incentives or compulsory
membership.

Public interest groups whose members
are vaguely interested in the group's
political goals. These groups tend to rely
on philanthropic and public sector grants
and a few large donors.

Intensity
of
Member
Interests

Proto–social movement organizations that
are highly reliant on support from other
organizations as they represent excluded
social groups. Many inter-governmental
groups as well.

Most large citizen groups with large,
active memberships. They rely heavily on
membership dues and offer more
purposive and solidary incentives for
membership.

FIGURE 2.2   Dimensions of Interest Group Organization

Trade and Professional Associations

The most numerous, if not the most passionate member-driven, interest groups are the **trade and professional associations**. The interest that binds their members together is what they do for a living, which means that theirs are fundamentally *economic* interests. Some associations do not even represent individuals but the companies they work for. The American Bakers Association represents individuals who make and sell baked goods, while the American Bankers Association represents corporations engaged in banking, though individual bank CEOs still decide whether to belong to the ABA. Some associations are well known, such as the US Chamber of Commerce (businesspeople and businesses), the American Bar Association (lawyers), and the American Medical Association (doctors). Others are a little more obscure, such as the National Rural Health Association (country doctors), the Toy Industry Association (toymakers), the Bond Dealers of America (banks and securities dealers), the Plasma Protein Therapeutics Association (plasma therapy professionals), and the Real Estate Roundtable (real estate development firms). Some have names that give them some flare, such as the Inflatable Advertising Dealers Association or the American Society of Nuclear Cardiology. Others try to make themselves sound less politically motivated, such as the American Petroleum Institute, which represents oil companies. Some like names that portray them as little persons struggling in the shadows of corporate Goliaths, like the Independent Oil and Gas Association. Some claim to represent broad economic interests when in fact they only represent a few well-heeled corporations, like the Financial Services Roundtable, which only represents the hundred biggest financial institutions in America. And every now and then entirely fake ones appear, such as the National Disabled Soldiers' League. It claimed to represent World War I veterans, but there were no members. League leaders pocketed all of the money they solicited except a little they spent to stage national conventions with hired "delegates" and "members" (Herring 1929, 27).

In Figure 2.3 I use the same data used in Figure 1.2 to chart the rise of trade and professional associations in American history. As I recounted there, these groups started to appear in the late nineteenth century as the Industrial Revolution gave rise to new trades and professions. When the country found itself faced with more complex economic and social problems, industries needed a more permanent presence in Washington to keep an eye on an increasingly proactive government (Aldrich et al. 1994, 227–34). The American Bankers Association, for instance, formed in 1875, when the federal government established and began to regulate a common currency with the 1864 National Bank Act (Hubbard 1995). Corporations also realized that it was not beneficial to them to be seen directly lobbying lawmakers after the fiascos of the Gilded Age, and instead invested in setting up associations to do it for them (Thompson 1985, 41–42). It is easy to see this in Figure 2.3, where the trend line indicating the number of trade associations born each year begins to rise in the late 1800s and early twentieth century.

Some associations were started at the urging of government. Part of the impetus to establish the Chamber of Commerce as an umbrella group covering all businesses came from President William Howard Taft, in 1912, to counter the umbrella union American Federation of Labor (Truman 1951, 85). The government pressured other industries to organize associations so production in support of World War I could be better coordinated. For instance, the government's Council of National Defense pushed the coal industry into forming the National Coal Association in 1917 (Truman 1951, 76). The trend line in

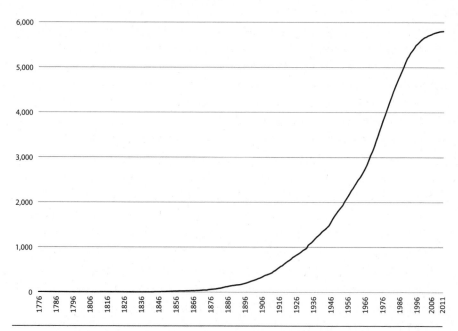

FIGURE 2.3   Historical Trend in the Total Number of Associations
Source: Lobbyists.info and *Washington Representatives*

Figure 2.3 continues to rise through the 1930s and 1940s, as the Commerce Department further organized industries into associations to instill some sense of self-governance in American industry without resorting to direct regulation, as well as assign them industrial classification codes to better target government support during the Great Depression (Lowi 1979, 79).

Some industries organized to ward off government regulation, as the American Association of Railroads did in 1934, after Roosevelt threatened a takeover because they were run so inefficiently (Truman 1951, 77). In 1919, after older organizations lobbying for national farm policy like the Grange declined, the American Farm Bureau Federation was formed. At the urging of Department of Agriculture officials, county farm bureaus (also originally created by the USDA) combined all over the nation to form this new agriculture advocacy group (Truman 1951, 90–91). Today just about every sector of the American workforce, from farm laborers to corporate boards, is represented by work-based associations. Indeed, one wonders if there is any profession in the United States still not represented by some trade group.

Business associations tend to seek government benefits aimed more exclusively at just their members, placing them on the left side of Figure 2.2. Some lobby for tax breaks, price supports, or subsidies for businesses or individuals practicing their profession. They also frequently defend their member businesses and professionals from regulatory restrictions on their freedom to operate. Surprisingly, though, sometimes these trade groups lobby *for* regulation because it gives their members a market advantage over foreign, and sometimes even domestic, competitors (Truman 1951, 78–79; Stigler 1971). While these benefits are only for members, the group's lobbyists may still portray the desired policy as a public good benefitting the nation. Tax breaks for an industry can be justified by a lobbyist because they might benefit the country through job creation or through the production of more commodities and goods, which then generate greater revenue for the public sector through corporate and individual income taxes. When regulations on companies are loosened, this directly benefits member businesses, but it is also portrayed as job creation by the US Chamber of Commerce, National Federation of Independent Businesses, and National Association of Manufacturers. Because there may be truth to these assertions, the division between private benefits restricted to just one section of society and public benefits available to everyone is often just a matter of perspective.

Many associations are organized into state and even county chapters, such as the county farm bureaus or county bar associations. These decentralized groups are more reliant on revenue from dues than are other types of groups, though many of their members can charge their dues to their companies or customers and sometimes even deduct them from their taxes (King and Walker 1991, 82–83). Most trade and professional groups are organized as nonprofits under section 501(c)(6) of the Internal Revenue Code, which exempts them from many federal income taxes, though not to the same extent as 501(c)(3) charities. According to Lobbyists.info, and displayed in Table 2.1, the plurality (only 12 percent) have annual budgets between $100,000 and $250,000, so they are not as wealthy as some might believe, though 11 percent have budgets over $5 million. About 87 percent employ only one to twenty-five staff members.

Members tend to join because they receive the exclusive, material benefits that Olson believed were important, such as cheap insurance, information about the latest innovations in their profession, and conventions in luxurious places. Others, usually corporate members, join so they can have a say in what their association lobbies for (Drutman 2012, 85). About 35 percent of these associations have at least one national convention a year for members in which they can socialize while the organization's official policy positions are decided, usually by committees of members specializing in different

Interest Group Type	Average Group Age	Average Number of Members	Number of Employees (modal category)	Annual Budget (modal category)
Trade and Professional Associations	51	11,965	1-25 (87%)	Under $10,000 (5%)
			Over 100 (3%)	$100,000-250,000 (12%)
				Over $5,000,000 (11%)
Citizen's and Public Interest Groups	31	133,478	1-25 (74%)	Under $10,000 (2%)
			Over 100 (11%)	$2,000,000-5,000,000 (19%)
				Over $5,000,000 (16%)
Labor Unions	79	200,014	1-25 (50%)	Under $10,000 (2%)
			Over 100 (27%)	$2,000,000-5,000,000 (22%)
				Over $5,000,000 (45%)
Inter-Governmental Groups	51	1,864	1-25 (82%)	Under $10,000 (11%)
			Over 100 (4%)	$250,000-500,000 (13%)
				Over $5,000,000 (12%)

TABLE 2.1 Characteristics of Interest Group Types in 2010
Source: Lobbyists.info

policy areas (Drutman 2012, 81). About 80 percent of associations sponsor professional journals, like the *Journal of the American Medical Association*, or newsletters with the latest research and statistics on the profession. Because associations try to be the sole and authoritative source of information regarding their members' professions, lawmakers, the media, and members alike often find these publications essential for policy making.

Some associations even provide what amounts to quasi-legal regulation of their professions, exerting control over them as if they were government agencies. They create and enforce common standards of practice and ethics of conduct, and some even expel violators from the profession. Much of this self-policing and self-regulation is backed by state and federal law, often at an association's request, and its voice carries tremendous influence regarding any changes to laws regarding the profession under its jurisdiction (Truman 1951, 97). Associations usually do this to head off government regulation and preserve their professions' independence. For example, physicians formed the American Medical Association in 1846 to prove that they were more than just blood-letters, but also to stay independent of both hospitals and the government (McAdam and Scott 2005, 20–21). According to the Lobbyists.info data, about 19 percent of associations set certification of education standards at special colleges or accredit special degrees at standard universities (business schools, law schools, and medical programs). Doctors, nurses, lawyers, physical therapists, specialized contractors, and many others are bound by association standards of practice and conduct. And, like medieval guilds, one must pass rigorous exams in order to become a licensed member of groups like the bar and medical associations, which grant the right to practice the profession.

Professional and trade associations, of course, also offer opportunities for political advocacy if members are so inclined, and group leaders even consider these to be important incentives (King and Walker 1991, 86–88), but the intensity of member interest in advocacy here is arguably less than it is for other group types. This places most associations in the top part of Figure 2.2. Many bankers are probably happy to go to Washington for a quiet chat with their local member of Congress on the group's annual **lobby day**, but do not expect a Million Bankers March on the National Mall any time soon. Although labor unions might take to the Mall, they are a special kind of restricted, economic interest group that seeks policy and employment benefits exclusively for their members. I discuss them in Chapter 3.

Inter-Governmental Groups

Inter-governmental groups are similar to trade and professional associations, but profoundly different in important ways.[3] Examples of inter-governmental groups are the National Governors Association (NGA), the National Conference of State Legislatures (NCSL), the National Association of Counties (NACo), the US Conference of Mayors, the National League of Cities, and dozens more representing states, cities, counties, and special-purpose districts (education, utilities, water, and so forth) before the national government. Like professional associations, many inter-governmental groups represent public officeholders, such as the NGA, the National Association of State Attorneys General, and the Conference of State Bank Supervisors, though it is the office itself that is represented rather than the person holding that office. Other inter-governmental groups represent public institutions, such as the NCSL, the National Association of Clean Water Agencies, and the International Association of Fish and Wildlife Agencies. Still others represent whole levels of government, such as NACo, the Council of State Governments, and the International City / County Management Association. These groups are similar to work-oriented interest groups in that their memberships are highly exclusive, but because they are drawn from government their members are much more politically inclined, which places them in the lower left quadrant of Figure 2.2. As Table 2.1 showed, these kinds of groups have fewer members than trade associations, but many have large budgets, thanks to the dues that are often paid with taxpayer money.

Inter-governmental groups arose in the twentieth century as the constitutional relationship between the levels of government began to shift power and responsibility up to Washington, DC (Schlozman and Tierney 1986, 55). With the Progressive Era, the New Deal, and the Great Society all expanding the role of national policy to replace (some might say "usurp") a variety of state and local responsibilities, these lower layers of government felt they needed to have coordinated representation in Washington. Because of this shared policy-making responsibility, some argue that it is not accurate to think of inter-governmental associations as interest groups. They are not groups of private citizens, but of official, and often popularly elected, policy makers exercising their public trust responsibilities, even if they often use many of the same lobbying tactics as other interest groups (Cigler 1995, 132). When the House Committee on Standards of Official Conduct held hearings on proposed (but ultimately failed) legislation to register lobbyists in 1975, the National Association of Counties argued that their members and organization staff should be exempted from any legal definition of "lobbyist" because as public officials they were the public's true representatives.[4]

Inter-governmental groups may actually be some of the most powerful of all of the types of interest groups because their members hold influential positions. Elected officials in Washington, DC, are of the same breed as those in states and cities. They travel the same career paths, serve many of the same constituents, and speak the same professional language. Often officials from the same state know each other well, perhaps as friends who got started in politics at the same time or as professional allies mobilizing resources to get each other elected and remain secure in office (though it is also possible that one is gunning for the other's office). If personal, mutually beneficial relationships between those who lobby and those who are lobbied are as important to political influence as scholars believe (see Chapter 6), then inter-governmental groups have a significant advantage over all the others. Yet it is perhaps not enough of an advantage for some members, as many cities and counties still hire private lobbying firms to pursue their interests—a pursuit that sometimes reaches arguably absurd levels. Take, for example, the California town of Half Moon Bay (population 11,234 but empty city coffers), which in 2008 and 2009 paid a lobbying firm $1,047,531 in a failed effort to secure financial bailout legislation (Maclachlan 2011).

Citizen Groups and Public Interest Groups

Scholars studying the changing political landscape of the 1960s were struck by what appeared to be an explosion of **cause-oriented groups** organizing to oppose what was believed to be the entrenched power of business in American politics (Knoke 1986). These new groups arguably conform more clearly to what people typically think of as interest groups. They differ from trade associations and inter-governmental groups in that their membership ranks are open to every citizen who identifies with the group's cause, who feels passionately about the interest the group represents, and who wants to be politically involved. This puts them in the lower right corner of Figure 2.2. At least this is true of the groups that actually have members. Political scientists do not agree on exactly what distinguishes citizen groups from public interest groups, but the difference often involves membership. Groups like the Sierra Club, lobbying for environmental conservation, and the National Rifle Association, protecting gun ownership rights, have large memberships organized into state and local chapters nationwide. Their members are passionate advocates for their causes, especially when their groups whip them into frenzies (Merry 2010). And *anybody* can join, which is why they are called **citizen groups**.

Interest groups like Defenders of Wildlife (lobbying for the environment) and American Land Rights Association (lobbying to keep property private rather than public) solicit contributions and donations from people they call members. But is somebody who only gives money really a member? These organizations may be lobbying for a cause that many people are sympathetic to and will give some money to support, such as preserving Rocky Mountain wolves or rolling back environmental restrictions on private landownership, but they are probably not going to go to group meetings or participate in public protests. These groups tend more toward the upper-right box of Figure 2.2 instead of the lower-right. Both the Environmental Defense Fund, which also lobbies for the environment, and the Mountain States Legal Foundation, which defends property rights in court, pretty clearly do not have any members, though they do solicit contributions. All four (Defenders of Wildlife, American Land Rights Association, Environmental Defense Fund, and Mountain States Legal Foundation) are **public interest groups** that, like citizen groups, lobby for causes many people in the United States support. But unlike citizen groups they work on behalf of these social interests without actually recruiting people to participate as members (and are therefore not accountable to them).

Passionate citizen activism through these kinds of interest groups can be found throughout American history. Some citizen groups are quite old, such as Sierra Club, which was started back in 1892 by famed naturalist John Muir. Sierra Club's original goal was to prevent the flooding of Hetch Hetchy Valley in California's Sierra Nevada mountains, though the group turned on Muir in the middle of that fight, and the valley is now a reservoir for the city of San Francisco (Righter 2006). A few other social groups emerged at the end of the nineteenth century to help labor unions fight for better working conditions, antitrust laws, and child labor laws (Clemens 1997). In his 1929 book *Group Representation Before Congress*, Pendleton Herring mentioned several citizen groups existing at that time: the American Taxpayers League, the Popular Government League, as well as the Anti-Saloon League and its opponent the Association Against Prohibition (1929, 22–24). Indeed, there is something of a cycle in American politics in which periods of abusive business practices in the pursuit of profit have led to popular revulsion, which in turn has led to the emergence of organizations promoting new views of the public interest at odds with the hyper-individualistic, pro-business policies of the time (Mierzwinski 2010).

Figure 2.4, however, shows a dramatic increase in the formation of citizen and public interest groups starting in the late 1960s, the very group explosion that caught the attention of political scientists. Subsequent growth has been steady, though they are still a clear minority in the national interest group community, with approximately 737 groups comprising 5 percent of all interest groups (see Figure 2.1). Because it is difficult to determine whether people who contribute to these groups really are members, it is hard to say

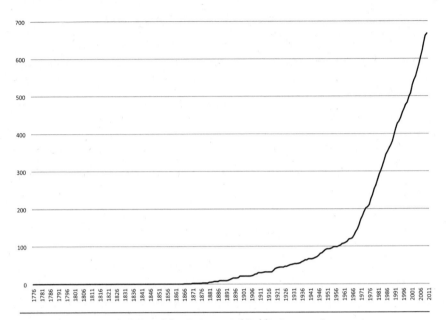

FIGURE 2.4   Historical Trend for Citizens and Public Interest Groups
Source: Lobbyists.info and *Washington Representatives*

whether they have more members than trade associations, though this is how it appears in Table 2.1.

Citizen groups have fascinated political scientists because they are so different from the older trade associations. Jeff Berry (1977) and Andrew McFarland (1984) were intrigued by the fact that citizen groups rely on dedicated members attracted by opportunities to express their political passions through advocacy. Members are drawn to join by purposive incentives, by opportunities to make a difference. Yet researchers also found that these groups are actually more dependent on the financial support of foundations and philanthropists, as opposed to member dues, than are trade and professional associations (Berry 1999, 25–26). Eighty-nine percent of citizen groups told Jack Walker that patron financing was critical to their survival (King and Walker 1991, 78). But as philanthropies have started directing their resources elsewhere since Walker's survey in 1983, many citizen groups have been forced to find new ways to aggressively fundraise (Nownes and Cigler 1995). As Table 2.1 shows, citizen groups today fundraise well: 35 percent of them have budgets over $2 million—significantly more than trade associations—though they like to argue that they are always at a disadvantage when compared to their business opponents (Zeller 2011).

Reliance on contributions and donations helps citizen groups keep member dues low, making it financially feasible for people to join. This, in turn, helps group lobbyists in their advocacy because they can point to the backing of a large membership when trying to establish their political legitimacy on Capitol Hill (Berry 1977). Large memberships give their lobbyists the grassroots (or at least what looks like grassroots) support they need to pressure elected officials when issues crucial to the groups' interests come up for votes. Citizen groups' grassroots advocacy includes flooding congressional offices with e-mails and phone calls, sending regular mail, and even staging highly visible protest marches. But low dues levels may also make citizen groups more apt to prioritize donor interests over member interests, creating conflicts of interest and concerns over who is really being represented in Washington.

As for public interest groups, just because they do not have actual members does not mean they do not provide representation to anyone. The government and philanthropies like the Ford Foundation were moved to fund these advocacy organizations because they provide services to, and advocate on behalf of, people who cannot represent themselves (Berry 1993). So, public interest groups that represent poor and homeless people, like the National Community Reinvestment Coalition, the National Coalition for the Homeless, and the National Low Income Housing Coalition, were formed. The National Women's Law Center was created to advocate for women's rights through the courts and in public policy. Many environmental advocacy organizations are public interest groups, such as the Environmental Defense Fund and the Natural Resources Defense Council, since rivers and forests, gray wolves and spotted owls cannot represent themselves (Bosso 1991).

Lack of members does not mean public interest groups are politically toothless either. Just look at the history of Ralph Nader, perhaps the best known founder of modern public interest groups. Drawing on years of personal research and information disclosed in lawsuits against General Motors, he made the case in his book *Unsafe at Any Speed* (1965) that GM's Corvair was prone to spins and rollovers but that GM suppressed these facts so as not to hurt consumer confidence in the car. Nader's book garnered much publicity, and GM was discovered tapping Nader's telephone and hiring private investigators to entrap him. Nader sued GM, won, and used the compensation to open the public interest group Center for the Study of Responsive Law (Vogel 1989, 104). The publicity pressured Congress to pass new consumer-friendly laws mandating auto safety standards and to create the National Highway Traffic Safety Administration. Success breeds imitation, and dozens of idealistic young lawyers and activists began setting up similar public interest groups with philanthropic support, many of them with Nader's aid and under his umbrella group, Public Citizen. This explains much of the dramatic upturn in the total number of citizen and public interest groups in the late 1960s, as seen in Figure 2.4.

The Politics of Tax Exemption

There is one more matter worth discussing: tax exemption. In 2013 this arcane tax issue was abruptly thrust into the political spotlight when the Internal Revenue Service (IRS) was accused by Republicans and Democrats alike of unfairly scrutinizing organizations connected to the Tea Party applying for tax-exempt status (Confessore 2013). It is a good example of how vague regulations can perhaps be abused by interest groups. Like trade associations, citizen and public interest groups are organized as nonprofits under the Internal Revenue Code's section 501(c), usually in the (4) category of social welfare organizations that do not have to pay income tax on money from member dues and donations. Many, though, are organized as 501(c)(3) charities to make it easier to raise money because contributors and members can deduct donations on their tax returns (Boris 1999; Reid 1999). And some organizations have parts of their operations classified under section (3) to do their charity work, and other parts under (4) to do their advocacy (Aviv et al. 2012).

Charitable nonprofits *can* engage in some limited political advocacy, but these limits are hardly limiting. Federal tax law says no charitable nonprofit can commit more than 10 percent of its time and resources toward actively influencing government officials on legislation, but this does not appear to include passively meeting with officials to consider contracts and services that nonprofits might offer, nor does it include efforts by nonprofits to organize people to lobby on their behalf (Reid 1999). Public interest groups organized as charities actually go out of their way to avoid using the word "lobbying," preferring the less pejorative term "advocacy" when doing this work (Reid 2000).

While most of the approximately 1.5 million charitable nonprofits in the United States (Reid 1999) are not true interest groups, they still work closely with the government. Since the 1980s the federal government has increasingly relied on nonprofits to provide social services (Smith and Lipsky 1993), such as counseling for abused women and alcoholics, mental health services, and economic development (DeVita 1999). Public sector outsourcing like this turns charities into implementers of policy, linking them to government in ways that some might call lobbying—especially if the government is not ideologically supportive of the services the nonprofits provide. Such concern led Ronald Reagan to try "defunding the Left" by cutting off federal grants to many nonprofits in the 1980s (Berry 1993). The concern may have been justified. Nonprofit leaders work in these low-paying, high-stress jobs because they are passionate about providing public support for the disadvantaged. If they see a proactive government as a partner in solving society's ills, would they not aggressively work to promote this partnership through advocacy? In fact, some are quite adept at it. Nonprofits seeking financial services for the poor have learned to use federal laws to pressure bank regulators to, in turn, pressure banks to lend and invest in low-income and minority neighborhoods (Holyoke 2004b; Casey, Glasberg, and Beeman 2011). These nonprofits may not be interest groups, but they certainly are political.

For these reasons some interest groups have had their charitable status challenged by their political opponents. In 2003, the petroleum industry–funded public interest group Public Interest Watch demanded that the IRS strip Greenpeace of its 501(c)(3) status because of its anti–oil drilling advocacy, though the IRS ended up exonerating Greenpeace (Stecklow 2006). This political scrutiny is starting to extend to groups with the 501(c)(4) classification as well, especially as many of these organizations have become more active in presidential and congressional campaigns. An example of this was seen in the lead-up to the 2008 presidential primaries, with Friends of the Earth backing former senator John Edwards (D-NC) and Americans for Fair Taxation backing former governor Mike Huckabee (R-AR) (Solomon and Mosk 2007).

These types of nonprofits, which include famous organizations like the Sierra Club and the National Rifle Association, are not as restricted in their advocacy as charities, but as social welfare organizations their advocacy is supposed to be primarily directed toward promoting social welfare, not toward winning elections. Recently, the public interest groups Democracy 21 and the Campaign Legal Center challenged the tax-exempt status of the fundraising groups Crossroads GPS and Priorities USA. They argued that while the 501(c)(4) classification does allow for some electioneering and contributing, it must be in the promotion of a broader social welfare cause, not just trying to win elections (see Aviv et al. 2012, 9).[5] Nor are (c)(4) organizations supposed to be spending all of their time pushing legislation. Common Cause has challenged the status of the conservative (c)(4) group American

Legislative Exchange Council, saying that the council just writes bills for legislators rather than pursues a social welfare goal (McIntire 2012). It remains
to be seen whether the IRS agrees that these organizations are abusing their
tax exempt status by being overtly political and cracks down on what well
may be political abuses of philanthropic tax exemptions. Unfortunately, the
IRS's rules regarding just how much political activity these nonprofit interest
groups can legally engage in is not at all clear, and it was this ambiguity that
led IRS staff to focus in on several small Tea Party organizations applying for
501(c)(4) status during the 2012 presidential election (Confessore and Luo
2013).

How Many Interest Groups Can There Be?

People who feel they do not have enough mail or e-mail in their lives should
join a cause-oriented, purposive incentive–driven interest group. Since they
share or sell their membership lists to one another, joining one guarantees a
flood of solicitation to join others (Godwin 1988). People must like solicitations because even though they have only so much money to spend in support
of political advocacy, only 11 percent of all people joining interest groups join
just one (Baldassarri 2011). But why would anybody support several groups,
especially if they appear to be advocating for very similar things? Is there a
meaningful difference between the Natural Resources Defense Council and
National Audubon Society that justifies joining both? How many organizations can one faction of people support? How many interest groups can
America support overall? Is not seven thousand plus interest groups enough?

The easiest answer comes from David Truman (1951), who said that the
size of the group community reflects the number and distribution of political
threats to formerly latent (unmobilized) social interests across the country. As
more threats arise in different areas of policy making, more groups mobilize.
Since existing interest groups are the primary source of political threats, the
actions of existing groups lead to the emergence of new groups that push
back. The result is an exponential increase in group mobilizations that only
ends when all possible latent interests in American society are no longer latent—when all of the mid-range interests of all people are represented by
some interest group. As one might suspect, this answer is too simple to explain all mobilizations.

What is called "niche theory" provides a more thorough answer. Each
group's size depends on the number of people sharing the interest it represents,

the **interest niche**, people who can be convinced to join using the three incentives described earlier in this chapter (Browne 1990). Therefore, whether more than one group can represent the same interest also depends on the size of the population with that interest, the willingness of people to join more than one group, the financial resources available, and how good each group is at recruitment (Gray and Lowery 1996; 1997). But instead of fighting each other to dominate the interest niche, many group executives try to divide it. They focus their attention on narrower subinterests, which allows them to parcel up the broader interest with other groups and share membership lists for fundraising, though subinterests can become only so small and refined before they are too small to support an interest group (Nownes and Lipinski 2005). So for everyone who cares about conservation generally, the Natural Resources Defense Council can represent those who care about wolves, while others can join the National Audubon Society to protect birds. Dedicated conservationists will join both. Overall, the more intensely people feel about an interest, the more that interest can be divided into subinterests, each represented by a separate interest group. In other words, the number of groups in America depends on the number of intensely felt interests.

The Diversity of Interests

There are many other entities identified in Figure 2.1 I did not discuss, like Native American tribes who lobby. And what about groups lobbying for foreign governments? What about lobbying by foreign governments themselves, or even by overthrown governments-in-exile? While space limits the number of group types I can discuss, some of these other groups are worth mentioning. Although Native Americans are represented by the Bureau of Indian Affairs (BIA) in the Interior Department, it is the kind of representation that leads many to wonder why Native Americans need enemies when they have friends like the BIA. Daniel McCool explains that Native Americans have, for decades, competed with farmers and their well-organized interest groups for federal money to build dams and irrigation systems. The National Irrigation Association and the American Farm Bureau Federation enjoy close relationships with successful dam-building agencies, like the Bureau of Reclamation and the Army Corps of Engineers, which have built dams and canals all over the country. Efforts by the BIA, responsible for helping Native Americans build similar structures, can be summed up in this anonymous quote from a BIA employee: "We began our first irrigation project in 1867 and we've never finished one yet" (McCool 1994, 112). So Native Americans have been forced to learn to advocate on their own, and have done it well, especially for BIA approval of casinos (Hansen and Skopek 2011; Boehmke and Witmer 2011).

Foreign governments are supposed to express their concerns through the State Department, but many also sign up lobbying firms for extra oomph. In 2008, 130 foreign governments hired lobbyists to represent them (Newhouse 2009). Since lobbyists contracted by foreign governments must disclose their work under the **Foreign Agents Registration Act**, we know that in 2008 the most intense lobbying was from Turkey, Libya, and the United Arab Emirates (Narayanswamy, Rosiak, and LaFleur 2009). Sometimes foreign governments shape American policy and opinion in more subtle ways, as seen in efforts by China, India, and Japan to endow centers for the study of their respective cultures on the campuses of American universities (Hrebenar and Thomas 2012). Sometimes it is less subtle and may also involve lobbying through organizations and PACs ostensibly representing sympathetic citizens living in the United States, like Israel's connections to known Washington heavy hitter the American Israeli Public Affairs Committee (Mearsheimer and Walt 2007). The concern, of course, is that regardless of what the specific requests of domestic-oriented interest groups are, there is an expectation that these requests benefit at least *some* Americans, but this may not be the case with foreign governments, or domestic ethnic groups lobbying to aid their "kin states" (Uslaner 2007). It is even murkier when the lobbying is done on behalf of former governments to shape US policy against the governments that overthrew them, as happened in the 1950s, when Tom Corcoran used his lobbying skills to aid Chiang Kai-shek and his government-in-exile in Taiwan against the new Chinese Communist government (Koen 1974; McKean 2004). Examples like these show just how influential foreign governments and the lobbyists they employ can be on American foreign policy.

In Summary

The main points in this chapter are:

- There are more noninterest groups lobbying in Washington than true interest groups, like corporations and hospitals that do not represent anybody but themselves.
- Some people join interest groups because they are offered valuable, tangible benefits that they cannot get anywhere else, while others join

because they feel strongly about political activism and are looking for a way to participate.

- Trade or professional associations only represent people practicing a particular profession, while citizen groups and public interest groups work on political causes that people feel strongly about, though public interest groups advocate on people's behalf rather than have active members.
- While member dues are an important source of funding, many interest groups are highly reliant on financial support from philanthropies and even the government.
- The more intensely people feel about their interest, the more groups will emerge to represent them, but will do so by subdividing the interest into narrower subinterests.

In other words, this chapter shows the many forms that mobilized interests can take.

Interest groups' forms and structures reflect both the kinds of interests that exist in society and the motivations behind joining a group. Studying the inner workings of these groups also shows us that there are different pathways to influence. Citizen groups can rely on their passion-driven members to provide grassroots advocacy; trade associations (whose members often lack this passion) employ quiet, personal lobbying; and memberless public interest groups rely on research and persuasive arguments. Tactics are therefore a consequence of organizational design and member or patron motivations, which I discuss in more detail in the second half of this book. But before I do that, I discuss in Chapter 3 how new interest groups are sometimes the product of major social changes in American society, and I look at how leaders interface with their members in Chapter 4.

Notes

1. See "About AAA," American Automobile Association, 2013, http://newsroom.aaa.com/about-aaa/.

2. I did much of the early data analysis for the Congressional Management Foundation for a project called Citizen Communication with Congress, and I worked on a couple of its reports. The report by Goldschmidt and Ochreiter (2008) is the one most pertinent to the data reported in this chapter and Chapter 4.

3. Much of the information in this subsection comes from my personal experience working for the National Association of Counties for four years.

4. See especially page 3 of the committee report *Lobbying—Efforts to Influence Governmental Actions* published by the Committee on Standards of Official Conduct, US House of Representatives, 94th Congress, 1st Session.

5. Gerald Hebert of the Campaign Legal Center and Fred Wertheimer of Democracy 21 made this challenge in a letter, dated September 28, 2011, to the commissioner of the Internal Revenue Service asking for a review of the 501(c)(4) status of the conservative groups, presumably as a first step in having their tax-exempt status stripped. I have this letter on file and will share it upon request.

CHAPTER THREE

Social Movements (Trying to Be Interest Groups?)

In 1932, one of the darkest years of the Great Depression, a small group of World War I veterans in Portland, Oregon, decided that the cash bonuses Congress promised to pay them way off in 1945 were needed now. So they set off to Washington to get them. Veterans all over the nation heard about the expedition on the radio and decided to join in. By train, bus, and car twenty thousand or so veterans came to the capitol city and set up camp by the Anacostia River. They called themselves the Bonus Army. They wore uniforms, waved flags, played music, ate communal meals, printed newspapers, banned alcohol, gave speeches, gained the support of military leaders, reminded the nation of their sacrifice, demonstrated outside of the Capitol, yelled at lawmakers, refused to leave when the Senate voted against them, and endured General Douglas MacArthur's tear gas (which sparked broad public sympathy). Finally, in 1936, the veterans got their bonuses.[1] They had pressured reluctant lawmakers to change policy, but the Bonus Army was a **social movement,** not an interest group.

Mass social movements like the Bonus Army can be found all through American history, though the Civil Rights Movement of the 1950s and 60s is arguably the modern archetype. After centuries of slavery and oppression, blacks and sympathetic whites organized a political campaign to end racial segregation and secure voting rights. Marches, tear-gassings, court challenges, attack dogs, and dramatic speeches on the Washington Mall all led to the Twenty-Fourth Amendment and the Voting Rights Act of 1965. Under sustained pressure, the American political system finally embraced African Americans and civil rights organizations, expanding the range of interests deemed worthy of government attention. Movements such as the women's suffrage movement, the Temperance (Prohibition) movement, the abolitionist movement, and even the Sagebrush Rebellion of the 1980s forced similar rearrangements of political power structures and policy. These movements shocked the political system by displacing interests favoring, and favored by, a policy status quo because they succeeded in portraying that status quo as suppressing their members' rights and interests. They expanded both the number of people involved in politics and the range of problems subject to government authority.

Social movements are both similar to and different from interest groups. They do not really conform to the romantic idea of an oppressed people spontaneously erupting into street demonstrations because they are tired of being oppressed. In fact, these demonstrations and marches are carefully coordinated by **social movement organizations** that must convince individuals to join and contribute resources and time to advocacy. Even the Bonus Army received support from the Veterans of Foreign Wars (Ortiz 2006). In this way, social movement organizations are similar to interest groups. But unlike most interest groups, they often must convince members to risk bodily harm in an effort to show lawmakers that existing policy is depriving them of rights enjoyed by everyone else in the society. Most modern-day interest groups never have to do this. For social movements, success means winning legitimacy in the eyes of the public and attention from leaders, often because these leaders think they can advance their own careers by becoming the aggrieved, but highly active, interest's champion. Ironically, achieving this success can mean that these social movement organizations become interest groups.

Cracking Open, Not Tearing Down, the System

Social movements have an almost respectable history in America. This is not surprising, since the nation's history began by revolting against a government that refused to recognize what many colonists felt were legitimate grievances. Revolutions, though, are not social movements. Revolutions destroy governments; social movements want to be included in government. Social movements want lawmakers to recognize their **grievances** to acknowledge that they have legitimate interests that are being harmed by existing policy, or lack thereof. Figure 3.1 shows the position of social movements on a continuum ranging from American society's rejection of a marginalized group's grievance to acceptance of that group's interests. Social movements occupy that

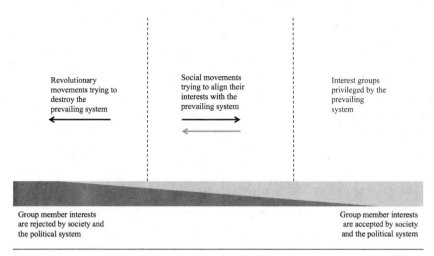

FIGURE 3.1   Orientation of Social Movements in Society and Government

middle space between support for the political system and a revolutionary desire to tear it down, but they want to move right (toward acceptance) on the continuum. Members of social movements accept prevailing social values and rights and believe their interests are consistent with those rights; their goal is to convince the public and lawmakers of this. Social movements want inclusion, to become interest groups supporting a new status quo that benefits them. But if lawmakers fail to help a movement, it may move left and threaten the political system.

American society and its political system have proven flexible enough to accommodate most movements and thus prevent revolution (Tarrow 1998, 21). Enduring class systems have made it difficult for Europeans to acknowledge the political legitimacy of new interests, but American society appears more inclined to reward a social group that stands up for itself. Americans embrace individual opportunity as well as collective morality (including religious values), and one or the other set of values tends to drive the lawmaking process at any given point in time (McFarland 1998, 13–15). Lawmakers today may justify new laws as essential for promoting individual opportunity, while next year their overriding concern may be collective morality. If a movement can align its grievance with whichever set of values is in ascendance, and show how the oppression its members suffer is contrary to those values, it may succeed.

Federalism divides the American government into many layers, and each layer is further divided in accordance with the doctrine of separation of powers into **venues**, like legislative committees, populated by lawmakers who embrace either individual opportunity or collective morality. This makes it easier for aggrieved interests to find inclusion somewhere in the political system (Tarrow 1998, 30–32). If the movement's grievance is the loss of personal freedom (Civil Rights, Tea Party), then it can try to convince lawmakers in a venue favoring individual rights that helping the movement is consistent with their principles of liberty. If a movement hopes to solve what it perceives as a social problem (e.g., drunkenness, abortion, environmental destruction), they might present their case to lawmakers prioritizing the collective good. That, plus some hard advocacy at the right moment, may result in the social movement finding inclusion in government and a redress of their grievance.

Social movements are motivated by the belief that the existing political order harms their interests in ways contrary to American values. The Whiskey Rebellion in the 1790s occurred because Appalachian farmers believed their whiskey income was being unjustly taxed by a government claiming to uphold individual liberty. The Temperance Movement of the early twentieth century believed that the individual freedom of a person to drink away all of their money, approved by the state due to its lack of prohibition, destroyed families and was contrary to the country's religious values. The women's and African Americans' voting rights movements argued that the government, which claims to support equal rights, was actually denying these groups' access to large parts of society by not protecting their rights to vote. The environmental movement of the 1960s argued that the collective moral obligations of humans to preserve nature were violated by a rapacious drive to strip the land of natural resources in support of economic individualism. And the 1980s Sagebrush Rebellion was led by western landowners who believed the government's sudden interest in environmental protection violated their individual right to own and use property. But simply having a grievance rooted in American values is not enough to create a movement that can compel the political system to change.

Recipe for a Successful Social Movement

What else is needed besides a good grievance to get a social movement going? Of the incentives for collective action laid out in the last chapter, only the purposive incentive applies to social movements. Members feel strongly about their grievance and want to actively fight to resolve it, but only if there is some hope of success and an organization can direct them.

Organizational and Societal Support

Inspired, charismatic leadership is necessary for a social movement to organize: somebody who symbolizes the oppression and bravely responds to it with a message of empowerment. Yet behind every leader, and therefore behind every movement, is a social movement organization that develops the message, builds lines of communication within the aggrieved population to spread this message, and crafts an advocacy strategy. No social movement can succeed without one (McCarthy and Zald 1977). Behind Martin Luther King Jr. and John Lewis were the civil rights organizations Southern Christian Leadership Conference and Student Nonviolent Coordinating Committee. Behind the Tea Party are Tea Party Express and FreedomWorks.

The social movement organization must convince the people it hopes to mobilize that they really have a legitimate grievance, and that what they want is in line with society's values. It must also convince them that they are entitled to the currently denied freedom or right, and that the government must be and can be convinced to rectify this indefensible circumstance. Message clarity may be a little harder to achieve, though, if there is more than one organization trying to direct the movement. Such lack of clarity hurt the Occupy Wall Street movement in 2011. Too many organizations like MoveOn.org, Rebuild the Dream, Progressives United, and several labor unions were all trying to be in charge, but were inconsistent in their messages to movement participants and to government leaders (Klein 2011). Not everyone agreed on what their grievance was or what they wanted government to do about it.

The Civil Rights Movement is an example of successful organization and coordination. African Americans were being denied their political rights, so the government, which promises equal rights for all its citizens, had to be shamed into guaranteeing those rights or risk losing its legitimacy. As sociologist Doug McAdam explains it, by the 1950s Southern blacks had developed strong—if nonpolitical—social institutions, notably black colleges and churches. These served as the original hubs for activism because they had developed tight social networks through which black people could be convinced that they had legitimate grievances, grievances that could be solved. These networks made it easier for early leaders to communicate empowering messages, convince members to act, and develop strategy (McAdam 1982, Ch. 5). Only after the civil rights marches and sit-ins began did purely political organizations like the Southern Christian Leadership Conference and

Student Nonviolent Coordinating Committee emerge to take over the job of directing the movement.

In addition to leadership and organization, successful movements need the support of other, already accepted social groups that can help bolster the aggrieved group's appearance of legitimacy, spread its message to the broader public, and provide financial and logistical support for demonstrations. They help make the powerless powerful. Sociologists Craig Jenkins and Charles Perrow (1977), for example, show how the efforts of California farmworkers to gain legal protections in the face of employer adversity failed in the late 1940s because they had no broad-based social support. Then, in the late 1960s, when religious and social welfare organizations openly and actively supported their cause, the farmworkers were able to gain the protections they sought. This support turned out to be as crucial to successful farmworker advocacy as the charisma and organizational acumen of Cesar Chavez.

Political Opportunity

Movements also need opportunities to succeed. It is romantic to think that movements create their own opportunities through passionate protests, but protests more often capitalize and expand on already existing opportunities than create new ones. Usually such political opportunities arise when the interests of the aggrieved group may be convincingly portrayed as consistent with dominant social values. As noted earlier, the United States goes through cycles in which an emphasis on collective morality as the legitimate basis for lawmaking is displaced by economic individualism (McFarland 1991). Then, when the pendulum swings too far in that direction, interest in the collective good reasserts itself. If current policy treats a social group harshly during times of stability, it is presumed that they brought it on themselves, and nothing is done to help them. But when new values begin reshaping public policy, there may be an opportunity for marginalized interests to link their grievances to now important social values and gain public sympathy. Radical ideas start to have the ring of truth, and would-be leaders of the oppressed group see that an opportunity has arisen and the time is right to demand justice (Meyer 1993, 455; Tilly 1978).

From the end of the Civil War to the early 1950s the plight of African Americans was largely ignored because ensuring political equality was not considered a legitimate government responsibility. But during the Cold War with the Soviet Union in the 1950s, this lack of attention started to look hypocritical. How could a wealthy and powerful nation promoting democratic rights and political equality around the world allow any of its own citizens to be systematically denied those rights? Without this shift in values, McAdam argues, the US Supreme Court might never have struck down racial segregation laws, or the Kennedy and Johnson administrations might not have pushed voting rights legislation. The Civil Rights Movement owes as much to these fundamental shifts in American social values as it does to the oratory of Martin Luther King and the willingness of tens of thousands of marchers to be arrested and beaten.

Lawmaker Response

Redress of aggrieved interests does not come for free. Democratic President Lyndon Johnson did not champion civil rights just out of a sense of morality. He expected African Americans, if given the right to vote, to vote for Democrats. Sagebrush rebels upset about environmental policies threatening their property rights were supported by Utah and Nevada politicians when it became clear that their anger would help elect Ronald Reagan to the White House and Republicans to Congress in 1980 (Skillen 2009, 121–124). The Tea Party movement may have arisen because many Americans were upset with their government handing out money to special interests with no apparent concern for the enormous public debt it created, but they depended on the organizational resources of Tea Party Express and the willingness of Republican members of Congress to be their champions, all under the (justified) assumption that it would benefit Republicans in future elections.

In sum, it is only after a grievance is defined and accepted by a group's members, after an organization is developed, after resources are secured, and after political opportunity is found that a movement emerges and begins the business of **grassroots protest**. Only then are marches and demonstrations planned to convince the broader public that the grievance is real. Only then are activists given colorful signs, papier-mâché caricatures of public officials, costumes to wear (or nothing to wear in some antifur protests), handcuffs to lock themselves to lampposts to resist arrest, and so forth. Only then can protestors get away with tying up traffic and blocking building entrances in the hope of shutting down some major event, as environmental, human rights, and union protestors shut down the 1999 meeting of the World Trade Organization in Seattle, Washington (Yuen, Rose, and Katsiaficas 2002). If the leaders have done a good job of framing the grievance as consistent with prevailing social values, nearly any aggressive police response can be portrayed as the state oppressing its own citizens, who simply want the same rights and liberties everyone else enjoys. Dramatic television footage of the beating and tear-gassing of civil rights marchers trying to cross the Edmund Pettus Bridge from Selma to Montgomery, Alabama, to demand their constitutional rights outraged Americans and moved Congress to pass the Voting Rights Act in 1965. Today the images and messages are often transmitted via YouTube and Facebook, but crowds of people still endure hardships in the name of their grievance to stimulate public support. It shows government leaders that a new interest has mobilized and that there may be political rewards for helping it.

Social Movement or Interest Group?

Successful social movement organizations change popular assumptions the public and lawmakers have regarding marginalized groups, making it acceptable for lawmakers to help out these interests and integrate them into the political system. Once this happens, they are not really social movement organizations at all; they become interest groups. This makes it difficult to tell interest groups from social movement organizations, especially since many interest groups try to portray themselves as leaders of social movements (Diani 2012). Citizen groups may have once led movements in the 1960s to convince lawmakers to enact environmental legislation, but their success forced them to transform from protest organization to interest group, though they may still have some of the trappings of a movement.

Figure 3.2 helps explain this transformation. The dimensions here are the extent to which a social group is excluded from policy decisions by the state (vertical axis), and the degree to which a social group can frame its grievance as legitimate given society's values (horizontal axis). People with a common grievance who lack this social support (high on the vertical axis and left on the horizontal) remain unmobilized and politically marginalized. Nothing is done to help them because their grievance is not considered legitimate. When social change makes it necessary to address the group's grievance (moving them to the right on the horizontal axis), its leaders are able to find the necessary resources and political support, and the movement will blossom. If the movement is successful, its guiding social movement organization will move into the lower-right square of Figure 3.2.

True interest groups are already accepted in the political system. Even if their policy demands are not always met, they are seen as legitimate

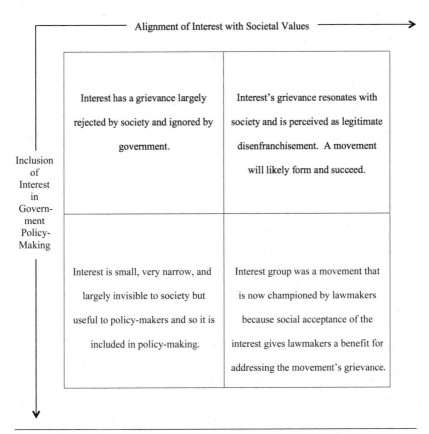

FIGURE 3.2   Dimensions of Social Movement and Interest Group Acceptance

participants in political deliberations. This is what social movement organizations want. When they get it, they are no longer supporting an outside
movement. They become an interest group with members and with a regular
seat at the table.[2] They are now expected to play by the rules of the system
that, ironically, they tried hard to break into by breaking the rules. Now they
are inside trying to cement their gains so that no future social movement can
take them away.

Outside to Inside: Organized Labor in American Politics

The history of American **labor unions** exemplifies this transition from
grievance-stricken social movement to consummate political insider. Although the American movement avoided much of the ideological class war-
fare that characterized European labor movements, its origins were no less

contentious. The shift from a near-subsistence agricultural economy to one of large-scale manufacturing after the Civil War created a big urban workforce in which individual workers were often seen as a commodity to be used up and replaced (Zeigler and Peak 1972, 236). Living close together around factories, rail yards, and mines helped workers develop a common sense of exploitation, though deep racial and ethnic divisions in the labor force made widespread organization and European-style class consciousness impossible to achieve (Greenstone 1977, 18–19). Starting with the Brotherhood of the Footboard (locomotive engineers) in 1863, unions formed to pursue a variety of goals, such as controlling who could work in an industry, protecting workers from arbitrary firing, ensuring good working conditions, and providing retirement benefits and health care. But early successes at organization were largely restricted to highly skilled workers in crafts and trades. Industrial workers did not unionize until the early twentieth century (Zeigler and Peak 1972, 240).

These unions were quickly attacked by businesses and even by the government, making the labor movement's early history quite bloody (Millis and Montgomery 1945). Dozens of union workers and their supporters, even women and children, were beaten by police in the Tompkins Square Riot of 1874; ten "Molly Maguires" (members of a secret society of coal miners) were hanged in Pennsylvania in 1877; thirty furniture workers were killed by federal troops at the Battle of the Viaduct in Chicago in 1877; Polish workers were shot by the national guard in Milwaukee's Bay View Tragedy of 1886; the Chicago Haymarket Riot of May 4 in 1886 (the original May Day) led to the wrongful execution of four; and eleven striking steel workers died in a clash with the Pinkerton Guards in 1892 (Millis and Montgomery 1945).

Early efforts at pulling separate unions together into a single, united movement by the National Labor Union in 1866 and the Knights of Labor in 1869 failed. Animosity between unions was too great and the benefits of unity too vague (Truman 1951, 68). The first lasting umbrella group, the American Federation of Labor (AFL), survived only because it tried to represent the skilled craft unions, which AFL felt had more in common with each other than with unskilled factory workers (Greenstone 1977, 23). Early leaders like AFL's Samuel Gompers also disdained politics, preferring to use strikes to deal with corporate management. Why even seek help from a government that was backing business and shooting strikers? In the second decade of the twentieth century, when Congress tried to create the social insurance plan many unions desired, Gompers dismissed it as an attempt to sway the loyalty of workers away from AFL (29). His faith in striking was justified with victories like the Great Southwest Railroad Strike against Union Pacific involving over two hundred thousand workers in 1886 and the seven-month strike of New York City garment workers, who succeeded in creating a **closed shop** where factories could only employ unionized workers (Millis and Montgomery 1945). Closed-shop rules became a union solution to the collective action problem—if you do not join, you do not work in the trade.

As early as the late nineteenth century, some in Congress tried to attract labor's political support with legislation like the Erdman Act of 1898, which prevented railroad companies from firing union workers, though it was later struck down by the Supreme Court. But some of labor's goals regarding child labor laws, restrictions on women's work hours, and old-age pensions fit well with contemporary religious and social values and thus found support from churches and women's suffrage groups and became law (Greenstone 1977, 27). These policies were championed by the Democratic Party, which, like many unions, had large numbers of Irish Catholics, drawing union members toward the party. Thus a connection through shared values, coupled with backing from other social groups, helped the early labor movement gain a foothold in Congress. Republicans, on the other hand, were largely anti-union, allying themselves with the militantly anti-union National Association of Manufacturers. Only the corporate trust-busting Republican Theodore Roosevelt enjoyed union support in the early years (29–30). In 1908 AFL supported the failed presidential campaign of William Jennings Bryan against William Howard Taft, who had upheld strike injunctions as a judge. However, the AFL were able to successfully get several congressional Democrats elected; they then rewarded labor with the 1914 **Clayton Act** exempting unions from the strike injunctions favored by the pro-business Taft (Truman 1951, 70).

Even as it tried to not become overly involved in politics, AFL used these successes to build a larger movement by attracting new members, even in the face of aggressive Republican antistrike legislation (Ziegler and Peak 1972, 241). Membership jumped from 278,000 in 1898 to 1,500,000 in 1906 and 2,500,000 in 1914 (Greenstone 1977, 24). Membership was over four million by 1920. But after World War I, the values driving American politics shifted toward individualism and economic opportunity (34). This helped business leaders portray closed-shop unions as communist, allowing management to come down hard on closed-shop unions, cut wages, and bring in workers to cross picket lines to undermine union control, all with congressional support (243). Belief among unions that government would help them faded, and AFL found itself unable to expand its membership, or even keep the numbers they had. Its choice to support workers striking against US Steel proved a disaster (Ziegler and Peak 1972, 242).

Everything changed again in 1929 with the Great Depression. The revulsion the public felt against business shifted dominant values back to caring for people hurt by the economic collapse (collective morality). Blue-collar workers were suddenly the symbol of American economic resilience and the willingness of government to care for its people. The AFL, however, was still reluctant to become politically involved, as Franklin Roosevelt's early New Deal programs only tangentially benefitted craft unions. Industrial workers, however, reacted enthusiastically and threw their support behind the Democratic Party. AFL started to lose control of the labor movement as industrial workers organized many new unions, such as United Auto Workers (UAW).[3] Union membership now jumped to over eight million. The Congress of Industrial Organizations (CIO) was formed in 1938 to act as the umbrella union for unskilled factory workers' unions, and thus became a rival to the AFL. The CIO provided substantial campaign support for congressional Democrats and worked hard to draft Roosevelt for a third term in 1940 (Greenstone 1977, 46–47).

Union loyalty to the Democrats was rewarded in 1935 with the **National Labor Relations Act**. Company workers could now form a union simply by voting for it, and management had to bargain exclusively with it, giving closed-shop unions a firm legal foundation. More importantly, the act also formally integrated the labor movement into the government through the National Labor Relations Board, an arm of the state with a vested interest in expanding the number and strength of unions in the United States (Greenstone 1977, 47). No example better shows how social movement organizations, which is what AFL and CIO were, become integrated into the political landscape as interest groups. They became especially allied with the Democratic Party, with union workers playing crucial roles in electing Democrats to Congress (Greenstone 1977, 9).

As World War II wound down, business leaders felt themselves once more on firmer political ground and began pushing back. At their behest Congress passed the **Smith-Connally Act** in 1943, making it illegal for unions to contribute to political campaigns, followed by the reviled (by unions) **Taft-Hartley Act** of 1947, reducing rights to strike and allowing states to enact **right-to-work laws** that let them outlaw closed-shop unions. So severe was the new threat that AFL and CIO overcame their differences and in 1955 merged to form the AFL-CIO, representing over thirteen million workers (Zeigler and Peak 1972, 247–248). Private sector unions started declining anyway. Business became better adept at stopping the organization of new unions, sometimes by simply closing plants and sending manufacturing jobs to right-to-work states or overseas. Union membership gains occurred, but did so in the public sector rather than the private, especially after President John F. Kennedy made it possible for federal workers to unionize (Zeigler and Peak 1972). Organizations such as the American Federation of State, County, and Municipal Employees and the American Federation of Teachers grew strong, while AFL-CIO lost members. AFL-CIO fractured in 2005, with UAW and the International Brotherhood of Teamsters breaking away over disagreement about political tactics (Asher et al. 2001). By 2010 there were over seven million workers in industrial unions, but they only represented seven percent of private sector employment, according to the US Bureau of Labor Statistics. Public sector unions, though, had over 7.6 million members, 36 percent of the public sector labor force.[4]

Although labor unions were so deeply integrated into the Democratic Party of the 1930s that they were nearly the same organization, today their influence in the party has arguably declined. In 1993 they failed to prevent Democratic president Bill Clinton and a Democratic Congress from approving the North American Free Trade Agreement, a trade pact that made it easier for employers to shift jobs out of the United States. Today labor also finds itself at odds with other major groups in the Democratic Party, especially environmental interest groups. Through the 1990s and early twenty-first century, labor groups struggled to convince Democrats to open the Arctic National Wildlife Refuge for oil exploration, as well as convince President Barack Obama in 2011 to approve building the massive Keystone XL Pipeline from Canada to Texas, both of which might create union jobs. They complained about the lack of support from political leaders as they fought companies trying to reduce retirement pensions during the Great Recession (Rutten 2011). Even with the differences between AFL-CIO and Teamsters papered over, because of the decline in membership the future of organized labor in the United States is uncertain. This is the case even for public unions, as evidenced by efforts by Republican governors in Wisconsin, Indiana, and Ohio in 2012 to eliminate the rights of state workers to bargain and strike as well as reduce government retirement pensions and health care benefits.

Countermovement Cycles in Business Advocacy

When a social movement succeeds, older interests that benefitted from the status quo have, to some extent, been pushed aside to make room for new ideas and policies. The result is a redistribution of resources. Sometimes these displaced interests fight back to make sure the new policies are never fully accepted by lawmakers and the public (Meyer and Staggenborg 1996; Holyoke et al. 2009). After a brief discussion of the labor movement, it makes sense to look now at the powerful interest labor pushed aside in the 1930s—American business—and how business fought back.

Perhaps no subject has obsessed political scientists as much as assessing the influence of business over government. Globe-spanning Fortune 500 companies and local small businesses are considered crucial to economic well-being, and therefore to voter happiness and government revenues. So what business leaders want matters to elected officials. There is, however, no monolithic business community or unified agenda of business interests. Studies of the interconnections between members of corporate boards of directors find too few broad cross-connections to conclude that any business leaders dominate the corporate community (Mintz and Schwartz 1983). Businesses compete with each other so much that it is hard to get them to work together. Most businesses do not lobby, do not contribute money, or are not especially active in their trade associations (Hansen and Mitchell 2000; Brasher and Lowery 2006), though most larger corporations are at least members of their associations (Drutman 2012).

Businesses, it turns out, tend to get into politics only when they need to create a new competitive advantage for themselves or when their primary customer is the government. Certainly the government's power to transfer wealth and shape markets through regulation can give a clever businessperson a decisive advantage over competitors (McCormick and Tollison 1981). Nobel Prize–winning economist George Stigler even argued that some corporations *want* regulation because it protects them from competitors, requires particular methods and standards of production that competitors might not master, and even guarantees minimum prices (Stigler and Friedland 1962; Stigler 1971; Barro 1973). According to this argument, regulation does not correct market failure when capitalism hurts society, but rather creates market failure by restricting the competition necessary to drive down prices. In highly concentrated industrial sectors the marginal benefits from regulation can actually make the difference between a company's success and its failure (Pittman 1976; Masters and Keim 1985; Andres 1985).[5]

So only businesses in fairly concentrated sectors are likely to lobby, at least until one or two become dominant, and then they let their industry trade associations (which they also dominate) do whatever advocacy is necessary to maintain the status quo (Munger 1988; Drope and Hansen 2009). Firms dependent on public spending, such as defense contractors, are also more likely to lobby (Boies 1989; Grier, Munger, and Roberts 1991; 1994; Hansen and Mitchell 2000). Businesses lobby when anticipating labor strikes, antitrust lawsuits, and new regulation of their industry (Pittman 1977; Hansen, Mitchell, and Drope 2005). For instance, when threatened with new regulations regarding copyrights and online privacy, several of the largest Internet companies, including Google, Facebook, Amazon, and LinkedIn, which until then had only intermittently lobbied, put both feet in by increasing their lobbying budgets (Google spent $9 million on lobbying in the first half of 2012) and funding a new interest group, the Internet Association (Kang 2012).

Political business historian David Vogel (1989) argues, however, that business's record of success in politics is decidedly mixed. In the 1870s industries such as railroads, steamship firms, and oil companies employed lobbyists like Sam Ward and Collis Huntington to lobby Congress for price controls, public subsidies, and public lands. Congress was so willing to comply that the Gilded Age is sometimes called the Great Barbeque because everyone could just come and get it (Jacob 2010). This excess led to an intense public backlash at the turn of the century (Thompson 1985). President Theodore Roosevelt was a Republican, but his vigorous push for anticorporate monopoly laws (trust busting), his support for many labor unions, and his promotion of laws banning child labor and requiring meat inspection standards placed him in the camp of the Progressives, who believed government had a duty to protect the physical and spiritual health of society by regulating American business (Clemens 1997). The Progressive Movement burned itself out by the 1920s with the disappointing end to Woodrow Wilson's presidency and the failed presidential campaign of Senator Robert La Follette of Wisconsin. Calvin Coolidge, Herbert Hoover, a Republican Congress, and a strong economy proved more business-friendly, as prevailing values in politics shifted from the collective morality championed by the Progressives to individual liberty, which favored business (Vogel 1989, 4).

As mentioned earlier, the Great Depression in 1929 changed everything once again. Franklin Roosevelt successfully ran for president on an antibusiness, pro-government platform and won overwhelmingly. The enactment of his enormous initial legislative package to solve the crisis and offer workers a "new deal" in the first one hundred days of his administration remains today's benchmark of presidential success. Roosevelt was proud of being called the great foe of the "economic royalists," so while he occasionally reached out to business through his new Business Advisory Council, corporate leaders felt the only way to defend themselves was to mobilize businesses big and small to stop the New Deal (Vogel 1989, 17; Young 2010, 14). When legislation was proposed to separate banks from Wall Street investment firms, a mixing many people believed led to the wild speculation that caused the stock market crash, some of the largest financial institutions set up shop for weeks in posh Washington hotels to lobby against the legislation (McKean 2004, 38, 51, 59). They even mounted their first public relations campaign to convince Americans that this separation was bad for business, but their efforts were all for nothing. The Glass-Steagall Act separating these industries passed in 1933 and remained until 1999.

Business remained poorly organized in Washington in the 1950s and early 1960s because political threats were fewer than during the New Deal era (Vogel 1989). Economic expansion was strong, a vibrant middle class was emerging, and the public was more concerned with the ideological struggle against the Soviet Union and communism than about whether what was good for American business was really good for Americans (a variation on the Chamber of Commerce's slogan "what helps business helps you" from the 1930s; Truman 1951, 228). Possibly as a consequence, the business community fell into in-fighting over support for open trade policies to build a global presence or support for the tariffs and trade barriers that preserved their markets in the United States (Bauer, Pool, and Dexter 1963, 61).

The political atmosphere changed again in the late 1960s, as popular interest in the collective health of American society returned to center stage. Indeed, Vogel argues that the political fortunes of business tend to nose-dive when the economy is strong because the public fixates on social health rather than individual economic opportunity (8). In this case what aroused public concern were the consequences of corporate success for consumers and the environment. Activist Ralph Nader's highly publicized exposure of dangerous manufacturing and marketing practices in the auto industry sparked similar investigations of water and air quality around factories, corporate advertising practices, pesticide usage, worker wages and benefits, and energy extraction and production techniques (Berry 1999). Congress responded to this shift in public sentiment with a host of new laws such as the Clean Air Act, the Clean Water Act, the National Environmental Policy Act, the Endangered Species Act, and the Consumer Credit Protection Act. Dozens of new citizen and public interest groups emerged with strong philanthropic support (recall Chapter 2), while business advocacy groups were almost nowhere to be seen

(Vogel 1989, 33–34). As long as the public believed that business could be regulated and forced to contribute to social goals without harming economic performance, government remained hostile toward the business community (Plotke 1992). Business leaders realized they needed to go on the offensive.

According to Vogel, business leaders responded by building up their trade associations so these interest groups could collectively convince Congress and the public that excessive regulation would have terrible consequences for the economy (1989, 173). Corporate-endowed think tanks such as the Heritage Foundation and the American Enterprise Institute produced peer-reviewed research that gave an empirically grounded, respectable academic voice to these arguments and showed how regulation increased market inefficiency. Greater costs from regulation, they argued, would always be passed on to consumers, and tighter corporate budgets from higher taxes and fees would decrease the supply of jobs. These were intuitive arguments the public could easily grasp. The US Chamber of Commerce was revived with infusions of new donations and members. It then led a fairly united effort to portray the energy crisis and economic downturn of the 1970s as a partial consequence of runaway regulation.

Money was aggressively raised and donated to pro-business Republicans (and a few Democrats), helping them take the Senate and make substantial gains in the House in 1980 (Jackson 1990). Perhaps their most successful strategy was making the small business entrepreneur, beloved in national myth, the poster child of all American business (Vogel 1989). Small business owners were mobilized through the National Federation of Independent Business to press their case in every congressional district, letting elected officials know how essential these entrepreneurs were to local economies and how they were suffering under all the red tape Washington created at the bidding of consumer and environmental "extremists" (Young 2010, 70; Fordham and McKeown 2003). The success of these tactics by businesses and their interest groups can be seen in the deregulation of the airline industry in 1978 and in the lack of new environmental laws after 1978.

Arguably—and many have argued it—the crowning achievement of the business counterattack was the election of Ronald Reagan. Business had already found it could beat back consumer group initiatives, such as President Jimmy Carter's Consumer Protection Agency, but the election of the pro–free market, antigovernment Reagan gave executives a sense of having a friend in the Oval Office. They probably wondered later about the quality of the friendship. A believer in the value of individual freedom to pursue economic opportunity on a level playing field, President Reagan aggressively moved to eliminate regulations protecting many businesses from competition. His not overly business-friendly Tax Reform Act of 1986 eliminated tax loopholes that benefitted many corporations (Vogel 1989, 243).

No president since Reagan has tried to aggressively regulate business. Trying to be a political centrist, Bill Clinton was probably the most business-friendly Democratic president in modern times. While many blame the Great Recession of 2008 on greed and carelessness in the financial industry, the government responded by extending credit to prop up big dying banks and auto manufacturers, and many business leaders like Tom Donohue of the Chamber argued that the way out of the Recession was to further reduce the tax and regulatory burden on business (Verini 2010). In 2010 the Chamber committed tens of millions of dollars to elect Republicans to the House of Representatives, making them the majority (Tate 2012). Similarly, companies like American Electric Power, Aetna, Prudential Financial, Dow Chemical, and Merck gave millions to tax-exempt nonprofits created to elect pro-business Republicans in 2012 (McIntire and Confessore 2012). Whatever its past failures, American business does not appear willing to let social movements displace it again.

Social Movement Protest in an Online World

The Arab Spring that swept the Middle East in 2011, toppling oppressive regimes in Egypt, Tunisia, and Libya, was made possible partially by online communication and social media (Shirky 2011). While dissident organizations and political parties handled much of the coordination of protests, the execution relied heavily on fast online communication. The revolution was not televised, but it was tweeted. The Internet has been a blessing for social movements because it makes it easy to swiftly assemble large numbers of people for a protest, send video messages to public officials, or post horrifying images of governments abusing their citizens to generate public support. Even in the United States, the Internet has changed the nature of social movement protest and interest group advocacy. In 2013, Latino advocacy groups staged "iMarches," using smartphones and social media to get their members to tweet senators in Washington, urging them to vote for immigration legislation (Romano 2013). A Pew study in 2007 found that 93 percent of teens use the Internet, often interacting with each other and sharing information on social media sites like Facebook (cited in Conroy, Feezell, and Guerrero

2012, 1535). It is too early to know what the political role of technology will be in the future, but many scholars predict that it may actually strengthen political participation and civil society (e.g., Norris 2001; Mossberger, Tolbert, and McNeal 2008).

Where the Internet suffers as an advocacy tool, and really as a means of political participation, is in quality. A recent study found that while participation in political groups via Facebook sites did increase a person's real-world participation, it did nothing to increase their political knowledge as they just repeated the misinformation and opinions of others in a kind of virtual echo chamber (Conroy, Feezell, and Guerrero 2012). A survey of congressional staff in 2010 by the Congressional Management Foundation found that while 87 percent believed the Internet made it easier for people to become politically involved, and 97 percent felt that it increased constituent contact with Congress, 65 percent believed that the quality of communication in terms of expressing concerns *fell* significantly as a result of the overuse of identical, generic e-mail messages. Fifty-three percent of respondents doubted that those who signed them had even read them. And about 97 percent felt that in-person contact is still the best way to influence elected officials (CMF 2011, 2–5).

It is certainly easier and quicker to email Congress now than it was in the past, as interest groups employ increasingly sophisticated contact forms on their websites, usually developed by third-party vendors like Capwiz that help individuals find their specific legislators based on zip codes and provide pre-written messages. After attempts were made to mail anthrax-filled envelopes to Capitol Hill in 2001, email was encouraged as an alternative means of contact; the email addresses of most congressional staff were made public (Fitch 2010a). But generic, identical emails are no more influential on members of Congress than form letters and postcards. Congressional letter-tracking software identifies boilerplate e-mails, making it easy for legislators to identify interest group–run, pseudo-grassroots advocacy campaigns that make it appear as if thousands of constituents care about an issue. Nothing replaces the personalized letter or e-mail recounting a heart-wrenching story of how some issue has affected a constituent. Those are the communications that get placed in front of a member of Congress and stick with him or her, not the hundred thousand identical emails that crash the Capitol Hill server (Fitch 2010a), irritating lawmakers and staff.

If thousands of identical postcards are useless **astroturf**, as former Senator Lloyd Bentsen (D-TX) allegedly labeled it (DeButts 1996, 67), rather than the passionate grassroots advocacy elected officials respond to and sometimes even fear, are thousands of duplicate e-mails good for anything? Not really. Online petitions, such as those created for any conceivable cause on Web sites like Change.org, are reported on Capitol Hill to be the least persuasive form of grassroots advocacy. Only identical physical postcards are more useless, and that is because most congressional offices can no longer record them in their contact-tracking software and usually throw them away (Fitch 2010a). Unless people signing an e-petition have actually included their personal signatures and addresses proving they are constituents, congressional offices generally ignore them. The online companies that run electronic petitions are probably more interested in collecting the personal contact information of everyone who signs them, as well as information on the kinds of causes they care about, and selling that data to interest groups (Shih 2011).

Where the Internet excels is in disseminating political information, even if the information is often inaccurate and highly opinionated. The CMF survey found that 57 percent of congressional staff felt that the ease of gaining political information through the Internet actually made legislators more accountable to their constituents (CMF 2011, 2). Three-fourths of them indicated they use social media like Facebook to learn about, and better understand, constituent concerns (6).

Not all that many interest groups use Facebook, though, and even fewer use it effectively. In interviews I did in 2012 with the American Society of Association Executives and the American League of Lobbyists, organizations representing many interest groups and for-hire lobbying firms, I asked about the extent of social media use. Although there was no firm data, the impressions these organizations had was that most trade associations used e-mail aggressively to communicate with members and lawmakers, but not social media. Many for-hire lobbying firms were barely even using e-mail, still preferring to go to Capitol Hill to meet legislators and staff in person. But many citizen and public interest groups are making real efforts to use social media, although they appear to only use tools like Twitter to send information on the latest developments regarding an issue to allied groups and media organizations. These groups were not necessarily using social media to interactively communicate with their members.

As for actual advocacy, there is little evidence of interest groups using social media effectively. Yet there are a few exceptions. In 2010 animal rights advocates in North Carolina were upset about alleged animal abuse and high kill rates at a shelter operated by Robeson County. When Governor Bev Purdue posted a comment on her Facebook page with a picture of her dog and said she was against using gas chambers to euthanize animals, she was bombarded with angry comments, many attached to pictures of dogs and cats, demanding she use her powers to close down the animal shelter.[6] That Governor Purdue had no such power mattered not at all. There were soon so many comments that Purdue had to shut down her Facebook page.[7] Activists may not have shut the shelter down, but they quickly got the governor's attention, and that was enough to declare victory. This is still the exception rather than the rule. To have an effective Facebook page, the interest group Common Cause employs a staff person (whom I interviewed) just to run its page, something few groups can afford to do. To keep people interested in the page, essential for its effectiveness, she posts new information and links at least twice a day. About 30 percent of Common Cause supporters check the page about twice a week, though some do so once an hour. Yet while Common Cause tries to link their site to the Facebook pages of public officials doing things the organization disapproves of so that its members can post negative comments there, perusing the page turns up little evidence that it does so frequently. I examined it for several days and found nearly all the posts were about sharing information, not taking action.

Video sites like YouTube also feature a few interesting advocacy stories. Before a Senate vote to eliminate Don't Ask, Don't Tell, the policy preventing gay military service personnel from acknowledging their sexual orientation, pop singer Lady Gaga recorded her own (failed) effort to call a senator on behalf of the Service Members Legal Defense Network and placed it on YouTube to encourage others to do the same (Hysom 2010). Two University of Colorado students did so with a YouTube appeal to Senator Michael Bennett (D-CO), who responded with his own video. Again, it is hard to know what the future of online advocacy will be, but it is important enough today that political consultants now offer seminars and online webinars for long-time lobbyists about how to use social media to pursue member interests.[8]

Virtual advocacy organizations have also emerged, but with very limited success. When rebuilding efforts in New Orleans by the government after Hurricane Katrina appeared to discriminate against people of color, activists created ColorofChange.org to raise money for a new civil rights campaign. They hoped they could mobilize people ordinarily lacking in political passion if all activists had to do was click a few links to contribute money and send complaints by e-mail to Congress (Thompson 2010). This online movement was initially successful, organizing a protest march in 2007 and creating a legal fund to defend several African American teenagers accused of assaulting a white student in Jena, Louisiana. Then donations dried up, and most of the eight hundred thousand members on their email list no longer respond. Other online organizations, such as Presente.org, which advocates for the DREAM Act, allowing young undocumented immigrants to gain resident status if they complete college or military service, have also experienced similarly mixed results.

Even professional Internet-activist companies have trouble sustaining protests. One such case is Change.org, a San Francisco–based Internet company that helps people with a cause collect signatures for their e-petitions, convinces others to participate in protests, writes press releases, and drops email "bombs" on public officials, overwhelming them with email that advocates for causes all over the world from Saudi Arabia to China and crashing servers. But Change.org has had difficulty convincing people to stay with the effort beyond the initial click. Said Jillian York of the Electronic Frontier Foundation of these Web sites and the "slacktivists" who initially respond to their appeals: "Social media tools can be very effective if they complement off-line campaigns, but I don't think signing a petition does anything useful" (Shih 2011). Activist websites are easy to set up, but participation is perhaps *too* easy: members acquire little sense of investment and commitment and thus are unlikely to stick with it. Clicking a few buttons is not the same as facing down police with tear gas, batons, and dogs. It is not even as intense, and therefore not as rewarding, an experience in political participation as picketing members of Congress.

In Summary

Here is the summary of the major points in this chapter:

- A grievance is a dominant interest held by a group of people that is being harmed by the government, through either existing policy or its refusal to enact policy.
- Social movements require a grievance that aligns with the dominant social values of the time, organization, and some hope of success to get started, along with broader social support and aid from political leaders in order to succeed.
- Success means the organizations backing the movement will be integrated into the political system as interest groups and must then play by Washington's rules.
- While the Internet is a great tool for spreading political information, it gives sympathizers of a cause too minimal of a sense of commitment

to make them truly dedicated activists, and therefore is a poor tool for encouraging meaningful and sustained political participation.

One point needs to be emphasized a little more. If a social movement succeeds in cracking open the political system, it must then learn to play by the rules of the institution it has worked to crack. Movements rearrange some of the pieces of the power structure that supported policies at the root of their grievance, forcing back older, more entrenched interests by making them accept the legitimacy of the movement's demands. They add their interest to the array of interests deemed worthy of government support, expanding the range of policy problems receiving government redress. This success is significant, but victory comes with costs, which may not be immediately apparent to the organizers of the social movement, who are now looking at careers as lobbyists. They must play by the rules and norms of the game they have struggled to join. The movement changed the beneficiaries of public policy and the values it enshrines, but not the way it is made. Activists-turned-lobbyists are now expected to work with lawmakers through the regular, institutionalized procedures of the political system. Bills will be introduced, other members of Congress will be lobbied, information packets developed, email campaigns launched—all with a united message that benefits their new legislative allies as much as their members. Other interest groups must be recruited as allies or bargained with as opponents. Because operating on the inside is much cheaper than staging protests, the group's staff are usually happy to oblige.

Passionate, dedicated movement members may not understand this transformation. They may not understand that further pursuing their interests now requires compromises with competing interests and paying attention to the needs of lawmakers. They may not understand the growing gulf between themselves and their leaders as the latter become part of the Washington social scene. While in many cases this simply leads to the loss of dispirited, disillusioned members, political scientist Anne Costain (1981) describes a much more dramatic result. At the 1975 national convention of the National Organization of Women (NOW), members forced out much of NOW's Washington staff for the crime of playing by Washington's rules, even though the professional activists had learned how to use them to the members' advantage.

Social movements are therefore embryonic interest groups, though not all interest groups start as social movements. The trade and professional associations representing businesses and white-collar professions certainly did not start out as street protests. Citizen groups, on the other hand, often started out as some kind of social movement, their origins grounded in passionate political activism. Sometimes they still try to keep the trappings of it and fire up large numbers of members just to keep them involved in the group. Of course the real difference between the two is that social movements represent interests truly excluded from regular politics but who have the opportunity and resources to break in, whereas interest groups are already on the inside.

Notes

1. "The Bonus Army: How a Protest Led to the GI Bill," *Radio Diaries*, National Public Radio, November 11, 2011, http://www.npr.org/templates/transcript/transcript .php?storyId=142224795. Authors Paul Dickson and Thomas Allen were interviewed about the Bonus Army and their book on the event (Dickson and Allen 2006).

2. The lower left area of Figure 3.2 is not directly relevant to this chapter but refers to those interests important to lawmakers perhaps because of campaign funding or because satisfying them is believed to be important for the well-being of society, even though society may not see it that way. Usually these are interests of a small number of individuals and are not perceived as affecting many citizens.

3. Surprisingly, General Motors supported the formation of the union.

4. See "Table 3: Union Affiliation of Employed Wage and Salary Workers by Occupation and Industry, 2011-2012 Annual Averages," Bureau of Labor Statistics, January 23, 2013, http://www.bls.gov/news.release/union2.t03.htm.

5. I am indebted to the work of Boies (1989) for providing a comprehensive overview of the economic theories of business lobbying.

6. See "Perdue's Facebook Page Slammed by Animal Rights Activists," *Under the Dome* (blog), Newsobserver.com, March 10, 2010, http://projects.newsobserver .com/under_the_dome/perdues_facebook_page_slammed_by_animal_activists.

7. I am indebted to the people I interviewed at Common Cause for this example.

8. I have on file a 2011 e-mail advertisement for one of these webinars from Lobbyists.info, the online subsidiary of Columbia Books, the publisher of *Washington Representatives*, from which came much of the data for this book.

CHAPTER FOUR

Lobbyists and Organization Management

Thomas J. Donohue, president of the US Chamber of Commerce, issued a call to arms to business leaders in November 2010. "We have never seen anything on this scale before," he said in his speech covered by the *Washington Post*, referring to a "regulatory tsunami" coming from the Obama administration (Dennis 2010). "It defies all logic and common sense." Obama's signature health care overhaul law had recently been enacted after a bitter battle in 2009, as had the Dodd-Frank financial reform bill mandating new regulations of investment firms, hedge funds, and credit default swaps designed to prevent another financial meltdown like the one in 2008. Calling these and other new laws "the biggest single threat to job creation," Donohue threw down the gauntlet. "We cannot allow this nation to move from a government of the people to a government of regulators." Having just invested millions of dollars to elect Republicans to Congress in the GOP landslide of 2010, he promised that the Chamber would go even further in its new campaign. "It is about representing our members," Donohue summed up for reporters.

Not all Chamber members thought so. The *Washington Post* reported a few days before Donohue's speech that "in 2008 a third of [the chamber's] income came from just 19 members—big companies to whom the chamber is beholden" (Vanden Heuvel 2010). If true, it helps explain why many small businesses, entrepreneurs, investors, and business groups abandoned the Chamber in frustration after Donohue's announcement. Some went on to form the American Sustainable Business Council to promote public policy that was as socially and environmentally responsible as it was supportive of profit making. They wanted to provide an alternative voice for American small business to the Chamber's megaphone. Some larger corporations such as Nike and Apple, and many local chambers, also left out of frustration, angry that their support was being used to advance the interests of a few corporate members with a profit-only political agenda. Monte Davis of the Homer, Alaska, chamber of commerce told National Public Radio reporter Aaron Selbig in 2011 that the US Chamber "doesn't represent us. They certainly don't do things politically that I think most people in Homer would agree with" (Selbig 2011).

As the US Chamber of Commerce story suggests, we should not assume that what group leaders want is exactly the same as what group members want. The interests of some members may match those of their Washington-based lobbyists, and sometimes lobbyists can convince members that their interests are all the same. But we cannot assume that those who lead and those who are led, the representatives and the represented, all want the same thing. Even if members do care about all the same issues and policies as their lobbyists, that may simply mean they were persuaded to believe it, perhaps manipulated into believing their interests were something other than what they had first thought. Those who run organized political groups often come from different backgrounds from those of the people they represent, and they certainly live different lives in Washington.[1] Lobbyists' interests may be quite different from those of the people they represent, and they might sometimes feel fine compromising member interests just to keep powerful lawmakers and other lobbyists in their professional and social circles happy.

In this chapter I talk about **lobbyists**, what they do, how they relate to interest group members, and why they sometimes prioritize the interests of some members over others or compromise all members' interests. Lobbyists are usually able to prevent the kinds of defections that the Chamber experienced. How members react to what their lobbyists do depends on what they know, but what members generally know about politics and policy in Washington, DC, including potential threats to their interests, comes from their lobbyists.

Information and Representation

Lobbyists as Informers

For all of the discussion in Chapter 2 about what interest groups provide their members in exchange for membership, one service went unmentioned: providing information. This is the service on which much of an organization's claim to be a legitimate representative of American citizens rests. An organization's staff is supposed to keep their members informed about what is happening in national politics that affects their interests. By most accounts, organizations take this responsibility seriously. Seventy-two percent of the lobbyists surveyed by political scientists Kay Lehman Schlozman and John Tierney (1986) in the 1980s responded that their organization spent "a great deal of time" communicating with their members (143). And that survey was done before mass e-mails and instant posts on Web sites, Facebook, and Twitter made it easy for a group to provide a steady flow of information to its members. In fact, group members today might suffer from an overabundance of information, both from their own interest group and from the Web sites, blogs, and Twitter accounts of an almost endless number of alternative, if factually questionable, online news sources.

Sometimes the information sent by interest group staff is passive: periodic updates from the Washington office about what is happening at the Capitol and how their lobbyists are always on the alert for anything threatening member interests. Some of these messages may be a chance for staff to show off their successes, taking credit (deserved or not) for favorable political and policy developments so that members will be impressed with the quality of the representation they are paying for. Other messages are intended to educate members, bringing new issues of concern to members' attention. These messages not only tell members what issues they should care about but also interpret the issues for members, teaching them why the lobbyists' proposed solutions are in members' best interests (Dexter 1969, 103–104). It is the organization's hope that once properly educated, members will spread the organization's interpretation of an issue and their policy solution to the broader public. Whether this amounts to member manipulation will be discussed later in the chapter.

Sometimes the information is proactive rather than passive, an urgent appeal for members to help defend crucial bread-and-butter issues by complaining to their local members of Congress or by writing angry letters to regulatory agencies. Cause-oriented citizen and public interest groups have learned to do this very well through the Internet (Bosso and Collins 2002). Often included in their online appeals are links to Web sites making contact easy in both form (an electronic form letter) and process (just click to send). Interest groups may also ask members to help recruit new members.

Members' Response to Information

Do members really want so much information from their interest group? Some do. The Congressional Management Foundation (CMF) research mentioned in Chapter 2 provides some insight here. When it comes to acquiring information on government and politics, 25 percent of people get it from a trusted interest group. Of that 25 percent, 22 percent get their information from the organization's Web site over any other means of communication (Goldschmidt and Ochreiter 2008, 16). People who want even more information can log in to the "Members Only" section of their group's Web site. Of the most politically motivated group members, those who frequently contact members of Congress, 73 percent said that they wanted their interest group to provide information on goings-on in Congress, and 78 percent said they wanted to be kept informed about the issues important to them (22).

So it appears that when an organization's staff dedicates time and resources to keeping their members informed, they are performing a desired service.[2] It is significant that politically active citizens rely so heavily on information provided by their interest group, especially since 70 percent of citizens contacting Congress said that they trust information from their group, but only 38 percent said they trusted information from their elected officials (Goldschmidt and Ochreiter 2008, 23–24). What a group says on its Web site, and how it interprets an issue, becomes the truth for many of its members. A group's lobbyist has a significant role as educator, but that also means there is potential for abuse.

When lobbyists prod their groups' members into action, the members take action. The CMF survey found that 60 percent of all interest group members contacted at least one member of Congress in the last five years; this was true of only 28 percent of nonmembers (Goldschmidt and Ochreiter 2008, 20). How members are contacting Capitol Hill is shown in Table 4.1, which uses the CMF data.[3] At least in 2008, e-mail was the overwhelming method of choice for advocacy. The data also shows that 43 percent of citizen contact with elected legislators was via the Internet in 2008, and 34 percent of that by e-mail (12–13). For their part, House offices reported receiving about three thousand to five thousand contacts of some type a month, and Senate offices around ten thousand (Fitch 2010a).

Participation in Interest Groups

Burning Out

The CMF survey also found that 69 percent of group members believed that group-driven campaigns to influence policy are good for representative government. But can even the most passionate members remain motivated

Method of Contact with Congress	Respondents Using Each Method
Contact form on House or Senate member's Web site	4%
Contact form on interest group's Web site	9%
E-mail	41%
In person	4%
Postal mail	7%
Public meeting	1%
Paper petition	3%
On-line petition	15%
Telephone	11%
Other	5%

TABLE 4.1   Methods of Interest Group Member Contact with Congress
Source: Poll conducted by Zogby International 2008 for (and provided to me by) the
Congressional Management Foundation

enough to stay deeply involved year after year? Take a look at the rate of
member participation in one interest group from the time of its birth until
five years later in Figure 4.1. Friends of Choice in Urban Schools, or FOCUS,
lobbies on behalf of the District of Columbia's charter schools, which are
schools free of government regulation of curriculum even though they are
funded with public money (Henig et al. 2004). Since it was founded in late
1998, I went to all of FOCUS's biweekly meetings until late 2003, meetings
to which all charter leaders were invited. The solid line in Figure 4.1 is the
percentage of school leaders who came to each meeting over the five-year
period, while the dashed line is the attendance rate of the original members
who founded FOCUS. The trend is clearly one of declining participation,
even by original members, though their line falls more slowly. What accounts
for such a decline?

One answer is that the passion members have for political change, at least
those drawn to the interest group by the purposive incentive discussed in
Chapter 2, is hard to maintain year after year. They get tired and burned out.
For instance, in two consecutive surveys of activists clashing over whether to
develop Lake Tahoe at the California-Nevada border, environmental politics

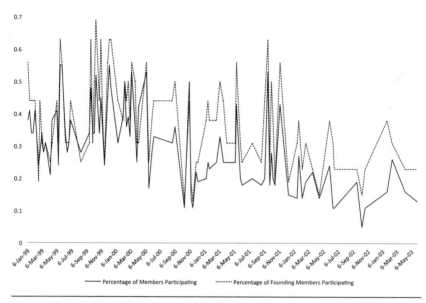

FIGURE 4.1   Percentage of FOCUS Members Participating Since Group's Founding
Source: Author's data

scholar Paul Sabatier (1992) found significantly fewer activists working in interest groups than in his first survey, even though the issue of development was still very much alive. It may be that people can only maintain a high level of activism just so long. Purposive-driven members join an interest group because they are attracted to a cause, but after a while the cause just does not spark the same fire in the belly that it used to. And they may realize that they are not quite as personally important to the group's success as they had originally believed, or were told to believe by the group's recruiters (Holyoke 2013a). Members may remain in the group to get the material benefits it provides, or just out of a sense of obligation and habit, but they might not be especially active. A major threat to their interests from competing interest groups may reignite their passion, but such bursts of participation are rarely sustained (Hansen 1985).

Original members are a little different. Brand-new groups are small and usually made up of the people who care most about the interest represented by the new group. After all, they are the ones taking the time and spending the money to get the group started. Original members more easily realize their personal importance to the small group's survival (Olson 1965). They likely have a greater sense of political efficacy and remain some of the organization's most passionate members, its "activist layer," as it grows and adds new members (Franke and Dobson 1985). But over time even founding members may become tired and complacent. Early victories mean they are now just defending the status quo, which is usually not quite as exciting, and they may look to "youngsters" to take over the cause for them. But newer members may be more interested in the goodies that come with membership, the material incentive, rather than the cause it stands for. This happened to FOCUS. In 1999 a few DC charter schools were fighting for their existence against a hostile local government, but by 2003 these public-private hybrid schools were an accepted part of the District's education landscape. The group's main enticement to join then became the aid it could provide new schools in finding buildings in which to hold class (Henig et al. 2004).

Managing Members

The participation decline in Figure 4.1 may also represent something more ominous: an effort by FOCUS's staff to manage a growing membership. Like any business or nonprofit, interest groups must institutionalize to survive, or they will perish when their founders pass on. Political scientist McGee Young (2010, 57) describes how the National Small Business Association was badly hurt by the death of its founder, DeWitt Emery, in 1955. It never really recovered, and is today a poor stepchild to its rival, the National Federation of Independent Business. To survive, an interest group must firmly establish its identity and reputation. Authority in the organization must be dispersed to other executives to give them a sense of commitment. Benefits for members must be consistently provided and expanded, meetings and conventions held on a regular basis, methods to routinely keep members informed must be put in place, and plans must be developed to keep the interest group's membership growing.

But the informal personal meetings and phone calls that members and lobbyists enjoyed in the group's salad days cannot continue as its membership swells to the thousands. The result is a sense of disconnect between members and the professional staff, leading to a sense of alienation on the part of members and, consequently, less interest in participation. Members are more likely to aid the interest group when its lobbyist makes a personal appeal in a meeting or phone call, but less so when the appeal comes in a form letter or generic e-mail addressed to "my friends." Group leaders compensate for the impersonal nature of these large and inflexible communication systems by making participation easier for members, linking them to Web sites with prepackaged, click-to-send letters. But this also means that information is flowing just one way, from leaders to members. It gives group leaders more control over what their members know and how they will react, getting members riled up when lobbyists think it might be strategically useful, but it also makes it easier for members not to respond.

Control of a one-way flow of information also makes it easier for group leaders to *not* report everything they are doing in Washington, keeping members in the dark while lobbyists work on issues that may not be in most members' interests. Why would leaders and lobbyists want to manipulate their members like this? One reason is that control of information may help them hold a divided membership together, a problem likely to arise as a group's membership grows (Moe 1980). Recall from the previous chapter that the AFL-CIO was a combination of many different trade and industrial unions. In 2005 the Teamsters Union, AFL-CIO's largest member, and a few other unions broke away after several fights over advocacy strategy, which issues were worth pursuing, and whose interests should be given priority. On the other hand, the American Bankers Association (ABA) appears to have succeeded where AFL-CIO failed. It claims to represent all banks, large and small, yet many members have accused ABA of being controlled by a few extremely large and wealthy banks whose interests are often harmful to smaller banks. Rival organizations emerged to represent smaller banks, such as America's Community Bankers and the Independent Community Bankers of America, asking what on earth a small bank could have in common with Citibank and Bank of America. Yet ABA has been able to hold its membership together by constantly telling members that there really are political issues important to both big and small banks.[4]

Another reason group leaders might want to control what their members know is that they want to use organizational resources to lobby on new issues that might attract new members. As I mentioned in Chapter 2, leaders usually want their organizations to grow. Bigger organizations representing larger, more diverse constituencies are given more attention and respect by lawmakers, and this makes their lobbyists more influential (Gray and Lowery 1997; Grossmann 2012, Ch. 5). Political scientist Robin Dale Jacobson (2011) shows how certain groups hoping to represent new interests only tangentially related to those of their core members changed their positions on immigration policy. They did it to appeal to broader audiences, even though it meant compromising the interests of their current members. Information control is the key to balancing acts like this—what members do not know will not hurt them—and it frees up lobbyists to do their job. The irony is in the fact that, as I showed in the previous section, members want to get political information from their interest group.

Who Are Lobbyists?

I will return to this discussion of member management later, but first let me clarify the role of lobbyists. Who are they? What do they do? Who becomes one? Lobbyists are people who advocate for the interests of other people before government officials. But they come with a seedy reputation. Journalists seem to have nothing but disdain for lobbyists, blaming them for most of the political system's ills because they apparently have the power to corrupt otherwise honest, if weak-willed, lawmakers (e.g., Birnbaum 1992; Drew 1999). Parents, don't let your kids grow up to be lobbyists! Lobbyists do not even like being called lobbyists. Their business cards tend to say "advocate," "liaison," "legislative director," "government affairs associate," or "government relations specialist"—anything but "lobbyist." Political scientist Lester Milbrath once asked several lobbyists if the job title fit them, but they refused to acknowledge that anything they did was **lobbying** (Milbrath 1963, 58).

On the other hand, there is also a view of lobbyists as fabulously wealthy people who attend all of Washington's best parties and are the real powers behind elected leaders. The lobbying directory *Washington Representatives* (2010, ix) reported that the highest lobbyist income in 2010 was $1,750,000 at Daryl Owen Associates.[5] Who would not want to join the ranks of this apparently wealthy, ruling elite? In his exposition of super-lobbyist Gerald Cassidy, journalist Robert Kaiser included pictures of Cassidy's beautiful mansion on Virginia's seashore. He also recounted that when lobbyist Robert Strauss was asked why so many people went into lobbying, Strauss responded "there is just so damn much money" (Kaiser 2009, 360).

By the Numbers

Thousands of people in Washington, state capitols, and county seats can be called lobbyists. *Washington Representatives* for 2010 lists 19,053 lobbyists in Washington alone, 206 of whom were once members of Congress. Lobbyists are employed by 15,609 organizations and corporations, and 2,384 private lobbying firms employ **for-hire lobbyists**, with powerhouse firm Patton Boggs employing the most at 154. We actually know a fair amount about who lobbyists are, where they come from, and what their career paths are from a 2012 survey of lobbyists by Lobbyists.info (3.2 percent margin of error; Rehr 2012, 3–6, 14):

- 70 percent are male, and the women who do lobby pretty much do it like the men (Nownes and Freeman 1998).
- 54 percent once worked for Congress and 26 percent for the executive branch before becoming lobbyists.[6]
- 27 percent are between ages thirty-six and forty-five; 27 percent are forty-six to fifty-five; 27 percent are fifty-six to sixty-five; 12 percent are younger than thirty-five; and 8 percent are over sixty-five.
- 40 percent are Democrats, 33 percent are Republicans, and 27 percent are independent or refused to say what party they support.
- 23 percent work for business and trade associations, 21 percent work for corporations, 18 percent work for independent lobbying firms (they are for-hire lobbyists), 16 percent work for think tanks, and 6 percent work for cause-oriented citizen and public interest groups.
- Only 80 percent are officially registered to lobby Congress under the Lobbying Disclosure Act of 1995.

As for making lots of money, research in the 1980s by John Heinz, Edward Laumann, Robert Nelson, and Robert Salisbury found that the plurality of lobbyists, 35 percent, earned between $30,000 to $59,000 annually (1993, 70–71). In 2011 this is about $63,000 to $124,000, which is certainly a good salary though hardly lavish. Only 9 percent were found to earn between $125,000 and $199,000, and only 8 percent earned more than $200,000 (or $421,000 today). Total 2009 lobbying sector profits, according to *Washington Representatives*, was $1.58 billion (Washington Representatives 2010, x).

Many lobbyists never dreamed that they would end up being lobbyists. Take Debbie Sease, the top lobbyist for the Sierra Club, who was profiled in 2011 by the western newspaper *High Country News* (Farrell 2011). Born in New Mexico, she became a passionate environmentalist in the early 1970s, just as the boom in new environmental interest groups and big new environmental laws was coming to an end. She and others, including the notable activist David Foreman, were hired by the Wilderness Society to take their passion to Washington—at least for a little while. Sease recalled, "I was only going to be here for a year. I didn't unpack my boxes." When the Carter administration dumped its support for legislation to designate millions of acres of land as untouchable by developers, her fellow environmentalists left

Washington in disgust. Foreman went on to start the much more radical, anti-DC group Earth First! But Sease stayed to fight the Reagan administration and discovered that she liked lobbying and was good at it. She moved on to lobby for the Sierra Club and frequently acts as the lead lobbyist for the whole environmental community. She says that the Internet keeps her in touch with members almost daily, which keeps her excited and helps her stay in touch with her group's principles.

Out of Government, into Interest Groups, and Back Again

As noted above, 80 percent of lobbyists came into lobbying from government jobs. Lobbyists told Heinz and his colleagues that government service helped launch their lobbying careers. Of the lobbyists interviewed, 70 percent said it gave them familiarity with issues, 80 percent said it taught them how the lawmaking process works, 59 percent said it gave them important contacts in Congress, 48 percent said it gave them contacts in the administration, and 47 percent said it helped them gain contacts with other lobbyists (Heinz et al. 1993, 115).

Because there are reasons to be concerned about government employees using their knowledge and contacts to make money in the lobbying world, the organization LegiStorm analyzed congressional staffing and lobbyist registration data for ten years and found that nearly 5,400 of today's lobbyists once worked on Capitol Hill. Almost 400 of them were once themselves representatives or senators (Farnam 2011). Many left the Hill fairly recently. Of the 19,053 lobbyists listed in *Washington Representatives*, 1,437 (or about 8 percent) once worked for a legislator in the 111th Congress (2009 to 2010). A little data analysis reveals that Democrats are just as likely as Republicans to leave staff positions in Congress for the lobbying industry.[7] Also, each legislative leader in 2010 had, on average, eight members of his or her staff leave to become lobbyists, while it was half that for nonleaders.[8] For committee chairs, on average nearly seven former staff members become lobbyists. It seems that knowing a powerful lawmaker makes one a hot commodity on the lobbyist job market. LegiStorm's research uncovered a whole network of ex-staffers for Senator Max Baucus (D-MT) now working for lobbying firms with business before the powerful senator's tax-writing Senate Finance Committee (Lipton 2013).

This is what is colloquially called the **revolving door**. Many ex-Hill people end up at well-known lobbying firms such as the Podesta Group (which has the most ex-Hill staff at eighteen, according to *Washington Representatives*

2010, vii) and major interest groups such as the US Chamber of Commerce. Why? Tony Podesta, founder of the Podesta Group, told the *Washington Post* that "people who are experienced in Washington tend to be better at doing this kind of work than people who have never worked in the government before." Often the reason is strategic. The Motion Picture Association of America hired former senator Chris Dodd (D-CT) to be its new president because for years Dodd had chaired the Senate committee that controlled many of the policies important to the group (Romm 2011). Conflicts of interest? Maybe. Citizens for Responsibility and Ethics in Washington found in 2011 that seven ex-congressmen were now lobbying for interests these legislators had supported with government appropriations while in Congress (Farnam 2012b).

The hiring of ex-legislators and legislative staffers as lobbyists (and the issue of who gets hired) has become a political issue. Interest groups and lobbying firms try to staff up with lobbyists of the same ideological persuasion as the party controlling Congress. For example, Republican staff members were in high demand in 1994 after their party gained control of the House and Senate (Stone 1996). Party leaders even threatened to shut several interest groups out of Congress if they did not hire Republican staff as lobbyists. For instance, the chief of staff for House Speaker Newt Gingrich (R-GA) insisted that the Electronics Industries Alliance (EIA) hire Rep. Bill Paxon (R-NY). Instead they hired Rep. David McCurdy (D-OK). In retaliation, Gingrich allegedly announced that Republicans would not talk to any EIA lobbyist and held up votes on bills that would implement treaties on intellectual property— something the EIA wanted. The chief of staff for Sen. Rick Santorum (R-PA) defended this move, saying, "At what point can you trust [Democrats lobbying for trade associations] that what you're sharing on inside strategy or tactics aren't going directly back to the Democratic leadership?" (Eilperin 1998b).

This problem reputedly became even worse in 2001, when lobbyist Grover Norquist of Americans for Tax Reform and House Majority Leader Tom DeLay (R-TX) created the K Street project to force lobbying firms to fire Democrats and hire Republicans (Eilperin 2001). Many firms, though, kept their Democrats even as they hired Republicans, hedging their bets that Democrats would return to power (Kaiser 2009, 267). Hiring from both parties may actually signal a decline in the influence of lobbyists. In the past, well-connected lobbyists like Lloyd Cutler, Clark Clifford, and Tom Corcoran could easily work with both parties, bringing competing groups of interests together to hammer out deals and resolve conflicts (Ignatius 2000). Today,

Lobbyist Professional Activity	Percentage Rating It Important
Alerting clients about important issues	84%
Developing policy positions and strategies	83%
Monitoring changes in rules and laws	62%
Maintaining informal contacts with government officials	62%
Providing written information to government officials	52%
Maintaining contacts with other lobbyist and elite allies	50%
Providing government officials with testimony	47%
Commenting to the press and contributing to speeches	44%
Mobilizing grassroots-member support	41%
Drafting bills and administrative rules	27%
Testifying at official proceedings	27%
Resolving internal organizational conflicts	23%
PAC fundraising	19%
Pursuing policy litigation	17%

TABLE 4.2   Activities Lobbyists Consider Important in Their Profession
Source: Adapted from Heinz et al. 1993, p. 99

though, lobbyists are pressured by the parties to take sides, with their access threatened (which kills a lobbyist's career) if they do not.

Perhaps even more interesting is that 605 congressional staffers in 2011 used to be lobbyists. When Republicans took over the House of Representatives that year, many new legislators recruited their senior staff from among the ranks of major lobbying firms and business associations (Farnam 2011). The door fully revolves. Government workers leave to make money as lobbyists, and some later return to work on the inside, possibly still biased toward the interest groups that recently employed them, and they could return to lobbying again in a couple of years for a lot more money. For instance, tax legislation passed in early 2013 resolving a fierce standoff between President Obama and Republicans controlling the House also contained special language that delayed Medicare restrictions on kidney dialysis drugs from taking effect for two years. This favored the pharmaceutical firm Amgen, even though the company was not specifically mentioned in the bill. Amgen contributed a great deal of money in 2012 to lawmakers, but its real ace in the hole was a former lobbyist who worked on the staff of the Senate Finance Committee but was apparently still sympathetic to his prior employer (Lipton and Sack 2013).

The second half of this book focuses on how lobbyists work to promote their members' interests in the different branches of government, but it is worth providing a little background information here. In Table 4.2 I use data from Heinz and colleagues (1993, 99) to show how important lobbyists feel the various aspects of their job are. The single most important item is informing interest group members and clients about what is happening in Washington, DC. This finding fits with the point made earlier in the chapter that this is what members want from their lobbyists. Some of the other items on the list regard collecting that information, such as monitoring changes in laws and administrative rules and talking to others. Resolving internal group conflicts, such as divisions in the membership, is another on the list, and a topic I will elaborate on momentarily.

Heinz and colleagues also found that lobbyists have about eight people in government that they talk to as part of their daily routine (96). Who might these contacts be? It is legislators on important committees and their staff about 31 percent of the time and legislative leaders about 14 percent of the time (159). It is with administrative agencies 18 percent of the time and the White House only 8 percent of the time. Understand, though, that when an issue important to their members is being debated, lobbyists will try to have a lot more contact with a lot more lawmakers and staff. And the reverse is true, that when they have no issue on the agenda, lobbyists leave busy lawmakers alone. Government officials have little time during the day for small talk, and lobbyists know it.[9]

Prioritizing Career Interests

None of this explains why lobbyists sometimes feel a need to exercise control over their members, but it is a starting point. Professional lobbyists have careers to advance, and this means they sometimes need to make choices that are not entirely consistent with what their members want. It should be clear now that lobbyists often do not stay at the same interest group, law firm, or public relations firm their entire career. They often move into the executive branch or Capitol Hill and then go back to lobbying. In this they are no different from people trying to advance careers in the corporate sector, where moving around is often expected. What is different about lobbyists, though, is that what they have to sell to a prospective employer is whom they have access to (who their contracts are) in Washington's power structure. A lobbying career means developing a larger portfolio of relationships with powerful figures—not just legislators, but also executive branch officials and other lobbyists. Who you know *does* matter.

Because lobbyists seek to advance their careers by finding better paying jobs at more influential interest groups and lobbying firms, the people they represent change frequently. Thus who they represent often becomes less important to their careers than remaining close to the policy makers they have built relationships with. *Remember this point.* Career-oriented lobbyists often place greater value on nurturing and maintaining these relationships than building close connections with members or clients. The larger and more diverse a lobbyist's portfolio of relationships with powerful people, the more likely he or she will be hired away from an interest group before learning much about that group's members, to say nothing of being committed to their cause. Most lobbyists are professional opportunists, and a strong portfolio of relationships is the currency they use to move up Washington's career ladder.

Many lobbyists do care about issues at least somewhat, and they may even have come up through the membership ranks of an interest group rather than out of government. But they have to be pragmatic. The ethical lobbyist puts the good of his or her members and clients before those of the officials with whom he or she has a relationship. The ambitious lobbyist does the opposite. The talented lobbyist makes sure the interests of these two "audiences" always appear aligned, even if they have to do some fast talking to convince everybody that is true. Lobbyists are, as political scientist Rogan Kersh (2002) argues, autonomous actors who often have considerable discretion to pursue whatever issues and positions they believe necessary to advance member interests—a skill they must have in order to be successful. At the same time their personal interests must also be served. When personal needs align with member interests, all is well, but what happens when they do not? How does a talented lobbyist avoid a situation in which he or she must choose between members and lawmakers? That brings us back to issues of member management.

The Politics of Interest Group Maintenance

Even at the best of times the amount of attention most interest group members pay to politics can be charitably described as selective. They vaguely understand political issues, often reducing complex issues to the question "Did we win?" in an us-or-them, do-or-die struggle (Baumgartner et al. 2009, Ch. 3). Most members do not care about most of the issues consuming so much time and energy in Washington because they do not believe the issues affect them. And most issues do not. It is the lobbyist's job to decide whether members should be made aware of an issue. Even if issues do affect group members, they may not care about them all that much. Lobbyists then have fairly wide latitude to solve these problems as they see fit, making it easy to solve them in ways that please the lawmakers with whom they have cultivated valuable relationships.

But sometimes members *really* care about an issue, especially if they were attracted to the interest group through the purposive incentive (members who joined for material benefits presumably do not care what the lobbyist is doing). If lobbyists find that their members' interests on these issues do not align with those of their Washington allies, they had better find a way to make them appear aligned. Their ability to use information to define issues and present them in simple us-or-them terms now becomes important, even if problematic from the standpoint of honest representation. A well-crafted message from the group's Washington office may convince even the most passionate, purposive-driven members that the issue they are so worked up about is not really that important, or that the position the group ought to take is different from what the members thought it should be. The "sensible" position the lobbyist promotes to members may actually be more pleasing to his or her allies in Washington.

Lobbyists manipulate members at their peril. If members suspect that their lobbyist's loyalties are pointed more toward the Washington establishment than their way, they might abandon the group (Hirschman 1970). Remember that interest group executives like their organizations to grow, but a reputation for poor representation is not going to help them do so. Exiting members is a big problem. An even worse problem for lobbyists and leaders is what happened to the National Organization of Women (mentioned in the last chapter). When members discovered that their Washington staff was making a lot of compromises with lawmakers and other interests groups, they rebelled and fired them all (Costain 1981).

Interest Groups and the Iron Law of Oligarchy

That leaders might use information to manage their members was predicted by French sociologist Robert Michels's **Iron Law of Oligarchy** in 1959.

Michels was thinking more about political parties, but his idea fits interest groups just as well. Living and working in Washington on a full-time basis means that lobbyists know much more about what is happening there than their members do. This is called **information asymmetry**. Michels's Iron Law predicts that as group memberships grow in size and diversity, leaders will have to use their control of information to highlight, via the group's communications structures, the issues the leaders believe are crucial and the positions they believe the group should take for the organization's benefit. More importantly, they may use information control to reshape member interests, encouraging them to believe that a new issue emerging on the government's agenda affects their interests—not because it does but because group leaders want to use it to claim new members that come with this new territory. Furthermore, differences between factions in the membership can be papered over by using information to convince members that their interests are largely the same. The American Bankers Association example I used earlier in the chapter illustrates this.

Another division between members that leaders and lobbyists might want to downplay is rooted in who contributes the most money to the interest group. Members who give more may be more important to its lobbyist. Since many groups use a sliding scale for determining how much each member should pay depending on their annual income, divisions in the membership by wealth frequently occur. Letting poorer members give smaller amounts seems benign, but it may make them less important to the group's leaders. The interests of wealthier members will be given priority, but the lobbyist may craft a message convincing all members that the position they are taking on the issue is in everyone's best interest. They can do this because they control the flow of information. Political scientist Dara Strolovitch (2006) finds cases of members being prioritized by socioeconomic status in many cause-oriented interest groups. To paraphrase George Orwell's *Animal Farm*, all members are equal, but wealthier members are more equal than others.

I do not want to end this section, though, with the impression that the decline in participation, as seen in Figure 4.1, is because lobbyists and group executives deliberately want to manipulate their members by controlling what they know. The division between members and leaders as anticipated by the Iron Law of Oligarchy, which results in members' sense of alienation, is often an unintended by-product of the leaders' need to cope with a large membership. It would happen even if the interest group employed the world's most faithful lobbyist. As organizations' memberships expand, leaders and lobbyists simply cannot keep interacting as frequently and as casually with their members as they did when the group was small. There are simply too many members who are potentially making too many demands and clamoring for too much attention. Thus it becomes rational and efficient, even essential, for leaders to use the apparatus of communication to impose these controls over members just so the organization can function (Arrow 1991). And as more and more interest groups base their offices in Washington, DC, and hire lobbyists from Capitol Hill and executive branch networks, the organization's leadership becomes ever more deeply embedded in Washington culture, further removed from their grassroots base. Now lobbyists need to manage their members in order to take maximum advantage of the organization's position in Washington with as little interference from members as possible.

Technology and the Erosion of Control

If lobbyists need to keep some control over what their members know, then the Internet may be their worst enemy. The online revolution has made it easy, or at least easier, for members to find out what is happening in Washington, DC, and even what their own interest group is doing, without depending solely on lobbyists for information. True, the information members find on many Web sites and blogs may not be accurate, but members are nowhere near as reliant on lobbyists for it as they once were. This, in turn, makes it much harder for lobbyists to manage the membership, suppress divisions among members, and frame issues and policy solutions in ways that benefit their Washington allies so lobbyists can advance their careers. However, the Internet may not help poorer members hold their lobbyists accountable. A recent study by the Pew Internet and American Life Project found that political Internet usage is skewed by annual income: those earning more money are using the Internet more frequently to find political information and contact government officials (Smith et al. 2009, 4) than those who earn less. Poorer citizens are left dependent on others to tell them what is going on. If the group's lobbyist is an honest purveyor of political information, then interest group membership may actually help poorer members keep tabs on their government, compensating for other socioeconomic barriers (Holyoke 2013b).

Time will tell, but political Internet usage being skewed toward wealthier individuals may change. Pew also found that not only are younger people using the Internet more frequently than older people, their use is less skewed by income, though they are often not looking for political information. Will the tech-savvy younger generation want to form virtual interest groups, whereby it might be easier to keep tabs on their lobbyists? Purely virtual communities may exist on Facebook and similar social media sites, but so far they do not appear to be anything like interest groups. Not yet anyway. The Pew study did find that 56 percent of citizens in political and civic groups do now communicate using the Internet, and 24 percent communicate with their interest group via social networking sites (Smith et al. 2009, 9). At the very least we can say the role of the Internet in interest group communication and management is becoming important.

Concerns for Interest Group Representation

Are members really so much at the mercy of their interest group leaders and lobbyists? At the beginning of this chapter I gave an example of members becoming so frustrated and angry with the Chamber's political activities that they quit. But as economist Albert Hirschman (1970) predicted, sometimes members will use their voices to force their group's leaders to account for actions seemingly at odds with member interests. An example of this is the re-action of members of the Nature Conservancy to a series of articles published in the *Washington Post* in 2003 about how the nation's largest and wealthiest environmental conservation organization was allowing the development of lands that its members assumed it owned to prevent them being developed.

According to the *Post*, the Conservancy had received a charitable gift from a family for $18.5 million that the interest group then pooled with other monies to buy 215 acres of land on Martha's Vineyard in Massachusetts from businesses owned by that same family. The family promptly deducted the entire contribution from their taxes. Half of the land purchased by the Conservancy was then resold to executives from Oracle and Goldman Sachs, as well as comedian David Letterman. Some development restrictions were imposed, but with enough flexibility to allow the buyers to still build enormous vacation homes (Ottaway and Stephens 2003). This, *Post* reporters found, was not at all an unusual deal for the Conservancy (Stephens and Ottaway 2003b). Although this "conservation development" strategy arguably did allow the group's leaders to place development restrictions on more land than they would be able to control otherwise, Conservancy members reacted angrily when they read the *Post*'s exposé. In a frantic burst of damage control, the Conservancy suspended its use of such deals and announced it would review other practices potentially out of line with member interests and values, such as inviting environmental fine–paying Fortune 500 executives to serve on its board of directors (Stephens and Ottaway 2003a). The group's president even mailed a personal letter to all the Conservancy's one million or so members in which the organization attacked the newspaper's "misrepresentations" but also apologized and promised to prioritize member values in all of its future land preservation deals.[10]

In Summary

Here is the summary of the chapter's main points:

- Active member participation in interest groups tends to decline over time, as a result of both burnout and group leaders trying to exercise greater control over their members.
- Lobbyists—the professionals who are responsible for representing the group's interests before lawmakers—often give a greater priority to the relationships they have developed with lawmakers than to faithfully pursuing their members' interests.
- This is because most lobbyists started their careers in government, where they made the important contacts necessary for having lucrative lobbying jobs, so their careers are dependent on preserving these relationships by keeping lawmakers happy.
- Consequently, lobbyists and other group leaders will often use their ability to control the information their members receive about Washington to make it appear that member interests are always being served, and indeed some control of information is required anyway just to hold a large and growing membership together.

In an ideal political world the interests of all group members would align perfectly with the policy positions their lobbyist promotes in Washington, DC. But this is often just not possible, even for the most well-intentioned lobbyist. For the less well-intentioned lobbyist more interested in promoting his or her personal career, his or her ability to control what members know makes it possible to keep allies in Washington happy without upsetting group members. Unfortunately it is not possible to know how often this happens in interest group politics. What the Chamber of Commerce story I used to open this chapter shows is that disalignment of interests does occur: the interests of a few powerful members and lawmakers were prioritized over those of smaller members, who reacted by leaving the organization to set up a countervailing group. The Nature Conservancy story, by contrast, shows how group leaders' control of information is not perfect. In this case it took enterprising journalists to show members that their interests and values were not being well represented, but once members realized this was the case, they reacted by forcing the leadership back into line rather than abandoning the group.

Members of other interest groups may not be so fortunate as to catch their lobbyists serving somebody else's interests. This is a problem for members and lobbyists alike, as the group ages and becomes more established, institutionalized, and even successful. What lobbyists must do to gain access and wield influence on behalf of their members in the three branches of government often requires them to reshape what their members want to make it more palatable to lawmakers. Otherwise the lobbyist would probably be ignored. How lobbyists gain access to, and exert their influence in, the three branches of government is what the second half of this book is about.

Notes

1. Not only is this assumption dangerous for understanding group politics, but Van Winden (1999) shows how dangerous it is for the study of interest groups and organizational politics as well.

2. This is from my own analysis of the survey data, as are all of the results aside from those citing the CMF report. The Congressional Management Foundation was kind enough to provide me with the report; in the spirit of full disclosure, I did much of the statistical analysis for it.

3. The table contains percentages of respondents reporting their last used method of contact with a member of Congress.

4. This observation comes from my own experiences working with banking association lobbyists in the late 1990s, when I worked for the banking committee of the New York State Senate.

5. This figure was calculated by dividing the firm's total income by the number of lobbyists it employed, so actual lobbyists there may not have made quite so much. Or they may have made even more!

6. It is interesting to note that in the 1980s study of Heinz et al. (1993, 115), 37 percent of lobbyists started in the executive branch and 32 percent in other government positions like members of Congress, so things have changed.

7. The difference between House and Senate could not be calculated because senators have a much larger staff of people who can become lobbyists.

8. Leadership means House Speaker, House and Senate majority or minority leaders, majority or minority whips, conference chairs, and anyone else listed on the legislative leadership rosters.

9. This observation about lobbyists' interactions with lawmakers comes from an interview I did in 2012 with a former legislative assistant.

10. Nature Conservancy letter to members, 2003. A copy of this letter is on file with the author and available on request.

CHAPTER FIVE

A Model of Interest Group Advocacy

Before moving on to the second half of the book, it is worth taking some time to use what has been learned from the first four chapters to think more carefully about how an interest group's internal dynamics shape its lobbying efforts. To do this I engage in a bit of what social scientists call modeling, which means using assumptions regarding the behavior of group members, government officials, and lobbyists to predict what they will do under certain circumstances. In other words, the model will show how lobbyists make decisions based on the motivations of policy makers, group members, and their own ambitions. It should help answer the question left hanging in the last chapter about how lobbyists balance competing group member and lawmaker pressures. It should also give some insight into lobbyists' capacity to meaningfully represent citizen interests before government.

Lobbyists in the Middle

As I explained in the last chapter, understanding interest group politics means seeing lobbyists as distinct from the people they represent, even as they pursue these people's interests by lobbying members of Congress, contributing money in elections, and filing lawsuits in court. This is not a pedantic distinction. Senators may act in ways inconsistent with the wishes of their constituents because they have to cope with demands from House members, presidents, bureaucrats, and other senators. So too with lobbyists. Indeed, it may be easier for lobbyists to be swayed by influences other than their own members because, unlike legislators, they do not have to publicly present themselves for validation or rejection in elections.

Sometimes lobbyists come out of their group's membership. Often, though, they come from other Washington interest groups or government institutions. This means their desire to advance the interests of their organization's members exists only insofar as it helps them build a successful and lucrative Washington career. A few ideologically motivated lobbyists like Sierra Club's Debbie Sease, mentioned in the last chapter, may stay with one group their entire career, but most try to move on to other groups that are larger, more prestigious, and better paying. Or they leave interest group employment and join a lobbying or public relations firm, perhaps bringing in their former group as a new client. If they go back to Capitol Hill, it is in a senior position they can use to build a heftier portfolio of contacts with powerful lawmakers to get an even better lobbying job afterwards. The mark of a successful lobbyist is a strong portfolio of relationships with important Capitol Hill lawmakers, presidential aides in the White House's West Wing, executives in administrative agencies, and other powerful lobbyists. Opportunities to move up in the lobbying profession depend on *what* you know and, most especially, *whom* you have access to, and more is better. Super-lobbyists like Sam Ward, Tom Corcoran, Charls Walker, Lloyd Cutler, and even Jack Abramoff advertised themselves almost exclusively in terms of whom they knew. From this, we can safely state the first assumption:

Assumption 1: Lobbyists want to advance their careers by building and maintaining personal relationships with government officials and by successfully representing member interests.

Like everyone, lobbyists have an interest they strive for; it is just that their interest may not be the same as the interests of the people they represent. They certainly have a professional interest in helping the people they are currently employed to represent, but when the needs of members clash with a lobbyist's need to maintain good relations with lawmakers, members sometimes fail to come first. Lobbyists believe in Shakespeare's line "To thy own self be true."

Interest Group Member Pressure

The pressures lobbyists must balance are a little more complex than they might seem at first. I have defined interest groups as people organized around some intensely felt desire or trait. But do not assume this means that all members want to pursue their common interest in exactly the same way. For instance, trucking companies have an interest in protecting themselves from heavy government regulation, a common interest that helps bond them together under the umbrella of the American Trucking Associations (ATA), their trade group.[1] Yet when it comes to government regulation of something like the number of hours a trucker can drive before taking a required break for sleep, members may sharply disagree. Some may want no government rule at all so that companies can set their own policy, or leave it up to the driver's discretion. Other members may feel that in the interests of public safety and their profession's image, and even out of regard for their drivers, there ought to be a uniform rule on driving time. In other words, though the ATA is a group of people with a common general interest, when it comes to specific issue questions such as how much regulation there should be regarding driving time (if any), they may sharply disagree with each other. This leads to the second assumption:

Assumption 2: Interest group members differ in how they would ideally like to see issues important to them resolved with public policy.

Members may also differ on how important they think the issue is. Regulations on driving time may be an important issue to ATA members, perhaps more than something like restrictions on carrying hazardous materials, but not as much as increases in fuel taxes or requirements to retrofit engines to comply with clean air standards. The latter two issues hit the trucking companies' bottom line hard and are thus the issues members *really* want their lobbyist to prioritize. Fuel taxes and engine retrofitting are also issues members are likely to follow closely, whereas issues less important to them, like driving hours, may fly under their radar entirely. Although one might think that members would be fairly united in how they would like to see their really important issues resolved with policy, there is no evidence in interest group research to support that conclusion, and so leads to the third assumption:

Assumption 3: Some issues are more important to members than others, and they will be more likely to be angry if their ideal positions on these issues are not precisely advocated by their lobbyist.

In discussing the internal workings of political groups, economist Albert Hirschman (1970) made a simple but important point. When faced with a leadership that does not appear to have their best interests at heart, members may do one of three things. They may loyally support the group anyway out of regard for the good of the whole, they may try to change the group by pushing out the unresponsive lobbyists and staff, or they may just quit the group entirely and take their dues with them as they exit. Except for some unions and a few professional organizations like bar associations, interest groups do not have compulsory membership. Members may quit at any time. So the fourth assumption states:

Assumption 4: Interest group members can quit their organization and are more likely to do so the more dissatisfied they are with the choices of its lobbyist.

Even when members are happy and pay their dues, there is another crucial limit on what lobbyists can do: money. Members only have so much money to give for group support. In Chapter 2, I tried to give some sense of the size of group budgets, and most are not all that large, even when they are supplemented by philanthropies, foundations, wealthy individuals, and the government. The costs of mounting major advocacy campaigns can be enormous, and apart from advocacy, groups also must allocate significant parts of their budgets to the nonpolitical activities and other benefits that members demand (and that may be more important to some members than the advocacy). The fifth assumption states the result of this fact:

Assumption 5: Lobbyists have limited resources for pursuing member interest advocacy.

The five assumptions outlined above are enough to start exploring how an ATA lobbyist might approach the driving hours issue. In Figure 5.1a, the horizontal line represents a continuum of possible policy outcomes. For this issue, the left side represents more restrictions on driving hours, and the right side represents fewer restrictions on driving hours, with some ultimate point to the far right indicating no restrictions at all. Following Assumption 2, a few members may want fairly tight restrictions, meaning their preferred policy outcome falls on the left side of the continuum. Other members want virtually no restriction, so they are on the right side, but the bulk of them want some restrictions, hence the "bubble" in the middle of Figure 5.1a.

Assumption 1 says that lobbyists always seek to advance their career interests, and part of that means doing a good job representing their members' interests in the political process. Since no counterpressures in the driving hours issue have been identified yet, it is safe to say that ATA's lobbyist wants to please the most members. Clearly that means supporting a policy at the center of the continuum, identified by the solid vertical line in Figure 5.1a, because there are more members there than at any other position. True, the majority of members are not quite at that specific position, but they are close. Unless they feel strongly about the number of hours, then, consistent with Assumption 3, the majority of members will be satisfied enough with their

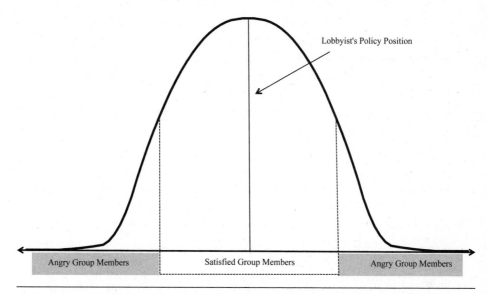

FIGURE 5.1A   Alignment of ATA Group Members on Hours of Driving Permitted

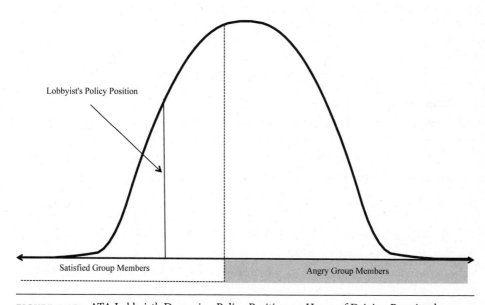

FIGURE 5.1B   ATA Lobbyist's Damaging Policy Position on Hours of Driving Permitted

lobbyist's choice. Assumption 4 holds that unhappy members will leave the group when it is not responsive to their wishes, thus limiting the resources that lobbyists have access to (as laid out in Assumption 5). But in this case few members are likely to leave because the lobbyist's position is the same as, or close to, the position that most of them prefer. They will continue to support ATA with their dues, and this keeps the lobbyist happy because he or she still has access to abundant resources for their job. So the lobbyist's choice is consistent with that part of Assumption 1 holding that lobbyists advance their careers by representing member interests.

A few members may be angry enough to leave the group, such as those on the extremes of the distribution in the shaded areas of Figure 5.1a. Of course if the lobbyist does *not* support the position acceptable to most members but instead supports a really severe restriction on driving hours on the far left side of the issue continuum, as shown in Figure 5.1b, the outcome would be different. In this situation, the lobbyist's position is far from what a majority of members want. Unless members really do not care about this issue at all, they will be very angry and may drop out of the organization, depriving the lobbyist of resources. Or there may be enough angry members to get rid of the lobbyist. Either outcome is a serious setback for the lobbyist's career and seemingly inconsistent with Assumption 1. No lobbyist would do this, would they?

Policy Maker Pressure

Lobbyists hold no official positions in government institutions and therefore cannot directly shape public policy. They have to convince others to do it for them. Members of Congress, presidential aides, administrative agency executives, and federal judges are all officials of the United States government and *are* responsible for making policy. This is why they are lobbying targets. It is why lobbyists need government officials to act on their behalf when new laws are made or old laws revised. It is also why interest groups need lobbyists. Somebody has to convince these officials to promote or defend group member interests, so the sixth assumption reads:

Assumption 6: Only elected and appointed government officials may directly influence the government's policy-making process.

Since policy maker support is critical to successful advocacy, lobbyists must find ways to persuade and pressure policy makers into acting on their members' behalf. I leave the details of how that happens for later chapters, but whether by enticements or threats, lobbyists make arguments that are meaningful to policy makers, arguments that convince them that it is in *their* interests to support a policy proposal that also happens to more or less be what the lobbyist's members want. Lobbying is the art of pursuing member interests by persuading lawmakers that their interests and member interests are one and the same.

Lobbyists start by understanding what the interests of government officials are. Members of Congress want to be reelected, or to become a senator, governor, or even president (Mayhew 1974). Many also want to make policy consistent with their own ideological beliefs, usually so they have an achievement to advertise when they run for reelection or for election to higher office (Dodd 1977). Appointed officials running administrative agencies that implement the laws Congress passes want larger budgets and less congressional oversight (Downs 1967; Balla 1998). Federal judges, and especially members of the US Supreme Court, with lifetime appointments and largely insulated from political pressures, simply want to advance their ideas of how the Constitution ought to be interpreted and how to make existing law consistent with that ideal (Segal and Spaeth 2002). Is this overly simplistic? Yes. Does this cynically rule out any notion of altruism or a desire to serve the public good? Certainly. But what this stripped-down view of policy maker motivation *does* provide is stated in the seventh assumption:

Assumption 7: All government officials seek to achieve professional and policy goals.

To summarize: group members have interests that manifest in how they want to see an issue, like how many hours a trucker can drive, resolved with public policy. But group members vary in just what they think these policy solutions should be, just as they feel more intensely about some issues than others and will be less tolerant of anything that falls short of what they consider an ideal solution. Policy makers also have interests that manifest as ideal solutions to issues, solutions that help them achieve their goals. But there is no reason to believe that members and policy makers all prefer exactly the *same* policy solutions, or anything even close. Lobbyists may also have personal opinions on how issues should be solved, but that is irrelevant. Never forget about Assumption 1: a lobbyist's job is to make sure policymaker and group member interests align, or at least appear aligned, or his or her career may be in jeopardy.

The Alignment of Interests

Finding a Champion

The issues that members of Congress are concerned with, and how they should be resolved, are largely determined by the policy positions that please their "reelection constituency," meaning the voters who voted for them in the past and hopefully will do so again (Fenno 1978). Lobbyists need legislators to influence policy in Congress, so lobbyists must persuade legislators that what group members want is more or less consistent with what their reelection constituencies want. Persuasion is easy if the lobbyist's members and a legislator's key constituents are one and the same, and they sometimes are. A legislator has every reason to help the part of his or her constituency that is in the interest group. But if they are not the same, then the lobbyist must convince the legislator that helping members will still help him or her be reelected or elected to higher office. This becomes harder for the lobbyist the further apart member and legislator policy preferences are (Ainsworth and Sened 1993). The legislator must be convinced that he or she has something to gain by helping people who are not his or her constituents. The group members may contribute money to the legislator's next campaign, or perhaps the group has members in many states other than the legislator's home state, which would be very useful if the legislator is running for president. Whatever it is, the lobbyist's group must be able to help the legislator achieve some personal or professional goal.

Look at Figure 5.2. The bottom part is the same graph of ATA member preferences for driving hours from Figure 5.1a, but the top part is different. The vertical black line in the top half shows that the legislator prefers a less restrictive policy when it comes to determining hours a trucker can drive. Perhaps the legislator is from a state where trucking is a major employer and he or she wants more industry support in the next election. Although the legislator is somewhat flexible about the ideal policy (is eight hours that different from seven and a half?), there are limits, shown by the tentlike dashed lines and gray areas in the top graph. He or she will not support a driving hours policy in the gray "vote no" zone. The white area around the legislator's preferred policy, however, represents the other proposals he or she could be persuaded by the ATA to support in exchange for votes in the next election. Take the proposal represented by the dashed vertical line. It is not ideally supported by most ATA members, nor is it the legislator's ideal solution, but it is

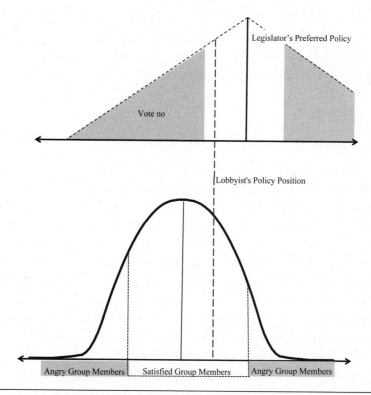

Legislator's Preferred Policy

Vote no

Lobbyist's Policy Position

Angry Group Members | Satisfied Group Members | Angry Group Members

FIGURE 5.2   Alignment of ATA Group Members and a Legislator on Hours of Driving

close enough to the solid vertical lines for the legislator to support it and still expect to have the votes of a plurality, perhaps even a majority, of truckers.

So the ATA lobbyist can advocate for a compromise everyone can live with. The dashed line connecting group members to the legislator in Figure 5.2 represents this policy compromise on the driving hours issue. It is still deep in the main bubble of group member preferences and also not in the legislator's "vote no" zone. The legislator can comfortably support this policy, and many—perhaps most—group members will also support it. Almost everyone more or less gets what they want. The legislator will push for the policy in Congress, which means the lobbyist's goal has been achieved, and his or her career remains in good shape.

But what if the policy that is acceptable to the legislator is *not* one that most ATA members would ordinarily support? Then, as suggested in the last chapter, the clever lobbyist might use ATA's communication systems to convince members that this policy does in fact serve the interests of trucking companies even better than they themselves had realized, in the hopes of changing the position of many, if not most, members. Legislators are harder to manipulate than a group's members, so usually the lobbyist will not try that tactic.

A Policy Most Everyone Can Support

There is one more assumption that needs to be laid out in response to a simple question: What about the rest of Congress? One legislator may be all a lobbyist needs to get a policy proposal introduced in Congress, whether as a new bill or an amendment to an existing bill, but it does not get the job done. No one is an island when it comes to making policy, whether it is a new statute, a new judicial precedent, or a new administrative rule. Both houses of Congress need majorities to move policies out of committee and through the parent chamber, with sixty plus votes often needed in the Senate to overcome a filibuster. Presidential executive orders and agency rules can be overridden by legislative statute or sometimes influenced by Congress (McCubbins and Schwartz 1984; Balla 1998); federal judicial decisions may be overturned by statute; and statutes, rules, executive orders, and lower court decisions can all be struck down by the Supreme Court as unconstitutional. It is a lawmaking *system* with many parts, and no lobbyist dares to forget it. So this brings us to the eighth assumption:

Assumption 8: Policy enactment requires the consent of many policy makers in several governing institutions.

This means moving beyond a simple alignment of group member interests with the interests of one lawmaker. To keep this simple I focus here on just the US House of Representatives. The House operates under straight majority rule, meaning a majority of representatives must be willing to vote for whatever policy is preferred by ATA members and the legislator in Figure 5.2. Since the lobbyist and legislator want the new policy enacted, they must choose another position on the number of driving hours, one that they think can pass the House. Yet the lobbyist, and to some extent the reelection-minded legislator, must still keep an eye on what group members will accept, making the balancing act even more precarious.

Figure 5.3 features the graph showing the legislator from Figure 5.2 in the middle. This legislator is now ATA's champion legislator because he or she believes that it is advantageous to help truckers and the ATA in the House.

Their interests are more or less aligned. In the bottom graph of Figure 5.3, I reformulate the distribution of ATA member preferences over the driving hours continuum so that the tentlike shape is a combination of all members' ideal positions and intensity of their feelings. If members were more united in their preferences for policy outcomes, and/or felt more strongly about this issue, then more members would leave the group the further the lobbyist's official position was from the solid vertical line—and the dashed tented lines would have steeper slopes. At the top of Figure 5.3 is a similar graph for the members of the House. Some care about trucking policy, while others couldn't care less, but the white space under the peak indicates the policy positions that would garner a majority of votes in the House. The vertical solid black line marks the position that would attract the most votes.

The lobbyist and the champion legislator know where the House collectively stands on the driving hours issue and what positions can win a majority. The policy acceptable to the most legislators and group members is marked by the dashed line running through all three parts of Figure 5.3. It is not what the champion legislator would ideally prefer, and it is not likely to gain anything more than a bare majority of votes in the House. It can just barely be sold by the lobbyist to enough ATA members to keep the group viable because it is fairly restrictive in the number of allowable driving hours. But for most group members and legislators it is better than nothing, and nothing would have been the result if the lobbyist had pushed a position that more ATA members would support, or one more ideally suited to the champion legislator's goals. That was impossible, so the lobbyist skillfully balances all of the competing pressures he or she is under, satisfying the demands of all eight assumptions, to produce a policy that at least passes the House and pleases more trucking companies than it angers. Lobbying is not only the art of persuasion; it is the science of the possible, though there is an art to making the possible look desirable.

Insights from the Model

There are several points to take away from this model. First, it provides insight into the real job of lobbyists. Lobbyists are sellers: people whose job it is to convince others, such as their members and the lawmakers controlling the levers of power, that achieving a policy outcome is in their interests. Second, it shows that lobbying is about compromise. Lobbyists must convince all parties involved to accept an outcome that is less than ideal because their

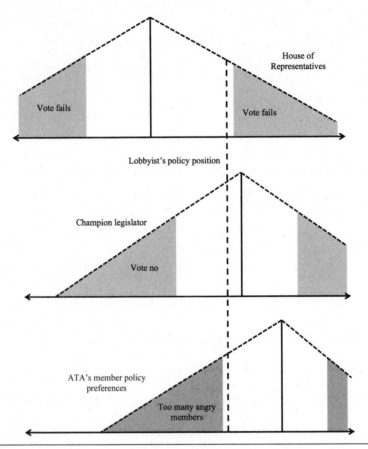

FIGURE 5.3   Balancing Interests in the Political System on Hours of Truck Driving

individual preferences are impossible to achieve given the current disposition of everyone else in the political system. Lobbyists have difficult jobs trying to balance these competing interests, finding the one position that enough people—group members, champion legislators, and other legislators—can all agree to and arriving at the best policy they can get. The lobbyist only needs to avoid picking a position that alienates too many of his or her members (the shaded region of the lower part of Figure 5.3). Lobbyists may, however, use their control of information to convince members that the policy compromise getting enacted into law is actually better than what members originally wanted. And this simple model fails to include senators, the president, the bureaucracy, other interest groups, and possibly the courts. It is not easy being a successful lobbyist!

Lastly, the ATA lobbyist also targeted a legislator who more or less already agreed with the position many ATA members wanted. This is important to understand. A well-known study in 1963 about lobbying on American trade policy revealed for the first time something that cuts against popular perceptions of lobbyists: lobbyists tend to lobby their allies, those lawmakers already supporting them, not their enemies (Bauer, Pool, and Dexter 1963). This model shows why. To get their jobs done, lobbyists must lobby their friends, legislators whose positions are relatively close to those of many group members. I will talk a lot more about this in the next chapter.

The Strategic Lobbyist

This abstract model is a useful foundation for understanding the basic steps of a lobbying campaign, which I will expand on in the second half of this book. Keep in mind, though, that there never really is a beginning or an end to lobbying on most issues.

Issue Selection

How do lobbyists decide which issues they should go lobby? First and foremost, if policy makers are looking at the membership's bread-and-butter issues, then the lobbyist had better go lobby those. Assumption 3 recognizes variation in how members feel about issues, but most members probably feel strongly about the core issues around which their group is organized. For example, all trucking companies worry about fuel costs. Members may not be aware of all the issues potentially affecting them that are being debated in Washington, but they will probably know if their most crucial issue is on the agenda. And members will be angry, and may even leave the group, if their lobbyist does not appear to be working hard on it. Overall, there are three parts to the decision on whether to lobby an issue: issue importance, membership cohesion, and probability of success.

This last relates to Assumption 5, the restriction on resources. Because resources are finite, lobbyists often must concentrate on what is doable, what issues can be lobbied with some hope of success, so that the members think these limited resources are being used well. Probability of success does not always matter, though. If lobbyists cannot or will not defend the group's turf by lobbying the membership's most basic issues, they lose members and make it hard to attract replacements. The fewer members in the group, the more it invites further encroachment from other groups hoping to steal away its remaining members. The interest group also loses its relevancy and legitimacy to policy makers as it shrinks. After all, fewer members means a legislator, or any political elite, has less to personally gain by championing the group's causes. But lobbyists need the assistance of, and relationships with, legislators and other political elites. To maintain their reputations and careers, lobbyists must use what resources they have to work on bread-and-butter issues regardless of whether they can win.

However, there is something to be gained by lobbying issues that are less important to members but can be easily won. A lobbyist cannot go for too long without showing some kind of activity and success before members wonder if the interest group and its lobbyist are really needed at all. A crisis does not have to be manufactured just to keep members interested (though that sometimes happens), but when there are no bread-and-butter issues on the government's agenda, it might be time to find little issues to blow out of proportion (remember that lobbyists control the flow of information to members). A good choice for an issue to pursue is one where member interests are already aligned with the interests of a champion lawmaker, and more or less aligned with the rest of the political system, so that victory will be easy and cheap. This way, the lobbyist gets something done for the group's members, small as it may be. The lobbyist could also take on an easy issue not overly relevant to their current members because that can be used by the group's marketing department to attract new members with slightly different interests. All of this keeps the lobbyist's career firmly on track.

Position Taking

Once the lobbyist has decided to lobby an issue, he or she must strategically decide what position to actually support, a choice known as **position taking**. I already showed how the ATA lobbyist strategically picked a position on driving hours he or she believed would pass in Congress, but there is another point to mention. Assumption 2 says that not all members want the same policy outcomes, and Assumption 3 says not all members feel strongly about the issue, so a strategic lobbyist would lean toward supporting the position desired by the members who are most likely to leave the group in anger if their position is not advocated, or the members that contribute most of the group's finite resources. The ATA example showed that the position chosen by lobbyists also depends on what champion lawmakers believe is in their best interests, along with what position the champion lawmakers and lobbyists believe can be supported by everyone else in the interconnected political system.

Whether the lobbyist can find a winning position affects issue selection. Why waste valuable resources and career credibility lobbying an issue when there is no position everyone else will support? If the issue at hand is one of great importance to members, but there is no winning position because everyone's interests cannot be aligned, the lobbyist must fight anyway and suffer defeat just to keep members happy and preserve the interest group's (and his or her own) integrity. Otherwise a careful lobbyist looks for issues vaguely important to members where it is possible to align interests around a position and lobbies for that. Supporting the winning position impresses members and lawmakers and thus helps the lobbyist's career.

Framing

Framing is all about persuasion. Once lobbyists know which issues they will be working on, they have to soften up the political system by convincing everyone involved that their chosen policy position is just common sense and should be made law. Lobbyists also block other positions from being considered by portraying them as radical and dangerous. As I mentioned earlier in the chapter, lobbyists are salespersons. They may be selling a little snake oil by overselling the benefits of their position, but if the selling is done well, it is possible for them to convince wary group members that a proposal capable of being passed by Congress is in their best interests. If the selling is done well, the lobbyist will persuade a would-be champion legislator that advocating this position on the group's behalf also furthers their interests. Then together legislator and lobbyist sell the benefits of this sensible position to everyone else in Congress and throughout the government. In other words, framing is how lobbyists align the interests of all of the members and lawmakers they must deal with.

Political scientists Frank Baumgartner and Bryan Jones (1993) found in a study of framing that it is easier for lobbyists to sell their positions when they can connect them to broader ideological beliefs most Americans share. If a policy proposal can be grounded in deeply held beliefs and myths, then it will be accepted as true, and nobody dares oppose it. If the American farmer is portrayed as the backbone of the country's economy and a symbol of its traditional values, who would oppose government subsidies and guaranteed crop prices? And what belief is more ingrained in Americans than the importance of owning a home? Real estate and mortgage banking groups love this. They can portray anybody challenging policies that support their industries as threats to the American Dream. Lobbyists for interest groups disadvantaged by policies that seemingly bolster such beliefs have a really difficult task. They must find a way to radically reframe the policy by disconnecting it from those myths.

Dramatic reframing, however, only happens when the cycle of a political system emphasizing individual rights shifts to one that emphasizes collective morality (or vice versa), which I discussed in Chapter 3. Labor unions and consumer groups in the 1930s and 1960s managed to crack the belief that what was good for business was good for America by reframing the debate, emphasizing the collective harm that unchecked business practices were wreaking on Americans. They never would have gotten workplace safety and truthful advertising laws passed otherwise. But their window of opportunity closed by the late 1970s, and their influence in Washington diminished. Belief in the value of individual entrepreneurship and faith in relatively unrestrained capitalism were too deeply ingrained to be displaced for long.

Framing ties into both issue selection and position selection. How an issue can be framed often determines whether the lobbyist decides to pursue it in the first place. Even if a competing group forces a threatening issue onto the government's agenda, a clever lobbyist can reframe it so that the political debate will lead to an outcome quite different from the one the competitor wants. Or the clever lobbyist can make it sound bizarre that the issue has come up at all and that working on it is a waste of taxpayer dollars. For years, the Motion Picture Association of America (MPAA) and other entertainment groups have been pushing legislation to make it illegal to download copyrighted movies and music from the Internet without paying for them—a policy that its lobbyists argue is in everyone's collective interests because illegal downloads will eventually destroy the film and music industries. In 2011, these groups and their champion legislators introduced the Stop Online Piracy Act (SOPA) as part of this effort. Opponents of SOPA hit back with even better framing: any regulation of the Internet is unnecessary government regulation of individual rights, it violates the First Amendment, and the legislators who supported SOPA would be targeted by thousands of angry downloaders in the next election (Martinez 2012). The opponents won, and SOPA was not enacted into law.

In sum, good framing makes it easier for policy makers and group members to believe that an issue is important to them and that the lobbyist's proposed policy solution advances their mutual interests. Good framing helps lobbyists balance the conflicting pressures from group members and lawmaker allies in assumptions 2, 3, and 7, with an eye toward saving resources by avoiding major battles, all (as always) in the service of being successful in their careers by keeping both group members happy and maintaining relationships with legislators and other political elites.

Choosing Tactics

Once a policy position has been selected, framed, packaged, and sold to members and policy makers, it is time to go about getting it made law. Again, this step feeds back on to earlier steps in the chain. Choice of advocacy tactics depends on how good of a job the lobbyist has done aligning everyone's interests. If successful, lobbying can be done quickly and quietly in personal meetings with champion lawmakers. This is usually called **insider lobbying**. When that is not possible, perhaps because the other side has done a better job framing the issue, then Assumption 5 (lobbyists have limited resources) becomes important. If expensive tactics will be needed to achieve policy goals, the lobbyist must think long and hard about not lobbying at all, which in turn depends on how crucial the issue is to group members.

All things being equal, most lobbyists prefer to do things quietly. Why attract needless attention that will just jeopardize control of a situation? Victory is easier and less expensive, and the achieved goal more in line with what members want, when only need-to-know government officials are involved. Other interests either are unaware of what is going on or do not perceive these actions to be encroaching on their interests, or both. In Figure 5.4 I lay out four different scenarios for a lobbyist's likely response to two sets of circumstances. The first is how important an issue is to group members and how unified they are in how they would like to see it resolved with policy. The second is how much resistance there may be from potential champion legislators in the political system because they have not yet been persuaded that the group's interest is their own.

When the interests of group members and their champion legislators can be aligned, either because they actually are aligned or because good framing has made it seem as if they are aligned, then members are relatively united and there is no resistance from the lawmaker (see the lower left quadrant in Figure 5.4). In this scenario, the lobbyist can operate quietly with the help of his or her champion in government by having meetings in smoky back rooms (actually, the Capitol building is smoke-free) far from the media spotlight

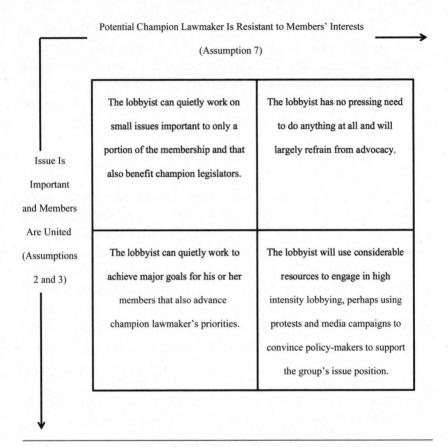

FIGURE 5.4   Choice of Advocacy Tactics in Response to Pressures

and even from the attention of most other policy makers. If members are not united and do not feel intensely about the issue, but it is easy to get support from lawmakers (the top left quadrant in Figure 5.4), then the lobbyist can quietly do some work for smaller subsections of his or her membership, such as a few big contributors. Or the lobbyist could pursue other policies that might bring some new members into the interest group. If no issue important to members is currently being considered in government, and lawmakers are not interested in helping the lobbyist work on the group's issues (the top right quadrant), then the lobbyist might as well take a vacation.

But when issues must be lobbied because they are crucial to the membership, but no policy maker has been persuaded that it is in his or her interest to be the group's champion (see the lower right quadrant in Figure 5.4), then the lobbyist must gather together all of the resources he or she can amass and wage a high-profile, often media-intensive advocacy campaign. This is called **outside lobbying**. If done right, this will put intense public pressure on policy makers to accept a reframing of the issue and realize that supporting the group means supporting themselves (Kollman 1998). It may mean commissioning a large number of studies showing logical, scientific support for a position, or a mass write-in campaign of members and sympathizers, or a large rally and march on a legislator's district office, or all of the above.

It is not always easy to get members focused on and fired up about an issue, so outside grassroots lobbying is sometimes very hard to organize. In 2013, even as legislation giving undocumented immigrants opportunities to earn citizenship was coming to the Senate floor, opposing interest groups like the Center for Immigration Studies had trouble getting their members focused on the issue when other issues also important to conservatives, such as the IRS targeting Tea Party organizations, were in the news. Said the center's executive director, Mark Krikorian, "There are so many scandals going on with the Obama administration that it's distracting a lot of people. The outrage can only be focused in so many directions" (Bolton 2013). Being expensive and difficult, member-intensive outside lobbying is only likely to occur on issues especially important to group members, since the financial costs and the political risks—for the lobbyist and for the group—are much higher.

Conflict and Compromise

Another part of the art of lobbying is knowing when to compromise. Lobbyists work hard to convince government allies that supporting a position is in their interests, but often there are countervailing pressures pulling these would-be champions in other directions. Assumption 8 says that policy makers need the support of other officials within and outside of their own institution to enact policy. Presidents, legislative leaders, and executive branch department secretaries all have their own interests and goals and are surrounded by other lobbyists for interests concerned with the same issue who are trying to convince them that they have mutual interests (Heclo 1978). Lobbyists must carefully consider issues, positions, and framing, and what they can do to win support rather than create enemies in the political system or in their group, while using as few resources as possible. Not an easy job.

Public advocacy battles quickly become expensive, but when the stakes are high on issues crucial to the membership, spending is necessary. So the advantage lies with the lobbyists who can command the most resources. Indeed, what makes groups like the AARP, the NRA, and the Chamber of Commerce so truly formidable is not just how widely accepted their framing of issues already is, but how plentiful their resources are in terms of money and broad-based group member support. Of course these groups also spend money on keeping lawmakers and the public convinced that their issues are consistent with American beliefs. Some lobbyists may even compromise early in a polit-ical struggle with an exceptionally powerful group, hoping perhaps to share its resources and ride its coattails to gain some minor policy success of their own (Hojnacki 1997; Holyoke 2009). Ultimately compromises of some sort happen, but they tend to favor the stronger interest groups.

Knowing how and when to lay aside the fight and begin talking and bar-gaining with competitors is another one of those special skills good lobbyists are prized for having. Still, the more a lobbyist finds him or herself in the lower right quadrant in Figure 5.4, the more they must fight to show members that they are committed to the cause and will not compromise, lest angry members abandon the interest group. If, however, the issue at hand is not of great importance to members, or if a group's members are so disunified that a variety of positions will please quite a number of them, then compromises are possible. Lawmakers usually like compromises because they do not have to choose winners and losers, which, in turn, keeps the relationship between the lobbyist and the lawmaker strong and the lobbyist's career on track. Never forget assumption 1.

In Summary

Here is a summary of this chapter's main points:

- Lobbyists are first and foremost interested in advancing their careers, which means balancing the needs of the members they represent against those of the lawmakers they depend on for access to govern-ment institutions.
- Lobbying is the business of finding and promoting positions that are ac-ceptable to most interest group members as well as the lawmakers lob-byists hope will champion their positions in the policy-making process.
- To convince group members and would-be champion lawmakers that the position chosen advances all of their interests, the lobbyist must choose issues carefully and pick positions that can win majorities in Congress and acceptance from other government institutions; this is

best done by framing the issue and position as consistent with broader American values and beliefs.

- Lobbyists prefer to conserve resources by working quietly with their champion lawmakers, but if members believe an issue is important, and there is no obvious champion, lobbyists must then mount high-profile and expensive grassroots advocacy campaigns to convince lawmakers that the group's position is worth supporting.

The social scientist cannot account for every possible factor potentially influencing human behavior, even of fairly rational people like lobbyists. It would be wrong to try. Instead, I tried to break down decision making into its most pertinent components, using as few variables as possible so that the results are useful for analyzing interest groups and lobbying. I claimed that a lobbyist's decision regarding what issue to take up, how to frame it, what position to take on it, when to fight, and when to compromise is largely explainable by the interaction of eight assumptions. I hope this model provides useful insight into lobbying, as we move into the second half of the book to see how lobbying is done in the three branches of government as well as the electoral arena.

Notes

1. American Trucking Associations is plural, referring to the fifty state associations that comprise ATA.

PART TWO

Lobbying
and Influence

CHAPTER SIX

Lobbying Congress, the Most Permeable Branch

In 1790, Senator William Maclay heard from Senator Pierce Butler that the vote of Rep. John Vining of Vermont might be bought for 1,000 guineas, but Butler suspected that the lobbyist most likely to approach the ethically challenged politician would probably haggle him down to a substantially smaller sum (Jacob 2010, 13). In 1833, Senator Daniel Webster wrote to Nicholas Biddle of the Bank of the United States that he (Webster) just might have to start listening to lobbyists opposed to that reviled institution's existence if his retainer from the Bank was not immediately "refreshed" (13). Fast forward to 2006, when Rep. Bob Ney (R-OH) was sentenced to prison for taking bribes from similarly prison-bound lobbyist Jack Abramoff.[1] Bribery by lobbyists appears to be a constant hazard for members of Congress. Fortunately this is not the norm. In fact, lobbyists do not need to bribe members of Congress in order to be influential.

Congress's responsibility for initiating the lawmaking process makes it an attractive target for interest groups and lobbyists, and its design and operations make gaining access to it relatively easy. John Heinz and his fellow researchers found that of all the lobbyists they interviewed, nearly a quarter had regular contact with *just* members of Congress, and another 57 percent had regular contact with members of Congress along with the executive branch (Heinz et al. 1993, 96). Congressional committees are especially attractive to lobbyists. Heinz and colleagues found that 31 percent of lobbyists have regular contact with committee legislators, far more than with party leaders, the White House, or executive branch officials (195). Since Congress requires the lobbyists walking its halls to register, it is easy to see just how attractive a target Congress is today. In the first quarter of 2011 there were about 12,600 people signed up to lobby, collectively spending $3.27 billion to do so.[2] But how is it done?

A Multiplicity of Pressure Points

There is no mystery regarding the legislative branch's popularity with lobbyists. Congress is where lawmaking formally begins, though most efforts at legislating, both noble and nefarious, tend to go nowhere. Interest group lobbyists know how to get bills moving and how to avoid the pitfalls that kill so many bills. They also know how to create those pitfalls. After all, many lobbyists began their careers on Capitol Hill and know where the right pressure points are to either initiate or kill any legislation that affects their group members' or clients' interests. And there are *many* pressure points in the legislative branch, which is another reason lobbyists are so attracted to it. At the very least there are 535 members of Congress, all of whom have the power to introduce legislation, offer amendments, raise new ideas in committee, or be the make-or-break vote on a bill.

Furthermore, as I show in Figure 6.1, each chamber, the **House of Representatives** and the **Senate**, divides into **committees** and **subcommittees**. Subcommittees are where new laws typically start. Every one of these subcommittees has fairly exclusive jurisdiction over some area of public policy, what political scientists call **policy domains**. The House Subcommittee on Water and Power (part of the Natural Resources Committee) has jurisdiction over all bills for building new dams and canals. The Senate Subcommittee on Strategic Forces (part of the Armed Services Committee) develops all legislation on national intelligence programs. Legislators serving on these subcommittees become experts on the policies within these domains. Rules and norms of operation usually insure that the legislative product of a subcommittee is not tampered with by other lawmakers, though this respect for expertise and autonomy has declined since 1995, as the needs of political parties have taken precedence.

Legislative decentralization favors interest groups and arguably helped stimulate their growth in the twentieth century. In 1911, members of the House became so frustrated under the heavy hand of Speaker Joseph Cannon (R-IL) that they rebelled and stripped the Speaker's office of much of its power. From that point forward control over policy shifted over to the committee chairs, formalized with the Legislative Reorganization Act of 1946

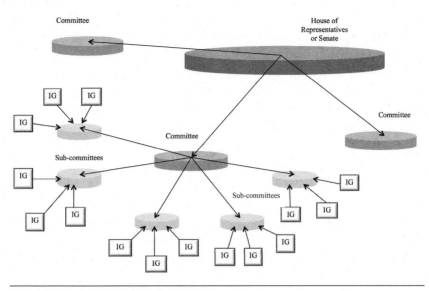

FIGURE 6.1   Lobbying a Decentralized Congress
IG = interest group

(Davidson 1990). Chairs now had tighter control of their agendas, jurisdiction over all bills addressing their committees' subject matter, and professional staff to conduct research and draft new legislation. In the House, norms of property rights and reciprocity further strengthened committee independence (Deering and Smith 1997, Ch. 3). **Property rights** allow legislators interested in a committee's policy jurisdiction to gain a seat on it and hold it in perpetuity (Jewell and Chi-Hung 1974; Benson 1981). **Reciprocity**, often just called *logrolling*, is the trading of votes between legislators, which helps ensure that bills approved by committees won't be changed by amendment on the floor of the House by members of other committees—lest the "favor" be returned. The emergence of similarly independent subcommittees in the early 1970s, with jurisdictions over increasingly narrow policy domains, further decentralized Congress (Davidson, Oleszek, and Kephart 1988). These changes served lawmakers' needs so well that even efforts at recentralization beginning in 1995, when Republicans took the majority, have only been marginally successful (Deering and Smith 1997, Ch. 2).

The changes of the early 1900s had another important consequence. The revolt against Speaker Cannon occurred in the Progressive Era, a time of good-government reaction against the corruption of the Gilded Age. Reformers sought greater government accountability to its citizens, to free legislators from their dependence on party bosses so they could better serve constituents during a time of great national change. Ending patronage appointments of party workers to office, pushing open party election primaries, limiting corporate contributions, and requiring the direct popular election of senators—all goals of the Progressives—resulted in rank-and-file legislators being more responsible for their own political survival instead of relying on their parties. This gave legislators an incentive to forge alliances with interest groups to help them secure their immediate goal of reelection and build their career-long policy-making "enterprises," which, in turn, made it easier for lobbyists to gain access to Congress (Mayhew 1974; Dodd 1977).

Decentralization and legislator independence benefits lobbyists for three specific reasons. First, most lobbyists only want to influence policy on a small number of issues important to the interests of their members and clients; they don't want to worry about every bill in Congress. Rather than try to lobby a powerful House or Senate leader who must balance hundreds of competing claims and has little time to give to any single interest group, most lobbyists focus just on the legislators on committees and subcommittees with jurisdiction over their issues. Second, because subcommittees usually only have about a dozen members, lobbyists concerned with policies within a subcommittee's jurisdiction can focus intensely on a manageable number of legislators. Thus decentralization makes lobbying efficient and effective.

Third, legislators on these subcommittees often *want* to help a lobbyist's members because the constituencies that legislators must keep happy in order to be reelected and the lobbyist's members are likely to overlap. This factor and an interest in the same policy domains mean lobbyists can build relationships with these few legislators by making themselves useful, even essential, parts of legislators' enterprises. Lobbyists use their substantial resources to provide ideas, draft legislation, give strategic and tactical advice, coordinate efforts to move bills, assist with constituency work, and, of course, provide election aid. Thus lobbyists often succeed in Congress by working quietly and, to most outward appearances, quite benignly.

The Constituency Connection

The Strength of Organized Constituencies

The idea that legislators give lobbyists access because it helps the former serve their **constituents** (or some of them anyway) may be a little difficult to accept, given the popular view of lobbyists working for some sinister "them" who want to exploit the rest of "us." Consider, though, the results of a 2005 survey by the Congressional Management Foundation of legislative offices on the types of contacts that influence a legislator's decisions. The foundation found that 99 percent of legislative offices surveyed rated constituent visits as having "some" or "a lot" of influence, with personalized letters and e-mails from constituents rating 96 percent and 94 percent, respectively (Fitch 2010a). More importantly, 96 percent of offices said that visits from a person representing constituents, namely their lobbyist, were influential. Lobbyists for interests not connected to a constituency, as well as the generic e-mails and e-postcards interest groups often send, were far less influential (Fitch 2010b).

The main point emphasized in the first half of this book is that most lobbyists represent organized groups of Americans who want (or do not want) something from their government. Legislators are elected by individuals who care enough about politics and policy to bother voting, so it is those individuals' wants and desires elected officials must be conscious of if they want to remain in office. The key here is that people who feel strongly enough about an issue to organize an interest group (with purposive-driven members) are also likely to be the same active voters their Senate and House representatives want to keep happy (Wright 1996).

Figure 6.2 helps make this concept clearer. Each bar represents all of the voting constituents of eleven legislators. The dark gray portions represent the percentage of constituents whose dominant interests are in housing and home ownership, the light gray represents the percentage whose interests are in farming and agribusiness, and the white represents those whose interests lie elsewhere. Urban lawmakers are likely elected predominantly by people in the housing industry; many of their key constituents are engaged in realty, home mortgage financing, home building, and housing development. In order to have influence over housing policy and consequently boost their reelection prospects, these legislators will seek seats on the House Committee on Financial Service's Subcommittee on Insurance, Housing, and Community Opportunity. For help in developing policies favoring a booming housing industry, legislators on this subcommittee turn to interest groups such as the National Association of Realtors (NAR), the Mortgage Bankers Association (MBA), and the National Association of Home Builders (NAHB). Lobbyists for these groups want to help members of the Insurance, Housing, and Community Opportunity subcommittee and will make themselves available to these legislators, providing information on how to serve the demands of their mutual constituents so that everyone can benefit. It is no different for rural, agriculture-oriented legislators who seek seats on the House Agriculture or Natural Resources committees and turn primarily to the American Farm Bureau Federation (AFBF), or commodities groups such as the American Corn Growers Association and the Produce Marketing Association, for information, strategy, and electoral aid in exchange for policy influence.

So when House members from Detroit, Atlanta, or Phoenix go to social events sponsored by home builder lobbyists, or closet themselves with lobbyists for mortgage bankers, it is not so much corruption as it is constituent service. For decades tobacco company lobbyists were portrayed as the very devil of American politics, buying votes in Congress to defend a dangerous product. But members of Congress supporting "Big Tobacco" tended to be from tobacco-growing congressional districts. Because tobacco lobbyists were good at helping their legislator allies stay in office until they gained enough seniority to block antismoking legislation, antitobacco interest groups had a long and difficult time gaining support for their policies. Tobacco lobbyists simply helped these lawmakers defend the interests of some of their mutual constituents, including the thousands who grew and processed tobacco.

A few interests have a strong presence in nearly every district and state because they have members widely dispersed around the country. The AARP is perhaps the most blessed in this way, as the expensive but thoroughly bipartisan-driven expansion of Medicare coverage for prescription drugs in 2003 proved.[3] Business and professional groups such as the US Chamber of Commerce, the National Federation of Independent Business, legal and medical groups, and even the National Audubon Society have similarly widespread membership. Consumer and other memberless public interest groups may claim they represent most Americans, but unless these people are dues-paying and card-carrying members, they rarely count when it comes to real assessments of interest group strength across congressional districts.

Is this fair to all constituents, including those who voted for the loser in the last election, or did not vote at all, or cannot create a group wealthy enough to employ a lobbyist? Absolutely not. From the standpoint of representational government, if elected officials are only paying attention to constituencies mobilized as interest groups, then who is looking out for the unmobilized or less critical constituencies the legislator is also supposed to be serving? Unless a public interest group lobbies on behalf of these citizens without requiring them to be members, which is true of interest groups like the National Community Reinvestment Coalition, which represents homeless people, then the answer is nobody. They are the casualties of interest group politics.

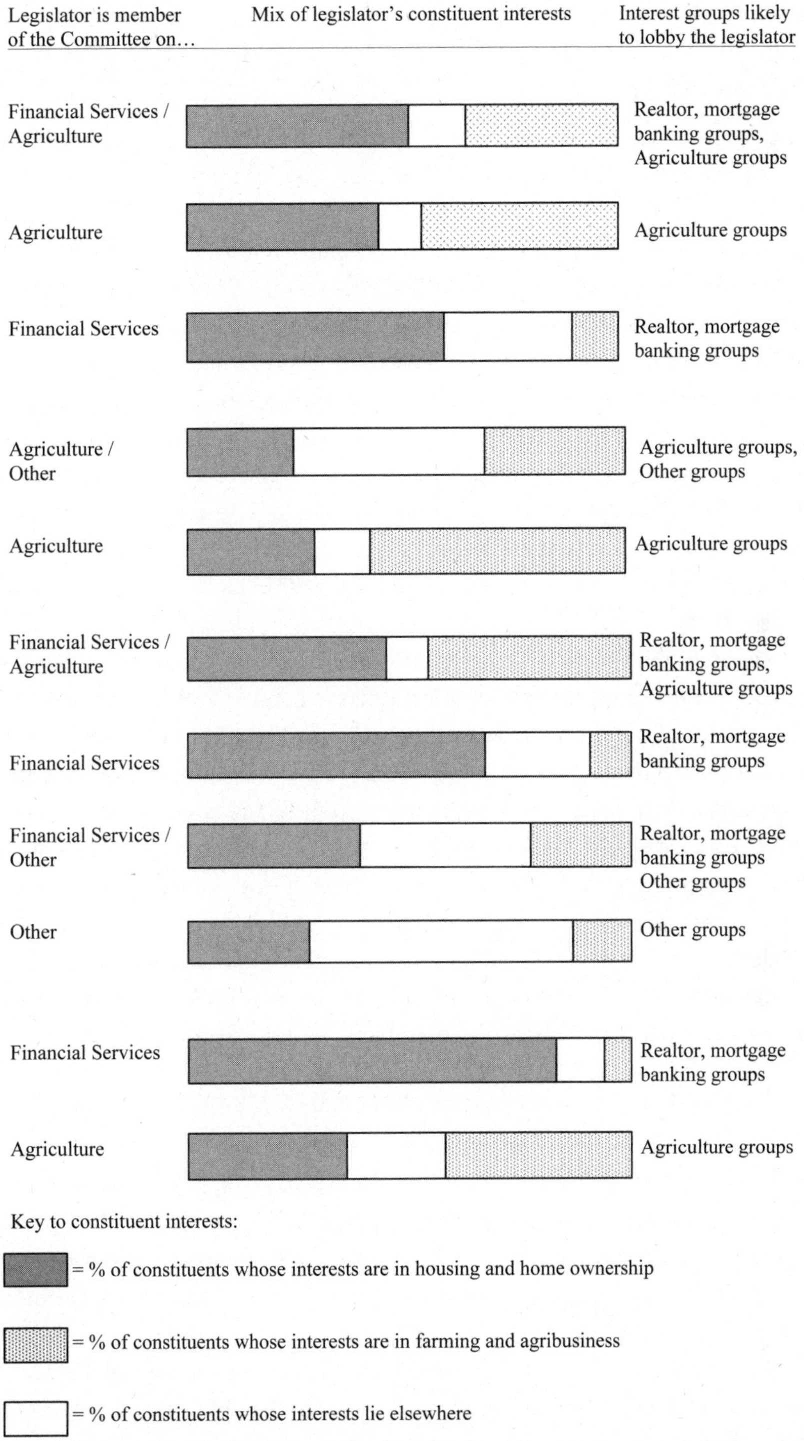

Legislator is member of the Committee on...	Mix of legislator's constituent interests	Interest groups likely to lobby the legislator
Financial Services / Agriculture		Realtor, mortgage banking groups, Agriculture groups
Agriculture		Agriculture groups
Financial Services		Realtor, mortgage banking groups
Agriculture / Other		Agriculture groups, Other groups
Agriculture		Agriculture groups
Financial Services / Agriculture		Realtor, mortgage banking groups, Agriculture groups
Financial Services		Realtor, mortgage banking groups
Financial Services / Other		Realtor, mortgage banking groups Other groups
Other		Other groups
Financial Services		Realtor, mortgage banking groups
Agriculture		Agriculture groups

Key to constituent interests:

= % of constituents whose interests are in housing and home ownership

= % of constituents whose interests are in farming and agribusiness

= % of constituents whose interests lie elsewhere

FIGURE 6.2   Legislators, Committee Preferences, and Constituent-Based Interest Group Allies

Information for Access

Legislators usually know who the electorally important constituents are and which interest groups represent them, but they still need help. They need to know just what these constituents and their interest groups want (e.g., job-stimulating subsidies or consumer-friendly regulation) or do not want (e.g., wasteful spending and job-killing regulation), and they need help formulating the best strategy for providing these politically active citizens with whatever it is they want (Ainsworth and Sened 1993). Just as citizen petitions in Great Britain and colonial America helped legislators know what constituents' concerns were and what might be done to solve them, the modern lobbyist as professional petitioner brings citizen concerns and ideas for remedies to elected members of Congress (Lawson and Seidman 1999). Bottom line: to learn which interest groups have real influence with a member of Congress, just look to see which groups of constituents are prominent in his or her district.

The help members of Congress need from lobbyists may vary depending on the legislator's own level of experience, connections, and **seniority** in Congress, and sometimes it is the legislator who ends up developing strategy for an inexperienced lobbyist who represents a common, crucial constituency. Once the policies and benefits their common constituents demand are achieved, a legislator expects the lobbyist to make it clear to the group's members just how hard the lawmaker worked, how essential the lawmaker was to the victory, and why he or she should be supported in the next election (Hansen 1991). In fact, as a rule lobbyists usually give legislators *all* of the credit. The voter guides many groups publish and the electoral endorsements they give are designed to show group members just how wonderful their elected official is (or not) (Fowler 1982).

Long-Term Investments

If lobbyists' information and services on behalf of key constituencies proves truthful and useful, legislators will ask for their help again and again, making the lobbyists trusted advisors and giving lobbyists what they need most: ongoing quality access to the lawmaking process (Milbrath 1963, 209–210; Wright 1996). This is not, strictly speaking, quid pro quo, in which both the legislator and lobbyist would be giving up something to get something else. While the lobbyist becomes an extension of the legislator's "enterprise"

(Ainsworth 1997), it is just as much the lobbyist's enterprise as it is the legislator's! As long as both parties benefit, they build and maintain a mutually advantageous relationship based on supporting the same people. The favored lobbyist advances the political interests of his or her group members but also advances his or her personal career by adding a legislator to his or her portfolio of relationships and becoming known as influential in the network of players in a particular policy domain. It is little wonder, then, that political scientists find lots of evidence of lobbyists lobbying legislators from districts where their interest groups are strong (Hojnacki and Kimball 1999, 1018). Lobbyists are lobbying their natural allies, their "friends."

For lobbyists, relationship building is an investment, often a very long-term investment. They see newly elected members of Congress as bundles of potential. Freshmen members of Congress have little idea how the institution, and the larger Washington community, works. They need help from lobbyists most in the early years of their careers. So it is really not surprising that many recently elected members of Congress arriving in Washington in early 2011 selected lobbyists to be their chiefs of staff (Smith and Eggen 2011), or that business lobbyists had to spend so much time and effort explaining to the new House Republicans why it would be economically and therefore politically disastrous to vote against raising the nation's debt ceiling in the fierce budget battles in the summer of 2011 (Rucker 2011). Nor is it surprising that in 2012 junior legislators on the House Financial Services Committee turned to Citibank lobbyists for help in drafting a bill reforming complex banking laws, letting the lobbyists write about seventy of the bill's eighty-five lines, even though it included an exemption Citibank wanted (Lipton and Protess 2013). Super-lobbyist Gerry Cassidy explained that this is just how he and his peers do business—building relationships by approaching junior members of Congress who badly need somebody's help to figure out how Washington works (Kaiser 2009, 284). Years later they reap the rewards of their investments.

The relationships lobbyists work to build with freshmen are sometimes so long-term that a lobbyist who lays its foundation never sees its fruition. The senior lobbyist must groom a replacement who will benefit from these budding relationships, as long as the senior properly instills in the junior a sense of the relationship's importance as they make the rounds on Capitol Hill.[4] For today's freshman may be tomorrow's committee chair or majority leader. Of course it is also possible that today's freshman is tomorrow's political roadkill if they are not reelected, something the lobbyist has an increasingly vested interest in preventing as the years go by.

Lobbyists also need to be careful about the accuracy of the information they give to legislators. If legislators find themselves embarrassed because they said something untrue, or made some foolish decision, because a lobbyist misled them, they will almost certainly retaliate by severing their relationships with that lobbyist, and will probably tell their colleagues in Congress to similarly shun the lobbyist. Legislators' careers often depend on getting accurate information from lobbyists, so they expect lobbyists to tell them the truth, even if it is a little one-sided. If they are so inclined, legislators can always double-check a lobbyist's information with the Congressional Research Service, the Government Accountability Office, or other lobbyists, so there is always pressure to be accurate (Allard 2008). A lobbyist's single greatest tool in the building and maintaining of the relationships they depend on for influence is a reputation for honesty, so being caught lying destroys their career. Lobbyist Bryce Harlow of Procter & Gamble, as quoted by lobbyist Joel Jankowsky, said, "If one lies, misrepresents, or even lets a misapprehension stand uncorrected—or if someone cuts corners too slyly—he/she is dead and gone, never to be resurrected, or even mourned" (Jankowsky 2006).

Circles of Friends

Insider Lobbying: Reciprocity and the Little Things

Everything described so far in this chapter is about how and why lobbyists form close relationships with a few legislators and how these friends of mutual need give lobbyists access to the lawmaking process. Working through lawmaker allies inside the institution like this is called insider lobbying. Yet lobbyists usually want, and very often need, more friends than just those lawmakers elected by constituents who happen to also be the people the lobbyist represents. Close, long-term, constituency-based friendships on relevant subcommittees are essential, but other allies are often valuable as well. In fact, these other allies *become* essential if a lobbyist does not have any constituent-based relationships with lawmakers. And many do not, but that hardly stops them from successfully pursuing their advocacy work. Figure 6.3 provides a visual aid for thinking about this arrangement. The innermost circle contains legislators with whom a lobbyist has built the tight, constituency-based relationships described in the previous section. They are the lobbyist's go-to allies on most issues important to their members.

The middle circle is made up of more casual acquaintances, lawmakers, and their staff who know a lobbyist from meetings, fundraisers, and social

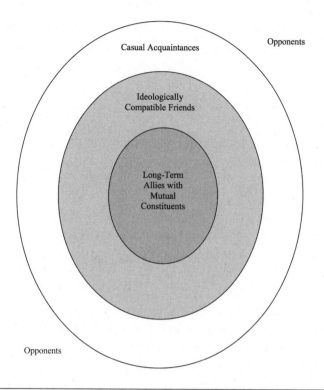

FIGURE 6.3   A Lobbyist's Circle of Friends in Congress

functions. Their connection is perhaps more an ideological one, or even just a shared interest in an issue like foreign affairs or national security. In this circle, legislator and lobbyist have shared beliefs, such as the value of tough environmental laws or the importance of strong pro-business policies, but because few of the lobbyist's members are constituents of the legislator, their connection is not as strong. A lawmaker representing a region where most employment is in the high-tech industry may be ideologically supportive of farmers and farm groups because he or she believes in hard work and entrepreneurialism, even though the legislator represents very few actual farmers. This legislator probably does not know much about farm issues, so when a farm bill comes up for a vote, he or she will be inclined to ask the farm lobbyist's advice just because they share the same basic worldview.

How do lobbyists make the connection to lawmakers if there is no natural constituent connection? How do they even get in the office door to start building relationships based on shared ideologies or common interests in the same issues? One way is to leverage even the smallest constituency tie. If there are a few farmers in a suburban lawmaker's district, a lobbyist may arrange to have them call the legislator's office a day or so before he or she comes to call, just to show that there is at least some small constituency connection. This softens up the legislator for the meeting.[5] Alternatively, a lobbyist who has already made a name for him- or herself as a powerbroker may be able to get meetings with lawmakers, especially young and impressionable lawmakers, just on the sheer basis of their reputation. This may also happen if the lobbyist works for a well-known, powerful interest group like the AARP, National Association of Manufacturers, National Rifle Association, or Sierra Club, though that would still require at least some common ideological bond.

If the lobbyist is not already well known, then it helps to be introduced by somebody who is—somebody the lawmaker already knows and trusts, such as another lobbyist or another lawmaker the target legislator trusts. Indeed, the ability to make introductions is one of the reasons ex-lawmakers and ex-legislative staff are hired by interest groups and lobbying firms. They can open doors and make connections between lobbyists and lawmakers. Very often these connections are made at Washington fundraisers.[6] Usually discussions at fundraisers are purely social, but it is still lobbying when telling a few jokes makes enough of an impression that the lawmaker and his or her staff will want to open the door to the lobbyist the next day during business hours.

Once the initial connection is made, lobbyists slowly build their influence and form relationships with lawmakers and their staff through what veteran lobbyist Thomas Susman calls the "reciprocity principle." Most of any lobbyist's influence, Susman argues, comes from doing lots of little things, providing lots of small services, for lawmakers and their staff (Susman 2006; 2008).[7] Once an introduction is made and an office door opened, the lobbyist might go to lunch with the staff (but not buy lunch these days), explain who they are, and talk a bit about issues in which they share a common interest. The lobbyist then offers him- or herself as a resource ready to be called upon for even the smallest bit of information or help. Perhaps the lobbyist will also offer to provide some research, write a speech or a press release, or help develop strategy and frame an argument for the lawmaker. He or she offers to help the lawmaker and staff make connections to other powerful people in Washington. Perhaps they might even help with some of the constituent work. Through it all, Susman explains, the lawmaker and staff, without quite even realizing it, become obligated—even indebted—to the lobbyist. Then, when the lobbyist genuinely needs the lawmaker's help, it would be the most natural thing in the world to give a few minutes of time, and even do something small, in return for the lobbyist who has apparently given so much so selflessly.

This reciprocal, favor-based relationship still cannot match one built on a constituency connection, and lobbyists are very careful about asking legislators to do something that is clearly contrary to their constituents' interests. In a head-to-head matchup, an elected official will almost always favor his or her constituents' interests over a lobbyist's requests, even if the lawmaker wants to help the lobbyist because they are personal friends. At least this is true for issues the legislator's constituents are likely to be aware of. Smart lobbyists only ask for help from sympathetic legislators on an issue without a constituent connection when the request is relatively small, such as support for a line-item appropriation or a small tax exemption favoring the lobbyist's members or clients. The lobbyist might tack on the smaller request after discussing another, bigger issue in which there is a constituency connection—a strategy a legislative aide I once interviewed calls the "Oh, while I have your attention" insider lobbying tactic. These little favors tend to be for something important to the people the lobbyist represents, something the legislator for personal or ideological reasons feels should be provided, and something the lawmaker's constituents are unlikely to ever find out about.[8]

There are also, from a lobbyist's point of view, even more legislators they could potentially have a peripheral relationship with (shown in the outer ring of Figure 6.3). This is the bulk of the House and Senate, lawmakers with whom the lobbyist just does not share any constituents or have enough of an ideological connection to form a bond. They are certainly not enemies (those are outside of the three rings in Figure 6.3); they are just indifferent to each other, at least until it comes time to vote on a bill the lobbyist wants passed or defeated. Even then, lacking a constituent connection, there is little the lobbyist can do except drop off or e-mail a report or position paper to the legislator's aide for that issue, usually a day or so ahead of the vote, and perhaps try to follow up with a phone call (Hojnacki and Kimball 1999, 1016). If a lobbyist does to decide to write a report, then, as the nonprofit research think tank the Independent Sector advises its members, they should make it short and to the point because, while everyone in Washington needs more information, nobody has much time for reading the information they get (Aviv et al. 2012, 7). Even then writing a report or position paper is probably not worth the time and effort. Congressional offices report getting about three to four feet of paper per week from various people, so the chance of one interest group's position paper getting read is truly remote (Fitch 2010a)!

Lobbyists are careful to remember which lawmaker is in which ring, often keeping databases on them that include information on where each legislator stands on an issue and whether there are important interest group members in that lawmaker's district who can talk to that House member or senator when a crucial vote comes up. This is an old practice. Peter Odegard (1928) describes the enormous card catalog system used by the Anti-Saloon League in the early twentieth century to track supporter, undecided, and opponent legislators. It contained information on sympathetic constituents in a congressional district who could be called on to help move a legislator from undecided to supporter. A similar system was used by the National Women's Party advocating for women's suffrage in the nineteenth century (Fitch 2010b).

Outside Lobbying

What happens to interest groups whose members are concerned with an issue, but do not have any allies on the committee with jurisdiction over it? Usually these are younger organizations that represent recently mobilized interests and consequently are not yet recognized as legitimate by members of the committee. Interest groups marginalized like this can do one or both of two things. One is to find another committee in Congress to lobby, though they would probably have an even tougher time getting recognized as legitimate in a committee that does not have jurisdiction over their issue. It would be better for them to try to find a way to be influential in the other branches of government, which I describe in chapters 7, 8, and 9. The second strategy is to try to find a way to gain legitimacy with, and the attention of, the committee that *does* have jurisdiction over their issue.

One well-honed path to gaining attention and legitimacy is to stage a large demonstration, called outside lobbying. The reason to bring tens of thousands of people with a common interest to wave signs, chant slogans, give speeches, and generally protest on the Washington Mall is to show elected officials that there is a prominent, geographically widespread, and politically active constituency being affected by a policy (or lack thereof), and lawmakers had better pay attention to this group if they want to avoid electoral retribution (Kollman 1998). Think of all the Million [Whatever] Marches. As I mentioned in Chapter 3, ambitious young politicians looking to secure their reelection prospects, and even build national constituencies for future elections, may be willing to embrace a highly energized but otherwise unrepresented constituency and be their champion. But it is usually hard to get members to come to Washington for a protest because they often have to pay their own way, so only the most passionate, purposive-driven members will do it. Most groups just do not have such diehards in their membership, so a practical (and cheaper) alternative is to ask members to corner their legislators at town hall meetings back home. What almost never works are thousands of identical postcards, identical e-mail messages, or online petitions. Lawmakers are not stupid. They know that if people signed these, they did not care enough to write a letter, make a phone call, or go to a protest, and they are often not constituents and probably never read the message they signed (Fitch 2010a).

Committees and Parties

The emphasis so far has been on finding allies in committees, which makes sense since committees are generally the first stage of the lawmaking process. But political parties also matter, even in the committees. Furthermore, since 1995 Congress, especially the House, has experienced a partial return to centralized agenda setting, as more power is accumulated by the party leaders (Deering and Smith 1997, Ch. 2). Lobbyists who ignore party loyalties and party leaders do so at their peril.

Partisanship in Committee Lobbying

Committees are natural targets because they are the birthplaces of legislation. Lobbyists spend most of their time there building mutually beneficial relationships with constituency-sharing committee members (Hojnacki and Kimball 1998, 782). Committees evolve their own cultures, and for committees in which a bipartisan spirit persists, lobbyists need not worry about whether the legislators they have built close relationships with are in the majority or minority parties (Fenno 1973). On famously bipartisan committees like agriculture and transportation, minority party legislators are lobbied just as frequently as the majority (Baumgartner et al. 1999, 161). Rank-and-file members of both parties are free to push amendments to committee bills on behalf of allied lobbyists and their mutual constituents (Hall and Wayman 1990). The lobbyist becomes like an extension of the committee staff—in fact, he or she may even have been a staff member of that committee in the past.

In bodies like the judiciary committee, in which a highly partisan culture prevails and chairs tend to be domineering, lobbyists close to the chair and majority party have significant advantages (Hojnacki and Kimball 1999, 1018). Chairs normally determine what issues the committee will take up each year, and they usually get the first stab at drafting all legislation addressing those issues. So when there is a powerful committee chair, lobbyists can find themselves in weaker positions because they all have to compete for one person's attention. Since powerful chairs can easily exclude them from future committee deliberations, lobbyists can be pressured to back the chair's or majority party's agenda—even when it conflicts with the interests of their members. Chairs prefer lobbyists to support committee legislation because unified interest group support is often seen as a proxy for public support (at least those parts of the public concerned with the issue), and that makes it easier to get the legislation through Congress. A chair may pressure interest groups into making painful compromises just to get this unity.

This phenomenon can often be seen at committee hearings. Hearings are usually carefully scripted events in which the chair showcases all of the interest groups backing his or her bill. Publicizing this support is especially important if a powerful group has opposed it in the past. Unless an issue important to members is getting a lot of publicity, lobbyists are less likely to suffer backlash from ill-informed group members than from angry chairs and will often support controversial legislation at public hearings when chairs pressure them to do so (Holyoke 2008).

Party Lobbying

Party agendas are always in the back of lobbyists' minds, even as they focus most of their efforts on committees. In the age of committee government from the 1940s to the 1970s, when parties in Congress were weak, lobbyists still kept a finger on the pulse of the majority party in the House and Senate (Truman 1951, Ch. 9). Ultimately party leaders control the calendars, decide when or if bills come up for floor votes, and often determine what the votes will be and what amendments will be offered and supported. Since holding onto the majority means holding onto power, it is unlikely that majority party leaders in any age would allow a bill to pass that they know will threaten their majority (Cox and McCubbins 1993).

Today, party leaders are the most powerful people in each chamber of Congress. Their goodwill, if not active support, is necessary if a lobbyist hopes to see his or her member's priorities made into law. Occasionally, a few lobbyists for interests ideologically aligned with a party even get to be its leader's regular counselors. A lobbyist for the Independent Insurance Agents of America (IIAA) I interviewed in 1999 proudly told me he was a member of House Majority Leader Tom DeLay's (R-TX) "Kitchen Cabinet," a group of lobbyists for Republican-compatible groups who met weekly to plot strategy. DeLay earned his nickname, "The Hammer," by blocking legislation desired by interest groups that were not actively helping the Republicans keep control of Congress and advance their party's agenda (Kaiser 2009, 264). Republican conference chair John Boehner (R-OH) had his Thursday Group, which also brought business and social conservative lobbyists together with Republicans (Jacobson 1995). Fourteen years later, in 2009, as House minority leader, Boehner invited banking lobbyists to meet on a recurring basis with Republicans to plan a counterstrategy to Democrats' efforts to craft new restrictions on the banking industry—what ultimately became the Dodd-Frank Act (Lipton 2010).

Most of the nineteen thousand plus lobbyists (the figure from *Washington Representatives*) do not get invitations to weekly party strategy meetings. Party leaders face enormous demands for their time from other legislators, executive branch officials, the press, each other, and even the president. Experienced lobbyists, however, know what the party positions on their issues are well in advance, as do the committee legislators they work with. Rather than count on lobbying leaders directly (though they will when they can), they propose bills suitable for the majority so that such consultations are unnecessary. On the highest of high-profile issues, though, control of legislation becomes an exclusive leadership decision, rather than a committee or subcommittee decision, and leaders become the prime targets of lobbying by all sides (Baumgartner et al. 2009, 157).

■ CASE STUDY ■

The Lobbying Campaign for the Financial Services Modernization Act

Congressional lobbying campaigns are often long and complicated. The groundwork frequently begins well before a bill comes up for a vote, assuming it ever does. (Most bills do not.) Because it helps reveal the subtleties and intricacies of lobbying generally, it is worth tracing the history of a successful large-scale campaign. This is the story of the Financial Services Modernization Act, perhaps the biggest rewrite of financial laws in American history.[9]

In the late 1990s, the banking, investment, and insurance industries wanted to repeal laws put in place during the Great Depression that prevented them from affiliating with each other and encroaching on each other's turf. The banking and investing industries already had some success in convincing friendly regulators to give them limited access to the other's long-forbidden territory. In the early 1980s, investment firms persuaded the Securities and Exchange Commission (SEC) to allow them to offer money market accounts that worked a lot like checking accounts but gave customers higher rates of return. In response, the Federal Reserve allowed banks to open securities-investing companies as long as their profits did not exceed 5 percent of the parent banks' assets. But with Wall Street of the late 1990s reaping record profits, more and more Americans put their savings into the stock market rather than into bank accounts.

The Office of the Comptroller of the Currency (OCC) in the Treasury Department, which regulates national banks, was sympathetic to their plight. The OCC began allowing banks to sell annuities everywhere and insurance in towns of five thousand people or fewer, which bankers assumed meant selling insurance nationwide as long as the bank was located in a small town. This upset the insurance industry, claiming that it was unfair of federal regulators to help out the banks in this way, especially when the insurance industry had no federal regulator to be their advocate. All three industries agreed that piecemeal regulatory decisions were not going to work in the long run. If there was going to be a brave new world of integrated, one-stop-shop financial institutions to benefit consumers, then Congress needed to create a consistent new legal structure.

STAGE ONE: THE POLICY WINDOW IS (PRIED) OPEN

The first and arguably most important step in an advocacy campaign is determining when the time is ripe to push for a new policy in Congress. Are there enough legislators at least willing to consider an interest group's proposal, with at least one willing to be the group's champion? Can a legislative proposal that meets the needs of the group lobbyist's members also make it through Congress? In this case, the window of opportunity opened when the Republicans took control of Congress in 1995 and expressed sympathy for the financial industry's problems with out-of-control regulators, cowardly courts, lost profit opportunities, and the alleged suffering of consumers because of archaic Depression-era laws. Lobbyists for all three industries believed that Republicans would be easier to persuade with a new policy proposal framed as embracing the American competitive spirit as well as consumer convenience. Let these industries compete to see which would emerge on top. Let consumers enjoy the "synergies" of banking, investing, and insurance products all offered by the same company. Interest groups preferring the now threatened status quo, such as independent insurance agents (not insurance companies) and pro-consumer citizen groups, argued that there was really no problem to be solved because none of these industries was really being hurt by current regulatory conditions, but that argument went nowhere with free-market Republicans.

STAGE TWO: DIFFERENT SIDES AND MAJOR PLAYERS

Policy contests are typically fights between only two sets of interests, usually one for and one against the status quo (Baumgartner et al. 2009, 157), but financial modernization had many. Once it became clear that Congress was willing to take up the issue, industry lobbyists began looking at their portfolios of relationships to find champions to promote their versions of what the new financial landscape ought to look like. The choices were not difficult. Remember that lobbyists tend to form close relationships with lawmakers who sit on the committees with jurisdiction over their issues. By being the chief advocates for the group's position in committee, these lawmakers can expect the group's support in the next election.

The policies lobbyists want usually make up only small portions of larger bills and are often inserted by a legislator ally on the committee. Sometimes they are added to a bill later as amendments, though voting on amendments may draw unwanted attention to the provisions lobbyists want. Financial modernization, though, was a large, complex issue that required its own mammoth bill. The trick for the lobbyists, then, was to make sure the committees getting jurisdiction over the bill were dominated by their legislator allies.

Large banks such as Citibank, Chase-Manhattan, and Bank of America along with their trade associations, the American Bankers Association and the Bankers Roundtable (which changed its name to the Financial Services Roundtable in anticipation of the bill's passage), sought champions on the committee they had worked with for decades, the House Banking Committee.

Unfortunately for them, the chair showed little interested in being their champion. Rep. Jim Leach (R-IA) was sympathetic to the banking industry's desire to get into the investing and insurance selling businesses, but refused to support a scheme in which banks established investment houses, insurance underwriting companies, and brokerage agencies inside their own bank structures, which meant that all of these new financial activities would only be regulated by the pro-bank OCC. Leach insisted that these entities be affiliated only with a bank in a holding company structure that allowed the SEC to continue regulating investment companies and allowed states to keep regulating insurance. Leach believed this would create a system of regulatory oversight fairer to consumers, but he also knew that Senate Banking Committee chair Alfonse D'Amato (R-NY) would insist on this arrangement. Leach wanted to solve this conflict, the most contentious part of the proposed legislation, sooner rather than later. The banks were not happy.

The investment industry, led by the Securities Industry Association and the Investment Company Institute, unsurprisingly agreed with Leach that it only made sense for them to remain regulated by the SEC. They had not expected Leach to help them but had pinned their hopes on Rep. Mike Oxley (R-OH), the chair of the House Commerce Committee's Subcommittee on Finance and Hazardous Materials. Yet, to their horror, Oxley wrote the most pro-bank version of financial modernization legislation. He did so because he hoped to replace retiring Commerce Committee chair Tom Bliley (R-VA) and wanted banking industry support when he campaigned to be chair of the committee. Even though the bill was in the banking committee, Oxley convinced House leaders to give his subcommittee jurisdiction as well and passed a bill that allowed banks to establish their own investment and insurance subsidiaries purely under OCC regulation.

The insurance industry, which includes both underwriting companies and independent insurance agents, was divided over whether or not to support the new integrated financial landscape being created in the House. The American Council of Life Insurers and American Insurance Association accepted it and even felt they might be able to compete with banks and investment firms. The Independent Insurance Agents of America and other agent interest groups really wanted to keep the status quo and opposed everything. These super-financial firms, they argued, would sell a mortgage loan and then force the poor, defenseless consumer to purchase home owners' insurance from a firm's own affiliate rather than let consumers turn to their local independent agent for advice. But if agent groups had to accept a proposal, they agreed with the insurance companies (and the investment industry) that they should all be able to remain with their traditional regulators. The states had decades of experience regulating insurance, whereas federal regulators knew little about it.

Insurance agents had a champion on the Banking Committee. Realizing that Leach's initial bill contained no actual guarantees that insurance would still be regulated by the states, they sought help from Rep. Sue Kelley (R-NY), who had a large number of agents in her district and was therefore an ally. Kelley often supported the moderate Leach against more conservative Republicans, so he was happy to return the favor by supporting her amendment guaranteeing state primacy in insurance regulation. Agents also assumed they had another champion, Rep. Gerald Solomon (R-NY). Solomon was himself a former insurance agent, and he chaired the powerful House Rules Committee, the committee all bills go to before going to the House floor for final votes. Everyone assumed he would help the insurance agents. But under pressure from the House Republican leadership to pass the bill wanted by the banking industry, he did not.

STAGE THREE: BUILDING COALITIONS

Usually the next step in a lobbying campaign is to build broad support among interest groups for a proposal at the committee stage by solving all of the conflicts that might prevent it from passing in later stages of the lawmaking process. Since there were, in 1997, two competing versions of financial modernization coming out of two House committees, resolving the conflict at the committee stage was impossible. Leach's bill was more balanced between the multiple interests, while Oxley's bill favored banks. Most legislators, however, do not like choosing between powerful constituencies. They especially did not want to vote for a bill opposed by independent insurance agents, whose grassroots strength was legendary. Nearly every congressional district has independent insurance agents, and they vote!

To resolve these differences and build a broad coalition backing a single bill when it came to the full House, Speaker Newt Gingrich (R-GA) appointed Republican conference chair John Boehner (R-OH) to mediate. Under enormous pressure from the insurance industry, both underwriters and agents, Boehner pushed Oxley to accept Leach's proposal supporting state regulation of insurance and forbid banks from directly owning insurance agencies and investment firms. The banking lobby reluctantly agreed, and with equal reluctance joined the other industry trade groups in forming the Financial Services Coordinating Council coalition to show unity behind the compromise. True unity remained elusive, as insurance agent groups IIAA, National Association of Professional Insurance Agents, Council of Insurance Agents and Brokers, and National Association of Life Underwriters formed a coalition opposing the bill. Also against Leach's bill, though largely invisible so far, were citizen and public interest groups like Consumer Federation of America, National Community Reinvestment Coalition, Common Cause, and US Public Interest Research Group. They opposed the very idea of a combined financial industry, but their champion, President Bill Clinton, was so far keeping quiet.

STAGE FOUR: GOING BEYOND HOUSE COMMITTEES

Boehner's success meant the House Republican leadership was behind financial modernization, which in turn meant the House Rules Committee would support the compromise bill. The rules committee determines which amendments, if any, may be offered to a bill on the House floor, so it essentially determines a bill's fate. Wise lobbyists supporting a bill remember to work this committee along with the party leadership to win a closed rule (no amendments allowed), guaranteeing that the proposal passes as is on the House floor. Dashing the hopes of the independent insurance agents, Boehner convinced rules committee chair Solomon to support Leach's bill without changes. Even so, grassroots lobbying by thousands of independent insurance agents nearly overwhelmed Republican Party discipline when the bill came up for a floor vote in 1998. Speaker Gingrich himself had to twist arms while the vote was in progress to get a majority, and it still passed by only one vote. Legislators were furious at being forced to vote against the insurance agents, and this was a big contributor toward Gingrich's ouster from the Speakership soon afterwards.

While coalitions are important for moving bills through the House, they are even more so in the Senate. Traditions of individual senatorial privilege backed by **filibuster** threats empower the minority party and make Senate floor debates unpredictable. Many a lobbyist's hopes have been shattered in the Senate, either by amendment (on which there are no restrictions), by personal senatorial holds preventing consideration of bills, or because frustrated majority leaders cannot come up with the sixty votes necessary to invoke **cloture** and bring bills to a final vote. Coalitions are almost the only way lobbyists can persuade large numbers of senators that a bill aligns with, or at least does not threaten, their electoral interests. Even though the Financial Services Coordinating Council had secured support from both Republican and Democratic senators, their hopes for passage in 1998 died because of Senator Phil Gramm's (R-TX) ambition.

Senate Banking Committee chair Al D'Amato (R-NY) was going into a difficult reelection and needed financial support from Wall Street firms. This is why he had always intended to support Leach's version of the bill, which was almost exactly what the investment industry had wanted from the beginning, and had championed the House deal supported by the Financial Services Coordinating Council. Most senators represent large and diverse constituencies, so the grassroots pressure of the insurance agents that was so influential in the House was too diluted to stop the bill in the Senate. D'Amato forced agents to accept the compromise bill by threatening to exclude them from all future negotiations. The bill failed anyway. Because he knew he would be the next banking committee chair if D'Amato lost reelection and could rewrite the bill to support his insurance agent allies, Senator Gramm filibustered financial modernization in 1998. The financial industry coalition begged Senate Majority Leader Trent Lott (R-MS) for help, but Gramm refused to relent, and Lott had to pull the bill off the schedule, killing it for the year. Even worse for the industry coalition, D'Amato lost his reelection, and Gramm became chair of the banking committee.

STAGE FIVE: THE CONFERENCE AND PASSING OF THE FINANCIAL SERVICES MODERNIZATION ACT

The Constitution requires all bills passed by the House and Senate to exactly resemble each other before going to the president for signature or veto. House and Senate leaders thus create ad hoc reconciliation, or conference, committees to hammer out the differences. Usually it is the members of the committees originally involved in writing the bills that sit on the conference committees, giving them what amounts to the last crack at the bill (Shepsle and Weingast 1987). This means lobbyists who enjoy close relationships with committee legislators have another great advantage. **Conference committee** bills cannot be amended, so they rarely fail to pass. If lobbyists win in conference, they are almost guaranteed to have won the overall struggle. If they cannot win in conference, then discretion may be the better part of valor, and they typically accept defeat rather than fight a hopeless battle. Only if the final compromise fundamentally threatens group member interests, so that supporting the conference bill would be seen by members as a betrayal, is it logical for lobbyists to mount a futile effort to kill it.

The financial modernization endgame unfolded quickly in 1999, driven by the merger of banking giant Citibank with the even larger Travelers Insurance Company into the first multiservice institution. The megacorporation now lobbied fiercely for a law to make its own existence legal. The House committees quickly repassed the compromise bill. Gramm, now chair of the Senate Banking Committee, ignored it. Industry coalition lobbyists then had the experience of a lifetime sitting in Gramm's office watching a senator personally rewrite legislation without any staff help. As they spoke with him, Gramm came to understand *why* the original compromise deal had been struck. Once "educated" by these lobbyists, he reluctantly agreed to support a bill that looked a lot like Leach's original 1997 bill, allowing all of the industries to be overseen by their traditional regulators. The Senate passed it, and the bill went to conference.

At the last moment, the Clinton administration stepped in with Treasury secretary Lawrence Summers telling Gramm, Leach, and Bliley (the largely uninvolved House Commerce Committee chair) that Clinton would veto the bill if some of the demands of pro-consumer citizen groups for stronger customer privacy provisions were not included. The financial industry was upset but agreed rather than risk a veto that would reset everything to square one. The Financial Services Modernization Act (often called Gramm-Leach-Bliley) became law in November 1999.

■   ■   ■

In Summary

Here is a summary of the chapter's main points:

- Lobbyists spend most of their time building and maintaining relationships with legislators on the committees holding jurisdiction over the issues important to the lobbyist's members.
- When the lobbyist's members are also important constituents of the committee legislator, the latter has every incentive to grant access to

the lobbyist and help him or her move legislation because helping the lobbyist's members helps the legislator get reelected.

- While lobbyists focus most of their attention on committee legislators, party leaders wield tremendous power in the modern Congress, so most lobbyists try to make sure their policy goals are consistent with, or at least not threatening to, the majority party agenda.
- Moving legislation through Congress is difficult because bills must be voted on many times and lobbyists have at most two years to get a bill through Congress before it dies, which means it is easier to defend the status quo by killing a bill than enacting new policy.

Lobbyists lose more than they win in their congressional advocacy efforts, at least on a year-to-year basis (Evans 1996). Legislative struggles, however, rarely ever end. As one lobbyist described it, "Almost nothing can be accomplished in 25 weeks and almost nothing can't be accomplished in 25 years" (Aviv et al. 2012, 4). In some years lobbyists and their congressional allies just cannot build enough support in committee to convince a chair to spend valuable time marking up their pet bill. Perhaps there are other public problems that need more immediate attention. Perhaps some great event, like an attack on the United States or an economic collapse, occurs, and "high politics" sucks up all of the political oxygen, shoving everything else off the agenda. Perhaps opposition from other interest groups is just too strong, and they are doing too good a job at framing the proactive lobbyist's proposal as a dangerous cover-up for the interest's greed. It is always easier to lobby against a proposal than for it (Schattschneider 1960; McKay 2012), especially in Congress, where bills have no more than two years to get to the president before they die, which advantages supporters of the status quo. As former Sierra Club lobbyist Tim Mahoney explained about a bill he was trying to kill, "You delay it, you run out the clock" (Farrell 2011, 14). Since overthrowing the status quo is difficult in a political system based on separation of powers, unless the political stars have really aligned, most lobbyists are smart enough not to try.

As financial modernization exemplified, even when lobbyists win, it is often not quite the win their members hoped for. Nothing passes in Congress without majorities, often super-majorities. Behind these majorities are large numbers of lobbyists all trying to make sure that a bill does not threaten the interests of their members or clients, with most having enough relationships in Congress to stop it. If one lobbyist's provision does not appear to threaten other interests, then all is fine and well, but in a world where thousands of groups are lobbying Congress, that is unlikely to happen. As I argued in

Chapter 5, lobbyists are serial compromisers, adjusting the provisions they are pushing and perhaps giving up some of what their members want in order to get something else they want. The trick for lobbyists is deciding how much they dare give up before compromise is no longer a better option than fighting or giving up. Lobbyists must be sensitive to the pressures their congressional allies are under as well as to the needs of their members. They often do not manage a complete victory, but they also rarely suffer complete defeat. Success in Congress is built on incremental gains, and patience is a particular virtue.

Notes

1. Technically, Representative Ney pled guilty to corruption and filing false disclosure statements.

2. "Lobbying Expenditures Slump in 2011," *OpenSecretsblog*, Center for Responsive Politics, January 26, 2012, http://www.opensecrets.org/news/2012/01/lobbying-expenditures-slump-in-2011.html.

3. Yet even AARP's influence has limits, which was apparent in 2011, when Congress criticized it for making a profit off of that very same law (Herger, Reichert, and Boustany 2011).

4. This insight comes from an interview I did with a lobbyist for the Independent Insurance Agents of America: his legitimacy was almost entirely due to a kind of coattail effect because he was being introduced to legislators by his group's senior lobbyist, who was well respected and established from decades of work.

5. This insight is from a 1999 interview I conducted with lobbyists for financial modernization.

6. This point regarding the importance of making connections at fundraisers was heavily emphasized by a lobbyist I interviewed for this project. For him it was the primary reason to go to fundraisers, to meet lawmakers and their staff, and to especially be connected to lawmakers he did not know through friends on the inside and outside who were also at the fundraiser. Indeed, he often would go to a specific fundraiser because he knew that a lawmaker he wanted to meet would be there, as well as a friend of his who could make the connection.

7. Susman himself attributes his thinking about the influential power of reciprocity to the research of the psychologist Dennis Regan, published in Cialdini (2001).

8. This "little favors" strategy is based on the many interviews I have had with lobbyists over the years, including responses to questions I asked about how they are able to get help from legislators with whom there is no constituency connection.

9. This case study is from interviews I did in 2000 and 2001 with lobbyists working on this bill.

CHAPTER SEVEN

Executive Branch Lobbying

In 2011 the American League of Lobbyists (ALL), an interest group representing lobbyists (yes, there really is one), announced its opposition to President Barack Obama's ban on executive branch employees in the White House and the bureaucracy accepting gifts from lobbyists. Employees would not even be allowed to accept free admission to events sponsored by interest groups. League leader Howard Marlowe described the administration's effort to disconnect the lobbying industry from the executive branch as the "dumbing-down of government" and said that "if [the proposal] is not withdrawn, this rule will prevent government workers from having even casual social contact with registered lobbyists" (Farnam 2011). Lobbying, he argued, keeps government in touch with the real world.

Lobbyists certainly are in contact with the executive branch: 26 percent do it regularly and many more on an occasional basis, according to Heinz and colleagues' study of lobbying (1993, 195). They probably feel they need to. Outsourcing of executive branch work to interest groups and private companies is a billion-dollar industry today, especially in national security, where private contractors are virtually a fourth branch of government. A private sector contractor's survival often depends on good lobbying (and with disturbingly little disclosure of how much money they spend on this lobbying; see Tau 2013). But is the public well served by this lobbying of the executive? The American League of Lobbyists claims they are because such communication allows different constituencies around the nation to have their voices heard as presidents assemble large governing coalitions (and prepare for reelection) and agencies prepare rules implementing acts of Congress. Certainly administrative rule making has profound and far-reaching effects on citizens and often determines who wins and who loses in policy conflicts.

How interest groups and corporations lobby the president and administrative agencies, however, is different from, and often less visible than, how they lobby Congress. In this chapter I explore executive branch advocacy and shed light on whether Marlowe is right or whether President Obama's proposed restrictions are, as the pro-ethics group Campaign Legal Center says, "long overdue" (Farnam 2011).

Lobbying the White House

Few people get to lobby the president. Those who manage it do it rarely. A survey of lobbying organizations in the 1980s found only 11 percent reported having any contact with the president and senior White House staff (Peterson 1992b). Congressional registration records for 1996 showed that only 8 percent of lobbyists working with Congress also contacted the White House (Holyoke 2004a). Yet lobbyists are not indifferent to the Oval Office, and presidents are only sometimes indifferent to them. But presidents run a serious risk when dealing with interest groups. If they are seen spending time with lobbyists, the public may wonder why a few special interests are being favored at the expense of the national constituency. President Bill Clinton's first political setback arguably came when he tried to fulfill a campaign promise to gay and lesbian groups to end discrimination in the military even though such a policy lacked broad public support (Pika and Maltese 2004, 97–99). The blowback led instead to Don't Ask, Don't Tell, a policy allowing gay people to serve only if they hid their sexual orientation. President George W. Bush never really escaped the perception that he was too close to the oil industry after Vice President Dick Cheney convened an energy task force of industry executives and their lobbyists to develop national energy policy early in his first term.

Different Needs

Presidents do sometimes need interest groups and lobbyists, just for different reasons than members of Congress. The president's constituency is the entire nation and cannot be dominated by any single interest group, unlike what happens in many House districts (Peterson 1992a, 224). In addition, a president's time in office cannot exceed eight years, making it almost impossible for lobbyists to develop the same mutually beneficial, long-term relationships they frequently build with legislators on the basis of shared constituencies.

Winning national elections means presidential candidates must assemble large coalitions of interests, but these groups are bound together by unifying themes rooted in broadly shared American values rather than hundreds of separate promises made to hundreds of groups (Seligman and Covington 1989).

Some interest groups may try to influence future presidential policy by lobbying party platform committees before national conventions (Fine 1994), but neither platforms nor campaign promises appear to bind presidents much once they are in office. Latino groups supporting President Obama in 2008 under the impression that he would dramatically change the nation's laws regarding the treatment of undocumented immigrants were sorely disappointed when he let the issue drop in face of Republican resistance in 2010. Other interest groups may try to get in on the ground floor of a new administration by lobbying a president's transition team, especially if they felt they made crucial contributions to the election or were excluded by the prior administration (Brown 2011). But modern presidents tend to run on promises of reform, so they risk their new political capital if they are seen cozying up to "special interests" on day 1.

Information regarding which constituencies to serve to guarantee reelection and how to move legislation through the maze of Capitol Hill is the currency in which lobbyists trade when they develop relationships with members of Congress. Presidents do not need this information. White House offices are staffed by some of the nation's best political strategists. With the considerable resources and expertise of the **Executive Office of the President** at their disposal, presidents have access to all the political and technical information they could ever want. If they have a problem with anything, it is that they have too much information. The services lobbyists perform for legislators are just not needed by the chief executive.

But this doesn't mean a president can ignore interest groups or run roughshod over too many of them. Doing so risks fracturing an electorate that might otherwise be supportive of a president's broad policy goals. Just ask President Jimmy Carter. Convinced he had a strong electoral mandate after defeating Gerald Ford in 1976, Carter used a president's unique ability to command media attention to try to push major policy changes, such as removing dams from rivers and reducing oil consumption. These policies were hostile to multiple interest groups, their congressional allies, and their mutual constituents. They pushed back hard, and Carter abruptly found his electoral support crumbling, leaving him too weak to fight off Ronald Reagan in 1980 (Gais, Peterson, and Walker 1984, 161). Reagan, too, left office blaming the entrenched power of "special interests" for resisting his efforts to reduce and reform social services (Peterson 1990, 539). The extent to which presidents dare take on interest groups en masse, or seek their assistance, is shaped by the political climate surrounding their presidency. So when do presidents reach out to interest groups?

Reaching Out

Political scientist Mark Peterson (1992b) argues that presidents are motivated by their need to maintain a reelection coalition and govern by moving a legislative agenda. From this I predict the level of outreach presidents will use with interest groups, as seen in Figure 7.1. Across the top of the figure is motivation—that is, the degree to which a president wants either to build a reelection coalition or to push a large package of status quo–threatening policies through Congress. Presidents in their first term cannot take their eyes off reelection, and this focus often limits the scope of the policies they try to enact, but presidents in their second term do not have this worry and are likely more concerned with leaving a legacy of substantial policy change contributing to the nation's well-being.

The vertical side of Figure 7.1 represents the political environment surrounding an administration, meaning the extent to which the public supports presidential policy goals. Presidents who win elections by large margins, such as Reagan's victory over Walter Mondale in 1984, have widespread public support for their policies. They can use the bully pulpit of their office—their ability to mobilize this broad public support—to pressure the ever sensitive Congress (Kernell 1993) and run over any interest groups that get in their way (Rankin 2006). When close elections or dramatic falls in public confidence deprive presidents of this ability to "go public," more subtle means must be found to influence national policy.

What does this combination of factors mean for how much a president reaches out to interest groups? First-term presidents who have lost public support (top left quadrant of Figure 7.1), perhaps because their policies do not match electoral promises or the economy has turned sour, but are keen on seeking reelection, must find ways to combine interest groups into a winning electoral coalition. That means winning the support of large interest groups. Presidents and their top advisors will aggressively seek opportunities to speak to big associations like the US Chamber of Commerce, the National Association of Manufacturers, National Association of Realtors, AFL-CIO,

	President's Primary Concern Is Reelection	President's Primary Concern Is Proactive Lawmaking
President Has Weak Public Support	Aggressive outreach to many interest groups with promises of rewards if they help form a new reelection coalition	Aggressive outreach to interest groups that have good connections on Capitol Hill to advance a few policy priorities
President Has Strong Public Support	Passive outreach to major interest groups in electoral coalition to insure they are not threatened by president's platform	Little outreach to interest groups except those already supportive of broad presidential policy priorities

FIGURE 7.1   Levels of Outreach from Presidents to Interest Groups

NAACP, and AARP to convince them that their agendas are aligned with the White House, probably by making promises benefitting these interests in the hoped-for second term (Pika and Maltese 2004). If governing, however, is the president's primary concern, but public support is too weak to browbeat Congress into passing their policies (top right quadrant of Figure 7.1), presidents may use lobbyists as back channels to reach out to legislators, as Obama and Treasury secretary Timothy Geithner did in 2011, when they quietly enlisted banking and finance lobbyists to press Republicans into voting to raise the nation's debt ceiling (Dash and Schwartz 2011).

But when presidents need interest group support, lobbyists can push them to prioritize policy changes lacking broad public support in exchange for votes and grassroots advocacy. Obama's abrupt announcement in 2012 that immigrants who came to the United States at a young age would no longer be deported was panned as a desperate effort by an embattled president to regain the support of Latino voters he had enjoyed in 2008, though in the end Latinos *did* support Obama's reelection by at least 71 percent (Diaz and Zogby 2012). Weak presidents in their second term need not worry about reelection, but they do worry about their legacy. Dwindling public support means less influence on Capitol Hill. Presidents must focus on the few policies still considered doable, and that means reaching out to lobbyists involved in the policy areas they still hope to influence for help in mobilizing congressional support or, more likely the case, finding ways to work around an obstinate Congress. The case study at the end of this chapter on Bill Clinton and environmental groups working on roadless wilderness legislation is a good example of this (see pages 181–184).

Presidents enjoying strong public support deal with interest groups on their own terms when they deal with them at all. They do not need group support for reelection (lower left quadrant of Figure 7.1) as long as their policy proposals do not strike too hard at the interests of groups connected to the president's party allies in Congress, such as organized labor for Democrats and Christian conservatives for Republicans. Popular second-term presidents (lower right quadrant of Figure 7.1) only need to work with interests already supporting their agendas. Indeed, it is more likely that many interest groups will try to reframe their desires to appear aligned with a president's agenda, hoping to hitch their desired policies to his star in the hopes that they will cruise through Congress on the president's popularity.

Formalizing Outreach

The relationship between interest groups and modern presidents (as laid out in Figure 7.1) can be seen in how and when past presidents reached out to particular groups. Franklin Roosevelt was perhaps the first to employ aides just to connect to specific groups in society he believed were essential to his electoral and governing coalitions. These special assistants were individuals who themselves had significant standing in crucial business, ethnic, and religious groups and could speak on their behalf (Pika 2009). Having liaisons did not actually give these groups access to the Oval Office, just the appearance of access, so Roosevelt could keep them as supporters.

In the early years of his administration, the crisis of the Great Depression and his strong mandate from the 1932 election gave Roosevelt the support he needed for moving major legislation through Capitol Hill. But as enthusiasm for New Deal policies cooled in the mid-1930s, Roosevelt built more durable political support by reaching out to organized labor, other blue-collar workers, African Americans, farmers, Catholics, and Jews to show opponents on Capitol Hill and in the business community that the nation was still on his side (Peterson 1992a, 230). Initially, these groups were more supportive of the New Deal than Roosevelt was of their interests, but this power dynamic changed as he lost public support and was forced to lean more heavily on these groups for electoral aid. For instance, Roosevelt had reservations about the National Labor Relations Act, a priority for organized labor, but he signed it into law anyway and was rewarded with enormous union support in the 1936 election (Greenstone 1977, 48). Lyndon Johnson similarly promoted his Great Society programs in the 1960s by establishing liaisons to carefully selected social interests that could act as his agents on Capitol Hill and in the public. These interest group allies were rewarded with new spending programs serving their interests (Peterson 1992b, 615).

The upper left quadrant of Figure 7.1 shows that presidents with weak public support and facing a difficult election will reach out to large numbers of interest groups. Reaching out was so important for President Gerald Ford that he opened an **Office of Public Liaison** (OPL) in the Executive Office of the President (EOP) staffed with aides tasked with reaching out to groups to learn what concerns they had and, implicitly, what the administration might do to gain their electoral support. His elevation to president after Richard Nixon's resignation had put him in the awkward position of being a national leader without a national electoral constituency that would support him in the 1976 election. The OPL gave him the institutional resources to build a large coalition of key interest groups around the nation to support his potential reelection (Pika 2009).

Ford still lost to Jimmy Carter, but the OPL became a fixture in the EOP. It is a point of contact specifically for interest groups, but one used differently by different presidents reflecting the strategies described in Figure 7.1. Carter initially used OPL to communicate with a few groups especially crucial for his reelection and then later used it to gain support from other interests determined by lobbyist Anne Wexler, his OPL director, as crucial for advancing his agenda. Carter needed the additional help when he realized that his heavy-handed approach to congressional relations had alienated allies, meaning that he had weaker public support than he originally thought. Carter's OPL was also willing to listen to organizations representing marginalized populations, such as gay rights groups (Kumar and Grossman 1986). Even if the interests of these groups did not end up on Carter's agenda, just finding OPL's door open with an aide willing to listen helped confer legitimacy on otherwise marginalized interests. What OPL became is another door in the government super-structure, one that seems to lead right to the president, though sometimes all that advocates find is an aide who politely listens without much action (Lucco 1992).

Defunding the Left

During Ronald Reagan's presidency, this door was even more of a dead end if a group's interests were not ideologically aligned with Reagan's agenda (Lucco 1992). More than his predecessors, Reagan preferred to use his communications and domestic policy offices rather than the OPL to reach out to the small number of interest groups he believed useful for promoting his agenda and shutting out everyone else (Peterson 1992b, 620). Interest alignment became the crucial factor for access as the partisan divide in Washington grew. By the first Bush administration, OPL was all but eliminated (Peterson 1992b, 623).

This was actually the least of the problems unaligned interest groups had in the 1980s. Elected with a solid mandate in 1980 and an even larger one in 1984, Reagan did not need widespread interest group support and aggressively moved against the left-leaning groups that he felt threatened his agenda (Berry 1993). What bothered Reagan was that many of these organizations received substantial funding from the very same federal government they were lobbying (Smith and Lipsky 1993; DeVita 1999). Indeed, 60 percent of all nonprofits in 1982 received some federal support, with 38 percent of all nonprofit revenue coming from public sources on top of the tax breaks many of these groups received if they held 501(c)(3) status (Salamon 1995, 63).

Once in office, Reagan began a campaign to reduce these organizations' influence by starving them of funds. Cutbacks in appropriations for social service contracts hit the operating budgets of many cause-oriented nonprofits hard (Wolman and Teitelbaum 1984). Yet, rather ironically, Reagan's attack turned out to be a great recruitment boon for many of these groups. Direct marketing technology was becoming widely used in Washington (Godwin 1988), and liberal groups' executives quickly learned how to use it to raise money and recruit members simply by alerting supporters that everything they had achieved in the 1960s and 70s was about to be lost (Berry 1993). Demonizing Reagan's Interior secretary James Watt led to one of the Sierra Club's most successful recruitment and fundraising drives ever. At the same time, business interests that had high hopes for Reagan were alarmed to learn that he was serious about reducing subsidies and tax breaks (Vogel 1989). Much of Reagan's 1986 Tax Reform Act came at their expense.

Reagan also supported the emergence of conservative public interest groups whose interests aligned with his and could help advance his agenda (Vogel 1989). Industries that were interested in deregulation (such as the trucking industry) and in union-busting (such as the airline industry) were delighted. The White House also supported the creation of conservative groups to develop alternative visions for public policy that Reagan's aides could incorporate into policy proposals, budget priorities, and even State of the Union addresses (Pika 2009, 556). These public interest groups were encouraged to sue the government to advance conservative interests, even as liberal groups were turning more to the courts because they were shut out of the Republican Congress and the Reagan White House (O'Connor and McFall 1992). Reagan did not break liberal interest groups, but he did populate the capitol city with many new, highly ideological conservative public interest groups.

Contemporary Presidents and Interest Groups

As the Cold War ended, the deference given to presidents as leaders during a time of national struggle began to evaporate, and many in Congress and the interest group community felt they were in stronger positions to oppose presidential foreign and domestic agendas (Skidmore 1993; Dietrich 1999). President Bill Clinton discovered this during his first year in office, when his public health care legislation was defeated by a nearly $100 million television campaign run by medical and insurance interest groups (Hacker 1999). Subsequent efforts to improve relations with interest groups fared no better. Clinton's selling of overnight White House visits and "coffees" to the leaders of interest groups crucial to his electoral triumph became a scandal. All this and more damaged his first years in office and convinced many business and conservative interests that the Democratic Party was out of touch enough with the public to be taken down, which they helped House and Senate Republicans do in the 1994 midterm election. Facing weakening public support, Clinton was forced to reach out even more to organizations that had helped elect him in 1992 to convince them to help again in 1996. The lines between governing and reelection during Clinton's first term became so blurred that much of his interest group outreach was handled by the Democratic National Committee rather than the withered OPL, and remained so even in his second term (Pika 2009, 559).

Interest group outreach in the George W. Bush administration was largely directed by chief campaign strategist Karl Rove, reflecting Bush's need to build an electoral coalition after his narrow, contested victory over Al Gore in 2000 (Pika 2009, 560–561). Close relationships were forged with large business and trade associations, such as the US Chamber of Commerce and the

National Association of Manufacturers, that sought tax and regulatory relief. Together they built the Tax Relief Coalition to push these parts of the president's agenda on Capitol Hill, where business groups already enjoyed close relationships with majority Republicans. The Office of Faith-Based and Community Initiatives, a new addition to the EOP, opened a line of direct communication between the White House and the social conservative interests that had delivered the 2000 Republican primary for Bush against Senator John McCain (R-AZ). To further strengthen his electoral coalition, Bush helped AARP expand Medicare prescription drug coverage for seniors in 2003 (Pika 2009). However, efforts in his second term to build a legacy of conservative policy change were less successful. By 2005, with unpopular wars in Afghanistan and Iraq, Bush no longer had the public clout to overcome interest group and congressional resistance to other conservative-backed proposals such as Social Security privatization (O'Connor 2005).

Although his refusal to accept public financing for his campaign left him heavily reliant on private contributions, President Barack Obama still promised to bring a new face to Washington, DC, by refraining from hiring lobbyists for senior staff positions. And, like presidents before him, he then decided that was an unwise strategy. Again, lobbyists know Washington better than almost any other person, and connections to key policy makers are their trade. For a new president trying to assemble an agenda and a governing team, especially one who had only spent a few years in Washington before becoming president, hiring lobbyists provided invaluable liaisons between the White House and Capitol Hill. By bringing in people such as Leon Panetta, an experienced lobbyist and ex-congressman, to be his CIA director, Obama may have broken a campaign promise, but it arguably helped him build a more effective governing team.

With a solid electoral win in 2008, Obama felt himself strong enough to try governing from the ideological middle. Perhaps this is best seen in his early moves on national health care, when he sought help from medical and insurance trade associations for his health care bill, which many of them initially gave. He also continued his predecessor's outreach to religious interests by retaining the Office of Faith-Based Partnerships, which some liberals hoped he would close (Landsberg 2012). But by late 2009, Obama found his public support beginning to erode. The last of his political capital was expended on enacting his health care legislation, only to find, as Bill Clinton had before him, that it cost him parts of his electoral coalition and once again put Republicans in control of the House of Representatives. This forced Obama to refocus on proving to liberal groups that he was still their friend as the 2012 election approached. This strategy proved successful, as he handily won reelection.

Lobbying the Bureaucracy

Most of the federal government exists in the executive branch beneath the Executive Office of the Presidency. Fifteen large departments, over two hundred independent agencies and government corporations, hundreds of regulatory agencies and bureaus, and nearly three million people employed in just civilian jobs: all have the responsibility for implementing (putting into effect) the laws enacted by Congress and the president. And even these numbers do not reveal the full scope of bureaucratic power and why interest groups and their lobbyists take implementation so seriously. **Implementation** is yet another opportunity for them to influence policy, for how public policy is put into practice by agency bureaucrats is how it really affects people. For interest groups excluded from congressional deliberations, it is a chance to pursue their members' interests in another venue. Even if the group's interests are well served by the way Congress wrote a new law, only a foolish lobbyist would assume that an agency's staff would implement it exactly as Congress intended. Lobbyists' efforts to bias implementation toward their members' interests are one reason why political scientist Charles Lindblom refers to agency decision making as the "science of muddling through" (Lindblom 1959).

Aligning Interests with Agency Missions

Just as the sweeping changes in Congress instituted by the Progressives in the early twentieth century made it easier for lobbyists to pursue member interests through Congress's committee system, good-government reforms to the bureaucracy also opened up executive agencies to lobbying. The Pendleton Act of 1883 created a federal **civil service system** that largely insulated executive branch staff from congressional and presidential control (Meier 1993, 33). This independence allows agencies to take seriously the policy missions defined in their establishing statutes, instilling them with their own mission-driven cultures (Downs 1967). Interest groups supportive of an agency's mission find that staff there welcome their input. And why not? After all, the interest group and the agency are united in their passion for advancing and protecting the same policies, designed to benefit a particular slice of the American public.

Political scientist Daniel McCool (1994) uses western water policy as an example to demonstrate the power of interest groups aligning with agencies—in this case, the US Bureau of Reclamation. In 1902, agriculture and business interests hoping to reap profits from farming and developing arid western land, which only needed water on it to be valuable, formed organizations such as the National Irrigation Congress to lobby for federal support of large dam and canal projects. At the same time, western lawmakers created a new irrigation subcommittee, and because Congress lets its members select their own committee assignments, these lawmakers all got seats on it. To serve the farmers and business leaders who were crucial to their reelection, these lawmakers took the advice of the National Irrigation Congress and created the Bureau of Reclamation to implement new water policy and new irrigation projects.

For nearly eighty years Reclamation happily did exactly what the interested parties wanted, building dams and canals all over the American west, most famously Hoover Dam on the Colorado River. When interest groups wanted more built, they went to Reclamation even before going to Congress, so that proposals for new water systems would be fully designed and their benefits to key constituencies made clear before asking committee lawmakers for authorization and funding. Because the Bureau's culture valued great engineering feats benefiting western constituencies, the legislators on the irrigation subcommittee and lobbyists representing related interest groups trusted it and protected it from attacks by others in Congress, as well as skeptical Interior secretaries, presidents, and, for many years, environmental interest groups (Reisner 1986). Nobody else in Congress, the executive branch, or the interest group community mattered. The autonomy of this network of legislators, lobbyists, and agency staff sharing the same interests was ultimately respected and protected because the rest of the government was divided into similar autonomous systems serving other interests—with everybody involved implicitly understanding that they must not interfere in others' policy territory (Lowi 1979).

The relationship McCool described in the example above is known as a **subgovernment** (McConnell 1966), though some prefer the term **iron triangle**, and is shown in the top part of Figure 7.2 (Cater 1964). Relationships among the creators of a policy (Congress), its implementers (agencies), and beneficiaries (interest groups) are so mutually advantageous in subgovernments that agencies end up defending and promoting the industries they are supposed to be regulating (Bernstein 1955; Stigler and Friedland 1962). This

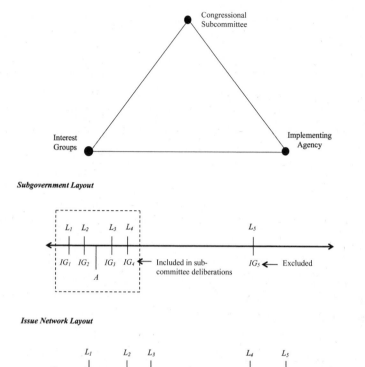

FIGURE 7.2   Subgovernments and Issue Networks

happens not because members of Congress and interest groups are forcing them to, but because the agency's staff want to. Agency staff believe that it is their mission to serve the industries their agency represents and promotes, and new staff are socialized to do the same. The costs to the public for policies favoring special interests are dispersed through the tax system. The lobbyist's job is to make sure the policy's benefits are clearly visible to their constituencies (their group members), so that their members will reward members of Congress with votes, who will in turn reward the agency with fat budgets, little oversight, and insulation from external political pressures (McCool 1994).

Subgovernment, or iron triangle, is an important concept to understand, for it is a consequence of the relationships lobbyists build with legislators discussed in the last chapter. In the middle portion of Figure 7.2, the five legislators on a subcommittee are marked with *L*s by where they would ideally like to see policy enacted on a liberal to conservative continuum of possible policy outcomes (like the hours of driving continuum in chapter 5). Interest groups concerned with the policy in the subcommittee's jurisdiction are listed as *IGs*. Their positions on the continuum reflect the desires of their members, who are the same constituents who keep the subcommittee legislators in office, which is why they are shown together on the same continuum in Figure 7.2. The upper continuum (middle of the figure) depicts a subgovernment layout, where a majority of legislators and interest groups agree on what policy should be and establish an agency with a mission to implement it at point *A*. Lobbyists for interest groups 1 through 4 are welcome at this agency because they share the same values as agency staff and desire to serve the same constituencies as the subcommittee legislators. Sometimes this means implementing the absurd. To make it easy to build a water system for Los Angeles, interest groups and irrigation subcommittee legislators easily convinced the US Forest Service to designate some scrub land as the Inyo National Forest so Reclamation could build a canal so L.A. could drain all of the water out of the Owens Valley in eastern California (Reisner 1986). Of course legislator *L5* and ally *IG5* are not happy, but their desires are considered far out of the mainstream and therefore excluded from subcommittee business and ignored by the agency.

Over time things may change. New interests championed by new legislators may find their way on to the subcommittee overseeing the agency and advocate for a new, perhaps radically different, policy. The result, displayed at the bottom of Figure 7.2, is more dispersed legislator-interest group preference pairs on the subcommittee, creating conflict where there had once been consensus. Any decision agency officials make now will displease somebody on the subcommittee, and may not please anybody. Oddly enough, though, the result of this subgovernment disintegration into what is called an **issue network** (Heclo 1978) is greater agency independence. The agency is now free to continue pursuing its original mission because the subcommittee's new members and their new lobbyist allies are not unified enough to use the lawmaking process to force the agency to do what they want (Niskanen 1971). That is why the agency's position, *A*, on the lower continuum is still the same as on the upper continuum. New staff members are still socialized into the agency's culture and will continue to implement policy in line with the original mission (Downs 1967). Groups whose interests still align with the agency's original mission continue to enjoy privileged access there. From everyone else's point of view, though, the agency has gone rogue.

For example, in 1982 the Federal Communications Commission (FCC), charged with regulating the telephone industry, broke up Bell Telephone Company on antitrust grounds. At the same time many legislators and interest groups supported the breakup. Then, as the communications industry began re-creating itself in the early twenty-first century, some in Congress now decided the FCC should be more accommodating of industry mergers. Public interest groups like Consumer Federation of America (CFA), however, still supported FCC staff who wanted to remain true to their original mission as a tough regulator. With members of Congress divided, FCC and CFA were able to prevent the reassembling of "Ma Bell" by denying the merger of T-Mobile and AT&T (Perine 2011).

Sometimes original missions are not clear, leaving an agency vulnerable to pressure from competing interest groups, both of which support part of its statutory mission (Gormley and Balla 2004, 82–83). Take the mission of the National Park Service (NPS) "to conserve the scenery and the national and historic objects and wild life therein and to provide for the enjoyment of the same in such manner and by such means as will leave them unimpaired for the enjoyment of future generations." The result? Environmental groups are pressuring NPS to "conserve . . . for future generations," while recreation groups threaten conservation by pushing NPS to allow more recreational development to enhance "enjoyment." Rather than clarity, there is inconsistent rule making and lots of lawsuits (Nie 2009).

The Administrative Procedures Act's Notice and Comment Period

Ironically, many of the tools created to encourage public participation in agency rule making make it easy for agencies to respond positively to interest groups that share their missions while ignoring others. In 1946 Congress passed the **Administrative Procedure Act** (APA), which requires most of the rules an agency proposes as part of any law it is responsible for implementing to be made available for public comment. Most agencies must publish proposed rules in the *Federal Register*, a daily government publication. The public is invited to read through it and send any comments on proposed rules to the proposing agency.

Unfortunately, few people know the *Federal Register* exists, much less how to find anything of concern to them in it, or understand what they are reading. Larger interest groups, however, have technical staff who understand the

Federal Register and can write responses pointing out the substantive and legal shortcoming of proposals they do not like (Golden 1998, 256). Agencies are not specifically obligated to change proposed rules as a result of comments but merely to take them into consideration. However, federal courts since the 1970s have pushed agencies to aggressively compile records of comments received and show how they responded—what are called **records of decision**—so that lawsuits over rules can be more easily resolved. This encourages agencies to respond to at least some comments (Rabin 1986). But whose?

The number of comments a proposed rule receives varies enormously, with many receiving none at all. It is the larger, more status quo–threatening proposals that have been found to attract the most interest group comments, especially those believed to have significant impacts on the economy (Kerwin 1999, 186). Yet scholar Marissa Golden finds little evidence that interest group comments have any effect on a rule's final form (1998, 252). Only when there was a high degree of consensus among commenters were proposals changed. Otherwise officials appear free to issue final rules reflecting their own policy preferences, citing only the comments they want to hear from groups whose interests align with their mission (261).

Other researchers argue that agencies are biased toward business interests, that comments from business groups are more likely to alter rules in their favor (Yackee and Yackee 2006). If true, it is not surprising. If agencies develop cultures institutionalizing and perpetuating their original statutorily mandated missions, then this would presumably advantage whatever interests were influential with Congress when an agency was created. As I showed in Chapter 2, business interests are, generally speaking, older than consumer protection and environmental interest groups, so they are more likely to have been involved in shaping the missions of all but the youngest agencies. Older agencies proposing rules that business groups see as threatening might be more likely to alter them in favor of those interests because the agencies believe that helping these businesses is consistent with their missions. Younger agencies may favor other interests. Business interests often accuse the Environmental Protection Agency of being beholden to the environmental groups that helped create it. Interestingly, since it became possible to file comments online, first allowed by the EPA in 1999, opponents and proponents of a rule proposed in the *Federal Register* are able to file comments later in time to refute claims made in comments by their competitors earlier in time, creating a strange kind of virtual dialogue (Gormley and Balla 2004, 98–99).

Advisory Committees

Highly privileged interest groups often get to influence a proposed rule before it is published for comment in the *Federal Register* (West 2004, 67). One way is through participation on **advisory committees** that help agency staff with numerous tasks like drafting rules. While the evolution of committees of advisors representing concerned constituencies supposedly goes clear back to the Washington administration (Petracca 1986, 83), their legitimacy, and thus the legitimacy of interest group participation in early rule making, came with the Federal Advisory Committee Act of 1972 (FACA). Today there are well over a thousand advisory committees (Balla 2003).

Sometimes Congress writes into law requirements that agencies form permanent or ad hoc committees of affected interests to consult as rules are developed. Congress does this to make sure that constituent interests important to them benefit from the agency's rules. Yet agencies often form these committees themselves. Certainly these committees can be effective tools for acquiring technical and political information the agencies need on the industries they regulate (Schlozman and Tierney 1983, 365), but advisory committees can also be a way to avoid irritating Congress and concerned (and favored) interest groups by getting advice from the latter on proposed rules before they go public.

So advisory committee seats are positions of privilege. Having a seat shows everyone else in the network of advocates within a policy domain that your interest's voice has greater resonance than others with the agency and its overseeing congressional subcommittee because you get the first crack at influencing a new rule (Petracca 1986, 84). Giving advisory committee seats to interest groups currently favored by the overseeing congressional subcommittee also ensures that the technical, economic, and social information the agency receives reflects the policy and electoral needs of the legislative subcommittee's members, who are the interest groups' patrons in Congress (Balla and Wright 2001). Following this advice keeps the agency on the legislative subcommittee's good side and ensures a future of generous budgets and little oversight, even if the rules it implements are biased toward those interests with advisory committee seats.

Do advisory committees favor business interests? Again, business interests likely worked with Congress to create many of the agencies, frame their missions, and establish their advisory committees—ensuring that business interests, aligned with Congress's intent, are served. So when it turns out that business and trade associations hold disproportionately more seats on advisory committees (Karty 2002), it is partially because opposing groups did not exist when many of these agencies' committees were constituted. Arguably agencies should expand the committees to include new voices, but since those voices are unlikely to support their missions, agency officials have little incentive to do so. It also means that there is a window-dressing quality to advisory committees. Since they are stacked with interests the agencies agree with, listening to committees gives agencies the appearance of stakeholder consultation and makes it easier for agencies to create rules reflecting their own missions.

Biased membership on advisory committees is still a cause for concern. For instance, a study found that when drug manufacturing industry representatives on the advisory committees of the Food and Drug Administration (FDA) vote together to recommend a new drug, it significantly speeds up FDA's approval process, possibly at the expense of additional testing to see if the new drug exhibits any dangerous side effects (Lavertu and Weimer 2011). Indeed, the *New York Times* found additional evidence that drug company lobbyists have been pushing FDA to approve drugs more rapidly in order to get them on the market (Pear 1996). Another study found that even when FDA advisory committee members had financial conflicts of interests—voting on the approval of drugs for companies they were connected to—they rarely recused themselves (Lurie et al. 2006). But do these studies really prove that the FDA is under the pharmaceutical industry's thumb? Or does it mean that the FDA is staying true to its mission to protect public health by listening to the recommendations of experts, even if the experts are employed by the pharmaceutical industry (Carpenter 2004)? If advisory committee members all vote to recommend a new drug, perhaps it means it really is safe for human use. It depends on one's point of view.

Might advisory committees be more effective if Congress forced agencies to expand them to include more diverse interests? Perhaps this would be a good way to get competing interests to resolve disputes before new rules are drafted. Unfortunately, one example shows that such well-meaning efforts may yield the opposite result. A flash point in environmental policy is the designation of lands as national monuments, which environmental groups want in order to preserve natural landscapes, but ranchers and developers decry as intrusions on individual rights to use private and public property as they see fit (Nie 2009). In the late 1990s, environmental groups asked Interior secretary Bruce Babbitt to designate Oregon's Steen Mountain as a national monument, even though some of the land around it was privately owned and most of the public land was being leased to ranchers for grazing by the Bureau of Land Management (BLM) (Ostlind 2011). Threatening to designate the entire 425,550 acres as a monument if an agreement was not reached, Babbitt pushed ranchers and public recreation advocates to sit down and bargain with the Oregon Natural Desert Association, the National Audubon Society, and the Wilderness Society, resulting in the Steen Mountain Cooperative Management and Protection Area Act of 2000. Development was forbidden on some lands, while others were kept open for recreation and to protect the property rights of ranchers in the monument's boundary.

To keep the process smooth and locally connected, the law mandated the creation of an advisory committee of local stakeholders to advise BLM and act as a forum for negotiating further conflicts between these interests. But BLM, which has long favored leasing land to ranchers (Skillen 2009), gave only two of the twelve seats to environmental groups. Environmentalists' fear of a deck stacked to favor ranchers appeared to be true when ranchers negotiated with an energy company to build wind farms, including over a hundred 415-foot turbines, on their portion of the monument without protest from BLM. The environmental groups were able to convince the committee to vote against the wind farm development, but only when many of the ranching interests were absent from the meeting. This meant there was no quorum, so the advisory committee's decision lacked authority. Now both sides are suing each other. In sum, rather than diffuse tension, the advisory committee actually made matters worse.

Regulatory Negotiation

Because public comments are in fact public, interest groups tend to only express their members' preferences rather than suggest compromises (Kerwin 1999, 197–198). Out of the spotlight, though, advisory committees can, the Steen Mountain example notwithstanding, create opportunities for bargaining among affected interests. Since the 1980s many agencies have tried to use various forms of negotiation to resolve the demands of competing interests before new rules are promulgated (Kerwin 1999, 197–202). When an agency knows that a proposed rule will pit organized interests against each other, it sometimes arranges for **regulatory negotiation**, or "reg neg," to occur before the rule is publicly released in the hope that compromises, if they can be reached, will save the agency time because it will not need to rewrite the rule again and again to try to accommodate warring interest groups. Agency officials also hope to head off costly litigation and spare legislators on the overseeing subcommittee the need to take awkward public positions pressuring the agency to favor one interest over others when they might prefer to avoid conflict entirely (Balla 2003).

Successful negotiations can also reduce the time between a rule's initial and final versions because affected parties become more invested in it and the process producing it (Langbein and Kerwin 2000). As with advisory committees, though, which interests are invited to negotiate depends on who is recognized by the agency, or by its overseeing subcommittee, as legitimate stakeholders. Furthermore, reg neg, like most forms of bargaining, only works when the differences between interests are not extreme; each side must believe it can give up something in return for gaining something else they can present to group members as a victory (Holyoke 2011, Ch. 5). Without trust in the negotiating process, faith that the other side will keep its word, and enormous patience, reg neg does not work. Stakeholders must be at least open to understanding other sides' concerns, but that is usually the hardest of all things to do. McCool (2002) describes how it took Interior Department officials years just to convince states, agricultural interests, and Native American tribes that negotiating over the apportionment of Colorado River water would yield a better outcome than more litigation. Deals were eventually reached because participants spent so much time together that they learned to respect each other. It also helped that Congress financially compensated every side that gave up a water claim.

Sometimes interest groups force other groups into regulatory negotiations. An example is how interest groups use the Community Reinvestment Act of 1977 to pressure regulators into demanding that banks provide investments and services in poor and minority urban communities as requirements for regulatory approval of corporate mergers (Haag 2000). As part of the approval process, agencies like the Federal Reserve hold public hearings and solicit comments on a bank's performance in low-income community lending and investing. Public interest groups representing the inner-city poor became adept in the 1990s at using this process to pressure banks (or "extort" as some bankers might say) into making major investments right before applications were filed. In return, these groups would testify in favor of a merger at agency hearings (Holyoke 2004b; Casey, Glasberg, and Beeman 2011). These groups were so good at applying pressure that banks and regulators would sit down with them to negotiate lending packages well in advance of filing merger applications (Santiago, Holyoke, and Levi 1998).

Environmental Impact Reports and Regulatory Scoping

The National Environmental Policy Act (NEPA) of 1969 requires agencies to write **environmental impact statements** (EIS) showing how a proposed public project minimizes potential environmental damage. The first step in this process is **scoping**, or holding public meetings to assess the range (or scope) of interests and public concerns related to the project. While interest groups known to be affected by a project may be contacted directly, scoping generally takes the form of open meetings in which any member of the public, and organizations representing mobilized public interests, may present their views. Scoping hearings give interests that might otherwise be excluded from policy debates the opportunity to be heard—even groups who may not really have a stake in the immediate issue at hand. Indeed, one of the most contentious aspects of democratic politics is determining who is, and who is not, a legitimate stakeholder with rights to be heard on an issue. An effective political tactic one group can use is to portray its opponents as not having a legitimate stake, being intrusive "outsiders" who really have no right to interfere in how an agency's rule is being developed.

As with notice and comment periods, information gained in scoping hearings need not influence the final EIS, and therefore approval of the project, but an official record of decision must be published by the agency detailing the comments received and what, if anything, was done about them and why. Even after drafting the EIS, the report must be made available for public comment before becoming official, all of which goes into the official record of decision. The paper trail NEPA requires forms a record of decision that makes it easy for interest groups to sue the agency over the EIS and its decision (Gormley and Balla 2004, 104). Again, transparency in the rule making actually benefits interest groups.

Sometimes interest groups can convince an agency to regulate an industry by invoking the requirements of NEPA and other environmental legislation, even though Congress has not explicitly given the agency that power. After a natural gas well exploded in Pennsylvania and sent possibly contaminated water into a river, the Natural Resources Defense Council and the state of New York pressured the Environmental Protection Agency to start regulating all natural gas and oil extraction by energy companies that used the controversial method of hydrological fracking. Surface water and groundwater were threatened, they argued, so EPA was obligated to regulate fracking under the Clean Water Act (Hobson 2011). Pennsylvania's natural gas industry complained that stretching EPA's mandate so far was not only unnecessary because state regulation (favoring energy companies) worked just fine, but also because if EPA got away with it, it would have a precedent for regulating just about everything anywhere anytime. This issue remains contested.

Sometimes interest groups create contention by convincing an agency whose jurisdiction intersects with that of another agency to claim sole jurisdiction. This pits agencies against each other. It recently happened when the Backcountry Horsemen Association convinced the US Forest Service to sue the National Park Service and the High Sierra Hikers Association, claiming that only the Forest Service could decide whether to permit or forbid the use of mules on Sierra Nevada camping trips (Tweed 2010, 96–97).

Limits of Influence

If every form of interest group influence on agency rule making was to be fully assessed, this chapter would never end. Suffice it to say that other efforts at fostering an open and transparent governing process have largely served to give interest groups more opportunities for influence. **Freedom of Information Act** (FOIA) and other "sunshine" requirements on agencies to make public most of the written materials, including e-mails, involved in rule making make it possible for lobbyists to track agency deliberation at almost every step. This means groups and their members have many opportunities to pressure agency officials into writing rules for the benefit of the interest group's members, either by directly pressuring agency officials or by threatening to get members of Congress involved or by filing lawsuits.

Despite this factor, there is little evidence that Congress can force an executive branch agency to adopt a rule it doesn't like. Congressional committees might try to influence agency decisions when the rules they promulgate are significantly different from what the committee wants, perhaps by holding public oversight hearings in which members of Congress can angrily accuse agency officials of ignoring Congress and the public (McCubbins, Noll, and Weingast 1987; Bawn 1997). Interest groups often play key roles in alerting committee legislators that agencies are going rogue, though they only do so when the groups do not themselves approve of what the agencies are doing (McCubbins and Schwartz 1984; Epstein and O'Halloran 1999). Yet there is little evidence that legislators can really rein in agencies (Balla 1998; Shipan 2004). Agency cultures are simply too deeply ingrained and their operations too complex for legislators to micromanage agency staff, especially when greater pressure on agencies can come from the president (Niskanen 1971; Moe 1987). Furthermore, the networks of political interests involved in issues are just too diverse and often at odds with each other for lawmakers to build enough unity to place intense pressure on an agency. In the end consistency between group interests and an agency's mission is the real key to executive branch influence.

■ CASE STUDY ■

Lobbying for the Roadless Rule

In the last years of the Clinton administration a number of interest groups launched what has been called the largest environmental advocacy campaign in history, and perhaps the first sophisticated use of Internet technology for grassroots advocacy, to protect those national forests and public lands still untouched by development.

STAGE ONE: BACKGROUND OF THE WILDERNESS CONFLICT

By the 1920s, roads were quickly being built all over the United States as a car culture began to emerge. Public lands agencies such as the Forest Service and the Park Service, along with the rest of the country, became caught up in the road-building craze (Sutter 2002). By building roads, and therefore creating easy access to public lands, these agencies opened the lands of the West, the mountain backcountry, and forests all over the nation for commercial and recreational use. Environmentalists like Aldo Leopold started to fear that if preserving some of the nation's still unspoiled, pristine lands was worthwhile, it had better be done fast by banning all future road development, while there was still wilderness to preserve. They established the Wilderness Society in 1935 to lobby the Forest Service to leave some land as wilderness.

But creating multiple-use land, or land designated for human use, is one of the Park Service's two goals as well as the Forest Service's main mission. This mission was too deeply ingrained in both agencies' cultures to allow them to be convinced that a lot more land should be closed to development (Nie 2004). So the Wilderness Society turned to Congress and in 1964 won passage of the Wilderness Act. Under this act Congress alone could require the Forest Service and Park Service to designate land as wilderness, where only roads absolutely necessary for management could be built, if at all.

The federal government owns enormous tracts of land in the western states, including most of Nevada and Utah, and suddenly a lot of this land was being walled off from mineral and energy development as well as tourism by the Wilderness Act (Skillen 2009). These were the keys to economic development in those states, and people there responded angrily in 1980 by electing to Congress many Republicans who were anti–public lands, an event now known as the Sagebrush Rebellion (Bosso 1991). The Sagebrush Rebellion made a policy of zero development of public lands and forests unthinkable because western Republicans in Congress now controlled committees with jurisdiction over government land agencies and insisted that these lands remain open for development (Nie 2009). The Wilderness Act required any new roadless lands and forests to be passed by Congress, but such bills were dead on arrival there, and western lawmakers took great pride in burying them.

STAGE TWO: THE EXECUTIVE BRANCH STRATEGY STARTS AT THE TOP

In the 1990s, interest groups like the National Audubon Society, Earthjustice, the Natural Resources Defense Council, and the Wilderness Society crafted an executive branch–oriented lobbying strategy called the Heritage Forests Campaign to pursue the preservation of undeveloped wilderness (Turner 2009). Pew Charitable Trusts, a philanthropic foundation, funded much of what became a $10 million campaign to convince executive branch officials that they had the administrative authority to protect forests and lands *without* legislation from Congress (Ring 2009a). Their first lobbying target was the man on top of the executive branch, President Bill Clinton.

By the late 90s Clinton was trying to find a legacy for his presidency but was hobbled by diminished public support after his impeachment. He needed environmental groups as much as they needed him. As Clinton's aide, George Frampton, the former head of the Wilderness Society, quietly worked with environmental groups to develop the idea of the president pressuring the

Forest Service into issuing a new rule to prevent road building in forests. They also convinced Clinton that he could use the Antiquities Act of 1906 to designate large pieces of public land as national monuments. President Theodore Roosevelt had used the Antiquities Act to stop development of Devil's Tower in Wyoming, so there was a precedent. Clinton agreed and used it to create the 1.9 million acre Grand Escalante Staircase in Utah as a nearly roadless national monument.

With the president also coming around to support a campaign to lobby the Forest Service, the Heritage Forests Campaign recruited several environmentally friendly religious organizations to broaden their base for the big push for roadless forests. Groups like Coalition on the Environment and Jewish Life crafted a letter to the president framing wilderness as a religious matter, which got them a rare meeting with John Podesta, Clinton's chief of staff. Podesta personally began working with Heritage Forests Campaign leaders to coordinate a massive grassroots campaign to pressure the Forest Service (Turner 2009).

STAGE THREE: PRESSURING THE FOREST SERVICE

In 1999, dozens of environmental organizations contributed their members' e-mail lists so the Heritage Forests Campaign could convince tens of thousands of activists to go to their Web site and send standardized e-mail postcards to the Forest Service demanding that it issue a roadless rule for hundreds of square miles of forests across the United States. The Heritage Forests Campaign also posted colorful banner ads on Yahoo.com and other Web sites, enticing casual users to visit their Web site, send an e-postcard, and then forward the link via e-mail to dozens of their friends (Turner 2009). Thousands responded. For their physical ground game, hundreds of student activists from the Heritage Forests Campaign's Green Corps were dispatched to malls and universities all across America to convince people to sign petitions and hand over their e-mail addresses to help the Heritage Forests Campaign become a true grassroots movement (Ring 2009a).

The beleaguered Forest Service agreed to consider a new roadless forests rule, and scoping meetings began in 1999. Activists, scientists, religious leaders, and even hunters and anglers were all encouraged by the Heritage Forests Campaign to go dominate these hearings. They came in overwhelming numbers, coming earlier than their opponents to take all of the speaking slots so that the Forest Service would only hear pro-wilderness demands (Ring

2009a). The Heritage Forests Campaign cleverly used new geographic information system software to find which scoping hearings were closest to which groups of advocates and direct them to the closest one, but also to make sure that there were always some advocates at every hearing (Turner 2009). The Heritage Forests Campaign's less organized opponents ended up with far less of a presence at the hearings than their numbers probably warranted.

A draft rule was published in 2000 at 796 pages; the public was given sixty-nine days to file comments (Nie 2004). President Clinton gave speeches invoking Teddy Roosevelt and his foresighted environmental efforts to help motivate activists to file comments supporting the rule. Of the 1.6 million comments received, which the campaign claimed was the most public comments on a proposed rule ever received, about 90 percent were nearly identical e-postcards and e-petitions supporting the rule (Ring 2009a). While identical e-mail and e-petitions technically count as one comment, when the Forest Service issued its final rule in early 2001 barring any future road building in 58.5 million acres of forest, it pointed critics of the agency and the rule to the mountains of comments the agency had received favoring the rule.

STAGE FOUR: THE NEVER-ENDING CONFLICT

The Heritage Forests Campaign won a major victory, but hardly the war. As I mentioned at the end of Chapter 6, struggles between competing interests rarely ever end. Roaring about radical environmentalists and activist agencies, congressional Republicans threatened to overrule the Forest Service with new legislation, but they could never muster the votes to do it. George W. Bush, the new president, placed a moratorium on all new administrative actions, which drastically slowed down but did not stop application of the roadless rule to miles of forests. The main theater of action, though, shifted to the federal courts. Several lawsuits were brought by conservative groups like the Mountain States Legal Foundation to overturn the rule, and then environmental groups brought more suits to force the Bush administration to fully implement the new rule (Ring 2009b). Both sides have had their successes and failures, but the new roadless rule remains the status quo today.

In Summary

Here is a summary of the chapter's key points:

- The president and executive branch agencies are often more influential in policy making than Congress, and as such are attractive lobbying targets.
- While agencies are lobbied more frequently than other parts of government, presidents are rarely lobbied, for they often do not need interest group support.
- Presidents are most in need of interest group support when their original electoral coalitions have deserted them or when they are too politically weak to pressure Congress into passing their agendas without support from interest groups on Capitol Hill.
- Efforts at creating government transparency and trying to involve the public more in rule making has made it easier for agencies to be lobbied by interest groups.
- The real key to an interest group's influencing an agency is to align its members' interests with the agency's mission and culture.

Is it easy for interest groups to influence agency rule making, or not easy enough? There seems to be a lingering concern about this question. Political scientist Cornelius Kerwin (1999, 159–160) points out that it was business interests in the late nineteenth century that began trying to use agency rules to reshape legislation they did not care for or extend the scope of legislation they liked. The notice and comments period imposed by the Administrative Procedures Act was to change this by empowering the public to watch agencies and influence rule making, but there is little evidence that any such inspired citizen vigilance has occurred. All that has happened is that more interest groups have learned how to pursue their members' interests through the institutionalized methods of communication with agencies.

In extensive work, political scientist Susan Yackee finds that interest groups may have even greater capacity to influence rules than had originally been suspected (Yackee 2006). Business and trade associations participate far more frequently than other group types and are far more influential over final rules (Yackee and Yackee 2006). Moreover, there is surprisingly little competition from other groups filing countercomments on proposed rules, meaning a fairly high degree of unanimity in comments pushing agencies in a particular direction is normal (McKay and Yackee 2007). In other words, significant fights during notice and comment periods pitting public interest and citizen groups against business interests are the exception rather than the rule. Notice and comment, and indeed most agency rule making, may assume a level playing field, but only one side tends to show up in strength. Many interests take a different tactic toward dealing with agencies: they go to court. It is not uncommon for agency heads to complain that most of what they now do is defend their rules in court, sometimes against litigation by all sides in a political dispute. As McCool (2002) described in the context of western water policy, often many marginalized interests, such as Native Americans, have little choice but to sue agencies because, in their opinion, agencies refuse to recognize their interests as legitimate.

CHAPTER EIGHT

Interest Groups
Going to Court

There is an often-told story about super-lobbyist Tom Corcoran going to the chambers of US Supreme Court justice Hugo Black to give his opinion on how a case ought to be decided (McKean 2004). When he realized Corcoran's intention, Black quickly ended the meeting and told the lobbyist never to speak to him again. Black then warned his fellow justices about Corcoran and recused himself from the case just because the conversation had taken place. So severe was Corcoran's breach of ethics that even Justice Felix Frankfurter, who as a law professor at Harvard University had started Corcoran on his Washington career, now snubbed him. While the incident hardly ended the career of one of Washington's most powerful men, it is a good example of how impervious the judicial branch tries to be to interest group influence. Members of Congress often want to work with lobbyists, the bureaucracy often must work with lobbyists, but the court tries to shut them out (Baum 2001, 89).

Still, many Americans believe the Supreme Court is fundamentally a political body no different from Congress. Whether or not the Court is a political body, groups are far from powerless when it comes to using it as a venue for pursuing their interests. While only a minority of interest groups, most notably the American Civil Liberties Union (ACLU), really specializes in lobbying the judicial branch, a significant number of groups, perhaps a majority, have at one time or another participated in some way before federal courts. Indeed, whereas it was once thought that interest groups only resorted to the judiciary when they were shut out of Congress and the executive branch, it is now clear that many powerful groups proactively go to court.

Shaping the Judiciary

In 1937 President Franklin Roosevelt declared war on the US Supreme Court after it struck down much of his early New Deal programs as unconstitutional. Since he could not change the minds of the justices, he decided to change the number of them by adding a few younger (and more New Deal–friendly) justices to "help" the older ones. Senators, who had to pass the court expansion legislation and then confirm new nominees, balked at such an obviously political maneuver, and Roosevelt's court-packing plan was shelved (Truman 1951, 490–491). Roosevelt's defeat, though, has not stopped interest groups from pursuing the same strategy. They have been trying to influence who becomes a judge since the Adams administration, when interests tied to the Federalist Party pressured Adams to appoint more federalist judges (Truman 1951, 490). And no wonder. Judicial scholar Thomas Hansford (2004b) shows that interest groups are more likely to pursue their goals in court when they believe judges share the same basic ideological beliefs as the groups' members because, unsurprisingly, they expect to win. But rather than wait for presidents to appoint sympathetic judges, some interest groups try to help the process along, or bring it to a stop, by influencing the **nomination and confirmation process**, the constitutional requirement that all judges and justices in the judicial branch be nominated for office by the president and confirmed by a vote of the Senate.

Judge Robert Bork is usually held up as an example of (or victim of, to many conservatives) successful interest group advocacy in the nominating process. Vigorous lobbying by liberal groups such as the ACLU and the National Organization for Women, which feared that Bork would roll back civil rights and abortion rights, led to a Senate vote against his nomination to the Supreme Court in 1987. A nomination that interest groups prevented from even getting off the ground was that of Harriet Miers. In 2005, President George W. Bush nominated Miers, then his White House counsel, to replace Sandra Day O'Connor. Not only was Miers opposed on the ideological left by interest groups, but she was also on the receiving end of much more damaging attacks from groups allied with Bush, such as Focus on the Family, who doubted her commitment to ending abortion. Bush withdrew Miers and nominated Samuel Alito instead.

Interest groups often involve themselves in high-profile Supreme Court nominations—145 lobbied on Bork and 81 on Clarence Thomas (DeGregorio and Rossotti 1995)—as well as appointments to lower levels of the federal judiciary (Caldeira, Hojnacki, and Wright 2000). They even attempt to influence appointments to the US Department of Justice. One such example is when thirty-six groups lobbied for the appointment of Edwin Meese to be Reagan's attorney general. These actions are not surprising: today's federal district judge or attorney general could be tomorrow's appointee to the court of appeals or the Supreme Court. Federal district judges very often make the only decision a case ever gets, and when rulings are appealed, their decisions are presumed to stand unless a compelling case is made otherwise. The Justice Department's solicitor general leads the government's legal team and enjoys the highest success rate before the Supreme Court. So lobbyists convince their members that lower-level judiciary and attorney general nominations matter—that the wrong judges will abuse the Constitution and the rights of the group's members—and lobbyists use that whipped-up anger to pressure senators to vote for or against nominees (Caldeira and Wright 1998).

Litigating for Policy Change: Risks and Rewards

Going to court is expensive and risky. It's expensive because lawyers experienced with the federal judicial system, especially the high court, charge a lot of money and often need to be retained for long periods of time. Going all the way to the Supreme Court can take years, but it is usually where interest groups want to end up. Individual plaintiffs may be satisfied with verdicts in lower federal courts on the merits of their cases, but interest groups are more interested in broad and lasting changes in **precedent**. Only the Supreme Court can create a new precedent that determines how the lower courts must interpret the law, including the Constitution, in future cases. It's also risky because it is hard to influence the opinions of judges and justices, especially when lobbyists cannot speak directly to them and there is no opportunity to earn their gratitude by contributing to elections or helping them serve some key constituency. Federal judges are not elected and thus have no constituents.

These two facts lead to a persistent belief among scholars that groups will not go to court unless there are no other options open to them (Olson 1990). True, interest groups excluded from the deliberations of congressional committees because they do not serve a recognized constituency or give contributions in elections can still try to use logic to convince judges of the merits of their policy positions. Court cases usually are challenges to the status quo, which makes them very risky bets because the status quo tends to win. Between 1946 and 2009 only 2 percent of all cases before the US Supreme Court seeking to overturn existing precedent (a status quo) succeeded, and only 6 percent of efforts to declare a federal, state, or local law unconstitutional succeeded.[1] Only a tiny fraction of cases appealed to the Supreme Court are heard. Interest groups must be desperate indeed to pin their hopes on the judiciary, but for those with deep enough pockets and a lot of persistence, the payoff can be enormous.

Perhaps the best-known example of an interest group overturning long-standing policy by working cases up to the Supreme Court is the National Association for the Advancement of Colored People (NAACP) and the public school desegregation cases. Ironically, the precedent of separate but equal laid down in *Plessy v. Ferguson* (1896) affirming racial segregation was the result of group litigation against segregation that backfired badly, which shows the risk of raising an issue before the Court in the first place. New Orleans–based Comité des Citoyens (Committee of Citizens) sponsored Homer Plessy's lawsuit against the East Louisiana Railroad and the state's laws requiring people of color to sit in specially designated rail cars. Plessy chose not to sit there, claiming the law violated his rights under the Fourteenth Amendment. The case went to the Supreme Court, but the Court ruled against Plessy by finding that segregation did not violate the Constitution as long as the public facilities provided were equal in quality.

The NAACP formed in 1909 to specifically use the judiciary to advance the cause of desegregation, which they felt would receive an icy reception on Capitol Hill and in the White House. Led by Thurgood Marshall, the NAACP's Legal Defense Fund sponsored several cases in which litigants were chosen not only because they could claim to have been harmed by segregation, and thus had **standing** (the legal right) to sue, but also because they resided in judicial districts likely to overturn *Plessy* (Vose 1959; O'Connor and McFall 1992). The first step in using a **litigation strategy** is selecting a **judicial district** that appears ideologically disposed toward the group's policy goals. After fifteen years of work, NAACP finally succeeded with the famous *Brown v. Board of Education* (1954) decision, but their success holds as much warning as promise for other interest groups considering the same strategy. Changing the status quo through the courts can succeed, but the NAACP only found success after committing enormous time and resources, and even then it took favorable political circumstances, such as the emergence of an ideologically sympathetic Supreme Court, to succeed. Indeed, perceptions of the policy preferences of the Court's justices, and their interest in engaging in the types of cases crucial to the interest group, have frequently been given as the primary reason for choosing to pursue policy goals in the judicial arena in the first place (Hansford 2004b). A more recent example of this strategy is the successful efforts of gun owners' rights groups to get a gun-permissive interpretation of the Second Amendment from a conservative-leaning Court, which I discuss in the case study at the end of the chapter.

Ideology and Interest Group Litigation

Much of the growth in litigation as a lobbying strategy came from activists who wanted to see more government intervention in society. Caught up in the heady days of the Kennedy and early Johnson administrations, when new public policy was considered the solution to social problems, a generation of Ivy League–trained young lawyers decided to direct their talents toward political activism rather than business careers (Vogel 1989, 97). Older organizations preferred working with Congress and the bureaucracy rather than risk the uncertainty of going to court (Morag-Levine 2003), but these ambitious lawyers believed the Supreme Court of the 1950s and 1960s under Chief Justice Earl Warren was willing to provide them with a constitutional foundation for government activism. They opened their own political law firms, such as the Environmental Defense Fund, National Women's Law Center, Institute for Justice, and Prisoners' Rights, to create new policy through lawsuits (they also have their own association, the National Lawyers Guild). These lawyers and organizations likely assumed that the justices on the Court were simply casting votes based on the same politically liberal beliefs they themselves shared, especially when there was no clear precedent. Years of research has found their assumption to be justified.[2]

Success in expanding civil rights, environmental protection, consumer protection, criminal rights, and the rights of women demonstrated clearly just how successful a judicial advocacy strategy could be when coupled to an ideologically sympathetic Supreme Court. So it is no surprise that when Richard Nixon and Gerald Ford started appointing more conservative justices in the 1970s, new, more conservative public interest law firms emerged hoping to use the judiciary to limit the role of government (Epstein 1986). Funded by business interests and conservative-leaning foundations, organizations such as the Pacific Legal Foundation and Washington Legal Foundation hoped to employ the Left's own tactics against it by using lawsuits that would give the increasingly conservative Supreme Court a chance to articulate a much stricter interpretation of the Constitution's Interstate Commerce Clause and Bill of Rights.

The **Interstate Commerce Clause** gives the federal government the authority to regulate business activity across state lines and had come to be the constitutional basis for most of its wide regulatory authority, whether it was clearly related to interstate commerce or not. The Bill of Rights also had become a source of new protections for those accused of crimes, which upset pro–law enforcement conservatives. But perhaps the greatest affront to conservatives, and their best evidence of liberal interest groups and Court gone wild, was *Griswold v. Connecticut* (1965), in which Justice William O. Douglas held that the Constitution implies, rather than specifies in its text, a right to personal privacy—a decision that was then used to justify a woman's right to have an abortion in *Roe v. Wade* (1973).

Even during the Reagan years, though, conservative public interest law firms did not quite equal their liberal counterparts in judicial advocacy. Scholars Karen O'Connor and Bryan McFall (1992) found that liberal groups were involved in 37 percent of Supreme Court cases from 1981 to 1987, either sponsoring cases or filing amicus briefs (see below), while conservative groups were only involved in 26 percent. Why conservative law firms were not as prominent during the Reagan presidency as one might expect, they argued, was because there was less perceived need for them. President Reagan was reshaping the entire federal court system with conservative appointees, and his solicitor general's office in the Justice Department was in a much better position to lead the conservative litigation charge than any interest group. Conservative lawyers found jobs in Reagan's Justice Department much more exciting than working for organizations outside of the administration. By the 1990s, however, out-of-power conservatives looked increasingly to the conservative Supreme Court as a preferred venue for advocacy against President Clinton's policies, and the number of lawsuits filed by conservative law firms increased.

Jurisdiction of Judicial Advocacy

Just because members of an interest group believe themselves to be wronged by existing court precedent or government policy does not mean they can sue the government in federal court. The courts may not actually have the legal jurisdiction to hear the case. When something happens that violates both state and federal law, the federal courts often cede jurisdictional responsibility to the states. This is not a problem for an interest group per se—it can sue in state court just as easily as in federal court—but it is a serious impediment if the group is trying to change federal law, which would apply to the entire nation rather than just the state. It is certainly a problem if the group wants to change Supreme Court precedent regarding how the Constitution is to be interpreted by all federal judges. Interest groups are usually going for the big payoff of nation-spanning rulings from the high court, so it is a major setback if their case ends up in a state system. However, while the American Civil Liberties Union may be good at convincing federal courts to take a case, many interest groups—even ambitious ones—don't have the experience and expert legal talent needed to do the same. But they can get some help from Congress.

To a considerable extent, judicial jurisdiction is determined by Congress, so it is unsurprising to find interest groups lobbying the legislative branch to increase or decrease the responsibilities of the judicial branch to make it easier to change national policy through the federal courts (or harder, if the group is defending the status quo). Part of the reason environmental groups benefitted so much from the enactment of the National Environmental Policy Act and the Endangered Species Act was that these laws extended federal judicial authority deep into land and water issues that had previously been just state and local concerns. Now, suddenly, it was possible to sue businesses as well as state and local governments in federal courts that environmentalists believed were more sympathetic to their causes (Nie 2008). Recall from the previous chapter that failure of an administrative agency to conduct a proper environmental impact statement or reach out to stakeholders, as indicated in its record of decision, is grounds for a lawsuit.

A similar approach was taken in the 1960s and 70s by attorneys' groups, such as the American Trial Lawyers Association, that pushed for changes in tort law to lower the threshold of harm necessary to bring suit in federal court when the alleged negligence of businesses or individuals was believed to have harmed somebody. Some interest groups have taken this a step further by convincing Congress to require that certain cases be decided by judges rather than juries (or vice versa) under the presumption that judges are more (or less) sympathetic to their arguments (Orren 1985). The influence that Congress has over judicial jurisdiction allows its members to better aid their interest group allies—thought federal judges probably don't enjoy the greater workload.

Standing to Advocate

Oliver Brown was the plaintiff named in *Brown v. Board of Education*, but most people probably think of the NAACP as the winning party in the lawsuit. Why is the interest group's name not in the case title? Because the NAACP could not bring the lawsuit directly, nor can most interest groups.

Interest groups can only sponsor somebody else, but that is more than enough to pursue member interests in court. The judiciary's rules of standing determine who has the right to file a lawsuit and be the plaintiff, and usually these require individuals to show that they have been directly harmed by a law passed by Congress, a rule promulgated by an agency, or the actions of another individual or organization (Baum 2001, 90–91).

The NAACP could not file an antisegregation case because as an organization it could not claim to have been harmed. Instead its strategists convinced thirteen parents to enroll their children in schools only accepting white children. Oliver Brown, for instance, tried to enroll his daughter, Linda, in segregated Sumner Elementary but was denied by the Topeka Board of Education. Now Brown could claim that he had been directly harmed by segregation policy and sue the school board. But lawsuits are very expensive, and so NAACP covered the cost and provided legal representation, much of it in the person of their chief lawyer, Thurgood Marshall—which was always NAACP's plan. Success breeds imitation, so it is no surprise that most of the major cases before the Court now are sponsored by one or more interest groups helping somebody who meets the standing requirements (Epstein 1993).

The 1960s and 1970s seem to have been a golden age for left-leaning interest groups seeking to articulate new rights for disadvantaged social groups, especially in the courts. The Supreme Court significantly loosened the standing rules in these years, making it easier for ideological, cause-oriented citizen and public interest groups to sue businesses and the government by sponsoring private individuals, who now had lower thresholds for meeting the harm qualifications (Orren 1976). One of the most dramatic expansions in standing rights came in the Endangered Species Act, which permitted interest groups to bring suit on behalf of threatened animal species, even though it was the animals being directly harmed and not the group's members. Pioneering this strategy was the Environmental Defense Fund, which helped several biologists sue the Interior Department to stop the building of Tellico Dam on the Little Tennessee River in the 1970s to save the endangered snail darter fish. The Audubon Society and the Sierra Club Legal Defense Fund similarly sued to save spotted owls in Washington and Oregon from extinction as a result of excessive logging of forests in the 1970s and 80s (Boyt 1993).

The loosening of requirements for standing has, unsurprisingly, swelled the amount of group participation before the courts and made litigation an indispensable weapon in every interest group's arsenal.[3] Consequently, many large interest groups, other than those that focus almost exclusively on legal work like the ACLU, Environmental Defense Fund, and Washington Legal Foundation, have now opened legal divisions to supplement their regular lobbying operations. Examples include the aforementioned Sierra Club Legal Defense Fund and the legal affairs division of the National Association of Realtors. But stretching the so-called zone of interest in the standing rules has made it a little difficult to determine just how the claims of harm made by a plaintiff can include other, third-party litigants that have managed to inject themselves into a case (Reitz 2002; Lindquist and Cross 2009). Conservatives, in particular, complain that the rules of standing are being abused by liberal interest groups and have tried to narrow the zone of interest, with Reagan-era appointees significantly less likely to grant standing in lawsuits against corporations or the government in which a party's claim of harm is not entirely clear (Rowland and Todd 1991).

One last point: standing to sue is not just a way to gain redress of grievances; it is also proof of political legitimacy. The standing of women and minorities before the courts itself was a heavily fought issue in the nineteenth and early twentieth centuries. In the infamous *Dred Scott* decision of 1857, an escaped slave was denied standing to sue for his freedom because the Supreme Court decided that he was property instead of a person. While the Constitution's Fourteenth Amendment subsequently conferred citizenship on everyone born in the United States, which would presumably include standing to sue, the recognition of these rights is slow and unclear even today (Ritter 2000). Do human fetuses have standing in court, as some antiabortion interest groups claim (McHugh 1992)? Standing, or lack thereof, also determines whether political leaders can be held accountable. A federal judge denied interest groups, and even the US Government Accountability Office, standing to sue Vice President Dick Cheney over public access to the records of his National Energy Policy Development Group (Halstead 2003).[4]

Who Sues and Why

Now to take a broader look at trends in interest group advocacy in the courts. As Figure 8.1 shows, it is significant but not consistent. Data on US Supreme Court cases from the 1946 to the 2009 terms assembled by judicial scholar Harold Spaeth and his colleagues show that direct group litigation, meaning lawsuits in which the interest group is named as either the plaintiff or the respondent, has grown only sporadically since the end of World War II.[5] And it was never common. Interest groups were litigants in only 8 percent of the

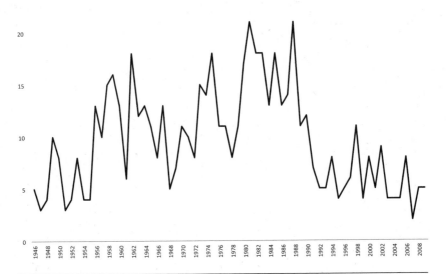

FIGURE 8.1   Number of Interest Groups Involved in Supreme Court Cases, 1946–2009
Source: Supreme Court Data Base (2011)

5,270 cases won by the plaintiff and in only 8 percent of the 2,975 cases won by the respondent. As you can see in the figure, interest groups' direct involvement increased more or less steadily from 1946 to 1962, fell drastically in the later 1960s, peaked again in the mid-1970s, went down and then went up to hit its highest peak in the 1980s, fell dramatically in the 1990s (as the total cases heard by the high court fell), and has remained relatively low since then.

In Figure 8.2, I break this trend line into the number of petitioner and respondent interest groups filing each year, but the figure requires some careful interpretation. Almost every case the Supreme Court hears is an **appeal,** so the organization listed as respondent, the defending party, on a case is likely the original plaintiff that brought the lawsuit in the first place. Because of this ambiguity, it is hard to draw clear conclusions from Figure 8.2. It may well be that the rise in the number of respondent groups in the 1980s is actually evidence of an increase in organizations suing the government. That explanation makes sense, given the political environment of the 1980s, in which liberal-leaning consumer and environmental interest groups frequently fought with President Reagan. They were not entirely shut out of Congress because the House was still under Democratic control, but Reagan

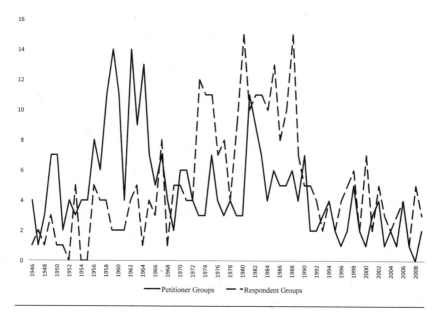

FIGURE 8.2 Number of Petitioner and Respondent Groups Involved in Supreme Court Cases, 1946–2009

aggressively tried to advance his policies through executive and administrative authority, which liberal groups could only challenge in court.

The trend in lawsuits by citizen groups, public interest law firms, and labor unions supports this explanation. Figure 8.3 shows the 1950s and 60s as the golden age of labor union litigation. After the anti-union Taft-Hartley Act in 1947, organized labor found itself increasingly in positions where it had to sue to overturn, or at least limit, anti-union legislation coming out of the Republican congresses. During the 1970s and 80s, though, there was a marked increase in citizen group and public interest law firm suits, which spiked during the later years of Republican presidents Nixon and Ford, and then again during the Reagan presidency, especially in the late 1980s, after Republicans lost the Senate and had to rely on administrative actions that liberal groups then tried to block in court.

Remember that conservative public interest groups were not strongly involved with the courts during the 1980s because much of their legal attention was focused on the Justice Department. So much of the legal advocacy in the judicial branch came from the left. The late 1960s and early 1970s was when these left-leaning public interest law firms almost exclusively pursued

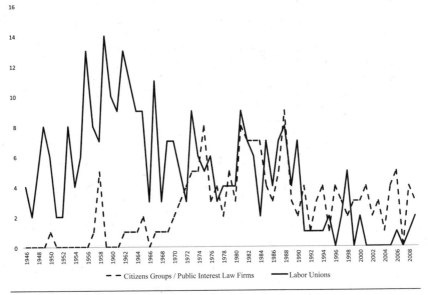

FIGURE 8.3   Number of Citizens Groups/Public Interest Law Firms and Labor
Unions in Supreme Court Cases, 1946–2009

ideological causes in the judicial branch, starting with Ralph Nader's Public
Citizen Litigation Group, funded largely from settlements with the companies
it sued. Along with organizations like the Environmental Defense Fund and
Natural Resources Defense Council, it saw the courts as not only another
venue for pursuing its mission but the only meaningful venue during the
Reagan years.

Some issues attract more interest group litigation than others. I break out
the litigation data in Table 8.1 by the number of groups involved in suits
within several general issue areas. Some issues hardly attract any group litigation at all. Civil rights, federalism, the extent of judicial power, and First
Amendment issues, though, clearly attract a lot of interest groups, along
with economic and labor issues (second column). Cause-oriented citizen
groups and public interest law firms (third column) are also concerned with
economic activity, but even more so with First Amendment civil liberties.
They are concerned with personal privacy and the scope of judicial power.
Freedom of speech, religion, and the press also concern these groups, along
with the right to an attorney, rights to privacy against potentially intrusive
law enforcement, equal protection, fair wages, discrimination, and political
representation. Labor unions are, unsurprisingly, primarily concerned with

Issue Area	All Interest Groups	Citizens Groups / Public Interest Law Firms	Labor Unions
Criminal Procedure	12	2	10
Civil Rights	37	13	16
First Amendment (civil liberties)	67	40	19
Due Process	8	4	0
Privacy	23	20	0
Attorneys	13	5	3
Unions	158	2	156
Economic Activity	110	38	8
Judicial Power	113	36	45
Federalism	58	3	51
Interstate Relations	1	0	0
Federal Taxation	9	2	0
Other Issues	1	1	0

TABLE 8.1   Interest Group Litigation Before the US Supreme Court by Issue
Source: Supreme Court Data Base (2011)

economic issues, but also federalism cases because many states have moved aggressively to limit union power. Unions have fought to keep issues important to them in federal venues rather than in the states.

The hard part is determining whether all of this interest group involvement actually affects the outcomes in cases. If the decisions of lower courts can be classified as ideologically liberal or conservative, on which side are interest group litigators most likely to be? The first two rows in Table 8.2 show that more interest groups are involved in a lower court case with a liberal decision rather than a conservative one. Whether group lobbyists *wanted* a liberal decision is unknown, but since the bulk of citizen and public interest groups tend to lean left (Berry 1999), their involvement just might be pushing a few decisions in that direction. This is not because they had any special influence over a judge, but because interest groups that specialize in the judiciary know which judicial districts will look favorably on their suit,

	All Groups	Citizens Groups / Public Interest Law Firms	Labor Unions
Lower court's decision is liberal	323	120	135
Lower court's decision is conservative	283	44	174
Supreme Court's decision is liberal	291	60	154
Supreme Court's decision is conservative	320	106	155
Court's decision did not change precedent	604	164	307
Court's decision changed precedent	11	4	3
Court ruled law was constitutional	579	143	307
Court ruled law was not constitutional	36	25	3
Plaintiff won	407 of 5,270 cases	122 of 5,270 cases	199 of 5,270 cases
Respondent won	208 of 2,975 cases	46 of 2,975 cases	111 of 2,975 cases

TABLE 8.2   Supreme Court Case Outcomes and Types of Interest Groups Involved
Source: Supreme Court Data Base (2011)

how to package the case for that judge or jury, and a dozen other things that only come with deep pockets and, perhaps more importantly, long experience litigating before the courts.

What about Supreme Court decisions? When it comes to an ideological connection between group advocacy and the Court's decisions, Table 8.2 suggests that more groups are involved in cases with conservative-leaning decisions than those with liberal-leaning ones, and that more citizen and public interest groups are involved in cases with conservative decisions than those with liberal decisions. While there certainly are some conservative public interest law firms, like the Washington Legal Foundation and Mountain States

Legal Foundation, this still suggests that the predominantly left-leaning public interest groups lose more than they win before the high court. After spending so much time and effort to get a case before the Supreme Court, is it really worth it? If the goal is to overturn precedent or have an act of Congress or a state legislature's law ruled unconstitutional, then the fifth through eighth rows in Table 8.2 suggest that it is perhaps not worth it. Out of respect for separation of powers, the Court infrequently strikes down statutes enacted by elected legislatures, which was a problem for liberal groups in the conservative 1980s. An even rarer event is the Court overturning its own precedents binding the rest of the federal judiciary.

In sum, when public interest groups are the challengers of the status quo, there is little evidence that they are getting anywhere at the Supreme Court. Of course when it comes to the consumer protection and environmental laws that these groups convinced Congress to enact in the 1960s and 70s, they are the ones defending the status quo, and they have the advantage. Basically the judiciary is a conservative institution in that judges and justices defer to the legislative and executive branches when they can, so challenging any policy status quo in the judiciary is an uphill battle. The payoff is enormous when successful, but it is a significant gamble of time and resources. Just look at the last two rows in Table 8.2. Petitioner groups win far more than respondent groups, but remember that in an appellate court it is likely that the petitioner group was originally the respondent and is actually defending the status quo! It is a common lesson in this book: status quo policies are hard to overthrow.

Friends of the Court: Filing Amicus Briefs

The most frequent way interest groups lobby the judicial branch is by filing **amicus curiae**, or "friend of the court," briefs, though surprisingly, this method may have even less impact than case sponsorship. The federal courts have long permitted individuals and organizations with a demonstrated stake in the outcome of a case to file briefs (legal arguments supporting the plaintiff or the defendant / respondent) with permission from the parties involved or from the Court itself (Baum 2001, 91–92). The idea is that courts are open to additional information on what social and economic interests in society might be affected by their decisions in cases, as well as additional arguments about what precedents are applicable, though filers are supposed to provide new information rather than repeat what has already been said (Spriggs and

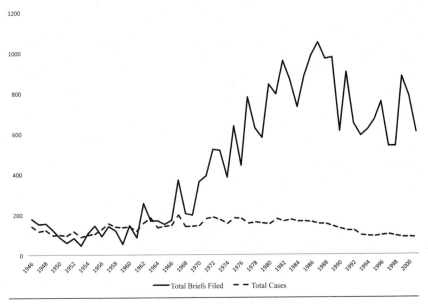

FIGURE 8.4   Total Number of Amicus Briefs (Merits) Filed in Supreme Court Cases, 1946–2001
Source: Paul Collins data set

Wahlbeck 1997, 366). Interest groups happily provide it. Figure 8.4 shows all of the amicus briefs filed by interest groups on all Supreme Court cases from 1946 to 2001, using data collected by judicial scholars Joseph Kearney, Thomas Merrill, and Paul Collins. Until the mid-1960s the number of amicus briefs was fairly equal to the number of cases heard by the Supreme Court (also shown in Figure 8.4 for comparison), but around 1966 the number of amicus briefs filed abruptly shot up over cases, peaking in the 1980s at over four times more briefs than cases. This is unsurprising, since the interest group explosion in Washington, including the new public interest law firms that specialized in lobbying the courts, occurred in the late 1960s.

As Figure 8.5 shows, there is no real difference in the trends between briefs filed on the petitioner side verses the respondent, though the number of "other" briefs filed by interest groups that believe they have something to say without actually supporting either side rose in the 1970s. In 1980, 841 amicus briefs were filed with the Supreme Court, which is more than the entire number of group-sponsored cases reaching the high court in the second half of the twentieth century. Clearly this is the most popular form of interest group participation before the Court, with nearly every case today accompanied by a pile of amicus briefs (Collins 2007, 61).

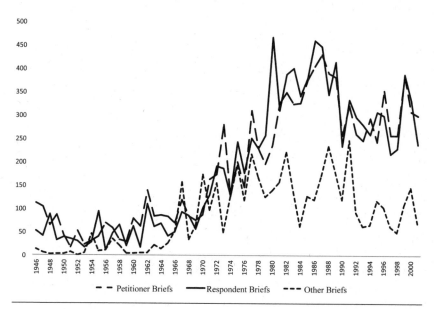

FIGURE 8.5   Number of Petitioner, Respondent, and Other Amicus Briefs
Source: Collins, 2007

The lower courts get interest group briefs too. Yet while the sheer number of amicus briefs filed is often greater at the federal district courts and the US Court of Appeals, the percentage of cases accompanied by amicus briefs fell as low as 6 percent of all cases before the appeals court in the 1990s (Martinek 2006, 807). The vast majority of federal cases live or die on the decisions of district or appeals court judges, but most interest groups are primarily interested in the high-profile, high-stakes battles before the Supreme Court, where precedent is set and questions of constitutionality decided with finality.

More seasoned interest groups, though, know the value of influencing appellate court decisions. Suits against the federal government are typically heard in the DC appellate circuit, but if one hopes for a more ideologically liberal appellate decision, then the Ninth Circuit in San Francisco is the venue of choice. When the Ninth Circuit takes up a case even tangentially connected to a group's member interests, the group may see an opportunity to influence the decision with a brief. And when it comes to amicus briefs in the appellate courts, there is some evidence that briefs filed by interest groups on behalf of appellants (those seeking to overturn district court decisions) may be a little more persuasive than those filed on behalf of appellees (Collins and Martinek

2010). So a clever liberal interest group that wants to try to influence a decision overturning a district court decision might sit it out if the case is in the DC circuit, but file a brief if it arises in the allegedly more liberal Ninth Circuit to influence the decision.

Influence or Cheerleading?

What do Supreme Court justices think of all these briefs? Do they care about these piles of third-party information? Most scholars are doubtful. In perhaps one of the most influential studies of amicus briefs, political scientists Gregory Caldeira and John Wright (1988) found that the only real influence amicus briefs had on the Court was on the question of **certiorari**—the decision made by the justices of the Court on which cases to hear. Supreme Court justices make two crucial decisions per case each term. The first is granting certiorari, and the second is the actual verdict. Caldeira and Wright claim that it is only on the first decision, the decision on what cases the Court will hear that term, that amicus briefs may be influential. And it is not the brief content that matters, but the sheer number of briefs filed for or against the decision to hear the case. The high court wants to hear cases of profound importance to the nation, but the justices do not have time to carefully read all of the information out there surrounding the thousands of cases appealed to them each year. They do not have time to read amicus briefs either. But a large pile of briefs on their desks may tip off justices that a case is significant because so many social and economic interests felt it necessary to file briefs on it. The justices are perhaps a little more inclined to accept it for that reason. Ironically, that means interest groups filing briefs against hearing a case are actually making it more likely the case will be heard.

This cynical view of amicus brief filing suggests lobbyists are ill-advised to spend time and money crafting arguments when only a brief's existence matters. So it is not surprising that political scientists James Spriggs and Paul Wahlbeck (1997) found in the Court's 1992 term that three-fourths of all amicus briefs filed just regurgitated information already found in plaintiff and respondent briefs. Moreover, they found that any new arguments in the amicus briefs were rarely even mentioned by the Court in their final decisions, a good indicator that the justices did not care much about the content and probably never read them. Why would interest group lawyers bother to even file briefs when it appears that the Court could not care less?

Thomas Hansford makes this all even murkier with his finding that interest groups tend to file briefs with the Supreme Court when they believe the ideological balance of the Court already favors their positions (2004b). This means interest groups are using resources to write briefs to convince judges to do something they are already likely to do. This might make sense if briefs influence the reasoning behind the Court's decision, but it is hard to imagine this is the answer if justices are not carefully reading them. Since many amicus briefs tend to say the same thing (Caldeira and Wright 1990), all that is being created is an echo chamber. Perhaps briefs to ideologically friendly justices are useful when they do not know much about the case's subject matter (Hansford 2004a; Collins 2007), but for the most part amicus briefs appear to be nothing more than legal cheerleading—competitive cheerleading, actually, for it appears that more briefs filed on one side of a case means more briefs will be filed on the other side (Solowiej and Collins 2009). So more and more briefs echoing each other are appearing on both sides of a case cheering the justices on, except that the justices themselves are mostly not listening.

A more satisfying explanation for why so many briefs are being submitted, one highlighted so many times already in this book, is that filing amicus briefs is all about group maintenance—pleasing current members and attracting potential members—not about changing policy. Organizations lobbying on the abortion issue, for instance, were found to be using their participation in Supreme Court cases to influence public opinion and fire up their activists (Wlezien and Goggin 1993). In other words, filing briefs, regardless of what they may or may not accomplish, is a high-visibility but low-cost form of lobbying (O'Connor and McFall 1992). Many Supreme Court cases receive enormous public attention. That is why large numbers of briefs appear to convince the Court to accept such cases on appeal. When highly salient, politically divisive issues are before the Court, such as abortion, what concerned interest group dares not be seen as involved? Not participating sends the message to members and congressional allies that the interest group and its lobbyist are spineless and ineffective, and therefore not worth supporting with dues and access. Yet because case sponsorship is enormously expensive and Court decisions are well outside of a group's control, participating by filing an amicus brief gives the appearance of pursuing member interests before the Court in a way that is relatively cheap, even if it is ineffectual. How would group members know better?

■ CASE STUDY ■

Second Amendment Lobbying

One of the most divisive issues in American society is gun ownership and the Constitution's Second Amendment. This case study details the story of the lobbying campaign for a gun ownership–friendly interpretation of that amendment.

STAGE ONE: LOBBYING TO SHAPE THE COURT

From the standpoint of many ideological conservatives, the 1950s and 60s were years when the US Supreme Court aggressively overturned precedents of the past regarding Constitutional interpretation to further an ideology that was, in their view, more about supporting government activism as a solution to social problems than about protecting existing freedoms and limiting government power (Kahn 1999). That the Court was being a political body more than a disinterested and unbiased interpreter of the law was not the problem for conservatives so much as it was seen as consistently ruling against conservative principles, such as establishing the right to privacy that became the foundation of *Roe v. Wade* in 1973. Conservatives felt that this situation needed to be changed. Richard Nixon, Ronald Reagan, and both Bush administrations worked to build a more conservative judiciary by appointing lawyers and law professors known for their support of limited government to federal judgeships, important offices in the Justice Department, and the Supreme Court (O'Connor and McFall 1992; Walker and Epstein 1993, 21). Many appointees were affiliated with the Federalist Society, an organization known for advocating the idea that the Constitution's text should only be interpreted as it would have been understood when ratified in the late eighteenth century—a view that, they claimed, supports limits on governmental powers.[6]

Throughout the 1980s and 90s, a variety of cause-oriented interest groups lobbied the Senate over the confirmation of judges to the federal courts and especially the Supreme Court. Nominees' known or assumed positions on issues like abortion, civil rights, affirmative action, civil rights of plaintiffs, and sometimes even gun ownership rights were given as reasons by lobbyists and activists to confirm or reject nominees (Caldeira, Hojnacki, and Wright 2000, 55). Some nominees were defeated, such as Kenneth Ryskamp and Bernard Siegan to the court of appeals and most famously Robert Bork to the Supreme Court. But the vast majority of nominees were approved, so Republican presidents and conservative interest groups like the Christian Coalition, Focus on the Family, and the Washington Legal Foundation were largely victorious in reshaping the Supreme Court and the rest of the judiciary along conservative lines (Walker and Epstein 1993, 154).

STAGE TWO: DEVELOPING THE LITIGATION STRATEGY

While it is natural to assume that prominent interest groups like the National Rifle Association (NRA) led the charge to bring Second Amendment and gun ownership litigation before a now more conservative Supreme Court, the strategy was actually developed and executed at the Cato Institute, a libertarian think tank (Doherty 2009). A number of state and city governments had enacted laws limiting the right to own and carry guns. One of the most onerous, from a gun rights point of view, was in the District of Columbia. In 1976 the District's city council passed a law forbidding residents from owning handguns and automatic or semiautomatic weapons. Legal guns kept at home had to be unloaded and disarmed by a trigger-locking device, which many residents argued made it impossible to use a gun in self-defense because it took too long to get it ready to fire.

Attorney Robert Levy at Cato decided that the severity of the DC law made it ideal for a lawsuit. He did not own a gun, meaning neither he nor Cato had standing to sue, so he recruited a number of people in DC to be plaintiffs in a case (Liptak 2007). One recruit was Dick Heller, who had originally tried to get the NRA to sponsor a case, but the NRA felt going to court was way too risky, that a negative decision by the Court would set back the whole cause of gun rights (Weiss 2007). The Court actually did not have much of a history with cases related to the Second Amendment, and the few existing decisions supported both restricted and unrestricted gun ownership (Halstad 2008). Even with more conservative justices, it was difficult to tell how the Court might rule.

In 2003, Heller and five other DC residents backed by the Cato Institute filed suit in federal district court arguing that the city law violated their

Second Amendment rights. The district court judge dismissed the suit, but an appeal to the DC Court of Appeals overturned the dismissal and then struck down the law as unconstitutional (Halstead 2008). When the District of Columbia challenged the standing of the plaintiffs to sue, saying they could not convincingly claim to have been harmed by the law, the Court of Appeals affirmed its decision in favor of Heller.

STAGE THREE: AT THE SUPREME COURT

The District of Columbia appealed to the US Supreme Court, and in 2007 the Court announced it would hear it, granting certiorari. The case quickly became very high profile and attracted the attention of many interest groups whose members were deeply interested in the Second Amendment, gun ownership, and public safety issues generally. Forty-seven groups filed amicus briefs supporting Heller and Cato (Coyle 2008), including the NRA and the Fraternal Order of Police. Twenty groups filed briefs against it, including the Brady Campaign to Prevent Gun Violence, the Anti-Defamation League, and the Educational Fund to Stop Gun Violence.

To a considerable extent, arguments came down to the meaning of the comma in the Second Amendment separating "A well regulated militia being necessary to the security of a free state," from "the right of the people to keep and bear arms shall not be infringed." Heller's lawyers argued that the Second Amendment gave an absolute right to unrestricted individual gun ownership, while opponents argued that it only applied to people serving in a state militia, presumably a state national guard (Halstead 2008). Oral arguments were heard by the Court in March 2008, and its decision was handed down on June 26 of the same year.

STAGE FOUR: RULING AND AFTERMATH

In a 5–4 decision, the Court ruled for Heller, giving a victory to the Cato Institute and, to a lesser extent, other gun rights advocacy groups like the NRA. The Court ruled that the Second Amendment granted an individual the fundamental right to own a gun in the home and thus struck down the DC law as unconstitutional. Just like all of the other examples and case studies used in this book, the Supreme Court's ruling was anything but the last word in the political conflict over gun rights. The NRA, probably reacting to criticism from its own members that it had nearly sat out the biggest Second Amendment case in American history, promptly filed lawsuits against Chicago and

San Francisco over their handgun bans (Halstead 2008, 21). Dozens of other lawsuits, many sponsored by interest groups, appeared in federal courts immediately after the ruling, challenging many local laws banning guns, though, surprisingly, challenges to these laws have largely failed (Winkler 2009).

■ ■ ■

In Summary

Here is a summary of the major points in this chapter:

- Courts can eliminate laws passed by Congress and administrative rules issued by executive branch agencies, so many interest groups believe it is to their advantage to pursue their members' interests in court, especially public interest groups set up as law firms.
- The ideological leanings of judges are usually believed to determine how cases will be decided, especially at the Supreme Court, so many interest groups lobby the Senate to confirm or reject the confirmation of judicial branch appointees.
- Opportunities to use lawsuits to overturn a law or administrative rule are shaped by the jurisdiction of the federal courts over areas of policy making as well as rules regarding the right (standing) to sue, so many interests group lobby to shape those rules.
- It takes a lot of time and money to sponsor cases all the way to the Supreme Court, and there is no guarantee regarding the outcome, so many interest groups are reluctant to pursue a direct litigation strategy.
- The most widely used strategy for lobbying the Supreme Court is filing amicus briefs, legal arguments designed to convince the Court to take or reject a case and how to decide the case if it is accepted for a hearing, but there is no evidence that the justices ever read these briefs or that they have any influence on how the justices make decisions.

Litigation is expensive and risky, so interest groups are only likely to choose this path when they think the courts, especially the US Supreme Court, are likely to rule in their favor, just as the NAACP felt its time had come in the 1950s, when the ideological tenor of the Court changed to favor expanding the rights of disadvantaged people. It is the alignment of interests that drives judicial lobbying strategies, just as it does for interest group lobbying everywhere else. Yet there are crucial differences. Judges and justices cannot be personally lobbied, so lobbyists cannot coordinate strategy with them as they do with members of Congress. Instead, lobbyists must carefully watch the courts and anticipate how a judge might rule on cases important to group members.

Another crucial difference is how court ideologies might be shaped. Federal judges are perilous to an interest group because of their lifetime appointments. Get the wrong one on the bench, and the interest group is stuck for a long time. Consequently, interest groups take elections to the White House and Senate even more seriously because who sits in the Oval Office and who controls the Senate determines who gets confirmed in these lifetime appointments. But once allies are installed in federal district court, the US Court of Appeals, and the Supreme Court, it is time for an interest group to sponsor some cases.

One final point is worth making. Going to court is an adversarial process designed to determine winners and losers. It tends to breed ill will and distrust among parties that can be hard to overcome in the future. As I explore in the next chapter, interest group lobbyists and other political elites must learn to work together in coalitions and partnerships, and this often requires crossing ideological lines. Not only is this useful for building consensus in Congress and the public, it is the only way to achieve anything in a political system of checks and balances. Going to court, however, has the opposite effect. It creates divisions and often prevents direct communication between competing interests. Yet, once again with some irony, the very cost and uncertainty of protracted litigation can force combatants to negotiate, compromise, and settle. Going to court signals to other parties that the plaintiff has little interest in settlement, which perpetuates political struggles that might be smoothed over in other venues. The courts may not be the venues of last resort, but perhaps they should be.

Notes

1. These percentages come from the Supreme Court Database 2011; see note 5 below for details.

2. Years of scholarship have given empirical support to the belief that Supreme Court justices do frequently cast votes consistent with their ideological beliefs, especially when there is no existing precedent. See Stidham and Carp 1987; Rowland, Carp, and Songer 1988; Segal and Spaeth 2002; Lindquist and Cross 2009.

3. Specifically, Reitz (2002) argues that Sandra Day O'Connor's opinion in *Allen v. White* (468 U.S. 737, 751 [1984]) was responsible for making it easier to claim harm was done in constitutional cases.

4. Halstead (2003) describes this situation in terms of the expansion of executive privilege at the expense of the legislative branch as a result of the security interests of the United States, as laid out in Executive Order 13292. Executive privilege becomes grounds for denying standing to interest groups and members of Congress demanding access to information from the Office of the Vice President.

5. This data set is assembled and periodically updated by Harold Spaeth, Lee Epstein, Ted Ruger, Keith Wittington, Jeffrey Segal, and Andrew D. Martin; it is available from the Supreme Court Database (2011), http://scdb.wustl.edu. I am using the data set updated through the first release in 2011 (downloaded on June 10, 2011). To identify "interest groups" I read through the name of every case and coded a dummy variable 1 if either the petitioner or respondent was identifiable as an interest group. Government litigants and private individuals were obviously not counted, and neither were businesses or other singular organizations such as hospitals and universities (what Robert Salisbury [1984] refers to as "institutions" that lobby intermittently). Names indicating the organization was a business, trade, or professional association were counted, as were organizations indicating that they were primarily advocacy organizations, and I also counted all labor unions and inter-governmental groups. When it was not immediately possible to determine if the organization was a political interest group, I researched it on its Web site, and if I still could not make a clear decision, the organization was not counted as an interest group. Distinctions between petitioner and respondent simply depended on whether the organization was listed first in the case before the "*v.*" (petitioner) or second after the "*v.*" (respondent). Unions were specifically identified using Spaeth and colleagues' petitioner / respondent type code 249; however, while environmental groups and consumer protection groups could be easily identified using such codes, activist organizations can appear in all categories, so these were visually identified by scanning the case names.

6. See "Our Background," The Federalist Society for Law and Public Policy Studies, n.d., http://www.fed-soc.org/aboutus/id.28/default.asp.

CHAPTER NINE

Friends and Foes of Convenience

Most people only think about interest groups pressuring lawmakers, not how they pressure each other. But lawmakers are only one set of pieces in the larger political game—and not always the most important pieces. Thousands of lobbyists for hundreds of interests feverishly try to persuade other lobbyists, journalists, lawmakers, agency officials, fundraisers, public relations specialists, and even scholars that their view of what issues are worth the government's attention and what public policy regarding those issues should be is right and everyone else's a wrongheaded waste of time. They often do it casually, for not only do lobbyists and other political elites work with each other on the same issues year after year, they also go to the same parties, gyms, vacation spots, restaurants, and social clubs. Work and play blur in Washington, and every casual conversation is subtle persuasion, as lobbyists try to convince others to support their agendas or to oppose other people's agendas. Success results in cooperation; failure means a fight.

"Nations have no permanent friends or allies; they only have permanent interests," Great Britain's Lord Palmerston famously said. Interest groups too! But even group members may have to keep their interests flexible if their lobbyist is going to achieve anything in a political system as dependent on bargaining and compromise as ours is. Yesterday's enemies may have to be today's friends, and sometimes it may be necessary to stab yesterday's friend in the back. In this chapter I explore this surprising and sometimes treacherous aspect of interest group politics. I explain what it means for interest groups to compete, why lobbyists for these competing groups fight, but also why they sometimes cut deals and lobby arm in arm with their new "friends," and how all of this influences lobbying strategy.

Competitive Differences and Strange Bedfellows

No two groups represent exactly the same economic or social interest, even if they do represent some of the same people. But many groups are still concerned with the same issues. That is inevitable with over seven thousand interest groups. The more members of one group believe their interests are threatened by policies that favor other interest groups on the same issue, the more competition there is between them. That, in turn, determines whom that group's lobbyist can call "friend" or "foe" at any given point in time. If members do not perceive their interests as threatened by anybody, there is no competition. The American Bankers Association does not need to worry about what the American Petroleum Institute, the American Soybean Association, and the Wilderness Society think about banking issues. Those groups don't perceive the issue as relevant to them, so there is no competition. But the National Community Reinvestment Coalition is concerned about banking issues and wants to pressure banks into lending more money to people from low-income communities, something bankers argue is too risky for them to do. Unsurprisingly these two groups are fierce competitors on just about every banking issue.

For groups whose interests do intersect, the degree of intersection determines how they will respond to each other. Look at an example of two interest groups that are both concerned with the issue of how much government-owned land in the Gulf of Mexico will be leased to oil companies for drilling. Representing hundreds of oil companies, and companies indirectly connected to the oil industry, the American Petroleum Institute (API) wants more land opened for drilling. The National Wildlife Federation (NFW) also cares about the issue, but its members want fairly significant limits on the area open for drilling out of concern for its impact on animal life in and around the Gulf. The top part of Figure 9.1 shows a continuum of possible policy outcomes on the issue (the horizontal line), with points to the right representing more miles of land in the Gulf open to drilling. As discussed in Chapter 5, group members do not all agree on which policy outcome best represents their personal interests, so both group memberships are represented as distributions of member preferences over the continuum (the triangles). Generally, though, API's members prefer more territory to explore and drill, while NWF's members prefer much less.

When one group's members collectively want an outcome quite different from the other group's members, we have **interest group competition**. As

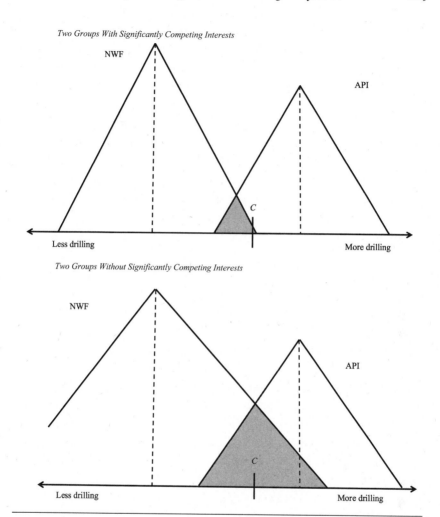

FIGURE 9.1   Positions of Two Groups on Gulf Oil Drilling

you can see in the top graph of Figure 9.1, even the average levels of drillable miles desired by the two groups' members (the dotted vertical lines) are far apart, indicating significant competition. A policy favoring a majority of one group's members is perceived by a majority of the other group's members as coming at their expense, and there is too little overlap (the shaded area) to create enough common ground for making compromises and building **lobbying coalitions** (Holyoke 2011, Ch. 2). Any agreement on how much territory to open for drilling, located in the tiny overlap of both membership distributions (like point *C* in the top graph), would be unacceptable to the vast majority of API and NWF members. They would not let their lobbyists agree to it. Angry members, believing themselves poorly represented, will leave the group, depriving it of resources and legitimacy (recall from Chapter 4). Or they will take out their anger by firing the lobbyist.

But what if NWF members are not at all unified about how much drilling there should be in the Gulf (see the bottom portion of Figure 9.1)? This broadens NWF's member distribution and creates a lot more overlap with API's members, perhaps creating enough common ground for both groups' lobbyists to strike a deal. In other words, a divided membership can decrease competition between competing groups. Competition between the two groups would also decrease if NWF's members didn't feel strongly about the oil-drilling issue and are thus more tolerant of policies not reflecting their ideal preferences. Several positions in the shaded overlap area of the bottom graph, including point C, are now potential compromises because many members of both groups prefer positions close to them. Perhaps that provides the two lobbyists with enough member support to now lobby together as a little coalition for a bill enacting policy at C.

Competition between interest groups is rarely this simple, though. Issues are usually more complex than simple questions of how much or how little to regulate oil drilling, and often a group's members only care about one part of each issue. This actually can make bargaining and coalition building much easier. Figure 9.2 expands upon the scenario in Figure 9.1. When the government leases land in the Gulf for oil drilling, it receives a royalty. What if some of these monies were to be spent on the upkeep of national parks? Now the issue NWF and API are competing over has two parts rather than one. One part is how much of the continental shelf is open to drilling, displayed on the horizontal axis. The other is how much royalty money goes to parks, displayed on the vertical axis. While NWF's members are not thrilled about oil drilling, they care more about having money for the parks. API's members, though, are interested in more drilling in the Gulf and are only concerned about park money in that it might mean paying higher royalties. This difference in emphasis makes it easier to strike a deal.

NWF's members would *ideally* like to see policy made at point *NWF*, but API, whose ideal policy is at *API*, would never agree to it. Instead, look at the two curved lines in Figure 9.2. They represent possible trade-offs between money for parks and available miles for drilling that the lobbyists for the two groups can consider. Every point on NWF's curve, for instance, is the maximum number of drillable miles its members would support for a

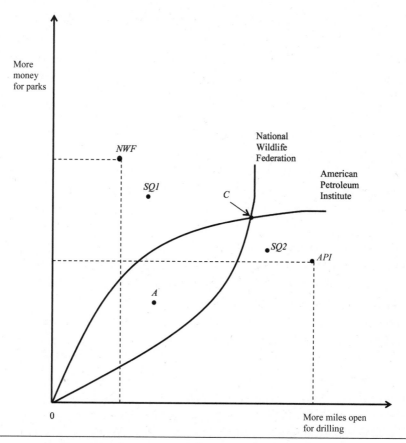

FIGURE 9.2   Bargaining Between Competing Interest Groups

corresponding amount of park money. NWF's lobbyist knows the group's members feel more intensely about park money than oil drilling, but many members also think there should be some Gulf oil drilling to reduce dependency on foreign oil. So, starting from zero, for every set increase in park money the NWF lobbyist demands, say for every $1 million, he or she is willing to open more miles of the continental shelf for drilling. After a while, NWF members start becoming increasingly uncomfortable with more drilling, so the NWF trade-off line starts to curve up and to the right. It does so because NWF members will tolerate progressively fewer miles of open shelf for drilling in exchange for another $1 million increase in royalties for parks. Finally, even though NWF members still want more park money, they will not support any more oil drilling in exchange, which is where NWF's curve becomes a straight vertical line. This works the same way for the API.

Every point on API's curve is the total amount of royalty money for parks the group's members will tolerate paying for the corresponding number of miles opened for drilling. API members are initially willing to be generous with royalty money for parks, but progressively less so because that is more money out of their profits.

Any position where API's trade-off curve is higher than NWF's is a possible deal between the two lobbyists, such as position A in Figure 9.2. But the two lobbyists would never make a deal at point A because they can find other trade-offs, yielding even more park money and more drillable miles acceptable to their members. Why would NWF's lobbyist agree to a deal at point A when he can get more money at point C, where the group's members will still tolerate opening some more of the continental shelf for drilling? Point C is actually the best trade-off possible because that is where the two curves intersect. Neither lobbyist can get the other to agree to a better deal than this.

It becomes more complicated if a status quo policy already exists, which it usually does. Say point SQ1 in Figure 9.2 is the current policy and provides NWF with more money for less drilling than API's lobbyist would ever accept because it is higher on the vertical axis than API's curve. SQ1 is closer to NWF than it is to point C, so NWF's lobbyist will not bargain with API because he knows the status quo is better than anything API will agree to. In other words, there can be no bargain in this scenario, and the NWF will fight to preserve the status quo. If the status quo was SQ2, then NWF's lobbyist would jump at the compromise at point C because it gives his members more of what they want than the status quo. But in this situation the API lobbyist would likely not support a deal at point C because the status quo (SQ2) is closer to what API members ideally want. So bargaining and coalition building depend on what trade-offs members will tolerate *and* what the alternatives to not bargaining are, including the status quo.

What this suggests is that a willingness to make trade-offs and compromises can make winners out of all groups. When the Environmental Protection Agency (EPA) proposed new fuel efficiency rules for large trucks and buses in 2011, these rules were praised by the Environmental Defense Fund, the Union of Concerned Scientists, and, surprisingly, the American Trucking Associations and the Engine Manufacturers Association (Eilperin 2011). Environmentalists wanted improved air quality and less reliance on fossil fuels, though it might mean more trucks on the road once they could be built to meet the new standards. Trucking companies wanted to eliminate the patchwork of state laws on emissions that made compliance difficult in favor of a single, national standard, even if it meant buying new, or retrofitting old, engines. Engine builders were delighted at the prospect of selling all of the new engines trucking companies would need to buy to comply with EPA's standards. Everybody gained something, so agreement was easy to reach, and they all backed the EPA's new rules.

Coalition Politics

Looking around Washington, DC, in the late 1980s, political scientist Robert Salisbury (1990) saw that what most lobbyists were doing they were doing together.[1] Apparently no lobbyist was so influential that he or she could go it alone with no regard for the interests of others. Instead, lobbyists worked in coalitions with peers whose member interests overlapped enough (as in the bottom graph of Figure 9.1) that they could all agree on a single policy to support. Competitors they could not compromise with usually formed opposing coalitions so that battles over issues and policies tended to be between packs of lobbyists (Sabatier and Jenkins-Smith 1993). Joining coalitions, however, means making compromises, and that means giving up something lobbyists' members want in order to accommodate competing groups. Why would lobbyists do that? What makes compromising member interests acceptable?

Coalitions Are Valuable

Lobbyists form or join coalitions to get something they would not have otherwise, which is usually the reason people compromise. Five potential benefits draw lobbyists to coalitions. First, they might gain connections to key policy makers in Congress or in the bureaucracy, perhaps even in the White House. As discussed in Chapter 6, building and maintaining relationships with lawmakers takes time and money. Some lobbyists just do not have the resources. Many lobbyists may also be vying for the attention of the same lawmaker, and if they lack a constituency connection, they are unlikely to get in the office door. Other lobbyists in a coalition, though, may have connections to a powerful committee chair or party leader they will share. But what do they get in return? Perhaps they get other contacts, perhaps access to other groups' financial resources, perhaps expectations of receiving help in the future (Hula 1999, Ch. 3; Holyoke 2009).

A second reason for building coalitions is information. The complicated, ever-changing political environment is difficult for even the most experienced lobbyist to keep track of. New bills or amendments threatening a lobbyist's members might suddenly appear from an unexpected quarter. Learning what is happening, who is doing what to whom, and sorting rumors from facts requires a network of trusted informants. Working in a coalition means everyone pools information and keeps each other informed (Hula 1999, Ch. 4).

Third, coalitions make it easier for lobbyists to impress group members by appearing to work on many issues simultaneously. Some coalitions last for years and collectively advocate on many issues year after year. No single lobbyist in the coalition works intensely on every issue, but if every lobbyist works hard on just one and shares the credit, then it appears to members that their lobbyist is working hard on lots of issues (Hula 1999, Ch. 3). Large, durable coalitions also show lawmakers that many groups representing a wide range of social or economic interests are united in their advocacy for or against a bill. Even if just one lobbyist in the coalition is doing the work on that issue, every group's name is mentioned in hearing testimony, is on the letterhead, and is listed on the press release. Every lobbyist gets some of the credit, and their united message is much more persuasive to lawmakers, since it appears that so many interests support it. Members back home can marvel at how many important issues are being covered by their superhuman lobbyist!

Fourth, large, well-known organizations with reputations for being influential can be attractive coalition partners (Hojnacki 1997). It is the lobbying world's equivalent of being seen with the "in" crowd. When opponents see a lobbyist in a coalition that includes powerful interest groups like AARP, the NRA, or the Chamber of Commerce, they may be more willing to cut deals and make compromises, fearing the costs of fighting such powerful organizations (Holyoke 2009).

Finally, lobbyists may join coalitions to please lawmakers. If this sounds strange, remember from Chapters 5 and 6 that lawmakers can exert tremendous pressure on lobbyists because they can easily cut off most lobbyists' access to governing institutions. Most legislators hate choosing which interest groups win and which lose on an issue because it often means choosing between groups of politically active constituents or supporters. Compromises, though, are easy to support, assuming constituents can all be convinced that the compromise is really in their best interest (which is part of the lobbyist's job). So when policy makers want to get legislation moved in Congress, or pull together support for a proposed executive branch regulation, they may push lobbyists into forming coalitions. They pressure lobbyists into cutting deals and then lobbying for legislation embodying those deals as a coalition to help convince majorities in Congress that these bills or agency rules enjoy broad public support (Ainsworth 1997; Holyoke 2011, Ch. 2). One example of this is detailed in the Chapter 6 case study (see pp. 149–156), when Senator D'Amato pressured insurance agents to support financial reform legislation.

Coalitions Carry Costs

Lobbyists spend much of their time trying to align the interests of members with those of lawmakers, and being in a coalition provides an opportunity to negotiate policy compromises on tricky issues so that policy makers and interest groups are all backing the same policy proposal. It also means making sacrifices, often by agreeing to support less dramatic changes in policy than group members may have wanted in order to keep coalition partners happy. As environmental lobbyist David Sirota said, "You are surrounded by people who subscribe to a certain set of narrow viewpoints. . . . Everything you hear at all times tells you not to rock the boat by actually doing what you came to Washington to do" (Farrell 2011, 13). Sirota's insight also suggests that making compromises may be harder for lobbyists representing cause-oriented citizen and public interest groups whose members and supporters are more passionate about their policy goals (Hula 1999, Ch. 8).

Participating in especially large, more ideologically diverse coalitions may demand even more significant compromises. Lobbyists find big coalitions attractive because they are more likely to win: groups that were potential opponents to a policy proposal have instead agreed to support the proposal and are invested in its success. It shows lawmakers that there is widespread support from many important constituencies for the proposal. But broad coalitions also put lobbyists in bed with very strange bedfellows. Sometimes the bedfellows are just too strange for principled group members to accept. Recall the example in Chapter 4 of the Nature Conservancy losing a lot of members just because its leaders agreed to a little land development in a compromise.

Unfortunately for lobbyists, being pressured by members to never compromise—refusing to make deals or join coalitions—also carries costs. Lawmakers like it when all of the competing interests surrounding a bill can find a way to cooperate because it reduces resistance to their favored policy proposals. By refusing to cooperate, lobbyists risk lawmakers excluding them from all future negotiations on the issue, making it likely they will end up with an even worse result than if they had shown a little willingness to bend. As former Sierra Club lobbyist Tim Mahoney said, regarding a public lands bill he opposed even after Senator Max Baucus (D-MT) had urged him to compromise, "We took the all or nothing approach. And we got nothing" (Farrell 2011, 15). His regret was echoed by Sierra Club lobbyist Debbie Sease, who also refused to compromise on the same bill: "Our grassroots wouldn't let me [accept the deal]. . . . Very, very nice areas are now clear-cut. . . . I look back and say, my God, if we had only taken that [deal]" (15). For the lobbyist it comes down to how united members are, how strongly members feel about the issue, and how big of a compromise the lobbyist is being asked to make. If members really feel strongly, then fighting the good fight and losing is a better choice for the lobbyist because it keeps them credible with members, though it may damage relationships with some allies in Congress.

Sometimes even highly principled interest groups find that bargains with the devil can be palatable if it makes it possible to achieve important goals. One such example of this is when the environmental advocacy group Center for Biological Diversity agreed not to file any more lawsuits challenging BrightSource Energy's efforts to develop large solar power fields in the Mojave Desert in exchange for a commitment from BrightSource that it would set aside company-owned land to preserve the habitat of the desert tortoise (Schwartz 2011). This exchange nicely reflects the hypothetical two-dimensional trade-off scenario in Figure 9.2, in this case a trade-off involving land for solar energy and tortoise habitat. But also realize that the Center had already brought BrightSource's project to a halt by suing the US Bureau of Land Management to stop granting permits to BrightSource. This is what motivated BrightSource to make a deal. Without credible threats, bargaining between competitors is nearly impossible. BrightSource had to fear the consequences of not getting the Center's support. The Center's attorney, though, admitted it was going to have to do some quick explaining to its members about why it made a deal with an energy company, but "I'd rather us get beat up a bit for having a 'secret agreement' that actually leads to additional tortoise habitat than one less likely to lead to those protections."

Electoral Coalitions

So far this chapter has all been about lobbying coalitions—interest groups working together to move or block legislation. There are also **electoral coalitions**, coalitions formed by interest groups to influence which party controls Congress and the White House. Often these coalitions reflect the same ideological division as the Democratic and Republican parties, with members of interest groups playing active roles in support of one or the other party (Heaney et al. 2012). Interest groups forming electoral coalitions are actually less surprising than interest groups forming lobbying coalitions. Political parties must try to represent broadly shared ideologies and general principles, not advocate for specific positions on specific issues, as interest groups do. Otherwise no party could pull enough factions together from around the nation to win the presidency. It is the same with interest groups in elections: they can focus on general principles rather than specific issues. This makes it easier for interest groups with differences on policy specifics, but all sharing the same broad political ideology, to form a coalition backing a party.

For instance, lobbyists for several environmental groups might compete with each other over how many square miles of forest to wall off from human development (see the Chapter 7 case study on pp. 181–184), but they all agree that conservation is good. Democrats are inclined to be supportive of that position, and Republicans are not, so all of these environmental groups can lay aside their specific differences to support the Democratic Party. Sometimes they coordinate with the parties so closely that it is hard to tell where the party ends and the interest groups begin. Of course, just because they work together in an electoral coalition does not mean these same groups will also join together in a lobbying coalition. Once environmental groups help Democrats take control of Congress, they will probably go back to fighting with each other over issues like exactly how many miles of natural forest to designate as wilderness.

Political scientist Paul Herrnson (2009) argues that as elections became more fiercely fought in the last couple of decades, interest groups were being pushed closer to the parties, creating semipermanent electoral coalitions in which interest groups almost exclusively supported candidates from one party or the other and directed their money as party operatives see fit. The fusion of labor unions into the Democratic Party in the 1930s is an older example, but it may be happening today on a larger scale. In 2010, business interests, under the banner of the US Chamber of Commerce, raised tremendous financial resources to elect Republicans to Congress, just as a coalition of conservative religious organizations did in the 1994 election. More interest groups today see their ability to advance member interests as tied to one party, and they believe that their chance to do so would be hurt if the other party was in power. Electoral coalitions may also be stronger than legislative coalitions because they can credibly threaten elected officials where it really hurts: the next election. In December 2012 an electoral coalition of about two dozen conservative antitax groups, including the powerful Club for Growth, derailed House Speaker John Boehner's (R-OH) legislation to raise taxes on millionaires by threatening to launch primary challenges to Republican lawmakers, even though voting on the bill was only a tactic to increase Boehner's leverage in a fight with President Barack Obama over whether to extend a series of tax cuts passed in 2001 (Montgomery and Helderman 2012).

Other Types of Partners

Coalitions are about more than just interest groups working with other interest groups. Influencing national politics in a media- and Internet-driven age means partnering with other kinds of organizations. In Chapter 3 I described how social movements use the media to promote their interests by putting well-crafted images of protest, and even violence toward movement members, in front of sympathetic audiences. Today television and Web sites frequently have advertisements from interest groups and public relations firms (frequent partners) that try to influence the way the public understands an issue, priming the public to support their proposal for addressing the issue (or leaving the issue alone). Recent controversies over gun violence had the Brady Center to Prevent Gun Violence running ads demanding restrictions on gun ownership because that will save lives, while the National Rifle Association ran ads demanding fewer restrictions on gun ownership because that will save lives.

In this example the media is passive, putting forward political messages that they do not create (but profit from), but that is not always the case. For example, filmmaker Michael Moore actively painted a sympathetic picture of the United Auto Workers and an unflattering one of General Motors executives in his documentary *Roger & Me*. And while UAW may not have explicitly developed and financed Moore's movie, it took the opportunity to show it to viewers all over the nation because the film gave unions an opportunity to frame corporate managers as soulless pursuers of profit at any cost. Another example is the movie *Thank You for Smoking*, which portrays a fictional tobacco lobbyist trying to defend an industry that knowingly promoted an unhealthy product. In one part of the movie the lobbyist even tries to make a deal with a movie producer to create a film promoting tobacco! Some media moguls also use the media properties they own to convey their political viewpoints. Once a supporter of Democrats Hillary Clinton and Barack Obama, Rupert Murdoch now opposes Democrats by aggressively giving money to interest groups like the US Chamber of Commerce and the Republican Governors Association (Rutenberg 2010). Moreover, the editorial pages of important publications Murdoch owns, most notably the *Wall Street Journal*, run pro-business editorials read by millions supporting the Chamber's policies and attacking those of Democrats.

Talk radio has proven to be an especially effective ally for some interest groups. Grover Norquist's group Americans for Tax Reform working with conservative talk radio is a good example of this. Sharing a disdain for taxes, and for any politician seeking to raise taxes, many conservative talk radio show hosts have taken up Norquist's antitax stand and aggressively attacked lawmakers who even consider voting for anything vaguely looking like a tax increase. Americans for Tax Reform does not create these radio shows, but media entrepreneurs know that antitax sentiment is strong in America and embrace that stance to draw listeners and boost ratings. Norquist's group simply supplies the message that these talk radio programs can play up and use to justify antitax feelings. Pacifica Radio out of Berkeley promotes distinctly liberal causes and is a popular outlet for left-leaning environmental and human-rights interest groups. What make these alliances possible are a shared political ideology and a need for each other's resources. Media organizations need information and policy experts to appear on their shows. Interest groups need outlets for their messages when they want to shape public opinion or raise public awareness regarding their framing of issues.

The difference between think tanks and interest groups is blurry, which is perhaps why they often make good coalition partners. Think tanks promote ideologically tinged policy proposals, often grounded in academic research, but they need the help of others to get their ideas before lawmakers (Rich 2005). They need the access that interest group lobbyists have, and often lobbyists need the ideas and research integrity think tanks provide to justify their own policy positions. The Manhattan Institute, for instance, develops and disseminates research promoting policies of consumer choice in K-12 education, such as charter schooling and vouchers, backed by years of rigorous, if ideologically driven, social science research. The institute's ideas are then promoted by interest groups like the pro–school choice Center for Education Reform (Henig 2009). Think tanks get interest group support in promoting their policy alternatives in the halls of government because the group's lobbyist helps lawmakers see the personal benefits in embracing the positions promoted by the think tank. Lobbyists add the tactical, constituent, and election-oriented edge to the think tank's message.

And sometimes interest groups and think tanks need the media as a third partner. Environmental groups and left-leaning think tanks praised and promoted the Al Gore documentary film *An Inconvenient Truth*, which made a strong case for human-caused global warming. Its creator, Davis Guggenheim, then went on to make *Waiting for Superman*, a movie criticizing traditional public education and teacher unions, which was embraced by groups like the Center for Education Reform and think tanks like the Manhattan Institute. It also won an award at the 2010 Sundance Film Festival, giving its political message more exposure than any interest group could ever hope for.

The Timing of Conflict and Cooperation

It should be clear now that forming coalitions is easy when lobbyists for competing interest groups all believe it is in their interest to cut a deal. Yet even when alliances are possible, lobbyists may still not want to compromise too early in the policy-making process, when lawmakers are still trying to decide just what a new policy ought to look like or whether it is even needed. When issues are first seriously raised in Congress, usually in a subcommittee with jurisdiction over their issues, lobbyists engage in position taking (recall this from Chapter 5). They try to persuade their allies on the committee why the issue should (or should not) be taken up and why the best policy just happens to be the one that gives their members everything they want. Anticipating a fight to get an issue raised and accepted by lawmakers, some lobbyists may form coalitions at this early stage to show broad public support for a new policy, but these are probably coalitions of groups that largely agree with each other to begin with. Deals requiring serious negotiation rarely happen at such an early point in the lawmaking process, for most lobbyists are still jockeying to define the issue and get their uncompromised policy priorities inserted into a new bill. Only after it becomes clear later on what lawmakers will and will not accept and what can actually get through Congress will lobbyists start negotiating and thinking about forming coalitions.

Once bills start to move, lobbyists must be ready to decide what versions of a bill they will accept after some negotiation and when to fight. But again, if legislators are successful in pressuring lobbyists to form a broad coalition behind a bill, it is risky for any single lobbyist not to jump on the bandwagon. Those who refuse to "join the team" may quickly find themselves excluded from the final negotiations before enactment, because lawmakers rarely want to significantly renegotiate a bill once it is moving forward (Holyoke 2011, Ch. 5). Such renegotiation would threaten deals already made and unravel the bill's political support. Remember that lobbyists depend on the goodwill of legislators for successful careers, so pressure from lawmakers is a powerful incentive to compromise. It is often more powerful than threats from angry group members, who may not realize their interests were even compromised in the final deal (their lobbyist certainly won't be telling them that). Resisting legislator pressure risks damaging the hard-won relationships lobbyists have built, so only on the issues most important to members will they resist compromise and go down in glorious defeat.

Competition and Venue Shopping

If a lobbyist cannot find enough coalition allies, or finds too many enemies, to advance member interests in a congressional committee without considerable struggle, he or she can try another committee. Or the legislature's other chamber. Or wait for implementation by the bureaucracy. Or go to court. Or abandon Washington entirely to pursue member interests in state capitols. This kind of strategizing is called **venue shopping**. It means appealing to government officials in other institutions of policy making who might be more sympathetic to the disadvantaged interest group than those in the current venue.

Lawyers do this all the time. If they believe a trial court in one judicial district is hostile to their clients' arguments, they try to have responsibility for the case transferred to another, more sympathetic district. Similarly, a lobbyist might try to shift policy-making authority from hostile venues to friendlier ones, perhaps by convincing a congressional committee of lawmakers with whom the lobbyist shares a constituent connection to claim jurisdiction over an issue, even if that means stepping on another committee's jurisdictional turf (Talbert, Jones, and Baumgartner 1995). Or a lobbyist may try to convince allies in an administrative agency to claim responsibility for implementing a policy he or she was not able to influence in Congress (McKay 2011). And as seen in Chapter 8, a lobbyist will go to court when prevailing ideology there favors his or her members' interests (Hansford 2004b). This is all venue shopping, and it is not just a matter of this venue *instead of* that venue, but very often this venue *and* that venue.

Multiple Venues, Multiple Opportunities

I emphasized in Chapter 6 that moving legislation through Congress is a long and arduous process: from subcommittee to committee then to the chamber floor in one house, repeat in the other house (often simultaneously), then (probably) to conference committee, and then finally to the White House. After that, the legislation moves to an implementing agency, or agencies, and perhaps a trial court, the court of appeals, and, possibly, finally the Supreme Court. And even that is not an exhaustive list of venues. Some congressional committee chairs, at the urging of lobbyists and in pursuit of their own goals, may try to expand their committee's policy jurisdiction by grabbing a bill that is supposed to go to another committee, or one that still does go to another committee (this is called multiple referrals). The result is an even greater number of access points for interest groups in the governmental superstructure and thus more chances for lobbyists to change and shape policy to a group's liking in a venue populated by lawmakers they have relationships with. Or lobbyists may try to kill a bill by preventing it from leaving a venue. Killing is easier because it only takes one negative committee or floor vote to do it. Group lobbyists and legislators happy with a bill the way it is already, of course, will try to reduce the number of venues it must go through to make enactment more likely.

The history of the Gramm-Leach-Bliley Act, the legislation that blended the banking, securities investing, and insurance industries discussed in Chapter 6, is a good example of strategic venue shopping. When banking groups began to suspect that House Banking Committee chair Jim Leach was not going to give them the results they wanted, they got a multiple referral that also sent the bill to the friendlier Commerce Committee. They expanded the number of venues to get what they wanted. When the legislation cleared the House and went to the Senate, these same interests found Senator D'Amato, chair of the Banking Committee, supportive and so convinced him to bypass Senate subcommittees entirely and just handle the bill quickly in the full committee. Here they shrank the number of venues to protect what they had gained.

Financial modernization also shows how some lobbyists throw their energies into some venues more than others. In 2001, I interviewed twenty-seven lobbyists who worked on financial modernization and walked them through the fourteen venues displayed in Figure 9.3. I asked each to rate whether the effort they expended to influence the issue in each venue was "intense" (scored 3), "moderate" (scored 2), or "none to minimal" (scored 1). I averaged these scores to produce the trend line in Figure 9.3. Congressional committees are clearly the most preferred venues, especially the committee where the legislation was first created, the House Banking Committee. So in venue shopping not all venues are equal. For example, being in on the ground floor

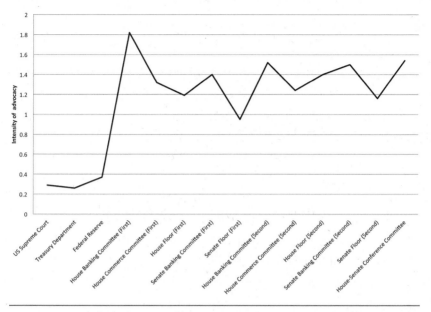

FIGURE 9.3 Level of Advocacy Across Venues on the Gramm-Leach-Bliley Act
Source: Author's data

of a new bill is so important that many interest groups will try to be involved there even if lawmakers on the committee are not the most hospitable.

Venue Shopping and Federalism

There is also a federalism side to venue shopping. Some lobbyists may feel that they would have a greater advantage in venues at lower levels of the American political system, such as city and county legislatures or local implementing agencies, rather than at the national level. A good example is in the debates over consumer choice in K-12 education. Charter schools are public-private entities created under state law to provide K-12 education largely free of government regulation, even though they receive public money (Henig et al. 2004). Since congressional Democrats made it nearly impossible to create a national charter school policy, and Republicans were reluctant to usurp traditional state control over K-12 education, school choice activists had to turn to state venues (Mintrom 2000). Once established, charter schools have been forced to lobby for their survival against teacher unions and school board associations, sometimes through their trade associations but often on their own (Holyoke et al. 2007).

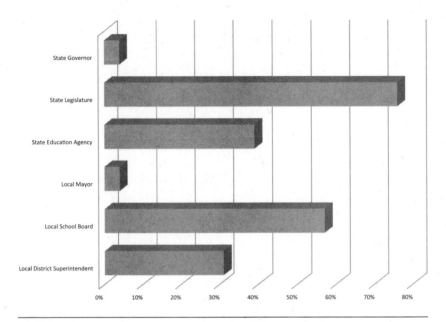

FIGURE 9.4   Percentage of Charter Schools Lobbying State and Local Venues
Source: Author's data

In 2003, several colleagues and I surveyed 270 charter school leaders in Michigan, Pennsylvania, and Arizona (see Brown et al. 2004). We asked how frequently they contacted elected and appointed lawmakers in state and local venues (see Holyoke, Brown, and Henig 2012). Each bar in Figure 9.4 indicates the percentage of school leaders lobbying a venue "moderately" or "frequently." Elected legislative venues, in this case state legislatures and local school boards, were clearly the venues of choice. They are the most susceptible to pressure from constituents who also happen to be the parents of charter school students. Furthermore, lobbying by schools only serving students from specific neighborhoods within cities rather than broader geographic areas (charter schools often do not have geographic limits on student recruitment) was clearly directed at local lawmaking venues rather than state. Why? When school leaders need to lobby on behalf of their students and their students' parents (their members), those representing a narrow geographic area are more likely to have a significant constituent presence in several school board districts, but only a single, larger state legislative district. The constituent connection is strong locally but diluted at the state level. Schools recruiting from a much wider geographic area may have more parent members in more state legislative districts and are therefore stronger in state venues as well as local venues. Yet because the constituent connection is such a powerful form of influence in representative democracy, regardless of whether it is state or local, advocates prefer legislative venues over all others.

There is something else important to note in Figure 9.4. Advocacy in all three state venues is greater than in their corresponding local venues. Not only is there a preference for elected legislators within a layer of government (horizontal venue shopping), but because higher venues bind lower venues but not vice versa in a federal system (the Tenth Amendment to the US Constitution not withstanding), there is a strategic preference for higher levels (vertical venue shopping). Victories at a higher level with the enactment of national or state law have a geographically broader impact, resulting in uniform national or state policy, rather than creating an inconsistent patchwork of local policies. So if an interest group can achieve its goals at the higher level, it will usually bypass local venues entirely.

The United States is nearly unique in how extensively its lawmaking venues are laid out horizontally and vertically in a federal system, though the European Union is shaping up to be a two-level system with national governments subject to a central government in Brussels, Belgium (see Constantelos 2007; Mahoney 2008). Here and in Europe, lobbyists take advantage of government complexity by venue shopping. Overall, the alignment of interests between lawmakers in a venue and group members matters most in choosing venues, especially when it is based on a constituent connection as it is in legislative venues. Structural features also matter, though they are secondary to interest alignment. That is, lobbyists prefer venues higher up the federal system because those decisions bind all of the lower venues as well, and they prefer lobbying legislative bodies. They also prefer venues where competing groups are weak (Holyoke 2003).

One important caveat on venue shopping: if lawmakers in any venue decide to take up an issue affecting a group's members, then the group's lobbyist must respond by lobbying that venue because that is where the action is. As discussed in Chapter 5, choosing not to lobby when issues important to members are being debated is dangerous to an interest group. Not lobbying means a lobbyist may be allowing competitor groups to have their way. It also signals to involved lawmakers that the group and its lobbyist are either not interested in the issue or incapable of defending its members' interests on it. It shows that the group is of no political consequence and should not be taken seriously. It also suggests to members that the lobbyist and his or her organization cannot represent their interests, and they may leave for another group whose interests are similar enough that it can reasonably claim to represent them. The wise lobbyist must at least give the appearance of working in that venue, if simply by going through the motions but expending little real effort and resources, sometimes called pro forma lobbying (Holyoke 2003). Or the lobbyist may join a coalition of other groups lobbying the issue but let the better-connected coalition partners do the heavy advocacy lifting (Hula 1999). Venue shopping provides many tactical opportunities, but they must be considered carefully by the lobbyist to make sure that even while he or she is working well with lawmakers, they are not simultaneously shooting themselves in the foot with group members.

■ CASE STUDY ■

Coalition Lobbying for Parks

One of the most impressive coalitions ever assembled in Washington was on an issue mentioned earlier in this chapter: opening government-owned land for drilling in exchange for money for parks conservation. It is worth telling the whole story to show how large, ideologically diverse coalitions of interest groups form but are also susceptible to defections when a better offer comes along.[2]

STAGE ONE: FRAMING A POLICY PROPOSAL

States share public land management responsibilities with the federal government, including wildlife management on those lands. While some of a state's expenses for this management come from fees paid by hunters using the land, the Pittman-Robertson Act of 1937 requires the federal government to help defray some of the cost. A decline in hunting and tighter federal budgets in the 1990s, though, led to a sharp decrease in the money states had to manage public lands and wildlife, even as public interest in nonhunting outdoor recreation increased. A small intragovernmental interest group representing state wildlife and parks departments, the International Association of Fish and Wildlife Agencies (IAFWA), decided they really needed to find a way to guarantee more federal funding to the states through Pittman-Robertson.

With Republicans in control of Congress, anything that looked like environmental legislation was dead on arrival, so IAFWA did three things. First, it underwent a strategic change of identity, as groups must do as situations warrant (Heaney 2004), presenting itself as a conservation and states' rights group rather than an environmental group. Second, it sought out as a legislative champion Republican representative Don Young of Alaska, a state with enormous public lands responsibilities and desperately in need of money to manage them. This gave Young a constituent-based reason to want to help, and as chair of the House Appropriations Committee controlling the federal purse strings, he was in a position to move new policy. Finally, knowing that Young could not get conservation legislation through the House without supporters on both sides of the aisle, IAFWA tried to form a coalition with groups from the die-hard states' rights Republican camp as well as the Democrats' environmental allies. While they were able to quickly sign up hundreds of interest groups as supporters, nearly all of them were environmental or otherwise left-leaning groups. The problem was that IAFWA's proposal was a new excise tax on recreation equipment that attracted the anger of antitax groups while scaring away outdoor recreation and hunting groups.

IAFWA's Senate champion, Mary Landrieu (D-LA), suggested a different approach. As a Louisianan, she knew all about oil drilling in the Gulf of Mexico. The continental shelf is federal land, so oil companies pay substantial royalties to the government for the right to drill there. Like Alaska, Louisiana needed money for its extensive public lands, especially for once-wildlife-abundant wetlands that they were desperately trying to preserve. She suggested simply diverting a portion of those royalties into the Pittman-Robertson fund. Brilliant.

STAGE TWO: ASSEMBLING THE GREAT COALITION

With the tax threat removed, antitax groups backed off, and recreation, hunting, and sporting groups like Ducks Unlimited agreed to join the coalition. As long as their members could hunt on those lands, they were all for well-funded land and wildlife management. More environmental groups also joined, supporting the idea of using oil money for conservation, though some feared this might also justify more Gulf oil drilling. Even some oil industry groups joined, probably hoping this would indeed lead to more oil drilling. By 1999 IAFWA had now assembled a jaw-dropping coalition of over five thousand local, state, and national interest groups (assuming Camp Fire Girls can be called an interest group).

The effort paid off in Congress. With over two hundred cosponsors, the Conservation and Reinvestment Act (CARA) passed the House in 2000, 315–102. Some supportive House members had reservations, fearing the bill might lead state governments to expand their public land holdings to claim even more money, or it would create more offshore oil drilling, but the pressure from such a large and diverse coalition to vote "aye" was nearly unbearable. The bill would have been enacted that year if it were not for President Bill Clinton.

STAGE THREE: IT ALL FALLS APART

The Chapter 7 case study told how in 2000 environmental groups persuaded Clinton to use his authority under the Antiquities Act to preserve more lands from development by designating them as national monuments. That broke the CARA coalition. Clinton's actions to place so much new land in the care of federal agencies as wilderness, restricting nearly all human use, required a lot more money at the federal level for public lands management. Environmental groups such as Defenders of Wildlife and Natural Resources Defense Council that had been uncomfortable with CARA because they feared it would lead to more oil drilling and more human use of public lands for hunting now switched sides to support Clinton's wilderness proposal. They pulled out of the CARA coalition and formed the Green Group coalition to convince Clinton that a large portion of the oil royalties should be used only for the new federal lands, with a much smaller portion going to the states. Deficit-minded Republicans on the House Appropriations Committee wanting to keep more money at the federal level defied their chair, Don Young, by agreeing. Hunting and oil industry groups unhappy with more restricted wilderness saw the new Clinton proposal backed by the environmental groups as a betrayal, so they abandoned the CARA coalition. IAFWA and its remaining allies were left with no choice but to support Clinton's new proposal with much less money for the states (many called it "CARA-Lite") and hoped they could get more in the future. As it turned out, they spent the next few years just fighting to keep what little they had.

STAGE FOUR: BIGGER IS NOT ALWAYS BETTER

The case study reveals the pitfalls of coalition politics. The CARA coalition was enormous in group numbers and, consequently, ideological breadth. As long as it could be kept together, it was powerful. It convinced Republicans to support environmental conservation. It convinced Democrats to embrace oil money. The larger and broader coalitions are, the more powerful they are when they can stay together and drive legislation forward. But it only worked as long as there was no viable alternative policy proposal. When Clinton's more environmentally friendly proposal appeared, the coalition fractured. And when it fractured, its support in Congress dropped because the show of broad interest group unity had been revealed as a façade. The CARA coalition's great weakness was that too many of its members did not trust each other; the bedfellows were too strange. Certainly the oil industry and hunting groups were wary of the environmentalists, but the environmental group community was also deeply divided internally (see Best and Nocella 2006). The die-hard group Defenders of Wildlife (and others like it) thought IAFWA was selling out environmentalism by allying with the oil industry and running away from the environmental label by calling itself a conservation group. As soon as a better opportunity came along, like Clinton's new federal lands policy, Defenders and other environmental groups took it. Once a coalition crumbles, its influence is gone for good because its power is in its unity. No unity, no influence.

In Summary

Here is a summary of the chapter's key points:

- Interest groups are competing when they are all interested in the same issue and each group's members collectively prefer different policy outcomes so that a final policy favoring one group is perceived as coming at the expense of other groups.

- Coalitions of groups can form if member preferences for policy outcomes overlap, or the members of one group are more concerned with a part of an issue that is less important to other groups so that trade-offs and compromises are possible.
- Lobbyists often want to form coalitions to share contacts and information, conserve resources, and please lawmakers, who themselves generally prefer that everyone get along rather than fight.
- Lobbyists can only compromise so far on an issue before group members feel betrayed, and lobbyists have less freedom to compromise when their members feel really strongly about an issue and are united on how they would like to see it resolved with policy.
- If lobbyists simply cannot win their case in one policy-making venue, there are many others in the American lawmaking system they can try, including venues at the state and local levels, though elected legislatures tend to be preferred.

Group competition is what creates a need for lobbying strategy, such as selecting policy-making venues where member priorities can be advanced because there are fewer competitors, or coalition allies have a lot of contacts there. Fear of competition can also convince opposing lobbyists to make deals and form coalitions. Joining coalitions is risky, though. On the one hand, it means compromising member interests. If members find out, it damages a lobbyist's credibility and jeopardizes member loyalty and support. On the other hand, reaching a deal with powerful competitor groups means resource-consuming fights have been avoided. Instead, the lobbyist has many of the resources of the coalition to draw on and can be on the winning side of more policy battles. Being on the winning side is usually the place an ambitious lobbyist wants to be. It builds up his or her reputation as a winner, which means other lobbyists will want to ally with him or her in the future, making it more likely that the lobbyist will win again. Winning advances a lobbyist's career, which, of course, is the basic motivation of these professional advocates.

But at what cost? Accommodating other interest groups to form coalitions, or giving the appearance of lobbying in a venue without committing real resources, raises serious questions about ethical representation. True, the American political system is fundamentally designed to push competing social and economic interests to compromise, but not at the expense of citizen interests. How far can and should lobbyists go to accommodate each other? When is true representation of member interests, even in the face of certain defeat, the better route? Moreover, building a coalition capable of pushing legislation through Congress often means that only the needs and interests of coalition members are being given attention by lawmakers. Unless they have enough resources to make their own voice heard over the coalition, groups left out never get a real chance to present their concerns or make their case to lawmakers. In other words, coalitions limit the range of policy alternatives lawmakers consider because they limit the voices that are heard in a political debate (Costain and Costain 1981). Can that be at all proper in a representative democracy? Before we explore the ethics of lobbying, there is one other area worth discussing, and that is campaign finance and financial contributions to politicians.

Notes

1. I have heard it said that Salisbury was seeing something new, but David Truman back in 1951 wrote that "rarely can any single group achieve its legislative objectives without assistance from other groups" (1951, 362).

2. The details of this case study come from interviews I conducted with several of the participants back in 2002 (see Holyoke 2011, Ch. 3).

CHAPTER TEN

Interest Groups, Elections, and Campaign Finance

A poll by CNN and the Opinion Research Corporation in June 2011 found that 86 percent of Americans believe elected lawmakers are influenced too much by those who contribute money to their campaigns, up from 77 percent in 1997. Polling director Keating Holland explained that "only one in eight [Americans] believe that Washington officials are mostly concerned about what is best for the country."[1] So the vast majority of citizens believe elections are for sale, being won by the person who raises the most money from well-heeled special interest groups rather than the candidate most concerned with constituent needs or the public interest.[2]

Interest groups are closely connected with campaign funding (and corruption resulting from this funding) in the minds of Americans, so much so that some readers may wonder why I waited so long to introduce this subject in the book. The truth is that while many interest groups are deeply involved in financing campaigns, a significant number of them stay away from elections. More importantly, these days most interest groups are, relatively speaking, small fry compared to other types of money collecting, bundling, and distributing organizations such as parties, leadership PACs, 527 organizations, and super PACs. These are *not* interest groups but ad hoc organizations created to raise and give enormous amounts of money to candidates for office, or spend it on their behalf. They do not represent members in any meaningful sense and often pursue ideological goals more akin to political parties, rather than the less partisan, more issue-specific interest groups. Nonetheless, because they are so closely associated with interest groups, I give these organizations some attention in this chapter.[3] The chapter's primary focus, however, is on interest groups in elections, what they do, what they give, and what they hope to get in return.

A Brief History of Electoral Contributing

In order to better understand the world of elections and campaign contributions, and the role of interest groups in this world, let's take a quick look at the history of campaign finance beginning in the early 1900s to the present day.

Early Origins and Trends

After decades of corruption, bribes, and everything the public tends to associate with the lobbying of Congress, at the beginning of the twentieth century this same body passed legislation forbidding corporations from contributing to political campaigns for national office. Since most late-nineteenth-century lobbying was done on behalf of corporations, this was a significant achievement, one in the "good government" spirit of Theodore Roosevelt's Progressive Era. In his book *PAC Power*, elections specialist Larry Sabato describes how turn-of-the-century party bosses like Republican chief Mark Hanna "shook down" businesses to build a campaign war chest for President William McKinley (1984, 3). It was Hanna who famously said, "There are two things that are important in politics. The first is money and I can't remember what the second one is." Ironically, though, after party "assessments" on American business were increased to help get him elected, Roosevelt turned on Hanna and his successors by persuading Congress to enact the first real limit on contributing. The result was the **Tillman Act** of 1907 banning direct contributions by companies to candidates for federal office. But like all efforts at reform, the act's main achievement was to stimulate creative thinking about other ways people and businesses could contribute, such as in-kind contributions of office space, equipment, and transportation, all seemingly given to candidates for free.

While business's political power declined during the Great Depression, the influence of labor unions grew. Tired of being steamrollered by unions during the New Deal years of the 1930s, business leaders began looking for a tough ally in Congress and found it in Senator Robert Taft (R-OH). Several labor strikes during World War II gave Taft and other congressional Republicans enough political support to enact the Smith-Connally Act over Franklin Roosevelt's veto in 1943. The new law banned unions from contributing to campaigns until the end of the war, and Taft later made the ban permanent with the Taft-Hartley Act of 1947 (over President Harry Truman's veto). Now neither unions nor corporations could contribute.

But money in politics is like water in riverbeds: no matter where you construct a dam, it will always find new ways to flow. Or perhaps the proverb "necessity is the mother of invention" is a better way to explain what happened next. Needing to find a way to remain influential in national politics after Smith-Connally, the Congress of Industrial Organizations (CIO) created a special new subsidiary organization called the Political Action Committee, or PAC, in 1943 to contribute to Roosevelt's reelection and keep congressional allies in office. Contributions totaling well over $1 million were raised for PAC in the 1944 election from individual union members (not union organizations) and were held in bank accounts entirely separate from the CIO's bank account—known as "separate segregated funds" in legal speak— and so was not technically considered CIO money (Sabato 1984, 5). Thus the Smith-Connally ban was circumvented. The CIO soon changed PAC's name to Committee on Political Education (COPE), but the original name stuck: PAC became the common name for all such campaign funding organizations (Zeigler and Peak 1972, 245).

Even though CIO's PAC helped reelect Roosevelt to a fourth term and increased Democratic control of the House of Representatives by twenty seats in 1944, corporations and business groups were wary of starting their own PACs because it was not yet clear how significant their long-term influence would be or whether they were legal. A few business PACs did emerge in the 1960s, such as the National Association of Manufacturers' Business-Industry PAC (BIPAC) and the American Medical Association's AMPAC, but most corporate money continued to be given by individuals, "bundled" together and distributed on Capitol Hill by lobbyists and often by members of Congress just as it was in the 1870s (Sabato 1984, 6).[4] Legitimacy for PACs came with the 1971 passage of the **Federal Election Campaign Act** (FECA), which also required the government to collect and make available data on who gave to PACs and which candidates or national parties received money from a PAC. The act became stronger with amendments in 1974 (after abuses in the 1972 presidential contest by Richard Nixon's campaign, when corporations were almost literally shaken down for money), setting up the contemporary legal structure for PACs and creating the **Federal Election Commission** (FEC) to regulate PAC activity and make all of the data available.

More importantly, FECA 1974 set clear contribution limits. Corporations and unions remained blocked from giving directly to candidates and parties, as were foreigners. Public financing based on an income tax checkoff system for presidential elections was created for candidates willing to limit the amount of money they spent and contributions they accepted from PACs and other sources. Contributions from individuals were severely limited, ironically making PACs more attractive for fundraising and contributing. An individual today can only give $2,500 to a candidate in a primary election, and then the same amount again to the same candidate in the general election. Individuals can, however, also give $5,000 to as many political action committees as they want each year, though the total they can give to all PACs cannot exceed $70,800. PACs themselves are limited to giving $5,000 per candidate per election, though they do not have a yearly limit on overall giving. Each can also give up to $15,000 annually to a national political party as well as $5,000 to another PAC.[5]

Most graphs of the total number of PACs in national elections, such as Figure 10.1, begin in 1974 because that was when the FEC declared PACs to be legal. First in was the Sun Oil Company, which established SunPAC, funded by company shareholders, executives, and ordinary employees. But only this **restricted class** of individuals could contribute to SunPAC, and the company could not pressure any of its employees to contribute. As other companies began establishing PACs that did solicit employee contributions, unions complained that employees were being exploited, which led Congress to further amend FECA in 1976 by limiting solicitations of employees to twice a year. Labor unions could still solicit their members without restriction, and if a business used a payroll deduction to make it easier for its employees to contribute, then that company's union could do the same. With this legal framework in place, everyone now felt more or less free to establish PACs, raise funds, and contribute to congressional and presidential races.

Another big event was the US Supreme Court's 1976 decision in *Buckley v. Valeo*, which held that spending money to influence elections was protected free speech under the First Amendment. Limits on how much individuals could spend on their own campaigns were struck down, and PACs were approved as a reasonable means of expressing political interests by giving. Contributing money to advance a political agenda or ideology was apparently no different from standing on a soap box to give a speech. And with this, the PAC era began: while the FEC recorded 608 PACs in 1974, by 2011 there were 4,859.

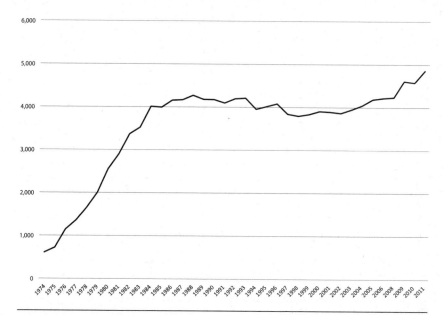

FIGURE 10.1   Total Number of PACs Registered with the Federal Election Commission, 1974–2011

Source: Federal Election Commission

Growth, Reform, and Innovation

Since the 1970s the political landscape has become crowded with further efforts to reform the campaign finance system; the more extreme efforts, such as banning PACs entirely, fizzled and died. There has been a lack of reform in spite of seemingly endless media stories about abuse and corruption, and a growing cottage industry of good-government interest groups like Common Cause, Center for Responsive Politics, and Center for Public Integrity advocating for stronger limits and disclosures. Political reporters, good-government advocates, and even scholars have laid the blame for the lack of reform not so much on PACs and interest groups as on their beneficiaries in Congress (e.g., Drew 1999).

As Figure 10.2 shows, the sheer amount of PAC money raised in races for the House of Representatives has risen dramatically, and this is only a portion of the total amounts raised by House candidates. If members of Congress are convinced that they need enormous campaign war chests to survive in office, what incentive do they have to enact reform legislation cutting off the supply? Ironically, though, even as they rake in PAC money, candidates on all

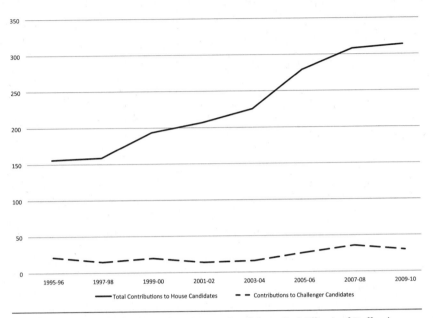

FIGURE 10.2   PAC Contributions to House Candidates (in Millions of Dollars)
Source: Vital Statistics on American Politics, 2011–2012

sides rail against alleged PAC and interest group corruption. In 1995, Republicans swept out Democrats, whom they accused of being beholden to special
interest groups, and promised to reform the House right along with the rest
of the Washington establishment. Then the new GOP members immediately
started raising money from PACs. Ann McBride of Common Cause told the
Washington Post, "The freshmen have become instant incumbents . . . raising
money like incumbents. It shows how rotten and corrosive the system is. . . .
It's not benign money, it's interested money." Of course newly elected representative Robert Ehrlich (R-MD) did not see it that way and replied in the
same article, "I don't see undue influence of any group. The fact is, the avail-
ability of PAC money helped me even the playing field" (Melton 1995). To
look at the amounts of PAC money contributed in recent elections, it seems
that a lot of "evening of the playing field" is required. Figure 10.2 shows that
total House contributions alone were over $300 million in the 2009–2010
campaign cycle, most of it going to **incumbents**, not those who challenge
incumbents (the dashed line). Moreover, Figure 10.3 shows that by 2010 total
PAC contributions in elections for national office reached nearly $1.2 billion.

   Gaps in FECA's contribution limits led to the emergence of **soft money** as
a way to circumvent limits in the late twentieth century. Federal election law
placed no limits on how much PACs could give to state and local political

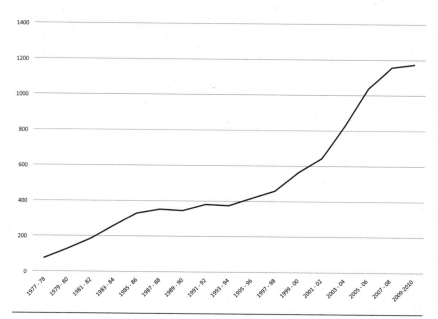

FIGURE 10.3   Total Federal PAC Spending (in Millions of Dollars), 1977–2010
Source: Vital Statistics on American Politics, 2011–2012

parties for what was loosely called "party-building activities." These parties could use the money to fund get-out-the-vote drives and advertising that shaped public opinion in elections. Soft money could *not* be used for anything that specifically advocated for or against a candidate for national office, but anything that builds a state or local party, turns out votes for that party, or shapes the issues driving a political campaign to favor that party is going to have significant impact on congressional and presidential races. It also frees the parties to spend other money directly on elections for national office. Richard Cook, a former Lockheed Corporation lobbyist, said, "You can call it giving to state parties, but it's close to legal bribery" (Stone 1995). During the 1990s, both Republican and Democratic parties brought in hundreds of millions of dollars from PACs through the soft money loophole, initially advantaging the Republicans but with Democrats catching up by the end of the century.[6]

Soft money was largely banned by the 2002 **Bipartisan Campaign Reform Act** (often called the McCain-Feingold Act after its Senate sponsors), giving creative campaigners an incentive to find new ways to go around the new limits. McCain-Feingold also prohibited advertisements funded by a contributor independent of the benefitting candidate that attacked the candidate's opponents thirty days before primary elections and sixty days before general elections. By the end of the twentieth century corporations, unions, and politically active nonprofits were frequently using this form of **independent expenditure** to influence elections by raising issues damaging to a candidate, even if the candidate was never mentioned and the ad was never approved by that candidate's opponent. But the issue-ad restriction in McCain-Feingold was struck down by the Supreme Court in 2007's *Federal Election Commission v. Wisconsin Right to Life.* The Court said that such ads could only be prohibited if they specifically attacked a candidate, not if they just shaped voter opinion by raising uncomfortable issues.

The rest of the issue-ad restriction was eliminated in 2010 by the Court in *Citizens United v. Federal Election Commission.* Recalling *Buckley v. Valeo,* the Court ruled that any legal restrictions on spending by corporations, unions, and nonprofits for issue advertising, even ads that *do* attack candidates, violate the First Amendment unless it is *clearly coordinated* with a candidate or party. Corporations, unions, and nonprofits can also give freely, the Court said, to other interest groups that create attack ads, though these interest groups still cannot coordinate their attacks with the benefitting candidate (see the Chamber of Commerce case study at the end of this chapter). Routing money like this through third parties makes it harder to track corporate and union money, since the receiving organizations generally do not have to disclose their contributors. Thus financial giants Goldman Sachs and Morgan Stanley can say they do not give political contributions when both gave to the California Public Securities Association in 2010 to support the association's political causes (Levey and Geiger 2011).

New Campaign Funding Organizations

With traditional soft money contributions slowing down after McCain-Feingold, new third-party advocacy organizations established under section 527 of the Internal Revenue Code started to appear as alternative conduits for giving. Most political parties, candidate campaign committees, and PACs are actually organized as section 527s, but the term **527 organizations** as used today refers to special groups that are not registered as PACs but still created solely to raise and spend money on independent expenditures like issue advertising. All they must do is not coordinate with a campaign or attack or promote candidates (like PACs), though they must periodically disclose who their contributors are. Well-known 527s associated with conservatives are Club for Growth, Swift Boat Veterans for Truth, and New Conservative Coalition; those on the left are People of Color United, America Coming Together, and MoveOn.org.[7] Much of their work has been on the same issue advertising and get-out-the-vote drives that state and local parties did when soft money was still legal, so in a real sense 527s are simply a new way to move soft money. Or rather, they were. Data from the Center for Responsive Politics shows that while 527s active at the national level spent nearly $442 million in 2004, by 2010 it was less than half of that and on track to be even half again by the presidential election of 2012.[8] Why? Because of super PACs.

Following the *Citizens United* decision, in 2010 the US Court of Appeals ruled in *SpeechNOW.org v. Federal Election Commission* that PACs can accept individual, corporate, and union contributions of over $5,000 if they do not coordinate their activities with campaigns or contribute money to campaigns. But unlike 527 organizations and ordinary PACs, purely independent expenditure–oriented **super PACs** *can* attack or promote specific candidates for federal office, including the presidency. Candidates benefitting from a super PAC's efforts can even attend its fundraisers so long as they do not personally solicit any money (Mann and Ornstein 2012, 154). Former FEC commissioner Trevor Potter summed it up, "This is pretty much the holy grail that people have been looking for" (Eggen and Farnam 2010).[9]

Super PACs were test-driven in the 2010 midterm election, spending $84 million total (Farnam 2010). In 2012, they became the preferred method for moving large amounts of money, though super PACs still must report their contributors to the FEC. Interestingly, many super PACs appear to be funded not by corporations and unions at all, but by exceptionally wealthy individuals such as Las Vegas casino owner Sheldon Adelson (giving to Winning Our Future, the Congressional Leadership Fund, and Restore Our Future), the brothers Charles and David Koch (giving to Americans for Prosperity and Restore Our Future), and George Soros (giving to Priorities USA Action and Majority PAC) (Eggen 2012). A few super PACs, though, are supported by unions such as Workers' Voice. Whether super PACs will last or be replaced when a new loophole in the campaign finance laws is found cannot be known now, just as the real influence of all of these PACs, 527s, and super PACs is hard to pin down.

Types of PACs

The more traditional, interest group–sponsored PACs come with colorful and sometimes comical acronyms, or "pacronyms" as the FEC calls them.[10] Some names are practical, like PORK PAC for the National Pork Producers Council. Some are more colorful, such as BAC PAC for Florida Building and Construction Trades Council, JAAMPAC for National Japanese American PAC,

SMACCPAC for Sheet Metal and Air Conditioning Contractors' PAC (or SMACC PAC for Student Mothers and Concerned Citizens PAC), SNACK-PAC for the Snack Food Association, WOLF-PAC for Working for Opportunity and Leadership Fund, and the now retired SIX PAC (an independent PAC unconnected to the beer industry). Some seemingly famous PACs are not PACs at all, such as AIPAC, which stands for American-Israeli Public Affairs Committee and is more of a standard interest group. Super PACs do not tend to use acronyms but prefer names that sound more like dramatic citizen-unifying calls-to-arms, such as Winning Our Future, Endorse Liberty, and Freedom PAC.

It is perhaps more useful to see traditional, interest group–connected PACs in terms of the types of groups they are affiliated with. In Figures 10.4 and 10.5 I break out the total number of PACs over time and their total contributions in federal campaigns by affiliation—whether it's with corporations, labor unions, or trade and professional associations, or they are unconnected. As you can see in the two figures, organized labor may have pioneered the PAC concept, but in terms of PAC numbers they are laggards. Corporations have traditionally dominated the PAC universe, which is not surprising, as they have few other ways of exerting political influence. Trade groups and labor unions, by contrast, see PACs as one tool among many to gain access and rely on them less. In terms of money contributed, however, there is some equality across types, with corporate PACs collectively contributing only a little (if $60 million can be a little) more than labor unions in the 2009–2010 cycle. In both numbers and contributions, though, it is the **nonconnected PACs** that are coming to dominate the universe of contributing organizations and the amounts contributed. These PACs are wholly independent of any parent organization and can solicit every American for money, though they still must comply with the same contribution and spending limits as group-connected PACs (meaning this category does not include super PACs).[11] The advantage of nonconnected PACs, and what makes them so attractive, is their freedom to solicit contributions from anyone, whereas corporate and labor PACs can only solicit from individuals connected to their organizations (employees, union members, stockholders, and so forth).

Why Form a PAC?

Nonconnected PACs aside, most interest groups establish PACs as complements to their larger lobbying efforts. For ideological reasons, though,

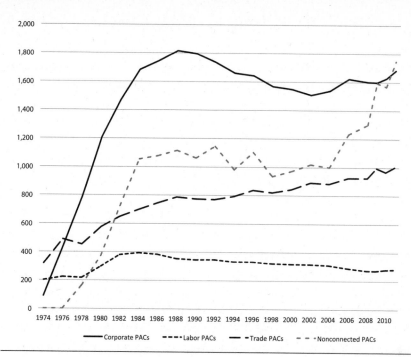

FIGURE 10.4   Number of Federal PACs by Type, 1974–2011
Source: Vital Statistics on American Politics, 2011–2012

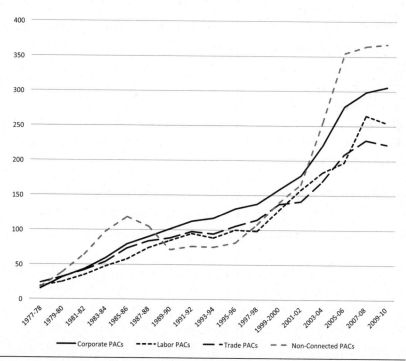

FIGURE 10.5   Contributions by Types of Federal PACs (in Millions of Dollars),
1977–2010

Source: Vital Statistics on American Politics, 2011–2012

some avoid them. Citizen groups warning of the corrupting influence of money in American politics can hardly turn around and create PACs, so most do not. Sometimes these good-government groups even try to use their PAC-less status to bolster their image of the little guy taking on the wealthy, business-as-usual crowd. But a few citizen groups do have PACs, such as Friends of the Earth, though these groups rarely have more than a few thousand dollars in their PACs.[12] Other interest groups simply do not see any need for one. AARP, perhaps the most powerful organized interest in the nation, has largely kept out of the PAC business. With several million older Americans ready to angrily call their elected officials on a moment's notice, storm Capitol Hill, or just vote useless legislators out of office, AARP has generally not seen any need for a PAC. So influential is AARP that its election recommendations and endorsements can actually direct the flow of its members' money to or away from candidates. Few groups, however, are in such an enviable position that they have the luxury of staying above the money game. In fact, many—and perhaps most—groups that form PACs do so to overcome the disadvantage of not having millions of dedicated group members. The weaker their other resources, the more need they have to make PAC contributions.

Corporations do not have any grassroots resources to draw on. Without any clear constituent connection, giving money is often the only way they can hope to influence policy decisions. Perhaps that is why some businesses have tried to stay out of politics, though many have discovered that ignoring the government is not a good business strategy. Microsoft refused to become involved in elections and lobbying until 1995, when the Federal Communication Commission (FCC) began taking a harder look at Internet use (Grimaldi 2000). Indeed, most high tech firms started contributing and lobbying in the 1990s to gain contracts and research and development credits, as well as to influence the way the FCC regulated the Internet (Hart 2001). On the other hand, IBM took itself out of the campaign game in 1976 (though not out of legislative lobbying) after its endorsements started alienating customers (Hart 2001, 1242–1243).

More broadly, corporations establish PACs and make financial contributions in elections because they understand what a powerful role government regulators play in trade policy, tax policy, and communications policy (just to name a few). Research by Neil Mitchell, Wendy Hansen, and Jeffrey Drope (2004) found that corporations form PACs and contribute when they expect (or fear) that issues important to them will emerge on the government's agenda but do not want to engage in other, more highly visible, and possibly customer-alienating forms of lobbying. Corporations also form PACs when they are highly reliant on government contracts, when they have unionized (or potentially unionizable) employees, when they have significant foreign operations, or when they see their opponents doing it.

What Does All This Money Buy?

Now the big question: Just what are all of these contributions buying? And that begs another question: What are donors primarily giving to? Do donors give to just one political party, meaning they are supporting a specific ideology, or are they pragmatically giving to both? The media often portrays contributions as buying the votes of lawmakers, and the public seems inclined to believe this. Political scientists, however, have largely rejected this portrayal as myth. While a few scholars claim that donations do influence official roll-call votes in Congress (e.g., Kau and Rubin 1981; Stratmann 2002), most come to the opposite conclusion. Henry Chappell (1981; 1982), for instance, found PAC money to have only a marginal influence on legislators' votes, and John Wright (1990) found essentially no correlation between PAC money and votes at all. Yet nobody would claim that money has zero influence, because why else would so much money exchange hands during election season? The connection between money and influence is subtle. The "currency is complex," says Janet Grenzke (1989), and most interest groups are using money to do one of two things: reshape the partisan and ideological makeup of Congress and gain access to key lawmakers.

Reshaping Congress: Ideological PACs

Up until when presidential candidates started opting out of the public finance program that restricted PAC donations, most interest groups focused their donations on candidates for Congress. As Figure 10.2 showed, incumbents have traditionally been the favored beneficiaries of PAC giving (Chappell 1982; Jacobson 1992), but more and more, these groups are trying to use their donations to reshape the partisan and ideological makeup of the House and Senate, especially nonconnected PACs and super PACs. They do it because they themselves tend to represent groups of highly ideological and highly motivated people in the electorate who prefer antigovernment conservatives to state-supporting liberals, or vice versa. Thus these PACs focus their electioneering efforts not on persuading lawmakers to help them in the legislating process but on using elections to oust legislators unsupportive of their PAC's political ideology and replacing them with true believers. Put another way, these **ideological PACs** are not trying to change minds in Congress; they are trying to change the bodies that make up the Congress. They aggressively support candidates in primary and general elections supportive of their ideology, even if the candidates are inexperienced challengers taking on entrenched incumbents.

Labor unions first used PAC contributions to influence electoral outcomes in favor of Democrats in the 1940s (Rudolph 1999), but most groups trying to reshape Congress through elections are fairly new to the political arena and tend to represent small but highly motivated and intensely partisan segments of the populace. They want to see policy reflect their values—their notions of right and wrong—and are happy to use the electoral process, and then the lawmaking process subsequently dominated by their ideological friends, to make it happen whether the rest of the nation wants it or not. They are found on both ends of the ideological spectrum. One of the earliest players of this PAC type was EMILY's List, a 527 organization devoted to electing pro-choice, Democratic women to office (a similar PAC, WISH, does largely the same thing for pro-life women; see Day and Hadley 2001). To give their efforts an extra kick, EMILY's List pioneered **bundling**, in which contributions from many individuals and groups are assembled and passed on to candidates. Because EMILY's List does not donate much of its own money, it complies with FECA limits and still wields considerable influence because it is presenting many other peoples' checks. Today many 527 organizations, super PACs, and nonconnected PACs use tactics like this to pursue the interests of their funders by changing Congress's ideological makeup.

So intense is the commitment of these organizations to advancing their ideological goals that they often prefer to support losing candidates who embrace their views instead of winners who, at best, are wishy-washy. This means ideological PACs are often likely to sponsor challengers against incumbents in long-shot races to prove their ideological commitment to their funders (Godwin 1988). They also tend to strictly align with one or the other parties more than most PACs. Political scientist Amy McKay (2010) shows that the more ideologically extreme a PAC is, left or right, the more closely it aligns itself with, and only donates to members of, one political party. And their numbers and influence appear to be increasing. While the Tea Party is more of a social movement than a PAC, it is backed by many PACs and super PACs, such as Crossroads GPS, Tea Party Express, and FreedomWorks, all spending millions to elect conservative, libertarian Republicans to Congress (Eggan and Farnam 2011). The Tea Party and their PACs are even willing to challenge moderate Republicans in primaries in an effort to not only reshape Congress but force the Republican Party in Congress to become more conservative. Thus the Tea Party blurs the lines between party, social movement, and interest group, with their ideological PACs and super PACs looking like extensions of political party funding operations. Or are the parties becoming extensions of these ideological PACs and their tens of thousands of supporters? It is hard to tell, but arguably these ideological PACs are both causes of, and symptoms of, the growing hyper-partisanship in modern politics.

Gaining Access and Other Little Things: Accommodationist PACs

What about the rest of the PACs? If nonideological PACs are not spending money to reshape Congress, what are they doing? Political scientist Frank Sorauf says it is all about gaining access (1992, 70). And it is true that most business associations and corporations just want a little time with lawmakers already in Congress. Let the limelight-loving crusader groups worry about ideology and party control; trade associations will be content with a few minutes with the right people and perhaps a little help where it counts in the lawmaking process in return for contributing at fundraisers.

To make giving and networking easier, members of Congress hold periodic fundraisers, many of which are actually sponsored by interest groups. While popular perception of fundraisers may be swanky evening black-tie banquets, research by the radio program Planet Money found that only 22 percent were held in the evening, and only 10 percent of those were dinners. In reality, 25 percent of fundraisers were breakfasts, and another 24 percent were larger affairs like hunting trips and golf outings (Planet Money 2012b). But whatever time of day they occur, the big fundraisers are headlined by powerful members of Congress with whom contributors want to get some face time. Contributing to get a moment with a committee chair is often worth the price of admission. Business lobbyist Stephen Brown told a *Wall Street Journal* reporter while he was waiting for a moment with Rep. Gerald Solomon (R-NY), "It's just our way of sending our appreciation for being able to have access" (Kuntz 1995). Solomon was chair of the powerful House Rules Committee and hosting a fundraiser to bring in deep-pocketed PACs to support a little-known colleague.

Broadly speaking, business and trade association PACs are **accommodationist PACs** in that their choices of contribution recipients are largely not swayed by political ideology or party affiliation. Their contributions may marginally influence House and Senate roll-call votes on the most nonideological and least visible issues (which is most of them; see Witko 2006), but these contributors mostly give to get some time with important lawmakers or with lawmakers who may one day be important. Access helps these groups get all of their bills and amendments lined up long before any roll-call votes take place. Contributions rarely carry a persuasive message, but they open doors so that a lobbyist has the chance to explain why it is in the legislator's own interest to aid the group behind the PAC. This is an important point. Contributions by accommodationist PACs are a supplement to interest groups' broader lobbying strategies (Wright 1990), something to help their lobbyists get on the crowded appointment schedules of busy legislators, or at least get meetings with somebody in legislators' offices other than interns, long before there are any roll-call votes (Langbein 1986).

I emphasized in Chapter 6 the importance lobbyists place on building relationships with legislators, usually with those whom a lobbyist's group has a constituency connection. Interest groups with these relationships contribute to help keep their allies in office. Those without connections give because it helps compensate for not having a shared constituency. Contributions help these lobbyists get appointments to see important legislators and convince them to help move a group's desired legislation out of committee. Or to offer an amendment to a committee bill containing language important to the group. Or to oppose other amendments harmful to the group. Or to simply give a crucial speech that positively frames the policy proposal favored by the group while portraying other policy alternatives as unfeasible and maybe even unpatriotic. The contributing group may also want a committee legislator to pressure a regulatory agency troublesome to the group's members to desist or face uncomfortable oversight hearings and budget cuts (Fellowes and Wolf 2004). So contributing does not just supplement a lobbying campaign; it helps make up for other weaknesses like lack of constituency-based connections. Since legislators are coming under greater pressure now to raise money for their parties, their incentive to accommodate groups that give a lot is also increasing (Currinder 2009).

Other Trends in Strategic Giving

A few other points about strategic giving by PACs are worth discussing, including the importance of committee jurisdiction, the role of leaders and

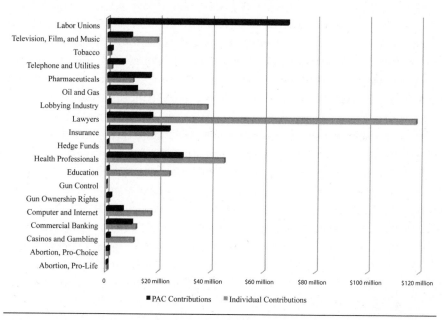

FIGURE 10.6   Individual and PAC Contributions by Issue or Industry, 2009–2010
Election Cycle

Source: Center for Responsive Politics

parties, why and how constituent connections matter, the timing of donations, and the pressure to give and the fear of retribution.

Committee Jurisdiction Matters

PACs tend to give to lawmakers on committees controlling policy important to the organizations (Gopoian 1984; Hall and Wayman 1990). Committee assignments are so important that when a PAC's longtime ally and contribution recipient leaves a committee, there is an observable decline in giving by that PAC to that legislator (Romer and Snyder 1984). Though the PAC may still give some support to the departing member if there is a constituency connection, with limited resources most of its money will go to current committee members so that its lobbyist can remain a part of the committee's business and culture. The smart lobbyist says yes to fundraising invitations from new legislators coming on to the committee whom he or she might have otherwise ignored; at the fundraiser the lobbyist can meet the new legislator and educate him or her regarding the group's interests in the committee while delivering a check.

Some committees' issue jurisdictions affect more segments of the public than others. Consequently, having a membership on those committees means you can attract more contributions. The Planet Money research mentioned earlier also found that over the last twenty years legislators on committees such as the House Ways and Means Committee, Financial Services Committee, and Energy and Commerce Committee, with jurisdiction over tax policy, banking policy, and energy policy, respectively, attract far more contributions than those on other committees. Alternatively, legislators on Judiciary, Natural Resources, and Administration bring in less than the average legislator (Planet Money 2012a). Similarly, some policy domains attract more contributions than others, both from PACs and from individuals. In Figure 10.6, I present data from the Center for Responsive Politics on PAC and individual contributions in the 2009–2010 election cycle. Labor union issues get the most PAC contributions (from labor unions), with health care next. Issues concerning lawyers get the most contributions from individuals (probably lawyers), though many are directed by lawyers' interest groups.

Parties and Leaders

Because accommodationist groups are so committee- and incumbent-focused, it is unsurprising to see that most PACs give to both parties, even in the highly partisan elections of recent years (Ronayne 2011). The Center for Responsive Politics breaks out the amounts given by over three thousand PACs to each party in the 2011–2012 electoral cycle, which I convert to percentages and graph in Figure 10.7. Each dot represents a PAC's ratio of Democrat to Republican contributions. If PAC giving was polarized by party, then the thick line of dots stretching from percentage-given-to-Democrats (vertical axis) to percentage-given-to-Republicans (horizontal axis) would not exist. Again, PACs are helping their parent interest groups concentrate on building relationships with key committee members, regardless of party. Once a relationship is established, groups spend heavily to keep that friend in office so they can rise in seniority and, consequently, become a more powerful friend. This is the secret of most PAC contributing: contributions are more about keeping friends in office than about pressuring lawmakers to change their votes. In fact, most lobbyists like to have allies in both parties to hedge their bets, for today's minority party could be tomorrow's majority.

Committee and party leaders get more contributions than junior members. Lobbyists who have built relationships with the chair of a key committee, or majority and minority leaders (especially the Senate minority), have an

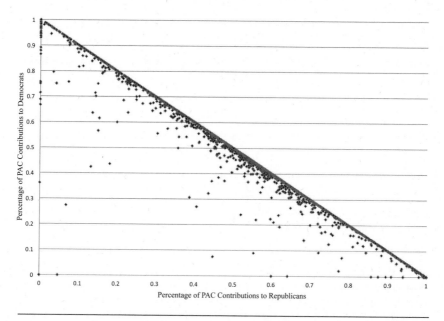

FIGURE 10.7   Percentage of PAC Contributions to Democrats and Republicans
Source: Center for Responsive Politics

enormous asset they want to preserve at all costs by keeping him or her in office, and they are willing to spend to do so (Rudolph 1999). Committee chairs largely determine which bills start the legislative process and which die. Among their many other powers, party leaders decide whether those bills will ever come up for roll-call votes in the House and Senate. So they get more money, and get it earlier, both to protect themselves and to build up their **leadership PACs**, which are a special kind of PAC lawmakers use to raise money from other PACs. The money is then redirected to the leaders' own party members (Currinder 2009). Some party leaders have tried to use their disproportionately greater power to pressure interest groups into giving to their party. Former House Majority Leader Tom DeLay (R-TX) famously kept a notebook on a table outside his office listing which groups had contributed to Republicans and which had not, and it was well known that those not listed as Republican "friends" might as well talk to a wall than ask him for help (Kaiser 2009, 264). Still, Figure 10.7 shows that most PACs contribute to both parties.

The Constituent Connection

The connections among lawmakers, constituents, and interest group members influence not only to whom money is given but how it is raised. PACs find it easier to convince their members to contribute when they promise to give that money to popular incumbents currently representing those members or to challengers who may oust incumbents detested by members (Wright 1985). This is not surprising, since group members are likely to have the strongest feelings about the legislators who represent them. Sometimes, to keep their members' support, PAC and interest group leaders negotiate with their members over which legislators will receive money in an election. This link between legislators and groups representing some of their constituents can be so strong that ideological differences between groups and legislators get pushed aside (Wright 1989; Hojnacki and Kimball 2001). It works well for the lobbyist, since the constituency connection is the prime tool for gaining access to a legislator and the foundation of their ongoing relationship. Giving PAC money to this lawmaker simply cements the relationship; pleasing constituent members by giving to that lawmaker is an added bonus. It helps the lawmaker, too, since taking PAC money raised outside of the district makes the legislator look like the pawn of outside special interests (Alexander 2005).

Giving on Time

It takes money to raise money in politics. Raising money early is crucial to elected officials, especially challengers, though incumbents can use early money to discourage potential challengers (Jacobson 1992). Interest group and PAC leaders understand this, and some, like EMILY's List, specifically contribute early to help favored candidates raise more money down the line (Box-Steffensmeier, Radcliffe, and Bartels 2004). Most PACs, though, are conservative about contributing early because they want to back winners. It is another reason why they favor incumbents (who nearly always win) and are often unwilling to take a chance on a challenger unless that challenger shows early on that they can win, usually through aggressive fundraising. For candidates challenging incumbents, this PAC mind-set makes raising money early extremely difficult. More ideological, nonconnected PACs and super PACs, however, are more likely to take risks on challengers who embrace their ideological positions, but they are still a minority. Nonideological PACs are likely to give significant amounts of money early only when a partisan wave is building that is likely to change the minority party, as happened in 1980 (Eismeier and Pollock 1986), 1994, and 2010. PACs may also give late in a race when there is a clear winner, and they tend to tread cautiously in close races, when no winner is clear. They may also give after the election to help the winner erase campaign debts. The winner may not appreciate the late-giving PAC as much as one that took a chance on him or her early, but it may be better to give later than never if an interest group hopes to gain a foothold with the new representative or senator.

Pressure and Punishment

Many lobbyists do not actually enjoy raising and contributing money but feel they have no choice. To them it is a "pay to play" system in which, more than ever, party and congressional leaders are pushing lobbyists to raise money and get involved in more campaigns. Failure to do so, lobbyists fear, means exclusion from the governing party's agenda and orders from House and Senate leaders to their rank-and-file members to stiff-arm noncontributing lobbyists (Justice 2004). Yet, despite stories about Rep. DeLay's friends and enemies notebook, there is little concrete evidence that legislators punish lobbyists who don't contribute to them (McCarty and Rothenberg 1996). Nevertheless, lobbyists are driven by fear of what could happen. If one party is on the verge of taking the majority, everything suddenly becomes partisan, and the pressure on lobbyists to favor only one party, regardless of how good it has been on the lobbyist's members' issues, can be enormous. Should one party be supported even if that means abandoning old friends in the other party? Generally lobbyists try to avoid abandoning investments in any of their long-time friends, for that sends a terrible message to all of the lobbyist's allies, and the abandoned friend might be back in power in the future but much less friendly.

Is the reverse true? Do lobbyists punish legislators who do not vote in their members' interests? The evidence is thin, partially because it is unclear under just what circumstances a group would try to punish lawmakers by withholding contributions. After votes in Congress by union-backed legislators for the labor-despised North American Free Trade Agreement (NAFTA) in 1993, unions actually did withhold money from Democrats, but this punishment was short-lived, and soon these lawmakers were again receiving the same amount of union money as before (Engle and Jackson 1998). Again, money is given to keep friends in office, not to buy roll-call votes. Friends may occasionally go off the rails and oppose contributors, but in many other, less visible ways, they can still help the interest group and its lobbyist. Moreover, the group has probably invested tremendously in building the relationship with this legislator and does not want to consider it all wasted, and anybody who defeats that legislator is going to be even less sympathetic to the group's interests. Furthermore, given contribution limits and the enormous amount of money candidates must raise, it is unlikely that losing the financial support of one or a few groups would hurt a legislator much. This is really the bottom line: when it comes to giving, individual interest groups (though not super PACs) are in the weaker position and more likely to be exploited as ATMs by lawmakers than being able to hold the lawmaking system in thrall. Money still has a dangerous influence, just not quite in the way that most people believe is true.

Endorsements and Campaign Support

There are several other important ways in which interest groups participate in elections apart from PAC contributions. One is **endorsements**. High-profile interest groups, particularly those with large memberships such as the NRA, the Chamber of Commerce, the National Education Association, the American Farm Bureau Federation, and AARP, are often looked to by members, and even many nonmembers, for advice on whom to vote for. Who do their leaders think is the best candidate in terms of their interests? Gaining an endorsement can make or break a candidate, especially a challenger, not only because the organization will urge its members to support the candidate, but also because money often follows endorsements from that group and others. It provides a cloak of legitimacy to a challenger candidate and consequently strips it from an incumbent who once enjoyed the endorsement.

As part of determining who is to be endorsed, some interest groups develop and publicly release scorecards that rate incumbents on how loyal they have been to the group's agenda. Groups like the NRA, the Chamber, Americans for Democratic Action, Americans for Constitutional Action, the AFL-CIO's Committee on Public Education, and many environmental groups select several roll-call votes in the House and Senate on issues considered crucial to their interests and calculate the percentage of times each incumbent voted for their group's position (Fowler 1982). Many incumbents, usually those desiring high scores but getting lower ones, complain that these score sheets ignore other important votes, or misunderstand the meaning of votes used, and therefore distort the incumbents' real level of support for the group's position. Indeed, these score sheets often do make incumbents look more ideologically extreme than they really are (Snyder 1992) or just get the lawmaker's ideology wrong (Groseclose, Levitt, and Snyder 1999). Some interest groups therefore use a much simpler method for determining endorsements. They endorse candidates willing to sign pledges promising to support the group's positions. The best example is Americans for Tax Reform, run by lobbyist Grover Norquist, which has convinced many lawmakers, mostly Republicans, to sign pledges that they will never, ever vote to raise taxes or anything that looks or smells like a tax—as determined by Norquist (Montgomery 2011).

Some interest groups do more than just endorse; they also act. Historically this took the form of operating phone banks on behalf of candidates, making calls to promote a candidate, and getting voters out to vote. Sometimes they provide transportation to polls or bring mail-in ballots to voters. Changes in technology and the loosening of laws restricting contributions for issue advertising have made it easier for many more interest groups to aggressively promote favored candidates and attack others. Beyond television ads, groups can use YouTube, click-here advertising on Web sites, and Facebook. Through these various advertising tactics, interest groups try shaping public opinion in those crucial weeks right before an election, when voters are starting to focus on candidates and issues.

One of the more interesting developments in the last couple of decades has been the emergence of religious organizations in electoral politics with tremendous ability to mobilize voters. Religion in American politics goes back to the nation's founding, but the emergence of the Reverend Jerry Falwell's Moral Majority in the early 1980s is usually marked as the beginning of modern religious activism in electoral politics. Promoting a conservative social agenda, including banning abortion and opposing same-sex marriage, while increasing government support for homeschooling, the Moral Majority used church sermons and religious television programs to promote political ideas and endorse candidates for office. The Moral Majority faded after the Reagan presidency but was replaced in the 1990s by the Christian Coalition, a more grassroots-oriented organization promoting much of the same agenda, but with an even greater focus on elections (Guth et al. 2007). Influential in the Republican takeover of Congress in 1994, instrumental in helping George W. Bush defeat John McCain in the South Carolina Republican primary in 2000, and aggressively remobilized by Karl Rove to help Bush defeat John Kerry in 2004, the Christian Coalition's mobilization strategy became the archetype of grassroots advocacy in elections at the beginning of the twenty-first century. Other religious groups have also sought to get into electoral politics, including the Catholic Church, which has repeatedly condemned abortion and threatened to excommunicate the Catholic Kerry for his pro-choice positions (Finer 2004). Opposition organizations such as Americans United for the Separation of Church and State have tried to use the First Amendment barrier to keep religion out of politics, but so far with little success.

■ CASE STUDY ■

Shifting Politics at the US Chamber of Commerce

Interest groups change strategies over time, and sometimes this means moving aggressively into the electoral arena to pursue member interests, both as a contributor to campaigns and as an independent spender on issue advertising. Perhaps no organization demonstrates this better than the US Chamber of Commerce.

STAGE ONE: FINDING ITS FEET

In 2012 the Chamber celebrated its hundredth anniversary. It had been established in 1912 at the urging of President William Howard Taft to defend all American businesses, large and small, against the growing power of organized labor (Truman 1951, 85). This mission has not always gone well. The Chamber has sometimes found it hard to convince small businesses that they have issues in common with globe-spanning corporations, and many small businesses find a better fit with the National Federation of Independent Business (Young 2010). The Chamber reached a low point in the 1960s, with a diminished number of members, a lack of respect from its members, and an incoherent political agenda (Vogel 1989, 34).

By the late 1970s everything began to change. Alarmed at the increase in the number of citizen and public interest groups on the ideological left blaming business for all of America's social ills, business leaders began organizing a counterattack. Part of this strategy was to breathe life and fire back into the Chamber of Commerce (Vogel 1989, 193). The Chamber's revival was noticed by Rep. Guy Vander Jagt (R-MI), chair of the National Republican

Congressional Committee. Business interests, Vander Jagt argued, would be better served if Republicans controlled Congress, and he contended that business PAC money ought to flow exclusively to the Republican Party (Jackson 1990).

STAGE TWO: IRRITATING FRIENDS

Business contributions certainly helped Republicans put Ronald Reagan in the White House in 1980, as well as take over the Senate and make gains in the House, but Rep. Tony Coelho (D-CA) starkly reminded groups like the Chamber that there were plenty of pro-business Democrats in Congress and that Democrats were not likely to get any weaker now, so business had better start supporting the Democratic Party as well (Jackson 1990). Whether or not Coelho's veiled threats were persuasive, the Chamber became a more bipartisan contributor in the 1980s and 1990s, supporting incumbents based more on individual voting records than the desire to favor one political party over the other. In other words, the Chamber became a true accommodationist group.

Nor were its positions on issues necessarily aligned with Republicans. In 1993, the Chamber came out in support of President Bill Clinton's health care legislation, as well as another Clinton priority, the North American Free Trade Agreement. Republicans were furious. Rep. John Boehner (R-OH), later Speaker of the House, encouraged businesses all over the country to dump their Chamber memberships in protest, and the Chamber was largely shut out when Republicans took the majority in 1995 until it replaced its president, Richard Lesher (Verini 2010).

STAGE THREE: RISING POWERHOUSE

The embattled Chamber hired Thomas J. Donohue as its president in 1997. His generous compensation, which was $4.9 million in 2011 (the second highest for an association executive just behind the Edison Electric Institute; see Stolberg 2013), reflected the Chamber's high expectations, and Donohue didn't disappoint. He quickly retooled the organization into a campaign heavyweight. The Center for Responsive Politics reports that Chamber campaign contributions went from around $3,000 in 1996 to about $72,000 in 1998 and then to about $558,000 in 2000.[13] Although its PAC contributions actually declined somewhat in later years, overall spending on lobbying and elections by giving soft money for issue advertising increased. In 2009, to oppose new financial sector regulation legislation, climate change bills, and national health care legislation, the Chamber spent around $120 million on lobbying and creating television advertisements, reputedly spending $800,000 a day right before the final votes on the health care bill (Verini 2010). By 2012, it was spending $136 million on lobbying, more than any other interest group (Stolberg 2013). The Chamber also created an enormous grassroots program in 2008, signing up about six million people. Participants were encouraged to work on get-out-the-vote drives and deluge Capitol Hill with calls and letters opposing bills such as the Affordable Care Act (Hamburger 2010).

Much of this spending on media campaigns and issue advertising came out of the Chamber's general fund, an unusual move for an interest group. But the money was quickly replaced, as the Chamber promptly raised nearly $250 million to fund its electoral programs in 2010, much of it from health care and pharmaceutical companies (Verini 2010). Because businesses were only donating to the Chamber's general fund, campaign finance and tax laws allowed their contributions to remain anonymous, even though the Chamber spent an equivalent amount of money from its general fund on its election-eering programs. Member businesses preferred the anonymity, not wanting to be seen spending money on politics because it might alienate shareholders and contributors. Robert Kelner of the lobbying firm Covington & Burling said of this, "In the past a lot of companies and wealthy individuals stood on the sidelines. That cloud has been lifted" (Hamburger 2010).

The Chamber's contributions and endorsements today pretty clearly tilt Republican. In 2008, 86 percent of the Chamber's political activities were in support of Republicans (Hamburger 2010). In 2010, it rose to 93 percent (Murray 2010). In 2012, while most of the millions being spent on issue advertising by business associations were positive in tone, the Chamber's attacks were mostly negative and against Democrats (Farnam 2012b). Chamber officials pointed to what they say were their nonpartisan voting scorecards showing how members of Congress voted on issues deemed crucial to business. Democrats tended to score poorly, so the Chamber claimed it had no choice but to fund and endorse candidates challenging these legislators (Murray 2010). It made no secret of its intent in 2012 to keep the House under Republican control, spending $50 million to do it (Tate 2012). Yet after it spent millions in fifteen Senate races, only two of which it won, many are once again questioning the Chamber's aggressive political strategy (Yang and Hamburger 2012).

STAGE FOUR: THE NEW MODEL?

Even though its ambitions to get a Republican majority in the Senate in 2012 failed, the Chamber may still be setting an example for other interest groups to follow. One consequence of the Supreme Court's *Citizens United* decision is to allow unions and corporations to contribute unlimited amounts of money to interest groups. As long as the groups use that money for issue advertising not directly connected to a campaign, they do not have to disclose their contributors. Companies like Merck, Dow, and Prudential are willing to reveal their Chamber contributions, some over $1 million, but many others are not. The Chamber's willingness to front for these companies ensures that they will keep on contributing to the Chamber's political efforts (Leonnig 2012).

Even super PACs must disclose their contributors, suggesting that the next big thing in campaign finance will be donating directly to interest groups like the Chamber, where contributor names can remain secret. Since the 1990s, nonconnected PACs, 527s, and super PACs had been pushing interest groups to the margins of electoral politics, but a new emphasis on using interest groups as conduits for spending on issue advertising may bring them back to the forefront in campaign spending. At least it will if the law remains unchanged. As Bruce Freed of the Center for Political Accountability said, "Corporations should operate on the premise that their political donations will be disclosed. Secrecy breeds abuse and undermines accountability" (Leonnig 2012). Freed's organization along with other good-government groups are pushing for a constitutional amendment overturning *Citizens United*, or at least a new law requiring the names of contributors to interest groups for issue advertising to be disclosed.

■ ■ ■

In Summary

Here are the key issues discussed in this chapter:

- Money plays an enormous role in American politics, and one that has been growing over time.

- Interest groups and their PACs are no longer the primary sources of this campaign money. That title goes to 527 organizations and super PACs that are not connected to interest groups, though this may change if interest groups are allowed to raise money from wealthy contributors without being required to disclose the names of these contributors.
- Interest group PACs do not buy votes in Congress, and it is not clear that any contribution does.
- Highly ideological PACs, and especially nonconnected PACs not affiliated with any interest group, primarily spend to reshape the governing ideology of Congress, often by spending to defeat incumbents opposed to their ideology.
- Accommodationist interest groups and their PACs spend money to help their allies in the legislature, with whom they have built long-term relationships, stay in office.

So the very worst form of corruption, vote buying, is perhaps more mythical than real.

In September 2011, during a particularly noxious partisan fight in Congress over whether to raise the nation's debt ceiling or risk default on debt payments, Howard Schultz, CEO of the coffee giant Starbucks, sent a letter to his customers claiming to have convinced over one hundred other business leaders to quit contributing to political campaigns until a solid, transparent debt-reduction plan was put in place.[14] But by the first quarter of the following year tens of millions of dollars had been raised by President Obama and Republican rivals for the presidential election, and no federal debt reduction master plan was in sight. What will it take to reduce the enormous amount of money flowing into American congressional and presidential elections? Quite a bit it would seem, given the Supreme Court's determination in *Citizens United* that contributing is protected free speech. But how serious is the problem? After all, even though all kinds of organizations, corporations, and billionaires spent well over a billion dollars in the 2012 election, most incumbents won, including President Obama, and the status quo in Washington remained (Eggen and Farnam 2012). Perhaps nothing changed because so much money was contributed to both parties, or perhaps some kind of saturation point was finally reached in American politics.

Perhaps the real problem in 2012 was that spending merely ensured that the political status quo prevailed, when dramatic change is what the nation needed. Keeping incumbent legislators in office makes it nearly impossible for new people with new ideas and representing new constituencies to meaning-fully challenge the status quo. That alone is cause for concern, as the economic and social challenges facing Americans continue to grow and change rapidly. Elected officials do little but often profound things to push their colleagues and the political system toward policies advantaging those interests. The fact that the people behind these interests are also constituents of these lawmakers is little solace, as it simply means some citizens become more equal than others. This strikes at the question of representation. If many interest groups are playing the money game and getting small but significant advantages in the policy-making process for it, then their members and their members' interests are elevated to a more privileged level than those of other constituents not so represented. And fair representation for all is the key to assessing the role of money in politics, and indeed the overall influence of interest groups in American policy making. That brings us to the last chapter and the biggest question: Are interest groups good for or detrimental to the process of representative government in the United States?

Notes

1. See CNN Political Unit, "CNN Poll: Two-Thirds Say Elections Are Usually for Sale," CNN, June 9, 2011, http://politicalticker.blogs.cnn.com/2011/06/09/cnn-poll-two-thirds-say-elections-are-usually-for-sale.

2. See CNN Opinion Research Poll, June 9, 2011, http://i2.cdn.turner.com/cnn/2011/images/06/09/rel10d-2.pdf.

3. There are plenty of good books on campaign finance, such as Currinder 2009 and Rozell, Wilcox, and Madland 2006.

4. Sabato (1984, 4) describes Oklahoma's Senator Bob Kerr as Capitol Hill's oil man, who had the task of collecting and distributing oil industry contributions to senators on the industry's behalf.

5. See "What Is a PAC?," Center for Responsive Politics, n.d., http://www.opensecrets.org/pacs/pacfaq.php, and Federal Elections Commission, *Federal Election Commission Campaign Guide: Corporations and Labor Organizations*, 2007, http://www.fec.gov/pdf/colagui.pdf.

6. See "The Disappearance of Congressional Soft Money," Center for Responsive Politics, n.d., http://www.opensecrets.org/bigpicture/congsoft.php?cycle=2010.

7. See "The Major Players: Active Advocacy Groups in the 2004 Election Cycle," Center for Responsive Politics, n.d., http://www.opensecrets.org/527s/527grps.php.

8. See "527s: Advocacy Group Spending," Center for Responsive Politics, 2013, http://www.opensecrets.org/527s/index.php.

9. In a publicity stunt to bring attention to super PACs, comedian Steven Colbert in 2011 applied for and received (by a 5 to 1 vote) FEC approval to form the

ColbertPAC, though it could only use donations to fund issue advertising appearing on his show, *The Colbert Report*.

10. The Federal Elections Commission provides a public master list of current pacronyms for 2009 at http://www.fec.gov/pubrec/pacronyms/Pacronyms.pdf.

11. See the *Federal Election Commission Campaign Guide: Nonconnected Committees*, May 2008, http://www.fec.gov/pdf/nongui.pdf, 1.

12. According to the Center for Responsive Politics, Friends of the Earth's PAC raised a little over $8,000 in 2011 and contributed none of it. They raised and gave nothing in 2012.

13. See "US Chamber of Commerce," Center for Responsive Politics, 2013, http://www.opensecrets.org/orgs/summary.php?id=D000019798&cycle=A.

14. I have this letter on file and will provide it on request.

Representation in the Interest Group Age

In his 1956 book *A Preface to Democratic Theory*, political scientist Robert Dahl discussed the promises and consequences of large numbers of competing interest groups, what is called pluralism, in democratic politics. He argued that interest groups should be embraced as something healthy in representative government because if public policies are going to affect some social or economic groups more than others, those people should be able to respond with greater influence than less affected citizens. Since political parties and elected officials often cannot provide effective representation for affected groups because they represent too many diverse constituencies already, interest groups are the vehicles of choice. The assumption of pluralism that groups of citizens are able to perceive threats to their interests and then quickly mobilize to effectively resist those threats has often been shown to be false (recall the collective action problem from Chapter 2), but Dahl's point was that the efforts of interest groups and their lobbyists to shape policies affecting them should not be hindered by government. It should be embraced as legitimate representation. Americans today, though, are not so sure. A 2006 CBS / *New York Times* poll found that 77 percent of the public believed that lobbyists regularly bribed lawmakers, and 73 percent believed that Congress favored special interests over their constituents (Jankowsky 2006). Even scholars have been skeptical of lobbying and have been calling for regulation for nearly a century (see Pollock 1927).

Ethics in Lobbying

So are interest groups and their lobbyists good or bad for American democracy? The only way to approach a question like this is to think about it in terms of honest representation, for that is the only justification any organization or person has for wielding political power in a representative democracy. What are citizens potentially getting from their interest groups and lobbyists? Reflecting on this question also provides an opportunity to summarize this book's main points. As I discussed in Chapter 1, the formation of interest groups is guaranteed under the First Amendment to the US Constitution as part of the freedom to assemble. Like social clubs, political parties, protests, and town hall meetings, interest groups are assemblies of citizens concerned with promoting an interest important to them, an interest that brings them together. That these citizens may never physically meet each other is irrelevant, especially today, when it is easy for people to communicate with each other without ever shaking hands. Creating an organization to pursue the collective interests of groups in society is legitimate and constitutionally protected.

So too is lobbying, for the First Amendment also guarantees the freedom to petition government for the redress of grievances. And as was discussed in Chapter 4, that agents, or lobbyists, are employed to present the petitions on behalf of citizens who have freely assembled is also not a problem as long as these agents present petitions that faithfully lay out the grievances of the assembled citizens and request the redress from government these citizens actually want. A lobbyist is employed to press a group's case before government officials, just as lawyers do on behalf of clients in court, just as stockbrokers do in the financial market, and just as real estate agents do in the housing market. As with elected officials and hired lawyers, the practice is ethical as long as the agent, the lobbyist, faithfully presents group members' concerns and follows accepted practice guidelines and rules. Any discussion of legitimacy and ethics in lobbying should be within these general principles.

A small army of good-government advocates, politicians, journalists, and even some scholars argue that what is going on now is far from ethical. Many have put forward proposals for reform, but before reviewing these proposals, a recap of the growth in groups, lobbyists, and spending is useful. Chapters 1, 2, and 4 provided data on the growth of interest groups and lobbyists in national politics. The overall interest group growth in the twentieth century and into the twenty-first has been enormous: at least eighteen thousand operating at all levels of the United States and even transnationally in 2011. Interest groups have also grown in terms of the diversity of the kinds of, and intensity of, interests represented. Representing these groups, along with corporations and other institutions in Washington, are over 19,000 lobbyists. The data that most concern critics of the lobbying industry are in Chapter 10:

interest groups' financial contributions reach into the billions, and lobbyists are constantly looking for new ways to avoid legal spending limits. The data in Chapter 4 on the number of ex-lawmakers in the lobbying industry and the huge salaries lobbyists earn also concern them. But does all of this suggest that something dramatic needs to be done to save the American republic from interest groups and lobbyists? Yes, but not because there are too many interest groups and lobbyists pressing their political causes in Washington and the states today. The real problem, as I see it, is the quality of the representation they are providing to citizens.

Think back to Chapter 5. Lobbyists try to find positions on issues that the greatest number of their members, or clients in the case of for-hire lobbyists, will accept, but they are also under enormous pressure to advocate for alternative positions that may not be so favorable to their members. In the context of honest representation in the political process, what arguably can be called lobbying ethics, *this* may be a problem. Pressure from government policy makers to modify group positions to fit the electoral needs of legislators or statutorily defined missions of agency officials, described in Chapters 6 and 7, or to find a position that can be supported by congressional majorities or survive challenges in court, described in Chapters 5 and 8, puts lobbyists in a bind. What they ought to do from an ethical standpoint appears to be in conflict with what they often must do to win, or at least to advance their personal careers.

In Chapter 9, I argued that compromise positions are the results of trade-offs between competing interest groups that allow members of all groups to gain part of what they want on the aspect of an issue they care about the most, with the alternative to a compromise usually being no policy gains at all. Whether the trade-off is the result of competition between groups or pressure from lawmakers for a compromise, or both, if the compromise really gives members something of what they want, especially when the alternative is nothing at all, then the lobbyist probably *is* serving his or her member interests by supporting it. This will be true at least as long as members are aware of and support the compromise. Similarly, if an alternative policy proposal serves members' long-term interests in ways they might not be immediately aware of, then the ethical lobbyist is right to promote such a position, but he or she must be careful about presuming to know the long-term interests of members. Members must come to believe that is true.

When a position not ideally preferred by an interest group's members still serves their interests and has a chance of becoming law, then not only is it the duty of the ethical lobbyist to support that position, but the lobbyist's role becomes one of member education. The lobbyist must convince members through reasoned argument supported by evidence that it is to their advantage—in their interests—to support the compromise policy. If the members cannot be convinced, then the lobbyist cannot support the compromise, regardless of how much pressure they are under from their friends in Congress to do so, or how much damage not compromising might do to the relationships the lobbyist has so carefully built. That is the ethical choice, but therein also lies the problem. Remember that the lobbyist has an incentive to support the compromise position regardless of whether members support it, because it is in their career interest to prioritize those relationships over faithfully representing members, especially since the lobbyist may be able to use the control they have over the interest group's information channels to convince members that they are being faithfully represented when that is not so. This is clearly *unethical* behavior and cannot be thought of as enjoying constitutional protection under the First Amendment because there is no honest representation of citizen interests.

Lobbying Reform

Unfortunately, current rules governing the conduct of lobbyists in Washington, DC, do not address this ethical problem of lobbyists not always faithfully representing their constituents. And the proposals for further lobbying reform or efforts to limit campaign spending don't either. Proposals for reform are more about getting accurate counts of the number of people in Washington who lobby and about recording lobbyists' contact with lawmakers than getting at the substance of this contact. Many proposals for reform also emphasize the need to limit, or even eliminate, money and campaign contributions in the lobbying profession, but even if this is worth doing for its own sake, such reforms also fail to address the threat to ethical representation. A few organizations have proposed ethics rules for lobbyists but seem reluctant to make their codes of conduct anything more than recommended guidelines without enforcement.

Lobbying Disclosure Act

The current lobbying laws were enacted in 1995 and require that people who lobby Capitol Hill register their activity and disclose how much money they and their organizations spend on it. Prior to this, the only registration law was enacted in 1946 and largely focused on individuals who had direct personal contact with lawmakers. It did not apply to contact with legislative staff or with anybody in the executive branch (ABA 2011, 1–2). Since face-to-face contact with elected officials has become rarer, with a growing number of congressional staff standing in for lawmakers, and a growing number of lobbyists competing for time with lawmakers, as well as rapidly growing demands on legislators' time that keeps them away from their Capitol offices, such a registration law makes little sense. It was also poorly enforced.

Republicans took control of both the House and the Senate in 1995 after a landslide election, partially caused by a widespread public perception that the Democrats had been corrupted by the lobbying industry. This created fertile ground for the lobbying reform law passed later that year. Under the **Lobbying Disclosure Act** (LDA), any lobbyist for a private lobbying firm, corporation, or interest group must register with the clerk of the House and secretary of the Senate. Lobbyists must disclose what issues they are lobbying and how much they are spending to do it, but only if they directly contact a lawmaker or his or her staff more than once to request specific legislative action on behalf of a client or group membership, and if they spend at least 20 percent of their time on such contacting activities (ABA 2011, 3, 5). The law by and large does not apply to contacting officials in the executive branch if the lobbyist is only contacting agency or White House officials. Lobbying firms must register for each client if the income they earn from contacting Congress on that client's behalf is at least $3,000 in a quarter year. Interest groups must register their lobbyists if the total they spend on lobbying is at least $11,500 in a quarter year (Straus 2011, 3; ABA 2011, 5).[1]

The LDA is really just about finding out who is lobbying, what issues are being lobbied, and how much is being spent on the practice. In that limited sense it has been relatively successful with very few prosecutions for failure to comply (ABA 2011, 5). The Government Accountability Office (GAO) in 2011 found that most lobbyists were correctly reporting their activities, and nearly all of those who were not in compliance became so after it was brought to their attention by the House clerk, Senate secretary, or the GAO (GAO 2011, 10–11). Yet the "one-time contact" exception and especially the "at least 20 percent of lobbyists' time" exception are proving to be significant loopholes. Also, the law's focus on the legislative branch means it fails to cover a significant portion of the lobbying of the executive branch, which in some ways is more extensive and influential than lobbying Congress. A recent survey of lobbyists found that only 80 percent of lobbyists were registered (Rehr 2012, 3), but since the sample came from the Lobbyists.info database, which includes large numbers of lobbyists who work purely with the executive branch and thus do not tend to register with Congress, 80 percent may actually be a pretty good rate of registration.

Honest Leadership and Open Government Act

Usually it takes major scandals for legislatures to enact reform that reduces their connections to interest groups and lobbyists (Ozymy 2012). So it is little surprise that after the public scandal involving lobbyist Jack Abramoff, Congress was under enormous pressure to enact further reform, which it did in 2007 (ABA 2011, 4). The **Honest Leadership and Open Government Act** (HLOGA) essentially banned all gift giving by lobbyists to legislators and their staff, creating harsher penalties for violating existing bans as well as adding new restrictions. Essentially HLOGA bans interest group–sponsored lobbying events, though not fundraisers that legislators hold for themselves and each other. It also requires lobbyists registered under LDA to file semiannual statements disclosing all of their contributions, and contributions from PACs their organizations are affiliated with, to candidates for federal office (Straus 2011, 6). Enforcement, though, has not been what many good-government advocates have hoped, with not a single prosecution for violation of HLOGA by 2011 (ABA 2011, 5). Congressional ethics committees, though, have seen their workload increase, as they try to decide what kinds of events and gifts from interest groups and constituents are still legal.[2]

Ironically, the result of HLOGA may be a greater dependence on campaign fundraisers as opportunities for lobbyists to connect with legislators and their staff. A for-hire lobbyist I interviewed for this book told me that he used to build his connections on Capitol Hill by taking legislative staff to lunch, which he would pay for, or holding briefing sessions for them that included food and drink. Lunches are still possible as long as everyone pays for themselves, and briefing sessions now come with very little food (Dwoskin 2012). Consequently, it is much harder to get legislative staff to go to them. In the Lobbyists.info report, slightly over half of lobbyists said HLOGA has made it harder to talk to congressional staff (Rehr 2012, 4). Efforts at doing so have moved to fundraisers, which means that some legislative staff now feel more pressure to attend these events in order to meet lobbyists. Other fundraisers and legislator-appreciation parties sponsored by interest groups and corporations have moved to party conventions (Herszenhorn 2008).

Whether this is a good thing depends on one's point of view. If lobbyists are seen as fundamentally corrosive to representational politics, then laws severing the connection between them and legislative staff are good. On the other hand, if lobbyists are providing valuable information to staff on what certain constituencies want, providing constitutionally protected representation, then this is a problem. The latter was the belief of slightly over half of the lobbyists in the Lobbyists.info survey (Rehr 2012, 4). The lobbyist I interviewed told me that today he spends only about 5 percent of his weekly time on Capitol Hill. Five percent! But he spends a lot more time at fundraisers for legislators around Washington, because legislative staff are often there, and it is his only chance to talk to them about issues important to his clients. About 42 percent of the lobbyists in the survey agreed with this assessment; only 34 percent believed HLOGA improved the profession's accountability (Rehr 2012, 7).

Executive Branch Restrictions

President Barack Obama tried to rectify the shortcomings in LDA's coverage of the executive branch when he came into office. The administration forbade lobbyists registered under the LDA, using LDA's rather narrow definition of "lobbyist," from giving gifts to officials in the executive branch, prevented lobbyists from serving on most advisory committees, and banned them from being hired into positions in the administration without a special waiver (Farnam 2011). These new restrictions had two results. The first was that several waivers were granted, including a high-profile waiver to a defense contractor lobbyist for a senior position in the Pentagon. The second was a noticeable decrease in the number of lobbyists registered under the LDA, about two thousand fewer in 2009 than in 2008 (Kirkpatrick 2010).

Another, again ironic consequence is that lobbyists for good-government citizen groups that have traditionally pushed for tighter laws on lobbying were themselves denied the opportunity to work for the Obama administration. A citizen group lobbyist I interviewed lamented this unhappy circumstance, feeling that he could have made significant contributions to the administration in a financial regulatory agency. More broadly, though, the president's restriction appears to have shifted the calculus of those advocates who are not quite sure they are lobbyists. In the past people who occasionally lobbied tended to play it safe by registering, but now that it is harder to lobby the executive branch or be employed by the executive branch if they are registered, they choose not to do so. Whereas some lobbyists thought that registering might actually look appealing to potential clients, now they find it a significant detriment, and so some in the profession are quietly lobbying without officially registering (Kirkpatrick 2010). The lobbying profession may be slowly going underground!

Even when interest group and corporate lobbyists do file disclosure paperwork, it is often hard for the public, or at least good-government groups like the Center for Responsive Politics and Citizens for Responsibility and Ethics in Washington, to get enough information about these lobbying efforts to make oversight effective. For instance, all corporations receiving contracts from the executive branch are required under a law called the Byrd Amendment of 1989 to file forms with every granting agency describing the money they spent lobbying for those contracts and proving that no federal contract money was used for lobbying. The law was written by the late senator Robert Byrd (D-WV), who was angry that the University of West Virginia hired super-lobbyist Gerry Cassidy to lobby for a contract rather than come to him directly (Kaiser 2009). Recently the Sunlight Foundation and the Washington news source *Politico* attempted to get copies of these disclosure forms from several agencies, including the National Security Administration and the FBI, but were told to file complicated Freedom of Information Act requests, which often takes years to be processed. Sometimes the requests were refused because the disclosure forms were classified in the name of national security. In some cases they did not get a response at all (Tau 2013). So much for executive branch lobbying disclosure.

Reform the Law or Self-Police the Profession

The Constitution ensures that interest groups and the lobbying profession will continue, so, if we assume more reform is needed, what should that reform look like? The greatest concern seems to be over who is still not registering as a lobbyist because they do not fall into LDA's narrow definition or because they dedicate less than 20 percent of their time to directly contacting (in person or electronically) lawmakers and staff—the so-called 20 percent loophole. A 2011 report by the American Bar Association (ABA), with input from many of the interest groups calling for improvements in LDA, recommends eliminating that loophole so that anyone spending any time trying to make contact with Congress would have to register (ABA 2011, vii). Members of Congress have been reluctant to eliminate this loophole because their constituents might think they have to register when they contact Congress, shutting out the very people lawmakers are supposed to be hearing from.

What may be a little more acceptable to legislators is expanding the definition of lobbyist to include more people who provide "lobbying support," currently defined to include "preparation and planning activities, research and other background work" (Straus 2011, 15). Proposals for new language would be broadened to include anybody in a lobbying firm or interest group who in any way provides substantive (rather than secretarial) support to a lobbyist, including planning broad strategy. This would rope in many ex-members of Congress who currently just provide consultation services for lobbying firms rather than engage in direct lobbying (ABA 2011, 13; Dwoskin 2012).

What about the lobbying profession policing itself? The report on HLOGA from Lobbyists.info said that nearly a majority of responding lobbyists thought some type of ethics training on what not to do should be offered, perhaps because 37 percent said they were unfamiliar with what the law says (Rehr 2012, 4 & 6–7). Can the lobbying industry police itself? This may sound like foxes watching henhouses, but it is being tried. The American Society of Association Executives, the trade association for trade associations, has a one-page list of ethics emphasizing the importance of lobbyists always keeping the wants and needs of interest group members foremost in mind, and only after that giving thought to a broader public interest.[3] It also emphasizes the importance of properly understanding and honestly discussing with members and lawmakers all sides of an issue as well as the public interest. (Never lie!) In other words, it emphasizes all of the qualities the public believes lobbyists lack. The proposal says nothing about enforcement, however. There would be no disbarring of lobbyists as there is of unethical doctors and lawyers.

The code of ethics by the American League of Lobbyists aims a bit more at for-hire lobbyists and is nearly four pages long. Yet it says much the same thing and has the same lack of enforcement.[4] It too emphasizes respecting client interests, but also keeping the client properly educated on what is happening and what the larger public interest might be beyond the client's specific interests. It also emphasizes charging reasonable fees, something Abramoff was not known for doing. In fact, it even recommends that lobbyists do a little pro bono advocacy for people who cannot afford them. The league offers ethics training and urges its members to take it, but only 13 percent or so of lobbyists are actually members of the league.[5] There is no way to know how many lobbyists are truly ethical in that they honestly represent their members' interests, but remember from Chapters 5 and 9 that lobbyists are often under significant pressure to compromise member policy preferences as they negotiate deals with lawmakers and competing interest groups. Members feeling betrayed can leave the group, but, as I emphasized in Chapter 4, they would know that the lobbyist wasn't representing their best interests probably only if the lobbyist told them. In other words, members and clients are at the mercy of the lobbyist's personal sense of ethics.

I would like to make three final points as I end this discussion of lobbying reform. First, while disclosure laws like LDA and HLOGA are worthy in and of themselves, in that they tell us more about who is lobbying and who in society is represented by them, they do little to ensure that interest group members are being properly represented. They are about who is lobbying, not what they are lobbying for. And while proposed ethical guidelines are about substance, they are unenforced. Stronger laws regulating the lobbying profession should perhaps require lobbyists to disclose information about exactly *what* position on an issue they are lobbying for at any given point in time. Essentially, this means making available to members the position papers they frequently provide members of Congress. More importantly, it means writing new position papers every time lobbyists choose to change their position, so they can be made available to members, clients, and the public.

Second, there may be some self-regulation of lobbying going on anyway. While legislators may pull lobbyists away from what their members ideally want in order to form coalitions, that does not necessarily mean they want lobbyists to misrepresent member or client interests. Legislators need lobbyists to honestly tell them what members or clients want, though not necessarily for entirely altruistic reasons. If lobbyists are representing important interests in a legislator's state or district, then that legislator's own future depends on knowing what constituents think. They rely on the lobbyist to keep them honestly informed as part of the relationship of exchanging information for access, as discussed in Chapter 6. True, as a matter of strategy, the legislator may push the lobbyist to compromise some of the members' or clients' interests to facilitate assembling coalitions and majorities in Congress, but it may only be within margins that lawmakers and lobbyists feel are acceptable compromises to constituent interests. Or not. The ethical issue arises depending on how this is done.

If the lobbyist uses his or her control of the distribution of information in the interest group to sell that compromise to members and clients, manipulating what they know, then this is unethical, even if it gets member constituents something instead of nothing in a policy debate and their interests are well served by the compromise. But if the lobbyist uses the flow of information to deliberate and reason with members so they themselves are convinced of the compromise's worth, this is ethical. It is the honesty in convincing members or clients of the value of these compromises that makes lobbying ethical and worthy of constitutional protection. As a practical matter, requiring disclosure of lobbying positions as they change may help keep lobbyists honest and ethical.

Finally, nothing in the model laid out in Chapter 5 or discussed here says anything about the public interest. In Chapter 1, I was skeptical about there even being a public interest to serve. The codes of ethics proposed by the lobbying trade associations mention the public interest as a secondary concern. More importantly, they suggest it is something lobbyists should encourage their members and clients to think about. If we do not normally expect a concern with the public interest to shape the choices and strategies of other agents we employ, such as lawyers, stockbrokers, and real estate agents, should we expect it of lobbyists? In practice most members and clients probably do not expect it, though the language lobbyists use to convince lawmakers of the merits of their members' interest may emphasize some notion of the public interest as a strategy.

Still, public policy is public: changes in law potentially affect everyone, not just the members of a single group. But it is the group members and clients who need to think about what the idea of a "public interest" means to them in regards to an issue and how important it should be as they give direction to their hired lobbyists. The ethical lobbyist's job is to pursue those members' interests in the public arena as best they can and as honestly as they can once those goals have been chosen. Lobbyists probably should remind members to consider the well-being of the public beyond their own interests when telling their lobbyists what to advocate for. Once members choose positions, however, that is what their lobbyists must advocate for. The ethical lobbyist only advocates for member interests, regardless of whether they are purely private or considerate of a broader public interest, and ensuring that lobbyists do this should be the goal of real lobbying reform.

Neopluralist Politics

Now let's take a step back and consider what it means to have a political system so heavily populated with interest groups. The growth in the overall number of interest groups has alarmed scholars. Their concern is that so many groups representing so many mobilized interests in the nation, all making policy demands on the government backed by threats of electoral reprisals, leads to two results. First, it forces the government to increase public spending so much, either through direct payments or by reducing public revenue by offering tax breaks for special groups, that it creates an enormous debt that cannot be reduced without angering some or all of these financially dependent interests (Mueller and Murrell 1986; Peterson 1990). Second, because they are so good at gaining access to Congress through its decentralized committee system, in which lawmakers have electoral incentives to get on committees from which they can direct policy benefits toward key constituencies organized as interest groups, groups with largely similar interests come to control different domains of policy making. This makes it impossible for the government to react in an emergency or serve any notion of the public interest because no major change in policy that threatens the status quo is possible. These interest groups essentially govern large areas of policy making that shut out groups and even elected officials with competing ideas (Lowi 1979; Peltzman 1980). Ultimately such paralysis could lead to the government's collapse (Olson 1982).

These long-term fears may not be just the product of concerned academics. A recent assessment of the government's major spending programs by Brookings Institution scholar Ron Haskins showed that most of the major social welfare programs, backed by a multitude of interest groups, have consistently grown from 1980 to 2011, with per-qualified person spending rising from $4,300 in 1980 to $13,000 in 2011 (dollar value adjusted for inflation), in spite of efforts by fiscal conservatives to cut them down (Samuelson 2012). In his 1961 farewell address, President Dwight Eisenhower warned Americans against the dangers of a large and still growing military-industrial complex, an enormous amount of spending on military programs promoted by the Department of Defense and numerous military contractors and their armies of lobbyists. In spite of his warning, defense spending has largely grown, and grown quite dramatically, since Eisenhower's time. Interest groups certainly appear able to defend their policy gains from attack—even from criticism.

Can this trajectory of growth be changed if interest groups and lobbyists are constitutionally protected?

Ironically, just as some have argued that the cure for the democracy-inducing paralysis of the two-party system is more parties and more democracy, it may also be the case that the only constitutionally acceptable solution to the problem of interest group dominance of government is mobilizing more citizens in interest groups to exercise countervailing power (Berry 1977; McFarland 1992). In Chapters 2 and 3, I described groups of citizens being mobilized by political entrepreneurs who argued convincingly that these citizens' interests were threatened by the policies of the governing elite. The solution in the 1960s to the perceived problem of business interests controlling public policy, framing the very policies that benefited them as serving the public interest, was for smart entrepreneurs like Ralph Nader and John Gardner to help unmobilized interests realize what was happening to them and organize them to fight back. Part of the reason we have so many interest groups in the United States is that efforts at domination by a few interest groups have sparked countermobilizations and intense competition. In that sense more interest groups is better, and any effort to reduce the influence of interest groups and lobbyists is dangerous. This is our age: an age of fierce interest group competition to prevent the very stagnation many scholars feared. There is even a term for it: neopluralism.

Neopluralism is like pluralism, which I explained in Chapter 2, in that it assumes American society can be thought of as a large number of overlapping interests. Citizens tend to be members, officially or unofficially, of several groups because they have multiple defining interests. Moreover, there are so many active or latent interests in society that any action to advance the needs and desires of one interest ends up affecting the interests of several other groups, probably in some detrimental way. In this sense neopluralism seems entirely consistent with evidence of the enormous number of mobilized interests in national politics today. What differentiates neopluralism from traditional pluralism is that it is often hard for some latent interests to realize they are threatened by existing groups, and even if they are aware of the threat, they still may not have the motivations or resources to mobilize (McFarland 2004). My concern here is with another problem with interest group representation that has not, I feel, drawn enough attention from other scholars.

Solving the problem of domineering groups by creating more groups as countervailing power only works in a neopluralist system if their lobbying is ethical. Ethical representation is legitimate in that representatives accurately and honestly express the desires and fears of the citizens who hire them to do the representing. Thousands of mobilized groups with overlapping interests competing to have their issues addressed in the political arena means legislators end up hearing a cacophony of demands, especially if they really are hearing from more than just a few privileged groups. How can they respond to so many interest groups and the people in them? If they cannot, then neopluralist politics is little better than a system dominated by a few, powerful interests. But, as I discussed in Chapters 6 and 9, the consequence of all of these competing groups and lobbyists is that they *must* bargain and compromise to build coalitions capable of advancing new policy or defending existing policy. The American federal government was designed to require negotiation and compromise, so that all proposed policy would be thoroughly debated before enactment or rejection, but it means that the interests of many, perhaps most, groups must be sacrificed to some extent—even if only in order to gain something else.

This finally brings the discussion to the main potential hope for interest group representation. In Chapter 5 I made the assumption that lobbyists are first and foremost concerned with advancing their own professional careers. Lobbyists are often pressured into accepting compromises that are not necessarily in their members' best interests, a problem that becomes worse as more groups and lobbyists enter the political arena. Indeed, this is a consequence of neopluralism. If all lobbyists used deliberation to convince all members to want to make compromises, then, in the aggregate, neopluralist politics means more citizens are honestly represented *and* more engaged in the political process, strengthening civil society (Mansbridge 1992).

Greater ability of citizens to watch their lobbyist representatives is therefore essential. Disclosure requiring lobbyists to file position papers, and amend those papers when deals are struck, may help members do a better job tracking shifts in positions their lobbyists are taking. Unhappy members can complain to their lobbyists and hold them accountable. The lobbyist then must convince members that it is to the members' advantage to accept a compromise, fulfilling the lobbyist's education role. Lawyers must always keep their clients informed on changes in settlement negotiations, and real estate agents must always inform their clients of changes in home purchase agreements. They risk their professional licensing if they do not. Lobbyists, too, can use technology to keep their members and clients informed and file new position disclosure statements. Members who are interested can track their lobbyist's efforts, as compromises are made or attacks launched against competing interests. Once lobbyists' personal career goals are more clearly aligned with serving member interests over pleasing lawmakers, there may be some hope in harnessing the expanding and increasingly competitive world of neopluralist group politics as a means of providing ethical and engaged political representation.

Final Thoughts

As I said back in the Introduction, most lobbyists are not Jack Abramoff, or even Sam Ward. Every lobbyist I have ever met, and I have met and interviewed well over a hundred, seems to have tremendous personal integrity. Many told me anecdotes about defying lawmakers because they could not, in good conscience, compromise member interests. Yet even the possibility of misrepresentation because of conflicts of interests arising from lobbyists' need to help lawmakers achieve their goals, as well as bargain with each other, is the unappreciated flaw in neopluralism. Problems with realizing that one's interests are threatened as well as the barriers to collective action that undercut classic pluralism are now fairly well understood. To some extent they are even minimized because the Internet makes information easily available and because there is more countervailing power being wielded by more interest groups. As for misrepresentation, since the Constitution's First Amendment says interest groups must be embraced rather than suppressed, and lobbyist connections to lawmakers accepted as a necessary part of this representation, any regulation enacted by lawmakers and good-government groups must seek to maximize lobbyist accountability to all of their members.

But what about the public interest? James Madison and others involved with designing the government hoped that people of integrity who valued the public interest over individual self-interest would be involved in government, even as they feared that this might not actually happen (see Federalist No. 51 about men not being angels). Should lobbyists take the public interest into account when they press for policy change or strive to maintain the status quo? Perhaps not. It is unclear what is meant by the "public interest" or the "national interest," but even if these terms were clearly defined I do not think it should be expected of interest group lobbyists. Lobbyists are representatives of mobilized interests. That is what they are paid to do, just as lawyers are paid to represent clients even if they know those clients are guilty of crimes. Lobbyists also do not make final decisions on public policy; they articulate and press the desires of specific groups. In our system of government, law-makers, elected or appointed, are supposed to consider the public interest as they make final decisions. The job lobbyists and the interest groups they work for are expected to do, and do with integrity, is to honestly and aggressively pursue the interests of the citizens they represent.

Notes

1. Technically, the original LDA required reports to be filed semiannually, not quarterly. It was changed to a quarter system in the Honest Leadership and Open Government Act of 2007.

2. This has also created a small cottage industry of lobbying compliance manuals, such as the one from Lobbyists.info, which, among other things, explains how to throw a legal holiday party.

3. This is not available online, but I have a copy of it and will make it available on request.

4. See "Code of Ethics," American League of Lobbyists, November 2010, http://www.alldc.org/ethicscode.cfm.

5. This is what I was told by the league's representative.

GLOSSARY

Accommodationist PAC—Political action committees that are not overly ideological or partisan in their contributing strategies. They tend to contribute to supplement the broader lobbying strategies of their affiliate interest group's lobbyist, giving to members of Congress with whom that lobbyist has built long-term relationships. Thus they tend to give nearly all of their contributions to incumbent candidates and worry less about which party controls Congress or the White House.

Administrative Procedure Act—Law enacted in 1946 that requires most administrative agencies in the executive branch to publish proposed regulations for public review and comment in the *Federal Register*, and then make changes to the rules based on that comment (or explain why they did not make any changes) before publishing the final version of the new rule. The law also gives the federal courts a role in reviewing the decisions of agencies.

Advisory committees—Formalized in the Federal Advisory Committee Act of 1972, even though they have existed in some form for most of the nation's history. They provide opportunities for interest groups to provide information and recommendations to administrative agencies on proposed rules before they are released for public comment. Some advisory committee memberships are mandated in law by Congress, with agencies required to listen to some interest groups, while others are created at the discretion of the agency.

Advocacy explosion—The dramatic increase in the number of interest groups operating in national politics beginning in the late 1960s, especially in the number of citizen and public interest groups.

Amicus curiae (friend of the court briefs)—Filed by individuals and organizations who are not direct parties in a federal case and containing additional information the third parties believe would be useful for the judges in a case to know. Amicus briefs must be filed with the consent of either party in the case or with the consent of the court. They may provide information on the merits (actual substance) of a case, or they may argue for or against an appeal being heard by a higher court.

Appeal—The constitutional right of an individual to request that a court higher in the judicial branch rehear a case because of some substantive or procedural error in the original case. Higher courts, however, are not obligated to accept the appeal.

Astroturf—A top-down directed advocacy campaign typically involving thousands of identical phone calls, letters, e-mails, or petitions being signed by people at the request of an interest group to give the appearance of widespread public support for an issue and the interest group's position.

Bipartisan Campaign Reform Act (McCain-Feingold Act)—Law enacted in 2002 that is the latest attempt to limit campaign contributions and other forms of campaign spending in federal elections. It was largely successful in banning unlimited PAC contributions to state parties for "party-building activities" (so-called soft money). It was less successful in preventing contributions from being used for issue advertising, which is where an organization spends money to develop advertisements in the media attacking or promoting a candidate, or even just raising issues uncomfortable to a candidate, without actually coordinating with the benefitting candidate's campaign.

Bundling—A PAC practice of convincing large numbers of individuals or other PACs to contribute money to a candidate, with the PAC collecting all of the contributions and giving them to the benefitting candidate in a single "bundle." This gives the impression that the bundling PAC is giving very large amounts of money, but the PAC is still not violating the FEC's limits on the amount of campaign contributions because it is merely passing along other contributors' money.

Cause-oriented group—An interest group that exists primarily to lobby the government for significant new policy affecting all citizens, not just any particular group, though only a particular group may want the new policy. It usually has an open membership, though some may have no membership at all. This is often a more general reference to citizen and public interest groups.

Certiorari—A writ (order) issued by the US Supreme Court to a lower court instructing the lower court that the Supreme Court has decided to hear the case in question on appeal. Usually four of the nine justices on the Supreme Court must vote to hear a case before certiorari (the appeal) is granted.

Citizen group—An open-membership organization that exists primarily to advocate for public policies desired by its members, though the policies would affect all citizens. These organizations typically have fairly significant numbers of members but often rely on foundation and philanthropic support for their operations.

Civil service system—Established by the Pendleton Act of 1883, which largely ended the old spoils-style system of staffing the federal government through patronage (members of Congress awarding jobs to their supporters) by requiring federal employees to be hired on the basis of merit, usually after passing a rigorous exam. The system also lays out explicit pay grades and provides significant protections for federal employees from being arbitrarily fired or demoted by the president or other senior government officials.

Clayton Act—Law enacted in 1914 that strengthened existing antitrust laws (laid down in the Sherman Act of 1890) to prevent the formation of business cartels and monopolies. It also specifically exempted labor unions from most forms of federal legal restrictions, including injunctions, thereby making it significantly easier for unions to strike and picket.

Closed shop—An agreement between an employer and the union representing the employees of a company. The employer agrees to only hire members of that union, and that an employee must remain a member of that union in order to remain employed at the company. This membership-for-employment requirement helps unions circumvent the free-rider problem. The Taft-Hartley Act of 1947 replaced closed shops with union shops, which are fairly similar. However, Taft-Hartley outlaws closed shops and union shops in states that have passed right-to-work laws.

Cloture—A motion in the Senate that brings debate on pending legislation to a close so that a vote can be taken. Passage of a cloture motion in the Senate requires at least sixty votes of all sworn senators, not just 60 percent of all senators present on the Senate floor. Since debate is presumed to continue if a cloture motion cannot be passed, it is closely connected to the strategy of filibustering legislation, preventing a bill from passing because debate cannot be brought to a close and therefore a vote cannot be taken. In actual practice senators rarely need to actively keep on debating to stop legislation.

Committee—A body composed of elected legislators of either the House of Representatives or the Senate. It has jurisdiction over a fairly well defined area of public policy making (a policy domain) and has the primary responsibility for writing all legislation affecting that area of policy. Parallel committees typically exist in the House and Senate with the same jurisdictions.

Conference committee—Also referred to as a committee on reconciliation, an ad hoc committee of members of both the House of Representatives and the Senate who are tasked with working out differences in legislation passed by their respective parent chambers. This is necessary because the Constitution requires that both House and Senate pass *exactly* the same bill before it goes to the president.

Constituents—Refers generally to any group of people who are represented in government by an agent who is accountable to them, such as an elected legislator, political party official, or interest group lobbyist. It is normally used, however, to refer to just the citizens who reside in a geographic congressional district or state and are thus represented by their elected member of the House and their two senators.

Electoral coalition—A formal or informal group of organizations, including interest groups as well as 527 organizations and super PACs, who coordinate their contributing and other electioneering activities in order to elect candidates sharing their political views.

Endorsement—An interest group's practice of formally announcing its support for a candidate for elected office. Often interest groups will use roll-call votes cast by incumbent members of Congress to determine whether they will support them with money and votes in the next election, creating an index of how much (or how little) the legislator supports the interest group. Interest groups then encourage their members, and other allied interest groups, to support their endorsed candidate with votes and contributions.

Environmental impact statement—Required by the National Environmental Policy Act of 1969 for any governmental project, or any project requiring governmental approval, that is deemed to be "significant and affecting the quality of the human environment." The EIS describes what positive and negative impacts the project will have on the environment and also lays out different versions of the project that may reduce the environmental impact in different ways. Failure to complete a proper EIS, and the ambiguity in just what qualifies as a proper EIS, is grounds for a lawsuit in federal court, potentially delaying or stopping the project.

Executive Office of the President—A series of executive branch offices that primarily exist to help the president manage the government. In the structure of the executive branch they exist between the White House and the bureaucracy proper.

Federal Election Campaign Act—Law enacted in 1971 and significantly amended in 1974 that updated the legal bans on campaign contributions by corporations and labor unions, and set limits on how much money could be contributed to people running for federal elected office from individuals and from political action committees (PACs). It also set rules on how candidates for federal office could raise money.

Federal Election Commission—The federal agency created by the Federal Election Campaign Act to administer federal election law, assess penalties on violators of that law, and collect and make publicly available data on where candidates raised money and how they spent it, as well as data on where PACs raised their money and to whom they contributed it.

Filibuster—Preventing action on a bill in the Senate because debate cannot be brought to an end. Senate rules allow senators to talk on the Senate floor for as long as they want and on whatever topic they choose before a final vote is cast on whether or not to pass a bill. Senators can force an end to debate by passing a cloture motion, but that requires the support of sixty or more sitting senators and is hard to achieve. In practice the threat of a filibuster is sufficient to stop a bill in the Senate without actually requiring senators to keep talking.

First Amendment—First article of the Bill of Rights in the US Constitution laying out guarantees of liberty. The pertinent part of the amendment for interest groups and lobbying is "Congress shall make no law respecting . . . the right of the people peaceably to assemble, and to petition the Government for a redress of grievances."

527 Organization—Generally refers to organizations created solely to raise money and then contribute that money in elections. The contribution amounts are unlimited and usually fund independent expenditures on issue advertising, raising a variety of campaign issues that aim to make an opponent candidate uncomfortable. These organizations cannot coordinate their activities with a candidate's campaign committee, nor can their contributions fund advertisements that directly attack or promote a candidate. For the latter reason 527 organizations are starting to be displaced by super PACs, which can attack candidates.

Foreign Agents Registration Act—Law enacted in 1938 that requires any person, American citizen or otherwise, acting on behalf of a foreign government in the United States to influence government policy in regard to that nation to register with the US Department of Justice. This includes all lobbyists hired to represent foreign governments and requires public disclosure of the financial arrangements between the foreign governments and the lobbyists hired to represent them.

For-hire lobbyist—A professional advocate who works for a private lobbying firm, or law firm with a lobbying practice, rather than for an interest group. He or she is typically contracted by individuals, corporations, or interest groups to represent them before government, often on very specific concerns and issues.

Framing—The advocacy strategy of shaping public and elite beliefs regarding an issue, including whether and how the issue should be addressed with public policy. This typically involves portraying an issue before lawmakers and in the media as in need of dramatic change if such change benefits the lobbyist's members, or requiring no change at all if the status quo benefits the members.

Free-rider problem—A barrier to convincing individuals to join and participate in interest groups. If the interest group charges a fee for membership and lobbies for policy benefits available to all citizens, there is no rational reason for individuals to join the group and pay the fee, since they will enjoy the benefits of the new policy whether or not they are members of the group. Interest group leaders overcome this problem by offering special material benefits, applying peer pressure, providing opportunities to fulfill political passions, or making membership compulsory to practice a profession.

Freedom of Information Act—Law enacted in 1966 that requires most federal administrative agencies to release documents and reports to citizens upon request, though documents of a top secret nature are excluded. Interest groups and journalists have frequently used the law to hold administrative agencies accountable, especially in court.

Grassroots protest—Occurs when an interest group or social movement organization is able to convince its members and sympathizers to participate in public events such as marches or speeches in order to show lawmakers that many people are being hurt by current public policy. It also shows lawmakers there is a large constituency whose loyalty lawmakers might win by championing their cause.

Grievance—The harm done to the interests of a group of people by existing public policy, usually because that group's interest is not recognized as legitimate by current policy makers.

Honest Leadership and Open Government Act—Law enacted in 2007 as the government's most recent effort to regulate the practice of lobbying. It amends the Lobbying Disclosure Act of 1995 by requiring lobbyists to submit reports on what issues they are lobbying and how much they are spending to lobby quarterly rather than every six months. It also sets fairly strict limits on the value of gifts, including food and drink, that lobbyists can provide to members of Congress, their staff, and executive branch officials.

House of Representatives—One of the two lawmaking chambers of the legislative branch, often referred to as the "lower house" and comprising 435 officials elected to two-year terms. Each member of the House represents approximately seven hundred thousand citizens in geographic districts, though every state is guaranteed one member of the House regardless of how small its population is.

Ideological PAC—A political action committee that contributes money almost exclusively to candidates who share its ideological and/or partisan beliefs, even though the candidate is challenging an incumbent and might very well lose. These types of PACs tend to be affiliated with one or the other major political parties and spend their money to help their allied party gain and maintain control of Congress and the White House.

Implementation—Putting into operation the legislation passed by Congress and signed into law by the president. Implementation is typically done by an administrative agency in the executive branch of the government and often requires the development and approval of regulations specifying exactly how the law will be carried out by the agency.

Incumbent—In an election for public office, the person who already holds the office and who is running to be reelected to another term in that same office.

Independent expenditure—Campaign contributions made by a PAC or other contributing entity to fund the creation of media advertisements to influence voters or other campaign activities. Depending on what type of organization is doing the contributing (regular PACs, 527 organizations, or super PACs), advertising created with this money may or may not attack a candidate. Under no circumstances can the use of independent expenditures be done in coordination with the benefitting candidate's campaign.

Information asymmetry—When one side in a relationship has more information about circumstances and choices of actions than the other side, allowing the advantaged side to potentially manipulate a situation to its benefit.

Insider lobbying—Advocacy for or against new policy usually done by a professional advocate in personal meetings with relevant lawmakers so that little or no public attention is drawn to the lobbying effort.

Interest (or self-interest)—Each individual's wants, desires, or beliefs about what would improve their personal fortunes or bring them happiness, or at least satisfaction. It is so defining a trait in an individual that they would be a different person if they did not possess that want, desire, or belief.

Interest group—An organization made up of people, or at least financial supporters, who all share the same general interest and who want to see this interest furthered through the government's public policy-making process.

Interest group competition—A state of conflict that exists when the wants, desires, and beliefs of one group, meaning that group of people's interest mobilized as an interest group, are perceived as harmful to the interest of another group of people should the first group's interest be supported by public policy.

Interest niche—The entire faction (or collection) of individuals who share a common want, desire, or belief, though not all of them may be members of an interest group organized to pursue that interest in the policy-making process. They may not be mobilized as an interest group at all.

Inter-governmental group—A type of interest group that represents government officials, and sometimes government institutions and whole governments, at lower levels of the federal system, including states, counties, legislatures, and special purpose districts.

Interstate Commerce Clause—A line in Article I, Section 8, of the Constitution reading "Congress shall have the power . . . to regulate Commerce with foreign nations, and among the several States, and with the Indian Tribes." This is frequently used to justify much of the federal government's power to regulate the activities of business and industry.

Iron Law of Oligarchy—Prediction by scholar Robert Michels that as organizations grow and age, they inevitably create rigid institutional structures that divide leaders from members, making it increasingly unlikely that the words and actions of leaders will be truly representative of their members' interests.

Iron triangle—A metaphor for the tight, exclusive relationships between a small number of interest groups with fairly similar interests, a congressional committee with jurisdiction over policy affecting these groups' interests, and the administrative agency responsible for implementing policies benefitting interest group members and members of the congressional committee. Everyone in the iron triangle benefits from this arrangement, so they have no incentive to include other interests, resulting in those interests being shut out of the policy-making process. The term "iron triangle" means much the same thing as "subgovernment."

Issue network—All of the interest group lobbyists, legislators, administrative agency officials, and other elites concerned with the same issues and policies (the same policy domain). Because they are all concerned with the same issues, they tend to know each other, exchange ideas with each other, lobby together, and sometimes compete fiercely against each other. As Washington has grown in terms of the number of mobilized interest groups seeking to influence the same policies, old, more exclusive relationships characterized by terms like "iron triangle" and "subgovernment" have dissolved into issue networks.

Judicial district—One of ninety-four federal judicial districts, each district staffed by a team of federal judges. Each state has at least one district. When a crime against federal law is committed in a district, or a lawsuit is filed against a person or entity within that district, that case is usually heard and decided by a federal judge in that district. Interest groups sometimes try to sponsor lawsuits by finding people who can claim to have been hurt by a federal law who reside in a judicial district believed to be sympathetic to the group's cause.

Labor union—A type of interest group representing workers in a relatively well-defined craft, profession, or industry. To overcome the free-rider problem in convincing people to join interest groups, labor unions require membership in order to practice that craft or profession or work in that industry. Labor unions represent both private and public sector workers.

Leadership PAC—A political action committee formed by a member of Congress rather than a corporation or interest group. These PACs raise money, but then the legislator running it recontributes that money to other candidates for office rather than use it for his or her own campaign. Often this is done by the law-maker to gain influence in Congress. The contributions help get the legislator elected to a party leadership post or become chair of an important committee.

Litigation strategy—A lobbying effort that uses the courts as the preferred venue for changing public policy or overturning existing judicial precedent. Interest groups using this strategy typically find an individual who can claim to have been harmed by current law, convince that individual to file a suit, and then provide the financial and legal resources to help that individual pursue his or her case.

Lobby day—One or two days of a year when a trade or professional association brings its members to Washington, DC, to meet in person with their respective members of the House and Senate to discuss issues of concern to the association. This is often done because members of Congress may be more responsive to appeals from their own constituents than from professional lobbyists representing those constituents.

Lobbying—The act of persuading public officials to change public policy or for there to be no change in current public policy. Those who lobby cannot directly influence the shape of policy, so they must persuade others to do it for them.

Lobbying coalition—A partnership among two or more interest groups to pool their informational and financial resources to advocate for or against legislation or administrative regulation. Some coalitions are ad hoc, only lasting for short periods of time on a single piece of legislation, while others are formal, last for years, and lobby on many different issues. Coalition members may have similar interests, but some ad hoc coalitions are made up of groups with different, often competing interests, who have struck deals they are now committed to see en-acted into law.

Lobbying Disclosure Act—Law enacted in 1995 that is the first systematic attempt to track lobbying activity and mildly regulate it since 1946. It requires all lobby-ists who meet with members of Congress or their staff, or with senior executive branch officials, for the express purpose of discussing action on legislation and who spend at least 20 percent of their time on lobbying semiannually to register their clients, what issues they are lobbying, and how much they are spending to do it with the clerk of the House or the secretary of the Senate. For-hire lobbying firms must register themselves if quarterly income from direct lobbying is at least $3,000, and interest groups must register if they spend at least $11,500 in a quarter on lobbying.

Lobbyist—A professional advocate for one or more organized interests before government officials. They may be directly employed by an interest group and therefore only lobby for that group's interests, or they may be employed in private firms and are contracted by many different clients to advocate on many different issues.

Material incentive—Some tangible, physical benefit that an interest group offers people in exchange for membership because something is provided that a person cannot get, or at least not easily, outside of the interest group. It is a way interest groups overcome the free-rider problem.

National Labor Relations Act—Law enacted in 1935 that created the National Labor Relations Board to manage relations between companies and their unions, thus formally tying unions to the government. The law also guarantees workers in a company the right to vote to unionize and, assuming the vote is for a union, requires the company's management to bargain exclusively with that union. This essentially creates closed-shop industries.

Neopluralism—A contemporary variation on the theory of pluralism in American politics. Neopluralism accepts pluralism's assumptions that society is fundamentally divided into many different, often overlapping groups of interests, which frequently mobilize for political action. It more or less accepts the pluralist idea that there ought to be some political advantage for groups of people who feel more strongly about a policy than others, but also acknowledges that many entrenched interest groups frame policies to prevent other, negatively affected groups from realizing their interests are being harmed, thus reducing interest group competition and perpetuating the status quo. Neopluralism recognizes that some groups of people have problems mobilizing even when they do realize their interests are being hurt by existing policy because of the free-rider problem in collective action.

Nomination and confirmation process—The Constitutional requirement that all senior officials in the executive branch, as well as all judges and justices in the judicial branch, be nominated for office by the president and confirmed by a vote of the Senate.

Nonconnected PAC—A political action committee (PAC) that is not affiliated with any corporation or interest group. Thus it can raise money from anybody, not just from a specific restricted group of people. Although they have been the fastest-growing type of PAC, and tend to use more of their money for independent expenditures rather than direct contributions to politicians' campaigns, they are still under most of the same spending restrictions as PACs affiliated with interest groups and corporations.

Office of Public Liaison—Created in 1975 by President Gerald Ford in the Executive Office of the President and designed to reach out to mobilized interests in society to learn their concerns, or at least act as a place in the presidency where interest groups can register their concerns with the administration. The office started to decline in importance during the Reagan administration.

Organized interest—A more general term for entities that lobby government. Many lobbying organizations, such as corporations and public interest groups, do not have anything recognizable as members and therefore do not really qualify as "groups," even though they have a definable interest they want to see reflected in public policy.

Outside lobbying—An advocacy strategy in which members and supporters of an interest group are encouraged to engage in highly visible forms of protest, such as staging marches and rallies, to get the attention of public officials and force them to realize that current policy is harming a mobilized group of people in the nation. The tactic is expensive and hard to control, so it is often only employed when there is no other way to get public officials to pay attention to an interest group.

Pluralism—The belief that the United States is composed of many different groups of citizens, with many citizens often in several groups, and that these groups compete with each other to advance their personal self-interests, even though that may harm the interests of other groups in society. In this view, public policy reflects a balance of power between competing groups in society, with policy favoring the interest group that is larger, has more resources, and feels more intensely about the issue in contention. "Neopluralism" is an updated version of this belief.

Policy domain—Sets of similar public policies regarding a particular topic, such as defense policy, environmental policy, or transportation policy. Sometimes called an "issue domain," the term also tends to include the networks of actors involved in making, defending, and changing those policies, such as members of the congressional committees with jurisdiction over them, the staff in administrative agencies responsible for implementing them, and the interest groups representing factions of the public affected by them. Terms such as "subgovernment," "iron triangle," and "issue network" refer to different types of relationships these actors have within particular policy domains.

Political Action Committee (PAC)—An organization established to raise money from members of an interest group if it is affiliated with one, or the general public in the case of nonconnected PACs. It then contributes that money to candidates in elections or spends it on campaign activities indirectly benefitting the favored candidate. The Federal Election Campaign Act of 1971 and 1974 lays out the modern rules for PACs, though they have been around since the 1940s, as well as restrictions on how much they can contribute to each candidate in each election. Data on how much money PACs raise, who it is raised from, who it is given to, and how much is given is collected and made public by the Federal Election Commission.

Position taking—The strategic action of staking a position on how an issue should be resolved with public policy. Members of Congress typically do this by supporting or opposing a bill in Congress, or an amendment to a bill. Lobbyists often select positions based on what will satisfy interest group members and allies in government, and what can actually get passed in Congress and signed by the president into law.

Precedent—The judicial rule requiring that cases exhibiting a set of circumstances later in time be decided in more or less the same manner as similar cases arising earlier in time so that there is consistency in how courts interpret the law.

Violation of precedent by the federal district courts often makes it more likely that the court of appeals or the even the Supreme Court will rehear a case on appeal. The Supreme Court largely gives itself final authority to determine precedent regarding interpretation of the US Constitution.

Property right—The tradition in Congress that once a legislator obtains a seat on a desired committee or subcommittee, they may keep that seat for the remainder of their career in the House or Senate.

Public good—A policy or benefit created and provided by the government that is available to everyone. Use of the benefit cannot be formally restricted to any particular group of people.

Public interest group—A type of cause-oriented interest group lobbying for policy affecting everybody in the United States. Although the usage of the term is not generally agreed on, it often refers to a type of advocacy organization that does not have official members, merely many financial supporters. Public interest groups often lobby on behalf of people in society, such as the poor and homeless, who cannot afford to financially support interest groups themselves.

Purposive incentive—The opportunity that interest groups offer people who feel passionate about public policy to become actively involved in working to achieve their desired policy goals. Offering this opportunity for political advocacy is one way that many interest groups entice people to join and overcome the free-rider problem.

Reciprocity—In Congress the tradition of one legislator voting to support legislation coming out of a committee that he or she is not a member of because, in exchange, legislators on that committee will then vote to support legislation coming out of the committee that the first member of Congress is a member of. The norm thus supports each committee's autonomy to create policy on issues within its jurisdiction without interference from others in Congress.

Record of decision—A compilation of input from citizens on proposed regulation and administrative actions that executive branch agencies must create as they write the final versions of new regulations, including efforts the agency took to solicit these opinions. Courts will often use this record to determine whether the agency fulfilled its mission to identify and include all stakeholders in an administrative decision when that agency's decision is the subject of a lawsuit.

Regulatory negotiation—Efforts by an administrative agency to bring together identified stakeholders that are contending over a proposed administrative rule and try to work out a compromise that minimizes harm to all sides even as it achieves the agency's goal of implementing the law. Also called "negotiated rulemaking."

Restricted class—The group of people from whom a political action committee (PAC) can raise money if that PAC is affiliated with an interest group or corporation. For example, only employees, shareholders, or executives of a company can contribute to that corporation's PAC. Only members of a labor union can be solicited for donations to its PAC. Nonconnected PACs do not have a restricted class of people from whom they can solicit donations.

Revolving door—An expression referring to the tendency of government officials to leave public employment to become lobbyists. They use their contacts and knowledge to further their lobbying careers. It also recognizes that lobbyists may go back into government service to further expand their portfolios of contacts, and perhaps favor their former employing interest while in public service.

Right-to-work laws—Part of the Taft-Hartley Act of 1947 and used by states to forbid closed-shop (or union-shop) unions. In these states a business cannot be forced to require all of its employees to be members of a labor union as a condition of employment. As of 2013, twenty-four states have right-to-work laws.

Scoping—The requirement under federal law that before administrative agencies draft and release a new rule, they must hold hearings to identify all of the stakeholder groups in society that may be affected by the new rule and listen to their concerns. These concerns should then be reflected in the draft of the new rule as indicated in the agency's record of decision.

Senate—One of the two lawmaking chambers of the legislative branch, often referred to as the "upper house." It is composed of one hundred officials elected to staggered six-year terms. Every state elects two senators regardless of its population size.

Seniority—A tradition in Congress whereby chairs of committees and subcommittees are awarded to members of the majority party who have served on the committee or subcommittee longest. Since 1995 seniority as the sole means of selecting chairs has been reduced to one consideration among others, including party loyalty and fundraising prowess.

Smith-Connally Act—Law enacted in 1943 that temporarily forbade labor unions from making contributions, direct or indirect, to campaigns for federal office. It also permitted the federal government to take over an industry for the duration of World War II if its operation was being disrupted by a union strike.

Social movement—A group of people bound together by a common interest and organized for political advocacy but whose interest is not recognized as legitimate by the existing political system. They use their advocacy, usually dramatic grassroots protests, to demonstrate how widespread their grievance is and to show that there may be political advantages for lawmakers who are willing to champion their cause.

Social movement organization—A semiformal or formal organization that coordinates the activities of members of a social movement, provides its leadership, develops strategy, and reaches out to public officials and other interest groups for support. If the social movement succeeds, the organization often transforms into a regular interest group.

Soft money—Money that PACs and other contributors give to state political parties for "party building activities," often involving voter registration and mobilization. Until 2002 there was no restriction on how much soft money could be contributed, but the Bipartisan Campaign Reform Act largely eliminated it.

Solidary incentive—The opportunity many interest groups offer their members to join, meet, and socialize with other members who share the same interests and, presumably, make friends. Offering the opportunity to socialize is one way that many interest groups entice people to join and overcome the free-rider problem.

Standing (to sue)—The right to bring a lawsuit in court because the person can credibly claim they have been harmed by the law. Rules of standing often make it impossible for interest groups to bring lawsuits on behalf of individuals, so instead the groups sponsor individuals in their suits. Rules of standing have been broadened by Congress through statute to make it easier to sue the federal government in matters such as the environment and consumer protection.

Subcommittee—A body composed either of elected legislators of the House of Representatives or Senate that is a subdivision of a larger committee. It has jurisdiction over a narrow, relatively well-defined area of public policy making and has the primary responsibility for writing all legislation affecting that area of policy. Parallel subcommittees often exist in the House and Senate with the same jurisdictions, though not in all cases.

Subgovernment—A collection of interest groups, a congressional committee, and administrative agency with similar interests in enacting, implementing, and maintaining a set of policies addressing closely related issues. These three sets of actors hold exclusive authority to create policy in this domain of policy making, essentially allowing the involved interest groups to control policy and manage their professions with minimal interference from the government. Other interests with contrary views of how the issues affecting them should be resolved with policy are excluded, which makes this arrangement nearly the same as iron triangles.

Super PAC—A special kind of political action committee that specializes in independent expenditures. Made legal by the Supreme Court's decision in *Citizens United v. Federal Election Commission*, and especially the court of appeals' decision in *SpeechNOW.org v. Federal Election Commission*, super PACs can spend unlimited amounts of money funding media advertisements attacking or promoting a candidate, which most other campaign organizations cannot do. However, they cannot coordinate their activities with the benefitting candidate's campaign committee.

Taft-Hartley Act—Law enacted in 1947 that makes permanent the prohibition on direct contributions by labor unions to candidates for federal office, which had already been enacted temporarily by Congress in the Smith-Connally Act of 1943. Taft-Hartley also gives states the right to enact right-to-work laws forbidding labor unions from insisting that companies only hire union members. It also places some restrictions on the rights of labor unions to strike and picket.

Tillman Act—The law enacted in 1907 that banned corporations from directly contributing their money to candidates in federal elections. It is effectively the first law to restrict the contributing of money to candidates in elections for national office.

Trade and professional associations—The most numerous type of interest group in national politics. Representing specific industries or professions, or subdivisions within those industries or professions, they are closed-member groups in that only individuals working in that industry or practicing that profession may join, though sometimes it is the corporation rather than the individual that is the member. Not only do these associations provide political representation, often they determine ethical standards of practice and conduct, essentially regulating the profession so that government does not need to become involved.

Venue—Any public institution, or subdivision of a public institution, with some type of policy-making responsibility. Examples include congressional committees and subcommittees, executive branch agencies, and the courts.

Venue shopping—The lobbying strategy of selecting one or more venues in which the interest group will work to pursue the political interests of its members. Usually venues are selected on the basis of interest alignment, meaning lawmakers there are sympathetic to the interest group, though venues that have already decided to take up an issue important to a group's members usually must be lobbied whether it is sympathetic or not.

REFERENCES

ABA (American Bar Association). 2011. *Lobbying Law in the Spotlight: Challenges and Proposed Improvements*. Report of the Task Force on Federal Lobbying Laws Section of Administrative Law and Regulatory Practice, American Bar Association, Washington, DC.

Abbott, Frank Frost. 1901. *A History and Description of Roman Political Institutions*. London: Elibron Classics.

Ainsworth, Scott H. 1997. "The Role of Legislators in the Determination of Interest Group Influence." *Legislative Studies Quarterly* 22 (November): 517–533.

———, and John Anthony Maltese. 1996. "National Grange Influence on the Supreme Court Confirmation of Stanley Matthews." *Social Science History* 20 (Spring): 41–62.

Ainsworth, Scott H., and Itai Sened. 1993. "The Role of Lobbyists: Entrepreneurs with Two Audiences." *American Journal of Political Science* 37 (August): 834–866.

Aldrich, Howard E., Catherine R. Zimmer, Udo H. Staber, and John J. Beggs. 1994. "Minimalism, Mutualism, and Maturity: The Evolution of the American Trade Association Population in the 20th Century." In *Evolutionary Dynamics of Organizations*, edited by Joel A. C. Baum and Jitendra V. Singh. New York: Oxford University Press.

Alexander, Brad. 2005. "Good Money and Bad Money: Do Funding Sources Affect Electoral Outcomes?" *Political Research Quarterly* 58 (June): 353–358.

Alexander, Raquel, Susan Scholz, and Stephen Mazza. 2010. "Measuring Rates of Return for Lobbying Expenditures: An Empirical Analysis Under the American Jobs Creation Act." Paper presented at the Annual Meeting of the National Tax Association, Chicago.

Allard, Nicholas W. 2008. "Lobbying Is an Honorable Profession: The Right to Petition and the Competition to Be Right." *Stanford Law and Policy Review* 19 (Spring): 23–68.

Andres, Gary J. 1985. "Business Involvement in Campaign Finance: Factors Influencing the Decision to Form a Corporate PAC." *PS: Political Science and Politics* 18 (Spring): 213–220.

Arrow, Kenneth J. 1991. "Scale Returns in Communication and Elite Control of Organizations." *Journal of Law, Economics, and Organization* 7 (January): 1–6.

Asher, Herbert B., Eric S. Heberlig, Randall B. Ripley, and Karen Snyder. 2001. *American Labor Unions in the Electoral Arena.* New York: Rowman and Littlefield.

Aviv, Diana, Erica Greeley, Rosemary King, and Katie Rader. 2012. *Beyond the Cause: The Art and Science of Advocacy.* Report by the Independent Sector, Washington, DC.

Bachrach, Peter, and Morton S. Baratz. 1962. "Two Faces of Power." *American Political Science Review* 56 (December): 947–952.

Baldassarri, Delia. 2011. "Partisan Joiners: Associational Membership and Political Polarization in the United States (1974–2004)." *Social Science Quarterly* 92 (September): 631–655.

Balla, Steven J. 1998. "Administrative Procedures and Political Control of the Bureaucracy." *American Political Science Review* 92 (September): 663–673.

———. 2003. "Between Commenting and Negotiation: The Contours of Public Participation in Agency Rulemaking." *I/S: A Journal of Law and Policy* 1 (1): 59–94.

———, and John R. Wright. 2001. "Interest Groups, Advisory Committees, and Congressional Control of the Bureaucracy." *American Journal of Political Science* 45 (October): 799–812.

Baran, Jan Witold. 2006. "Can I Lobby You? Don't Let One Bad Abramoff Spoil the Whole Bunch." *Washington Post,* January 8.

Barro, Robert. 1973. "The Control of Politicians: An Economic Model." *Public Choice* 14 (Spring): 19–42.

Bauer, Raymond A., Ithiel de Sola Pool, and Lewis Anthony Dexter. 1963. *American Business and Public Policy: The Politics of Foreign Trade.* New York: Atherton.

Baum, Lawrence. 2001. *The Supreme Court.* 7th ed. Washington, DC: Congressional Quarterly Press.

Baumgartner, Frank R., Jeffrey M. Berry, Marie Hojnacki, David C. Kimball, and Beth L. Leech. 2009. *Lobbying and Policy Change: Who Wins, Who Loses, and Why.* Chicago: University of Chicago Press.

Baumgartner, Frank R., and Bryan D. Jones. 1993. *Agendas and Instability in American Politics.* Chicago: University of Chicago Press.

Baumgartner, Frank R., and Beth L. Leech. 1998. *Basic Interests: The Importance of Groups in Politics and Political Science.* Princeton, NJ: Princeton University Press.

Bawn, Kathleen. 1997. "Choosing Strategies to Control the Bureaucracy: Statutory Constraints, Oversight, and the Committee System." *Journal of Law, Economics, and Organization* 13 (April): 101–126.

Benson, Bruce L. 1981. "Why Are Congressional Committees Dominated by 'High Demand' Legislators? A Comment on Niskanen's View of Bureaucrats and Politicians." *Southern Economic Journal* 48 (July): 68–77.

Bentley, Arthur F. 1908. *The Process of Government: A Study of Social Pressures.* Chicago: University of Chicago Press.

Bernstein, Marver. 1955. *Regulating Industry by Independent Commission.* Princeton, NJ: Princeton University Press.

Berry, Jeffrey M. 1977. *Lobbying for the People: The Political Behavior of Public Interest Groups.* Princeton, NJ: Princeton University Press.

———. 1993. "Citizen Groups and the Changing Nature of Interest Group Politics in America." *Annals of the American Academy of Political and Social Science* 528 (July): 30–41.

———. 1999. *The New Liberalism: The Rising Power of Citizen Groups.* Washington, DC: Brookings Institution Press.

Best, Steven, and Anthony J. Nocella, eds. 2006. *Igniting a Revolution: Voices in Defense of the Earth.* Oakland, CA: AK Press.

Birnbaum, Jeffrey H. 1992. *The Lobbyists: How Influence Peddlers Work Their Way in Washington.* New York: Random House.

Bishop, Morris. 1968. *The Middle Ages.* Boston: Houghton Mifflin.

Boehmke, Frederick J., and Richard Witmer. 2011. "Indian Nations as Interest Groups: Tribal Motivations for Contributions to U.S. Senators." *Political Research Quarterly* 65 (March): 179–191.

Boies, John L. 1989. "Money, Business, and the State: Material Interests, Fortune 500 Corporations, and the Size of Political Action Committees." *American Sociological Review* 54 (October): 821–833.

Bolton, Alexander. 2013. "Conservatives: Public Backlash to Immigration Reform Is Coming." *The Hill*, June 1.

Bonnett, Clarence E. 1935. "The Evolution of Business Groupings." *Annals of the American Academy of Political and Social Science* 179 (May): 1–8.

Boris, Elizabeth T. 1999. "Nonprofit Organizations in a Democracy: Varied Roles and Responsibilities." In *Nonprofits and Government: Collaboration and Conflict*, edited by Elizabeth T. Boris and C. Eugene Steuerle, 3–30. Washington, DC: Urban Institute Press.

Bosso, Christopher J. 1991. "Adaption and Change in the Environmental Movement." In *Interest Group Politics*, edited by Allan J. Cigler and Burdett A. Loomis, 151–176. 3rd ed. Washington, DC: Congressional Quarterly Press.

———, and Michael Thomas Collins. 2002. "Just Another Tool? How Environmental Groups Use the Internet." In *Interest Group Politics*, edited by Allan J. Cigler and Burdett A. Loomis, 95–114. 6th ed. Washington, DC: Congressional Quarterly Press.

Box-Steffensmeier, Janet M., Peter M. Radcliffe, and Brandon L. Bartels. 2005. "The Incidence and Timing of PAC Contributions to Incumbent U.S. House Members, 1993–94." *Legislative Studies Quarterly* 30 (November): 549–579.

Boyt, Jeb. 1993. "Struggling to Protect Ecosystems and Biodiversity Under NEPA and NFMA: The Ancient Forests of the Pacific Northwest and the Northern Spotted Owl Comment." *Pace Environmental Law Review* 10 (Spring): 1009–1050.

Brady, Henry E., Kay Lehman Schlozman, and Sidney Verba. 1999. "Prospecting for Participants: Rational Expectations and the Recruitment of Political Activists." *American Political Science Review* 93 (March): 153–168.

Brady, Henry E., Sidney Verba, and Kay Lehman Schlozman. 1995. "Beyond SES: A Resource Model of Political Participation." *American Political Science Review* 89 (June): 271–294.

Brasher, Holly, and David Lowery. 2006. "The Corporate Context of Lobbying Activity." *Business and Politics* 8 (1): 1–23.

Brown, Heath. 2011. "Interest Groups and Presidential Transitions." *Congress and the Presidency* 38 (2): 152–170.

———, Jeffrey R. Henig, Natalie Lacireno-Paquet, and Thomas T. Holyoke. 2004. "Scale of Operations and Locus of Control in Market Versus Mission-Oriented Charter Schools." *Social Science Quarterly* 85 (December): 1035–1051.

Browne, William P. 1990. "Organized Interests and Their Issue Niches: A Search for Pluralism in a Policy Domain." *Journal of Politics* 52 (May): 477–509.

———. 2001. *The Failure of National Rural Policy: Institutions and Interests.* Washington, DC: Georgetown University Press.

Caldeira, Gregory A., Marie Hojnacki, and John R. Wright. 2000. "The Lobbying Activities of Organized Interests in Federal Judicial Nominations." *Journal of Politics* 62 (February): 51–69.

Caldeira, Gregory A., and John R. Wright. 1988. "Organized Interests and Agenda Setting in the U.S. Supreme Court." *American Political Science Review* 82 (December): 1109–1127.

———. 1990. "Amici Curiae before the Supreme Court: Who Participates, When, and How Much?" *Journal of Politics* 52 (August): 782–806.

———. 1998. "Lobbying for Justice: Organized Interests, Supreme Court Nominations, and the United States Senate." *American Journal of Political Science* 42 (April): 499–523.

Carpenter, Daniel P. 2004. "Protection Without Capture: Product Approval by a Politically Responsive, Learning Regulator." *American Political Science Review* 98 (November): 613–631.

Casey, Colleen, Davita Silfen Glasberg, and Angie Beeman. 2011. "Racial Disparities in Access to Mortgage Credit: Does Governance Matter?" *Social Science Quarterly* 92 (September): 782–806.

Cater, Douglass. 1964. *Power in Washington: A Critical Look at Today's Struggle to Govern in the Nation's Capital.* New York: Random House.

Chappell, Henry W., Jr. 1981. "Campaign Contributions and Voting on the Cargo Preference Bill: A Comparison of Simultaneous Models." *Public Choice* 36 (2): 301–312.

———. 1982. "Campaign Contributions and Congressional Voting: A Simultaneous Probit-Tobit Model." *Review of Economics and Statistics* 64 (February): 77–83.

Cialdini, Robert B. 2001. *Influence: Science and Practice.* 4th ed. New York: Pearson.

Cigler, Beverly A. 1995. "Not Just Another Special Interest: Intergovernmental Representation." In *Interest Group Politics*, edited by Allan J. Cigler and Burdett A. Loomis, 131–153. 4th ed. Washington, DC: Congressional Quarterly Press.

Clark, Peter B., and James Q. Wilson. 1961. "Incentive Systems: A Theory of Organizations." *Administrative Science Quarterly* 6 (September): 129–166.

Clemens, Elisabeth S. 1997. *The People's Lobby: Organizational Innovation and the Rise of Interest Group Politics in the United States, 1890–1925.* Chicago: University of Chicago Press.

CMF (Congressional Management Foundation). 2011. *Communicating with Congress: Perceptions of Citizen Advocacy on Capitol Hill.* Washington, DC.

Collins, Paul M., Jr. 2007. "Lobbyists Before the U.S. Supreme Court." *Political Research Quarterly* 60 (March): 55–70.

———. 2008. *Friends of the Supreme Court: Interest Groups and Judicial Decision Making.* New York: Oxford University Press.

———. and Wendy L. Martinek. 2010. "Friends of the Circuits: Interest Group Influence on Decision Making in the U.S. Court of Appeals." *Social Science Quarterly* 91 (June): 397–414.

Confessore, Nicholas. 2013. "Uneven I.R.S. Scrutiny Seen in Political Spending by Big Tax-Exempt Groups." *New York Times*, May 13.

———, and Michael Luo. 2013. "Groups Targeted by I.R.S. Tested Rules on Politics." *New York Times*, May 26, 2013.

Conroy, Meredith, Jessica T. Feezell, and Mario Guerrero. 2012. "Facebook and Political Engagement: A Study of Online Political Group Membership and Offline Political Engagement." *Computers in Human Behavior* 28 (September): 1535–1546.

Constantelos, John. 2007. "Interest Group Strategies in Multi-Level Europe." *Journal of Public Affairs* 7 (February): 39–53.

Costain, Anne N. 1981. "Representing Women: The Transition from Social Movement to Interest Group." *Western Political Quarterly* 34 (March): 100–113.

Costain, W. Douglas, and Anne N. Costain. 1981. "Interest Groups as Policy Aggregators in the Legislative Process." *Polity* 14 (Winter): 249–272.

Cox, Gary W., and Mathew D. McCubbins. 1993. *Legislative Leviathan: Party Government in the House.* Berkeley: University of California Press.

Coyle, Marcia. 2008. "Amicus Briefs Are Ammo for Supreme Court Gun Case." *National Law Journal*, March 10.

Currinder, Marian. 2009. *Money in the House: Campaign Funds and Congressional Party Politics.* Boulder: Westview.

Dahl, Robert A. 1956. *A Preface to Democratic Theory.* Chicago: University of Chicago Press.

Dash, Eric, and Nelson D. Schwartz. 2011. "A Mobilization in Washington by Wall Street." *New York Times*, July 30.

Davidson, Roger H. 1990. "The Advent of the Modern Congress: The Legislative Reorganization Act of 1946." *Legislative Studies Quarterly* 15 (August): 357–373.

———, Walter J. Oleszek, and Thomas Kephart. 1988. "One Bill, Many Committees: Multiple Referrals in the U.S. House of Representatives." *Legislative Studies Quarterly* 13 (February): 3–28.

Day, Christine L., and Charles D. Hadley. 2001. "Feminist Diversity: The Policy Preferences of Women's PAC Contributions." *Political Research Quarterly* 54 (September): 673–686.

DeButts, C. Read. 1996. "In Defense of Grassroots Lobbying." *Campaigns & Elections* 17 (December/January): 67–68.

Deering, Christopher J., and Steven S. Smith. 1997. *Committees in Congress.* 3rd ed. Washington, DC: Congressional Quarterly Press.

DeGregorio, Christine, and Jack E. Rossotti. 1995. "Campaigning for the Court: Interest Group Participation in the Bork and Thomas Confirmation Processes." In *Interest Group Politics*, edited by Allan J. Cigler and Burdett A. Loomis, 215–238. 4th ed. Washington, DC: Congressional Quarterly Press.

Dennis, Brady. 2010. "Chamber of Commerce Leader Pledges to Fight Health-Care Law, Financial Overhaul." *Washington Post*, November 17.

DeVita, Carol J. 1999. "Nonprofits and Devolution: What Do We Know?" In *Nonprofits and Government: Collaboration and Conflict*, edited by Elizabeth Boris and C. Eugene Steuerle, 213–233. Washington, DC: Urban Institute Press.

Dexter, Lewis Anthony. 1969. *How Organizations Are Represented in Washington.* New York: Bobbs-Merrill.

Diani, Mario. 2012. "Interest Organizations in Social Movements: An Empirical Exploration." *Interest Groups and Advocacy* 1 (May): 26–47.

Diaz, Manny, and John Zogby. 2012. "The Latino Vote in 2012 and the Depth of the GOP Problem." *NJ Today*, November 27. http://njtoday.net/2012/11/27/opinion -the-latino-vote-in-2012-and-the-depth-of-the-gop-problem/.

Dickson, Paul, and Thomas B. Allen. 2006. *The Bonus Army: An American Epic.* New York: Walker.

Dietrich, John W. 1999. "Interest Groups and Foreign Policy: Clinton and the China MFN Debates." *Presidential Studies Quarterly* 29 (June): 280–296.

Dodd, Lawrence C. 1977. "Congress and the Quest for Power." In *Congress Reconsidered*, edited by Lawrence C. Dodd and Bruce I. Oppenheimer. New York: Praeger.

Doherty, Brian. 2009. *Gun Control on Trial: Inside the Supreme Court Battle over the Second Amendment.* Washington, DC: Cato Institute.

Downs, Anthony J. 1967. *Inside Bureaucracy.* New York: HarperCollins.

Drew, Elizabeth. 1999. *The Corruption of American Politics: What Went Wrong and Why.* Secaucus, NJ: Birch Lane.

Drope, Jeffrey M., and Wendy L. Hansen. 2009. "New Evidence for the Theory of Groups: Trade Association Lobbying in Washington, D.C." *Political Research Quarterly* 62 (June): 303–316.

Drutman, Lee. 2012. "Trade Associations, the Collective Action Dilemma, and the Problem of Cohesion." In *Interest Group Politics*, edited by Allan J. Cigler and Burdett A. Loomis, 74–96. 8th ed. Washington, DC: Congressional Quarterly Press.

Dwoskin, Elizabeth. 2012. "Lobbyist on Incremental Mission to Restore Lobbying's Good Name." *Bloomberg News*, July 7.

Eggen, Dan. 2012. "Soros Donates $1.5 Million to Pro-Obama Super PACs." *Washington Post*, September 27.

———, and T. W. Farnam. 2010. "New 'Super PACs' Bringing Millions Into Campaigns." *Washington Post*, September 28.

———. 2011. "Corporate Contributions Have Surged for New Republican Leaders in House." *Washington Post*, January 22.

———. 2012. "Spending by Independent Groups had Little Election Impact, Analysis Finds." *Washington Post*, November 7.

Eilperin, Juliet. 1998a. "Lobbyists' Last-Minute Maneuvering Pays Off for Many Clients." *Washington Post*, October 25.

———. 1998b. "No Democrats Need Apply, House GOP Tells Lobby." *Washington Post*, October 14.

———. 2001. "Taking a Right Turn on K Street." *Washington Post*, March 14.

———. 2011. "Fuel-Efficiency Rules Set for Heavy-Duty Trucks and Buses." *Washington Post*, August 9.

Eismeier, Theodore J., and Philip H. Pollock III. 1986. "Strategy and Choice in Congressional Elections: The Role of Political Action Committees." *American Journal of Political Science* 30 (February): 197–213.

Engel, Steven T., and David J. Jackson. 1998. "Wielding the Stick Instead of the Carrot: Labor PAC Punishment of Pro-NAFTA Democrats." *Political Research Quarterly* 51 (September): 813–828.

Epstein, David, and Sharyn O'Halloran. 1999. *Delegating Powers: A Transaction Cost Politics Approach to Policy Making Under Separation of Powers.* New York: Cambridge University Press.

Epstein, Lee. 1986. *Conservatives in Court.* Knoxville: University of Tennessee Press.

———. 1993. "Interest Group Litigation During the Rehnquist Court Era." *Journal of Law and Politics* 9 (Summer): 715–717.

Evans, Diana. 1996. "Before the Roll Call: Interest Group Lobbying and Public Policy Outcomes in House Committees." *Political Research Quarterly* 49 (June): 287–304.

Everitt, Anthony. 2007. *Augustus: The Life of Rome's First Emperor.* New York: Random House.

Farnam, T. W. 2010. "72 Super PACs Spent $83.7 Million on Election." *Washington Post,* December 4.

———. 2011. "Revolving Door of Employment Between Congress, Lobbying Firms, study Shows." *Washington Post*, September 12.

———. 2012a. "Industry Trade Groups Investing Big in Positive Political Messages." *Washington Post*, October 13.

———. 2012b. "Seven Ex-Lawmakers Now Lobby for Groups that Got Earmarks." *Washington Post*, January 27.

Farrell, John A. 2011. "The Westerner in D.C." *High Country News*, May 2.

Fellowes, Matthew C., and Patrick J. Wolf. 2004. "Funding Mechanisms and Policy Instruments: How Business Campaign Contributions Influence Congressional Votes." *Political Research Quarterly* 57 (June): 315–324.

Fenno, Richard F., Jr. 1973. *Congressmen in Committees.* Boston: Little, Brown.

———. 1978. *Home Style: House Members in Their Districts.* Boston: Little, Brown.

Fine, Terri Susan. 1994. "Interest Groups and the Framing of the 1988 Democratic and Republican Party Platforms." *Polity* 26 (Spring): 517–530.

Finer, Jonathan. 2004. "Kerry Says He Believes Life Starts at Conception." *Washington Post*, July 5.

Fitch, Bradford. 2010a. *Citizen's Handbook to Influencing Elected Officials: A Guide for Citizen Lobbyists and Grassroots Advocates*. Washington, DC: The Capitol.net, Inc.

———. 2010b. "New House Calendar Benefits Grassroots Advocates." Congressional Management Foundation. http://pmpu.org/category/projects/communicating -with-congress/.

Fordham, Benjamin O., and Timothy J. McKeown. 2003. "Selection and Influence: Interest Groups and Congressional Voting on Trade Policy." *International Organization* 57 (Summer): 519–549.

Fornara, Charles W., and Loren J. Samons II. 1991. *Athens from Cleisthenes to Pericles*. Berkeley: University of California Press.

Fowler, Linda L. 1982. "How Interest Groups Select Issues for Rating Voting Records of the Members of the U.S. Congress." *Legislative Studies Quarterly* 7 (August): 401–413.

Franke, James L., and Douglas Dobson. 1985. "Interest Groups: The Problem of Representation." *Western Political Quarterly* 38 (June): 224–237.

Gais, Thomas L., Mark A. Peterson, and Jack L. Walker. 1984. "Interest Groups, Iron Triangles, and Representative Institutions in American National Government." *British Journal of Political Science* 14 (2): 161–185.

Gamm, Gerald, and Robert D. Putnam. 1999. "The Growth of Voluntary Associations in American, 1840–1940." *Journal of Interdisciplinary History* 29 (Spring): 511–557.

GAO (Government Accountability Office). 2011. *2011 Lobbying Disclosure: Observations on Lobbyists' Compliance with Disclosure Requirements*. GAO-12-492. Washington, DC.

Gardner, John W. 1972. *In Common Cause*. New York: Norton.

Godwin, R. Kenneth. 1988. *One Billion Dollars of Influence: The Direct Marketing of Politics*. Chatham: Chatham House.

Golden, Marissa Martino. 1998. "Interest Groups in the Rule-Making Process: Who Participates? Whose Voices Get Heard?" *Journal of Public Administration Research and Theory* 8 (April): 245–270.

Goldman, T. R. 2012. "Forget Creativity: Can Lobbying be Taught?" *Washington Post*, November 18.

Goldschmidt, Kathy, and Leslie Ochreiter. 2008. *Communicating with Congress: How the Internet Has Changed Citizen Engagement*. Washington, DC: Congressional Management Foundation.

Gopoian, J. David. 1984. "What Makes PACs Tick? An Analysis of the Allocation Patterns of Economic Interest Groups." *American Journal of Political Science* 28 (May): 259–281.

Gormley, William T., Jr., and Steven J. Balla. 2004. *Bureaucracy and Democracy: Accountability and Performance*. Washington, DC: Congressional Quarterly Press.

Gray, Virginia, and David Lowery. 1996. *The Population Ecology of Interest Representation: Lobbying Communities in the American States*. Ann Arbor: University of Michigan Press.

———. 1997. "Life in a Niche: Mortality Anxiety among Organized Interests in the American States." *Political Research Quarterly* 50 (March): 25–47.

Graziano, Luigi. 2001. *Lobbying, Pluralism, and Democracy*. New York: Palgrave.

Greenstone, J. David. 1977. *Labor in American Politics*. Chicago: University of Chicago Press.

Grenzke, Janet M. 1989. "PACs and the Congressional Supermarket: The Currency is Complex." *American Journal of Political Science* 33 (February): 1–24.

Grier, Kevin B., Michael C. Munger, and Brian E. Roberts. 1991. "The Industrial Organization of Corporate Political Participation." *Southern Economic Journal* 57 (January): 727–738.

———. 1994. "The Determinants of Industry Political Activity, 1978–1986." *American Political Science Review* 88 (December): 911–926.

Grimaldi, James V. 2000. "Microsoft's Lobbying Largess Pays Off." *Washington Post*, May 17.

Groseclose, Tim, Steven D. Levitt, and James M. Snyder Jr. 1999. "Comparing Interest Group Scores across Time and Chambers: Adjusted ADA Scores for the U.S. Congress." *American Political Science Review* 93 (March): 33–50.

Grossmann, Matt. 2012. *The Not-So-Special Interests: Interest Groups, Public Representation, and American Governance*. Stanford: Stanford University Press.

Guth, James L., Lyman A. Kellstedt, John C. Green, and Corwin E. Schmidt. 2007. "Getting the Spirit? Religious and Partisan Mobilization in the 2004 Elections." In *Interest Group Politics*, edited by Allan J. Cigler and Burdett A. Loomis, 157–181. 7th ed. Washington, DC: Congressional Quarterly Press.

Haag, Susan White. 2000. *Community Reinvestment and Cities: A Literature Review of CRA's Impact and Future*. Washington, DC: Brookings Institution Press.

Hacker, Jacob S. 1999. *The Road to Nowhere: The Genesis of President Clinton's Plan for Health Security*. Princeton, NJ: Princeton University Press.

Hall, Richard L., and Frank W. Wayman. 1990. "Buying Time: Moneyed Interests and the Mobilization of Bias in Congressional Committees." *American Political Science Review* 84 (September): 797–820.

Halstead, T. J. 2003. "'The Law: Walker v. Cheney': Legal Insulation of the Vice President from GAO Investigations." *Presidential Studies Quarterly* 33 (September): 635–648.

———. 2008. *District of Columbia v. Heller: The Supreme Court and the Second Amendment*. Washington, DC: Congressional Research Service.

Hamburger, Tom. 2010. "U.S. Chamber of Commerce Grows Into a Political Force." *Los Angeles Times*, March 8.

Hannan, Michael T., and John Freeman. 1977. "The Population Ecology of Organizations." *American Journal of Sociology* 82 (5): 929–964.

Hansen, John Mark. 1985. "The Political Economy of Group Membership." *American Political Science Review* 79 (March): 79–96.

———. 1991. *Gaining Access: Congress and the Farm Lobby, 1919–1981*. Chicago: University of Chicago Press.

Hansen, Kenneth N., and Tracy A. Skopek, eds. 2011. *The New Politics of Indian Gaming: The Rise of Reservation Interest Groups*. Reno: University of Nevada Press.

Hansen, Liane. 2006. "A Lobbyist by Any Other Name?" National Public Radio. http://www.npr.org/templates/story/story.php?storyId=5167187.

Hansen, Wendy L., and Neil J. Mitchell. 2000. "Disaggregating and Explaining Corporate Political Activity: Domestic and Foreign Corporations in National Politics." *American Political Science Review* 94 (December): 891–903.

———, and Jeffrey M. Drope. 2005. "The Logic of Private and Collective Action." *American Journal of Political Science* 49 (January): 150–167.

Hansford, Thomas G. 2004a. "Information Provisions, Organizational Constraints, and the Decision to Submit an Amicus Curiae Brief in a U.S. Supreme Court Case." *Political Research Quarterly* 57 (June): 219–230.

———. 2004b. "Lobbying Strategies, Venue Selection, and Organized Interest Involvement at the U.S. Supreme Court." *American Politics Research* 32 (March): 170–197.

Hart, David M. 2001. "Why Do Some Firms Give? Why Do Some Firms Give a Lot? High-Tech PACs, 1977–1996." *Journal of Politics* 63 (November): 1230–1249.

Heaney, Michael T. 2004. "Outside the Issue Niche: The Multidimensionality of Interest Group Identity." *American Politics Research* 32 (November): 611–651.

———, Seth E. Masket, Joanne M. Miller, and Dara Z. Strolovitch. 2012. "Polarized Networks: The Organizational Affiliations of National Party Convention Delegates." *American Behavioral Scientist* 56 (12): 1654–1676.

Heclo, Hugh. 1978. "Issue Networks and the Executive Establishment." In *The New American Political System*, edited by Anthony King, 87–124. Washington, DC: American Enterprise Institute Press.

Heinz, John P., Edward O. Laumann, Robert L. Nelson, and Robert H. Salisbury. 1993. *The Hollow Core: Private Interests in National Policymaking*. Cambridge, MA: Harvard University Press.

Henig, Jeffrey R. 2009. *Spin Cycle: How Research Is Used in Policy Debates: The Case of Charter Schools*. New York: Russell Sage Foundation.

———, Thomas T. Holyoke, Natalie Lacireno-Paquet, and Michele Moser. 2004. "Privatization, Politics, and Urban Services: The Political Behavior of Charter Schools." *Journal of Urban Affairs* 25 (February): 37–54.

Herger, Wally, Dave Reichert, and Charles Boustany. 2011. *Behind the Veil: The AARP America Doesn't Know*. http://waysandmeans.house.gov/News/DocumentSingle.aspx?DocumentID=232179.

Herring, E. Pendleton. 1929. *Group Representation Before Congress*. Baltimore: Johns Hopkins University Press.

Herrnson, Paul S. 2009. "The Role of Party Organizations, Party-Connected Committees, and Party Allies in Elections." *Journal of Politics* 71 (October): 1207–1224.

Herszenhorn, David M. 2008. "Congressional Crackdown on Lobbying is Already Showing Cracks." *New York Times*, January 3.

Hirschman, Albert O. 1970. *Exit, Voice, and Loyalty: Responses to Decline in Firms, Organizations, and States*. Cambridge, MA: Harvard University Press.

Hobson, Margaret Kriz. 2011. "Pollution Worries Surface Along with Energy Trove." *CQ Weekly* May 9, p. 993.

Hojnacki, Marie. 1997. "Interest Groups' Decisions to Join Alliance or Work Alone." *American Journal of Political Science* 41 (January): 61–87.

——, and David C. Kimball. 1998. "Organized Interests and the Decision of Whom to Lobby in Congress." *American Political Science Review* 92(December): 775–790.

——. 1999. "The Who and How of Organizations' Lobbying Strategies in Committee." *Journal of Politics* 61 (November): 999–1024.

——. 2001. "PAC Contributions and Lobbying Contacts in Congressional Committees." *Political Research Quarterly* 54 (March): 161–180.

Holland, Tom. 2005. *Rubicon: The Last Years of the Roman Republic.* Random House.

Holt, James Clarke. 1992. *Magna Carta.* 2nd ed. New York: Cambridge University Press.

Holyoke, Thomas T. 2003. "Choosing Battlegrounds: Interest Group Lobbying Across Multiple Venues." *Political Research Quarterly* 56 (September): 325–336.

——2004a. "By Invitation Only: Controlling Interest Group Access to the Oval Office." *American Review of Politics* 25 (Fall): 221–240.

——. 2004b. "Community Mobilization and Credit: The Impact of Nonprofits and Social Capital on Community Reinvestment Act Lending." *Social Science Quarterly* 85 (March): 187–205.

——. 2008. "Interest Group Competition and Cooperation at Legislative Hearings." *Congress and the Presidency* 35 (Autumn): 17–38.

——. 2009. "Interest Group Competition and Coalition Formation." *American Journal of Political Science* 53 (April): 360–375.

——. 2011. *Competitive Interests: Competition and Compromise in American Interest Group Politics.* Washington, DC: Georgetown University Press.

——. 2013a. "A Dynamic Model of Member Participation in Interest Groups." *Interest Groups & Advocacy* 2 (October): 278–301.

——. 2013b. "The Interest Group Effect on Citizen Contact with Congress." *Party Politics* 19 (November): 925–944.

Holyoke, Thomas T., Heath Brown, and Jeffrey R. Henig. 2012. "Shopping in the Political Arena: Strategic State and Local Venue Selection by Advocates." *State and Local Government Review* 44 (March): 1–13.

Holyoke, Thomas T., Jeffrey R. Henig, Heath Brown, and Natalie Lacireno-Paquet. 2007. "Institutional Advocacy and the Political Behavior of Charter Schools." *Political Research Quarterly* 60 (June): 202–214.

——. 2009. "Policy Dynamics and the Evolution of State Charter School Laws." *Policy Sciences* 42 (February): 33–55.

Hrebenar, Ronald J., and Clive S. Thomas. 2012. "The Rise and Fall and Rise of the China Lobby in the United States." In *Interest Group Politics*, edited by Allan J. Cigler and Burdett A. Loomis, 297–316. 8th ed. Washington, DC: Congressional Quarterly Press.

Hubbard, J. T. 1995. *For Each, the Strength of All: A History of Banking in the State of New York.* New York: New York University Press.

Hula, Kevin W. 1999. *Lobbying Together: Interest Group Coalitions in Legislative Politics.* Washington, DC: Georgetown University Press.

Hysom, Tim. 2010. "Lady Gaga and the Evolution of Constituent Communications." Congressional Management Foundation. http://pmpu.org/category/projects /communicating-with-congress/.

Ignatius, David. 2000. "So Long, Super Lawyers." *Washington Post*, June 11.

Jackson, Brooks. 1990. *Honest Graft: Big Money and the American Political Process.* Washington, DC: Farragut.

Jacob, Kathryn Allamong. 2010. *King of the Lobby: The Life and Times of Sam Ward, Man About Washington in the Gilded Age.* Baltimore: Johns Hopkins University Press.

Jacobson, Gary C. 1992. *The Politics of Congressional Elections.* 3rd ed. New York: HarperCollins.

Jacobson, Louis. 1995. "Washington's a Movable Feast for Conservatives." *National Journal*, November 25.

Jacobson, Robin Dale. 2011. "The Politics of Belonging: Interest Group Identity and Agenda Setting on Immigration." *American Politics Research* 39 (November): 993–1018.

Jankowsky, Joel. 2006. "Lobbying and Lobby Reform: A Practitioner's Viewpoint." *Extensions* 14 (Fall): 20–24.

Jenkins, J. Craig, and Charles Perrow. 1977. "Insurgency of the Powerless: Farm Workers Movements (1946–1972)." *American Sociological Review* 42 (April): 249–268.

Jewell, Malcolm E., and Chu Chi-Hung. 1974. "Membership Movement and Committee Attractiveness in the U.S. House of Representatives, 1963–1971." *American Journal of Political Science* 18 (May): 433–441.

Justice, Glen. 2004. "New Rules on Fund-Raising Bring Lobbyists to the Fore." *New York Times*, April 20.

Kahn, Ronald. 1999. "Institutional Norms and the Historical Development of Supreme Court Politics: Changing 'Social Facts' and Doctrinal Development." In *The Supreme Court in American Politics: New Institutionalist Interpretations*, edited by Howard Gillman and Cornell Clayton, 43–59. Lawrence: University Press of Kansas.

Kaiser, Robert G. 2009. *So Damn Much Money: The Triumph of Lobbying and the Corrosion of the American Government.* New York: Vintage Books.

Kang, Cecilia. 2012. "Web Giants Launch Lobbying Group." *Washington Post*, September 19.

Karty, Kevin D. 2002. "Closure and Capture in Federal Advisory Committees." *Business and Politics* 4 (2): 213–238.

Katel, Peter. 2005. "Lobbying Boom: Should the Industry Be Regulated More Closely?" *CQ Researcher* 15 (26): 613–636.

Kau, James B., and Paul H. Rubin. 1981. "The Impact of Labor Unions on the Passage of Economic Legislation." *Journal of Labor Research* 2 (Fall): 133–145.

Kearney, Joseph D., and Thomas W. Merrill. 2000. "The Influence of Amicus Curiae Briefs on the Supreme Court." *University of Pennsylvania Law Review* 148 (3): 743–853.

Kernell, Samuel. 1993. *Going Public: New Strategies of Presidential Leadership*. Washington, DC: Congressional Quarterly Press.

Kersh, Rogan. 2002. "Corporate Lobbyists as Political Actors: A View from the Field." In *Interest Group Politics*, edited by Allan J. Cigler and Burdett A. Loomis, 225–248. 6th ed. Washington, DC: Congressional Quarterly Press.

Kerwin, Cornelius M. 1999. *Rulemaking: How Government Agencies Write Law and Make Policy*. 2nd ed. Washington, DC: Congressional Quarterly Press.

King, David C., and Jack L. Walker Jr. 1991. "The Origins and Maintenance of Groups." In *Mobilizing Interest Groups in America: Patrons, Professions, and Social Movements*, by Jack L. Walker Jr., 75–102. Ann Arbor: University of Michigan Press.

Kirkpatrick, David D. 2010. "Law to Curb Lobbying Sends It Underground." *New York Times*, January 18.

Klein, Ezra. 2011. "A Tipping Point for Occupy Wall Street." *Washington Post*, August 25.

Knoke, David. 1986. "Associations and Interest Groups." *Annual Review of Sociology* 12: 1–12.

Koen, Ross Y. 1974. *The China Lobby in American Politics*. New York: Harper & Row.

Kollman, Ken. 1998. *Outside Lobbying: Public Opinion and Interest Group Strategies*. Princeton, NJ: Princeton University Press.

Kumar, Martha Joynt, and Michael Baruch Grossman. 1986. "Political Communication from the White House: The Interest Group Connection." *Presidential Studies Quarterly* 16 (Winter): 92–101.

Kuntz, Phil. 1995. "A Day in Washington Is Just Another Day to Raise More Dollars." *Wall Street Journal*, October 23.

Landsberg, Mitchell. 2012. "Obama Praised—and Pummeled—On Matters of Faith." *Los Angeles Times*, April 8.

Langbein, Laura I. 1986. "Money and Access: Some Empirical Evidence." *Journal of Politics* 48 (November): 1052–1062.

———, and Cornelius M. Kerwin. 2000. "Regulatory Negotiation Versus Conventional Rule Making: Claims, Counterclaims, and Empirical Evidence." *Journal of Public Administration Research and Theory* 10 (July): 599–632.

Lardner, Richard. 2009. "House Pushes Ban on Peer-to-Peer Software for Federal Employees." *Huffington Post*, November 18.

Lavertu, Stéphane, and David L. Weimer. 2011. "Federal Advisory Committees, Policy Expertise, and the Approval of Drugs and Medical Devices at the FDA." *Journal of Public Administration Research and Theory* 21 (April): 211–237.

Lawson, Gary J., and Guy Seidman. 1999. "Downsizing the Right to Petition." *Northwestern University Law Review* 93 (Spring): 739–766.

Leech, Beth L., Frank R. Baumgartner, Timothy M. La Pira, and Nicholas A. Semanko. 2005. "Drawing Lobbyists to Washington: Government Activity and the Demand for Advocacy." *Political Research Quarterly* 58 (March): 19–30.

Leonnig, Carol D. 2012. "Corporate Donors Fuel Chamber of Commerce's Political Power." *Washington Post*, October 18.

Levey, Noam N., and Kim Geiger. 2011. "Much Corporate Political Spending Stays Hidden." *Los Angeles Times*, April 24.

Lindblom, Charles E. 1959. "The Science of 'Muddling Through.'" *Public Administration Review* 19 (Spring): 79–88.

Lindquist, Stefanie A., and Frank B. Cross. 2009. *Measuring Judicial Activism*. New York: Oxford University Press.

Liptak, Adam. 2007. "Carefully Plotted Course Propels Gun Case to Top." *New York Times*, December 3.

Lipton, Eric. 2010. "A G.O.P. Leader Tightly Bound to Lobbyists." *New York Times*, September 11.

———. 2013. "Tax Lobby Builds Ties to Chairman of Finance Panel." *New York Times*, April 6.

———, and Ben Protess. 2013. "Banks' Lobbyists Help in Drafting Financial Bills." *New York Times*, May 23.

Lipton, Eric, and Kevin Sack. 2013. "Fiscal Footnote: Big Senate Gift to Drug Maker." *New York Times*, January 13.

Lowi, Theodore J. 1979. *The End of Liberalism: The Second Republic of the United States*. 2nd ed. New York: Norton.

Lucco, Joan. 1992. "Representing the Public Interest: Consumer Groups and the Presidency." In Petracca 1992, 242–262.

Lurie, Peter, Christina M. Almeida, Nicholas Stine, Alexander R. Stine, and Sidney M. Wolfe. 2006. "Financial Conflict of Interest Disclosure and Voting Patterns at Food and Drug Administration Advisory Committee Meetings." *Journal of the American Medical Association* 295 (April): 1291–1298.

Lux, Sean, T. Russell Crook, and David J. Woehr. 2011. "Mixing Business with Politics: A Meta-Analysis of the Antecedents and Outcomes of Corporate Political Activity." *Journal of Management* 37 (January): 223–247.

Maclachlan, Malcolm. 2011. "Little Cities Spend Big on Lobbyists." *Capitol Weekly*. http://www.capitolweekly.net/article.php?xid=zppncn2v8ed4jd.

Mahoney, Christine. 2008. *Brussels Versus the Beltway: Advocacy in the United States and the European Union*. Washington, DC: Georgetown University Press.

Mann, Thomas E., and Norman J. Ornstein. 2012. *It's Even Worse Than It Looks: How the American Constitutional System Collided with the New Politics of Extremism*. New York: Basic Books.

Mansbridge, Jane J. 1980. *Beyond Adversary Democracy*. Chicago: University of Chicago Press.

———. 1990. "Self Interest in Political Life." *Political Theory* 18 (February): 132–153.

———. 1992. "A Deliberative Theory of Interest Representation." In Petracca 1992, 38–47.

Martinek, Wendy L. 2006. "Amici Curiae in the U.S. Court of Appeals." *American Politics Research* 34 (6): 803–824.

Martinez, Jennifer. 2012. "SOPA Becoming Election Liability for Backers." *Politico*, January 10.

Masters, Marick F., and Gerald D. Keim. 1985. "Determinants of PAC Participation among Large Corporations." *Journal of Politics* 47 (November): 1158–1173.

Mayhew, David R. 1974. *Congress: The Electoral Connection*. New Haven, CT: Yale University Press.

McAdam, Doug. 1982. *Political Process and the Development of Black Insurgency, 1930–1970*. Chicago: University of Chicago Press.

———, and W. Richard Scott. 2005. "Organizations and Movements." In *Social Movements and Organization Theory*, edited by Gerald F. Davis, Doug McAdam, W. Richard Scott, and Mayer N. Zald, 4–40. New York: Cambridge University Press.

McCarthy, John D., and Mayer N. Zald. 1977. "Resource Mobilization and Social Movements: A Partial Theory." *American Journal of Sociology* 82 (May): 1212–1241.

McCarty, Nolan, and Lawrence S. Rothenberg. 1996. "Commitment and the Campaign Contribution Contract." *American Journal of Political Science* 40 (August): 872–904.

McConnell, Grant. 1966. *Private Power & American Democracy*. New York: Knopf.

McCool, Daniel. 1994. *Command of the Waters: Iron Triangles, Federal Water Development, and Indian Water*. Tucson: University of Arizona Press.

———. 2002. *Native Waters: Contemporary Indian Water Settlements and the Second Treaty Era*. Tucson: University of Arizona Press.

McCormick, Robert E., and Robert D. Tollison. 1981. *Politicians, Legislation, and the Economy: An Inquiry into the Interest-Group Theory of Government*. Boston: Martinus Nijhoff.

McCubbins, Mathew D., Roger G. Noll, and Barry R. Weingast. 1987. "Administrative Procedures as Instruments of Political Control." *Journal of Law, Economics, and Organization* 3 (Autumn): 243–277.

McCubbins, Mathew D., and Thomas Schwartz. 1984. "Congressional Oversight Overlooked: Police Patrols Versus Fire Alarms." *American Journal of Political Science* 28 (February): 165–179.

McDonald, Forrest. 1979. *Alexander Hamilton: A Biography*. New York: Norton.

McFarland, Andrew S. 1984. *Common Cause*. Chatham, NJ: Chatham House.

———. 1991. "Interest Groups and Political Time: Cycles in America." *British Journal of Political Science* 21 (July): 257–284.

———. 1992. "Interest Groups and the Policymaking Process: Sources of Countervailing Power in American Politics." In Petracca 1992, 58–79.

———. 1998. "Social Movements and Theories of American Politics." In *Social Movements and American Political Institutions*, edited by Anne N. Costain and Andrew S. McFarland, 7–19. Lanham: Rowman and Littlefield.

———. 2004. *Neopluralism: The Evolution of Political Process Theory*. Lawrence: University Press of Kansas.

McHugh, James T. 1992. "What Is the Difference Between a 'Person' and a 'Human Being' Within the Law?" *Review of Politics* 54 (Summer): 445–461.

McIntire, Mike. 2012. "Conservative Nonprofit Acts as a Stealth Business Lobbyist." *New York Times*, April 21.

———, and Nicholas Confessore. 2012. "Tax-Exempt Groups Shield Political Gifts of Business." *New York Times*, July 8.

McKay, Amy. 2010. "The Effects of Interest Groups' Ideology on Their PAC and Lobbying Expenditures." *Business and Politics* 12 (2): 1–21.

———. 2011. "The Decision to Lobby Bureaucrats." *Public Choice* 147 (February): 123–138.

———. 2012. "Negative Lobbying and Policy Outcomes." *American Politics Research* 40 (January): 116–146.

———, and Susan Webb Yackee. 2007. "Interest Group Competition on Federal Agency Rules." *American Politics Research* 35 (May): 336–357.

McKean, David. 2004. *Peddling Influence: Thomas "Tommy the Cork" Corcoran and the Birth of Modern Lobbying.* Hanover: Steerforth.

Mearsheimer, John J., and Stephen M. Walt. 2007. *The Israel Lobby and U.S. Foreign Policy.* New York: Farrar, Straus, and Giroux.

Meier, Kenneth J. 1993. *Politics and the Bureaucracy: Policymaking in the Fourth Branch of Government.* 3rd ed. Belmont, CA: Wadsworth.

Melton, R. H. 1995. "PACs Weigh In with Freshmen; Group Contributions Represent 45 Percent of 1995 Donations in House." *Washington Post*, August 15.

Merry, Melissa K. 2010. "Emotional Appeals in Environmental Group Communications." *American Politics Research* 38 (September): 862–889.

Meyer, David S. 1993. "Protest Cycles and Political Process: American Peace Movements in the Nuclear Age." *Political Research Quarterly* 46 (September): 451–479.

———, and Suzanne Staggenborg. 1996. "Movements, Countermovements, and the Structure of Political Opportunity." *American Journal of Sociology* 101 (May): 1628–1660.

Michels, Robert. 1959. *Political Parties: A Sociological Study of the Oligarchical Tendencies of Modern Democracy.* Translated by Eden and Cedar Paul. New York: Dover.

Mierzwinski, Edmund. 2010. "Colston E. Warne Lecture: Consumer Protection 2.0– Protecting Consumers in the 21st Century." *Journal of Consumer Affairs* 44 (3): 578–597.

Milbank, Dana. 2012. "Come to Think of It, Jim DeMint and the Heritage Foundation Make Sense." *Washington Post*, December 7.

Milbrath, Lester W. 1963. *The Washington Lobbyists.* Chicago: Rand McNally.

Millis, Harry A., and Royal E. Montgomery. 1945. *Organized Labor.* New York: McGraw-Hill.

Mills, C. Wright. 1956. *The Power Elite.* New York: Oxford University Press.

Mintrom, Michael. 2000. *Policy Entrepreneurs and School Choice.* Washington, DC: Georgetown University Press.

Mintz, Beth, and Michael Schwartz. 1983. "Financial Interest Groups and Interlocking Directorates." *Social Science History* 7 (Spring): 183–204.

Mitchell, Neil J., Wendy L. Hansen, and Jeffrey M. Drope. 2004. "Collective Action, Pluralism, and the Legitimacy Tariff: Corporate Activity or Inactivity in Politics." *Political Research Quarterly* 57 (September): 421–429.

Moe, Terry M. 1980. *The Organization of Interests: Incentives and the Internal Dynamics of Political Interest Groups.* Chicago: University of Chicago Press.

————. 1987. "An Assessment of the Positive Theory of 'Congressional Dominance.'" *Legislative Studies Quarterly* 12 (November): 475–520.

Montgomery, Lori. 2011. "Among GOP, Anti-Tax Orthodoxy Runs Deep." *Washington Post*, June 5.

————, and Rosalind S. Helderman. 2012. "Boehner Abandons Plan to Avoid Fiscal Cliff." *Washington Post*, December 20.

Morag-Levine, Noga. 2003. "Partners No More: Relational Transformation and the Turn to Litigation in Two Conservationist Organizations." *Law and Society Review* 37 (June): 457–510.

Mossberger, Karen, Caroline Tolbert, and Ramona S. McNeal. 2007. *Digital Citizenship: The Internet, Society, and Participation.* Cambridge: MIT Press.

Mueller, Dennis C., and Peter Murrell. 1986. "Interest Groups and the Size of Government." *Public Choice* 48 (2): 125–145.

Munger, Michael C. 1988. "On the Political Participation of the Firm in the Electoral Process: An Update." *Public Choice* 56 (3): 295–298.

Murray, Matthew. 2010. "Chamber Watch: Business Group 'Central' to GOP Gains." *Roll Call*, November 12.

Narayanswamy, Anupama, Luke Rosiak, and Jennifer LaFleur. 2009. *Adding It Up: The Top Players in Foreign Agent Lobbying.* Report by the Sunlight Foundation and ProPublica.

Newhouse, John. 2009. "Diplomacy, Inc.: The Influence of Lobbies on U.S. Foreign Policy." *Foreign Affairs* 88 (May/June): 73–92.

Nie, Martin. 2004. "Administrative Rulemaking and Public Lands Conflict: The Forest Service's Roadless Rule." *Natural Resources Journal* 44 (Summer): 687–742.

————. 2008. "The Underappreciated Role of Regulatory Enforcement in Natural Resource Conservation." *Policy Sciences* 41 (April): 139–164.

————. 2009. *The Governance of Western Public Lands: Mapping Its Present and Future.* Lawrence: University Press of Kansas.

Niskanen, William A., Jr. 1971. *Bureaucracy and Representative Government.* Chicago: Aldine-Atherton.

Norris, Pippa. 2001. *Digital Divide: Civic Engagement, Information Poverty, and the Internet.* Cambridge, MA: Harvard University Press.

Nownes, Anthony J., and Allan J. Cigler. 1995. "Public Interest Groups and the Road to Survival." *Polity* 27 (Spring): 379–404.

Nownes, Anthony J., and Patricia K. Freeman. 1998. "Female Lobbyists: Women in the World of 'Good Ol' Boys.'" *Journal of Politics* 60 (November): 1181–1201.

Nownes, Anthony J., and Daniel Lipinski. 2005. "The Population Ecology of Interest Group Death: Gay and Lesbian Rights Interest Groups in the United States, 1945–98." *British Journal of Political Science* 35 (April): 303–319.

O'Connor, Karen, and Bryant Scott McFall. 1992. "Conservative Interest Group Litigation in the Reagan Era and Beyond." In Petracca 1992, 263–281.

O'Connor, Patrick. 2005. "Social Security in Limbo." *The Hill,* June 1.

Odegard, Peter. 1928. *Pressure Politics: The Story of the Anti-Saloon League.* New York: Columbia University Press.

Olson, Mancur, Jr. 1965. *The Logic of Collective Action: Public Goods and the Theory of Groups*. Cambridge, MA: Harvard University Press.

———. 1982. *The Rise and Decline of Nations: Economic Growth, Stagflation, and Social Rigidities*. New Haven, CT: Yale University Press.

Olson, Susan M. 1990. "Interest-Group Litigation in Federal District Court: Beyond the Political Disadvantage Theory." *Journal of Politics* 52 (August): 854–882.

Orren, Karen. 1976. "Standing to Sue: Interest Group Conflict in the Federal Courts." *American Political Science Review* 70 (September): 723–741.

———. 1985. "Judicial Whipsaw: Interest Conflict, Corporate Business and the Seventh Amendment." *Polity* 18 (Autumn): 70–97.

Ortiz, Stephen R. 2006. "The 'New Deal' for Veterans: The Economy Act, the Veterans of Foreign Wars, and the Origins of the New Deal." *Journal of Military History* 70 (April): 434–435.

Ostlind, Emiline. 2011. "Strife Mounts at Steens: Wind Farms Test a Longstanding Effort to Cooperate." *High Country News*, May 2.

Ottaway, David B., and Joe Stephens. 2003. "Landing a Big One: Preservation, Private Development." *Washington Post*, May 6.

Ozymy, Joshua. 2012. "Keepin' on the Sunny Side: Scandals, Organized Interests, and the Passage of Legislative Lobbying Laws in the American States." *American Politics Research* 41 (January): 3–23.

Pear, Robert. 1996. "Lawyers and Lobbyists Help Guide Effort by Republicans to Speed Drug Approvals." *New York Times*, March 4.

Peltzman, Sam. 1980. "The Growth of Government." *Journal of Law and Economics* 23 (2): 209–288.

Perine, Keith. 2011. "Wireless Merger, or Empire-Rebuilding?" *CQ Weekly* May 30: 1110–1112.

Peterson, Mark A. 1992a. "Interest Mobilization and the Presidency." In Petracca 1992, 221–241.

———. 1992b. "The Presidency and Organized Interests: White House Patterns of Interest Group Liaison." *American Political Science Review* 86 (September): 612–624.

Peterson, Paul E. 1990. "The Rise and Fall of Special Interest Politics." *Political Science Quarterly* 105 (Winter): 539–556.

Petracca, Mark P. 1986. "Federal Advisory Committees, Interest Groups, and the Administrative State." *Congress and the Presidency* 13 (1): 83–114.

———, ed. 1992. *The Politics of Interests: Interest Groups Transformed*. Boulder: Westview.

Pika, Joseph A. 2009. "The White House Office of Public Liaison." *Presidential Studies Quarterly* 39 (September): 549–573.

———, and John Anthony Maltese. 2004. *The Politics of the Presidency*. 6th ed. Washington, DC: Congressional Quarterly Press.

Pittman, Russell. 1976. "The Effects of Industry Concentration and Regulation on Contributions in Three 1972 U.S. Senate Campaigns." *Public Choice* 27 (Fall): 71–80.

———. 1977. "Market Structure and Campaign Contributions." *Public Choice* 31 (Fall): 37–52.

Planet Money. 2012a. "The Most (and Least) Lucrative Committees in Congress." National Public Radio, April 6. http://www.npr.org/blogs/money/2012/04/06/149714908/the-most-and-least-valuable-committees-in-congress-in-1-graph.

———. 2012b. "Where Money Meets Power in Washington." National Public Radio, April 4. http://www.npr.org/blogs/money/2012/04/04/150004648/where-money-meets-power-in-washington.

Plotke, David. 1992. "The Political Mobilization of Business." In Petracca 1992, 175–198.

Pollock, James K., Jr. 1927. "The Regulation of Lobbying." *American Political Science Review* 21 (May): 335–341.

Putnam, Robert. 2001. *Bowling Alone: The Collapse and Revival of American Community.* New York: Simon and Shuster.

Rabin, Robert L. 1986. "Federal Regulation in Historical Perspective." *Stanford Law Review* 38 (4): 1189–1326.

Rankin, David M. 2006. "Featuring the President as Free Trader: Television News Coverage of U.S. Trade Politics." *Presidential Studies Quarterly* 36 (December): 633–659.

Rauch, Jonathan. 1994. *Demosclerosis: The Silent Killer of American Government.* New York: Times Books.

Rehr, David K. 2012. *The Honest Leadership and Open Government Act: Five Years Later.* Lobbyists.info and the Graduate School of Political Management, George Washington University, Washington, DC.

Reid, Elizabeth J. 1999. "Nonprofit Advocacy and Political Participation." In *Nonprofits and Government: Collaboration and Conflict,* edited by Elizabeth Boris and C. Eugene Steuerle, 291–325. Washington, DC: Urban Institute Press.

———. 2000. "Understanding the Word 'Advocacy': Context and Use." In *Structuring the Inquiry into Advocacy,* vol. 1, edited by Elizabeth J. Reid, 1–8. Washington, DC: Urban Institute Press.

Reisner, Marc. 1986. *Cadillac Desert: The American West and Its Disappearing Water.* New York: Penguin Books.

Reitz, John C. 2002. "Standing to Raise Constitutional Issues." *American Journal of Comparative Law* 50 (Autumn): 437–461.

Rich, Andrew. 2005. *Think Tanks, Public Policy, and the Politics of Expertise.* New York: Cambridge University Press.

Righter, Robert W. 2006. *The Battle Over Hetch Hetchy: America's Most Controversial Dam and the Birth of Modern Environmentalism.* New York: Oxford University Press.

Ring, Ray. 2009a. "Roadless-less." *High Country News,* November 9.

———. 2009b. "The Wicked Witch of the West." *High Country News,* November 6.

Ritter, Gretchen. 2000. "Gender and Citizenship After the Nineteenth Amendment." *Polity* 32 (Spring): 345–375.

Romano, Lois. 2013. "Latinos Push Immigration Reform on Social Media." *Politico,* May 27.

Romer, Thomas, and James M. Snyder Jr. 1994. "An Empirical Investigation of the Dynamics of PAC Contributions." *American Journal of Political Science* 38 (August): 745–769.

Romm, Tony. 2011. "Dodd to Lead MPAA." *Politico*, March 1.

Ronayne, Kathleen. 2011. *Dueling Donations: Lobbyists Lining Pockets of Both Democratic and Republican Party Committees*. Center for Responsive Politics, Washington, DC.

Rowland, C. K., Robert A. Carp, and Donald Songer. 1988. "Presidential Effects on Criminal Justice Policy in the Lower Federal Courts." *Law and Society Review* 22 (1): 191–200.

Rowland, C. K., and Bridget Jeffrey Todd. 1991. "Where You Stand Depends on Who Sits: Platform Promises and Judicial Gatekeeping in the Federal District Courts." *Journal of Politics* 53 (February): 175–185.

Rozell, Mark, Clyde Wilcox, and David Madland. 2006. *Interest Groups in American Campaigns*. 2nd ed. Washington, DC: Congressional Quarterly Press.

Rucker, Philip. 2011. "As Debt Ceiling Vote Nears, the Pressure's On House Republican Freshmen." *Washington Post,* April 17.

Rudolph, Thomas J. 1999. "Corporate and Labor PAC Contributions in House Elections: Measuring the Effects of Majority Party States." *Journal of Politics* 61 (February): 192–206.

Rutenberg, Jim. 2010. "News Corps. Donates $1 Million to U.S. Chamber of Commerce." *New York Times*, October 1.

Rutten, Tim. 2011. "A Tipping Point for Labor in America." *Los Angeles Times*, February 19.

Sabatier, Paul A. 1992. "Interest Group Membership and Organization: Multiple Theories." In Petracca 1992, 99–129.

———, and Hank C. Jenkins-Smith. 1993. *Policy Change and Learning: An Advocacy Coalition Approach.* Boulder: Westview.

Sabato, Larry J. 1984. *PAC Power: Inside the World of Political Action Committees.* New York: Norton.

Salamon, Lester M. 1995. *Partners in Public Service: Government–Nonprofit Relations in the Modern Welfare State.* Baltimore: Johns Hopkins University Press.

Salisbury, Robert H. 1969. "An Exchange Theory of Interest Groups." *Midwest Journal of Political Science* 13 (February): 1–32.

———. 1984. "Interest Representation: The Dominance of Institutions." *American Political Science Review* 78 (March): 64–76.

———. 1990. "The Paradox of Interest Groups in Washington: More Groups, Less Clout." In *The New American Political System*, edited by Anthony J. King, 203–230. 2nd ed. Washington, DC: American Enterprise Institute Press.

Samuelson, Robert J. 2012. "Here's What Washington Really Does." *Washington Post,* April 29.

Santiago, Nellie R., Thomas T. Holyoke, and Ross D. Levi. 1998. "Turning David and Goliath into the Odd Couple: The Community Reinvestment Act and Community Development Financial Institutions." *Journal of Law and Policy* 6 (Fall): 571–651.

Schattschneider, E. E. 1960. *The Semisovereign People: A Realist's View of Democracy in America.* New York: Holt, Rinehart and Winston.

Schlozman, Kay Lehman, and John T. Tierney. 1983. "More of the Same: Washington Pressure Group Activity in a Decade of Change." *Journal of Politics* 45 (May): 351–377.

———. 1986. *Organized Interests and American Democracy.* New York: Harper & Row.

Schwartz, Noaki. 2011. "Striking Unusual Peace: Activists, Rivals Swap Silence for Conservation." *Fresno Bee* (Fresno, CA), July 31.

Segal, Jeffrey A., and Harold J. Spaeth. 2002. *The Supreme Court and the Attitudinal Model Revisited.* New York: Cambridge University Press.

Selbig, Aaron. 2011. "Alaska Town Leaves U.S. Chamber, Citing Politics." National Public Radio, September 30. http://www.npr.org/2011/09/30/140944826/alaska -town-leaves-u-s-chamber-citing-politics.

Seligman, Lester G., and Cary R. Covington. 1989. *The Coalitional Presidency.* Chicago: Dorsey.

Shepsle, Kenneth A., and Barry R. Weingast. 1987. "The Institutional Foundations of Committee Power." *American Political Science Review* 81 (March): 85–104.

Shih, Gerry. 2011. "Change.org: Activism or 'Slacktivism'?" *Bay Citizen* (San Francisco), June 30.

Shipan, Charles R. 2004. "Regulatory Regimes, Agency Actions, and the Conditional Nature of Congressional Influence." *American Political Science Review* 98 (August): 467–480.

Shirky, Clay. 2011. "The Political Power of Social Media: Technology, the Public Sphere, and Political Change." *Foreign Affairs* 90 (January/February): 28–41.

Skidmore, David. 1993. "Foreign Policy Interest Groups and Presidential Power: Jimmy Carter and the Battle over Ratification of the Panama Canal Treaties." *Presidential Studies Quarterly* 23 (Summer): 477–497.

Skillen, James R. 2009. *The Nation's Largest Landlord: The Bureau of Land Management in the American West.* Lawrence: University Press of Kansas.

Smith, Aaron, Kay Lehman Schlozman, Sidney Verba, and Henry Brady. 2009. *The Internet and Civic Engagement.* Washington, DC: The Pew Research Center.

Smith, R. Jeffrey, and Dan Eggen. 2011. "Lobbyists Flock to Capitol Hill Jobs." *Washington Post*, March 17.

Smith, Steven Rathgeb, and Michael Lipsky. 1993. *Nonprofits for Hire: The Welfare State in the Age of Contracting.* Cambridge, MA: Harvard University Press.

Snyder, James M. Jr. 1992. "Artificial Extremism in Interest Group Ratings." *Legislative Studies Quarterly* 17 (August): 319–345.

Solomon, John, and Matthew Mosk. 2007. "Nonprofits Become a Force in Primaries." *Washington Post*, December 5.

Solowiej, Lisa A., and Paul M. Collins Jr. 2009. "Counteractive Lobbying in the U.S. Supreme Court." *American Politics Research* 37 (July): 670–699.

Sorauf, Frank J. 1992. *Inside Campaign Finance: Myths and Realities.* New Haven, CT: Yale University Press.

Spriggs, James F. II, and Paul J. Wahlbeck. 1997. "Amicus Curiae and the Role of Information at the Supreme Court." *Political Research Quarterly* 50 (June): 365–386.

Stanley, Harold W., and Richard G. Niemi. 2011. *Vital Statistics on American Politics, 2011–2012*. Washington, DC: Congressional Quarterly Press.

Stecklow, Steve. 2006. "Did a Group Financed by Exxon Prompt IRS to Audit Greenpeace?" *Wall Street Journal*, March 21.

Stephens, Joe, and David B. Ottaway. 2003a. "Nature Conservancy Suspends Land Sales." *Washington Post*, May 13.

———. 2003b. "Nonprofit Sells Scenic Acreage to Allies at a Loss." *Washington Post*, May 6.

Stidham, Ronald, and Robert Carp. 1987. "Judges, Presidents, and Policy Choices: Exploring the Linkage." *Social Science Quarterly* 68 (June): 395–402.

Stigler, George J. 1971. "The Theory of Economic Regulation." *Bell Journal of Economics and Management Science* 3 (Spring): 3–26.

———, and Claire Friedland. 1962. "What Can Regulators Regulate? The Case of Electricity." *Journal of Law and Economics* 5 (October): 1–16.

Stolberg, Sheryl Gay. 2013. "Pugnacious Builder of the Business Lobby." *New York Times*, June 1.

Stone, Peter H. 1995. "Labyrinth of Loopholes." *National Journal*, November 25.

———. 1996. "Desperately Seeking Republicans." *National Journal*, November 16.

Stratmann, Thomas. 2002. "Can Special Interests Buy Congressional Votes? Evidence from Financial Services Legislation." *Journal of Law and Economics* 45 (October): 345–373.

Straus, Jacob R. 2011. *Lobbying Registration and Disclosure: Before and After the Enactment of the Honest Leadership and Open Government Act of 2007*. Washington, DC: Congressional Research Service.

Strolovitch, Dara Z. 2006. "Do Interest Groups Represent the Disadvantaged? Advocacy at the Intersections of Race, Class, and Gender." *Journal of Politics* 68 (November): 894–910.

Supreme Court Database. Washington University, St. Louis. 2011. http://scdb.wustl.edu.

Susman, Thomas M. 2006. "Lobbying in the 21st Century: Reciprocity and the Need for Reform." *Administrative Law Review* 58 (Fall): 737–752.

———. 2008. "Private Ethics, Public Conduct: An Essay on Ethical Lobbying, Campaign Contributions, Reciprocity, and the Public Good." *Stanford Law and Policy Review* 19 (Spring): 10–22.

Sutter, Paul S. 2002. *Driven Wild: How the Fight Against Automobiles Launched the Modern Wilderness Movement*. Seattle: University of Washington Press.

Talbert, Jeffrey, Bryan Jones, and Frank Baumgartner. 1995. "Nonlegislative Hearings and Policy Change in Congress." *American Journal of Political Science* 44 (May): 383–405.

Tarrow, Sidney. 1998. "'The Very Excess of Democracy': State Building and Contentious Politics in America." In *Social Movements and American Political Institutions*, edited by Anne N. Costain and Andrew S. McFarland, 20–38. Lanham: Rowman and Littlefield.

Tate, Curtis. 2012. "Cash Flows into California House Races." *Sacramento Bee*, October 7.

Tau, Byron. 2013. "Contractor Lobbying Info Under Wraps." *Politico*, July 7.

Thomas, Andrew P. 1993. "Easing the Pressure on Pressure Groups: Toward a Constitutional Right to Lobby." *Harvard Journal of Law and Public Policy* 16 (Winter): 149–194.

Thompson, Christopher. 2007. "Can McDonald's Alter the Dictionary?" *Time*, June 5.

Thompson, Krissah. 2010. "Activist Groups Take Full Advantage of New Media Outlets to Spread Their Message." *Washington Post*, December 27.

Thompson, Margaret Susan. 1985. *The "Spider Web": Congress and Lobbying in the Age of Grant*. Ithaca, NY: Cornell University Press.

Tichenor, Daniel J., and Richard A. Harris. 2002. "Organized Interests and American National Development." *Political Science Quarterly* 117 (4): 587–612.

Tilly, Charles. 1978. *From Mobilization to Revolution*. Reading, MA: Addison-Wesley.

Truman, David B. 1951. *The Governmental Process: Political Interests and Public Opinion*. New York: Knopf.

Turner, Tom. 2009. *Roadless Rules: The Struggle for the Last Wild Forests*. Washington, DC: Island.

Tweed, William C. 2010. *Uncertain Path: A Search for the Future of National Parks*. Berkeley: University of California Press.

Uslaner, Eric M. 2007. "American Interests in the Balance? Do Ethnic Groups Dominate Foreign Policy Making?" In *Interest Group Politics*, edited by Allan J. Cigler and Burdett A. Loomis, 301–321. 7th ed. Washington, DC: Congressional Quarterly Press.

Van Winden, Frans. 1999. "On the Economic Theory of Interest Groups: Towards a Group Frame of Reference in Political Economics." *Public Choice* 100 (July): 1–29.

Vanden Heuvel, Katrina. 2010. "Chamber of Commerce Backlash." *Washington Post*, Nov. 2.

Verini, James. 2010. "Show Him the Money." *Washington Monthly*. http://www.washingtonmonthly.com/features/2010/1007.verini.html.

Vogel, David. 1989. *Fluctuating Fortunes: The Political Power of Business in America*. New York: Basic Books.

Vose, Clement E. 1959. *Caucasians Only: The Supreme Court, the NAACP, and the Restrictive Covenant Cases*. Berkeley: University of California Press.

Walker, Jack L., Jr. 1983. "The Origin and Maintenance of Interest Groups in America." *American Political Science Review* 77 (June): 390–406.

———. 1991. *Mobilizing Interest Groups in America: Patrons, Professions, and Social Movements*. Ann Arbor: University of Michigan Press.

Walker, Thomas G., and Lee Epstein. 1993. *The Supreme Court of the United States: An Introduction*. New York: St. Martin's.

Washington Representatives. 2010. Washington, DC: Columbia Books.

Weiss, Debra Cassens. 2007. "NRA Had High Court Misgivings." *ABA Journal*, July 30.

West, William F. 2004. "Formal Procedures, Informal Processes, Accountability, and Responsiveness in Bureaucratic Policy Making: An Institutional Policy Analysis." *Public Administration Review* 64 (January): 66–80.

Winkler, Adam. 2009. "The New Second Amendment: A Bark Worse Than Its Right." *Huffington Post*, January 2.

Witko, Christopher. 2006. "PACs, Issue Context, and Congressional Decisionmaking." *Political Research Quarterly* 59 (June): 283–295.

Wlezien, Christopher B., and Malcolm L. Goggin. 1993. "The Courts, Interest Groups, and Public Opinion About Abortion." *Political Behavior* 15 (4): 381–405.

Wolman, Harold, and Fred Teitelbaum. 1984. "Interest Groups and the Reagan Presidency." In *The Reagan Presidency and the Governing of America*, edited by Lester M. Salamon and Michael S. Lund, 297–329. Washington, DC: Urban Institute Press.

Wright, John R. 1985. "PACs, Contributions, and Roll Calls: An Organizational Perspective." *American Political Science Review* 79 (June): 400–414.

———. 1989. "PAC Contributions, Lobbying, and Representation." *Journal of Politics* 51 (August): 713–729.

———. 1990. "Contributions, Lobbying, and Committee Voting in the U.S. House of Representatives." *American Political Science Review* 84 (June): 417–438.

———. 1996. *Interest Groups and Congress: Lobbying, Contributions, and Influence.* Boston: Allyn and Bacon.

Yackee, Jason Webb, and Susan Webb Yackee. 2006. "A Bias Towards Business? Assessing Interest Group Influence on the U.S. Bureaucracy." *Journal of Politics* 68 (February): 128–139.

Yackee, Susan Webb. 2006. "Sweet-Talking the Fourth Branch: The Influence of Interest Group Comments on Federal Agency Rulemaking." *Journal of Public Administration Research and Theory* 16 (January): 103–124.

Yang, Jia Lynn, and Tom Hamburger. 2012. "For U.S. Chamber of Commerce, Election Was a Money-loser." *Washington Post*, November 8.

———. 2013. "In Budget and Debt Fight, White House Finds Unlikely Alliance with Business Groups." *Washington Post*, October 12.

Young, McGee. 2010. *Developing Interests: Organizational Change and the Politics of Advocacy.* Lawrence: University Press of Kansas.

Yuen, Eddie, Daniel Burton Rose, and George Katsiaficas, eds. 2002. *The Battle for Seattle: The New Challenge to Capitalist Globalization.* New York: Soft Skull.

Zeigler, L. Harmon, and G. Wayne Peak. 1972. *Interest Groups in American Society.* 2nd ed. Englewood Cliffs, NJ: Prentice-Hall.

Zeller, Shawn. 2011. "Suspect Data Hurts Environmentalists' Cause." *CQ Weekly*, May 2.

INDEX